GREAT STORIES

OF

THE SEA AND SHIPS

GREAT STORIES OF THE SEA & SHIPS

EDITED AND WITH AN INTRODUCTION BY N·C·WYETH

ILLUSTRATED BY PETER HURD

NEW YORK
CASTLE

Published in 1986 by
Galahad Books
166 Fifth Avenue
New York, NY 10010

By arrangement with David McKay and Company

This edition distributed by Castle Books, a division of Book Sales, Inc.,
110 Enterprise Avenue, Secaucus, New Jersey 07094

LIBRARY OF CONGRESS CATALOG CARD NUMBER: 86-80454
ISBN: 1-55521-094-5

PRINTED IN THE UNITED STATES OF AMERICA

FOREWORD

THE VAST majority of us are landsmen, and we die landsmen. A vast majority of us will never gaze upon the long horizon of the open sea, nor feast our eyes upon the brilliant and dazzling spectacle of green crystal water bursting its mountains of force against a granite headland. The magic of stilled ocean waters lying in the sun like a wide flung placque of burnished steel, reflecting in strange patterns the towering clouds of a noonday sky can be but a fanciful dream. The endless and variable pageant of the sea's moods can live only in our imaginations. Its myriads of voices, from the languid night-whisperings of an incoming tide suckling the endless fringes of weed-hung crannies of the shoreline, to the earth-shaking thunder and crash of raging seas, the piercing obligato of its swift gale whistling and screaming in high minor cadences—eerily seductive, frightening, portentous, cataclysmic! To all this we must listen through the silences and dream its music.

And yet the appearance and voice of the sea is a tangible heritage to all who inhabit the earth. The sea is universally ancestral. The crimson thread of lineage reaching back through the generations, through the centuries of generations perhaps, may become dim and obscure and lost sight of entirely, yet it is there, weaving its devious and mystifying way toward that original source of life, the great waters of the earth. The sun and the sea brought life to this planet. Before these powers we stand in awesome regard and appreciation.

From the dawn of creative literature, the subject of man and his relation to the sea has occupied a dominant position. The wild and seductive call of the blue water is second only in importance to that foundation urge of mankind—the sublime magic of love and the forces of pro-genitation.

Verily, some minute portion of the salt seas must move in the blood stream of all mankind. Lulled, mayhap, into temporary apathy by a period of ancestral absence from the maritime scene, yet with what suddenness and brilliance are our sensatory faculties aroused by the magic of a poet's report of the sea, its sailors and ships.

Ships! Those mistresses of the flood which men have built and served since time immemorial. From the earliest coracle made of skins stretched on a wicker frame, or a crude hull hewn from a solid log, through the infinite transitions of wooden vessels conceived and made in every shape, size, and rig imaginable, and thence down to our own time of steam and steel, the romance of ships and the men who sailed them is undiminished.

I feel secure in asserting that there is hardly a page in the present volume but what contains a livid spark which will ignite and explode into pure brilliance some dormant joy which is linked to the sea. One will find, in these stories, its ineffable beauty, its dynamic and ruthless power, and its teeming romance.

N. C. WYETH
Port Clyde
Maine

CONTENTS

ILLUSTRATIONS

In the beginning God created the heaven and the earth. And the earth was without form, and void: and darkness was upon the face of the deep. And the Spirit of God moved upon the face of the waters.

And God said, Let there be light: and there was light. And God saw the light, that it was good: and God divided the light from the darkness. And God called the light Day, and the darkness he called Night. And the evening and the morning were the first day.

And God said, Let there be a firmament in the midst of the waters, and let it divide the waters from the waters. And God made the firmament, and divided the waters which were under the firmament from the waters which were above the firmament: and it was so. And God called the firmament Heaven. And the evening and the morning were the second day.

And God said, Let the waters under the heaven be gathered together unto one place, and let the dry land appear: and it was so. And God called the dry land Earth; and the gathering together of the waters called he Seas: and God saw that it was good.

GENESIS I: 1—10

THE MERMAID

Hans Christian Andersen

FAR OUT at sea the water is as blue as the bluest cornflower, and as clear as the clearest crystal; but it is very deep, too deep for any cable to fathom, and if many steeples were piled on the top of one another they would not reach from the bed of the sea to the surface of the water. It is down there that the Mermen live.

Now don't imagine that there are only bare white sands at the bottom; oh no! the most wonderful trees and plants grow there, and such flexible stalks and leaves, that at the slightest motion of the water they move just as if they were alive. All the fish, big and little, glide among the branches just as, up here, birds glide through the air. The palace of the Merman King lies in the very deepest part; its walls are of coral and the long pointed windows of the clearest amber, but the roof is made of mussel shells which open and shut with the lapping of the water. This has a lovely effect, for there are gleaming pearls in every shell, any one of which would be the pride of a queen's crown.

The Merman King had been for many years a widower, but his old mother kept house for him; she was a clever woman, but so proud of her noble birth that she wore twelve oysters on her tail, while the other grandees were only allowed six. Otherwise she was worthy of all praise, especially because she was so fond of the little mermaid princesses, her grandchildren. They were six beautiful children, but the youngest was the prettiest of all, her skin was as soft and delicate as a roseleaf, her eyes as blue as the deepest sea, but like all the others she had no feet, and instead of legs she had a fish's tail.

All the livelong day they used to play in the palace in the great halls, where

from "Fairy Tales" by Hans Christian Andersen

living flowers grew out of the walls. When the great amber windows were thrown open the fish swam in, just as the swallows fly into our rooms when we open the windows, but the fish swam right up to the little princesses, ate out of their hands, and allowed themselves to be patted.

Outside the palace was a large garden, with fiery red and deep blue trees, the fruit of which shone like gold, while the flowers glowed like fire on their ceaselessly waving stalks. The ground was of the finest sand, but it was of a blue phosphorescent tint. Everything was bathed in a wondrous blue light down there; you might more readily have supposed yourself to be high up in the air, with only the sky above and below you, than that you were at the bottom of the ocean. In a dead calm you could just catch a glimpse of the sun like a purple flower with a stream of light radiating from its calyx.

Each little princess had her own little plot of garden, where she could dig and plant just as she liked. One made her flower-bed in the shape of a whale, another thought it nice to have hers like a little mermaid; but the youngest made hers quite round like the sun, and she would only have flowers of a rosy hue like its beams. She was a curious child, quiet and thoughtful, and while the other sisters decked out their gardens with all kinds of extraordinary objects which they got from wrecks, she would have nothing besides the rosy flowers like the sun up above, except a statue of a beautiful boy. It was hewn out of the purest white marble and had gone to the bottom from some wreck. By the statue she planted a rosy red weeping willow which grew splendidly, and the fresh delicate branches hung round and over it, till they almost touched the blue sand where the shadows showed violet, and were ever moving like the branches. It looked as if the leaves and the roots were playfully interchanging kisses.

Nothing gave her greater pleasure than to hear about the world of human beings up above; she made her old grandmother tell her all that she knew about ships and towns, people and animals. But above all it seemed strangely beautiful to her that up on the earth the flowers were scented, for they were not so at the bottom of the sea; also that the woods were green, and that the fish which were to be seen among the branches could sing so loudly and sweetly that it was a delight to listen to them. You see the grandmother called little birds fish, or the mermaids would not have understood her, as they had never seen a bird.

"When you are fifteen," said the grandmother, "you will be allowed to rise up from the sea and sit on the rocks in the moonlight, and look at the big ships sailing by, and you will also see woods and towns."

One of the sisters would be fifteen in the following year, but the others,—well, they were each one year younger than the other, so that the youngest had five whole years to wait before she would be allowed to come up from the bottom, to see what things were like on earth. But each one promised the others to give a full account of all that she had seen, and found most wonderful on the first day. Their grandmother could never tell them enough, for there were so many things about which they wanted information.

None of them was so full of longings as the youngest, the very one who had the longest time to wait, and who was so quiet and dreamy. Many a night she stood by the open windows and looked up through the dark blue water which the fish were lashing with their tails and fins. She could see the moon and the stars, it is true, their light was pale but they looked much bigger through the water than they do to our eyes. When she saw a dark shadow glide between her and them, she knew that it was either a whale swimming above her, or else a ship laden with human beings. I am certain they never dreamt that a lovely little mermaid was standing down below, stretching up her white hands towards the keel.

The eldest princess had now reached her fifteenth birthday, and was to venture above the water. When she came back she had hundreds of things to tell them, but the most delightful of all, she said, was to lie in the moonlight on a sandbank in a calm sea, and to gaze at the large town close to the shore, where the lights twinkled like hundreds of stars; to listen to music and the noise and bustle of carriages and people, to see the many church towers and spires, and to hear the bells ringing; and just because she could not go on shore she longed for that most of all.

Oh! how eagerly the youngest sister listened, and when, later in the evening she stood at the open window and looked up through the dark blue water, she thought of the big town with all its noise and bustle, and fancied that she could even hear the church bells ringing.

The year after, the second sister was allowed to mount up through the water and swim about wherever she liked. The sun was just going down when she reached the surface, the most beautiful sight, she thought, that she had ever seen. The whole sky had looked like gold, she said, and as for the clouds! well, their beauty was beyond description, they floated in red and violet splendor over her head, and, far faster than they went, a flock of wild swans flew like a long white veil over the water towards the setting sun; she swam towards it, but it sank and all the rosy light on the clouds and water faded away.

The year after that the third sister went up, and being much the most ven-turesome of them all, swam up a broad river which ran into the sea. She saw beautiful green, vine-clad hills; palaces and country seats peeping through splendid woods. She heard the birds singing, and the sun was so hot that she was often obliged to dive to cool her burning face. In a tiny bay she found a troop of little children running about naked and paddling in the water; she wanted to play with them, but they were frightened and ran away. Then a little black animal came up, it was a dog, but she had never seen one before; it barked so furiously at her that she was frightened and made for the open sea. She could never forget the beautiful woods, the green hills and the lovely children who could swim in the water although they had no fishes' tails.

The fourth sister was not so brave, she stayed in the remotest part of the ocean, and, according to her account, that was the most beautiful spot. You could see for miles and miles around you, and the sky above was like a great glass dome. She had seen ships, but only far away, so that they looked like sea-gulls. There were grotesque dolphins turning somersaults, and gigantic whales squirting water through their nostrils like hundreds of fountains on every side.

Now the fifth sister's turn came. Her birthday fell in the winter, so that she saw sights that the others had not seen on their first trips. The sea looked quite green, and large icebergs were floating about, each one of which looked like a pearl, she said, but was much bigger than the church towers built by men. They took the most wonderful shapes, and sparkled like diamonds. She had seated herself on one of the largest, and all the passing ships sheered off in alarm when they saw her sitting there with her long hair streaming loose in the wind.

In the evening the sky became overcast with dark clouds; it thundered and lightened, and the huge icebergs, glittering in the bright lightning, were lifted high into the air by the black waves. All the ships shortened sail, and there was fear and trembling on every side, but she sat quietly on her floating ice-berg watching the blue lightning flash in zigzags down on to the shining sea.

The first time any of the sisters rose above the water she was delighted by the novelties and beauties she saw; but once grown up, and at liberty to go where she liked, she became indifferent and longed for her home; in the course of a month or so they all said that after all their own home in the deep was best, it was so cozy there.

Many an evening the five sisters interlacing their arms would rise above the water together. They had lovely voices, much clearer than any mortal, and when a storm was rising, and they expected ships to be wrecked, they would sing in the most seductive strains of the wonders of the deep, bidding the seafarers have no fear of them. But the sailors could not understand the words, they thought it was the voice of the storm; nor could it be theirs to see this Elysium of the deep, for when the ship sank they were drowned, and only reached the Merman's palace in death. When the elder sisters rose up in this manner, arm-in-arm, in the evening, the youngest remained behind quite alone, looking after them as if she must weep, but mermaids have no tears and so they suffer all the more.

"Oh! if I were only fifteen!" she said, "I know how fond I shall be of the world above, and of the mortals who dwell there."

At last her fifteenth birthday came.

"Now we shall have you off our hands," said her grandmother, the old queen dowager. "Come now, let me adorn you like your other sisters!" and she put a wreath of white lilies round her hair, but every petal of the flowers was half a pearl; then the old queen had eight oysters fixed on to the princess's tail to show her high rank.

"But it hurts so!" said the little mermaid.

"You must endure the pain for the sake of the finery!" said her grandmother.

But oh! how gladly would she have shaken off all this splendor, and laid aside the heavy wreath. Her red flowers in her garden suited her much better, but she did not dare to make any alteration. "Good-by," she said, and mounted as lightly and airily as a bubble through the water.

The sun had just set when her head rose above the water, but the clouds were still lighted up with a rosy and golden splendor, and the evening star sparkled in the soft pink sky, the air was mild and fresh, and the sea as calm as a millpond. A big three-masted ship lay close by with only a single sail set, for there was not a breath of wind, and the sailors were sitting about the rigging, on the cross-trees, and at the mast-heads. There was music and singing on board, and as the evening closed in, hundreds of gaily colored lanterns were lighted—they looked like the flags of all nations waving in the air. The little mermaid swam right up to the cabin windows, and every time she was lifted by the swell she could see through the transparent panes crowds of gaily dressed people. The handsomest of them all was the young prince with large dark eyes; he could not be much more than sixteen, and all these festivities were in honor of his birthday. The sailors danced on deck, and when the prince appeared among them hundreds of rockets were let off making it as light as day, and frightening the little mermaid so much that she had to dive under the water. She soon ventured up again, and it was just as if all the stars of heaven were falling in showers round about her. She had never seen such magic fires. Great suns whirled round, gorgeous fire-fish hung in the blue air, and all was reflected in the calm and glassy sea. It was so light on board the ship that every little rope could be seen, and the people still better. Oh! how handsome the prince was, how he laughed and smiled as he greeted his guests, while the music rang out in the quiet night.

It got quite late, but the little mermaid could not take her eyes off the ship and the beautiful prince. The colored lanterns were put out, no more rockets were sent up, and the cannon had ceased its thunder, but deep down in the sea there was a dull murmuring and moaning sound. Meanwhile she was rocked up and down on the waves, so that she could look into the cabin; but the ship got more and more way on, sail after sail was filled by the wind, the waves grew stronger, great clouds gathered, and it lightened in the distance. Oh, there was going to be a fearful storm! and soon the sailors had to shorten sail. The great ship rocked and rolled as she dashed over the angry sea, the black waves rose like mountains, high enough to overwhelm her, but she dived like a swan through them and rose again and again on their towering crests. The little mermaid thought it a most amusing race, but not so the sailors. The ship creaked and groaned, the mighty timbers bulged and bent under the heavy blows, the water broke over the decks, snapping the main mast like a reed, she heeled over on her side and the water rushed into the hold.

Now the little mermaid saw that they were in danger and she had for her own sake to beware of the floating beams and wreckage. One moment it was so pitch dark that she could not see at all, but when the lightning flashed it became so light that she could see all on board. Every man was looking out for his own safety as best he could, but she more particularly followed the

The little mermaid could not take her eyes off the ship.

young prince with her eyes, and when the ship went down she saw him sink in the deep sea. At first she was quite delighted, for now he was coming to be with her, but then she remembered that human beings could not live under water, and that only if he were dead could he go to her father's palace. No! he must not die; so she swam towards him all among the drifting beams and planks, quite forgetting that they might crush her. She dived deep down under the water, and came up again through the waves, and at last reached the young prince just as he was becoming unable to swim any further in the stormy sea. His limbs were numbed, his beautiful eyes were closing, and he must have died if the little mermaid had not come to the rescue. She held his head above the water and let the waves drive them whithersoever they would.

By daybreak all the storm was over, of the ship not a trace was to be seen; the sun rose from the water in radiant brilliance and his rosy beams seemed to cast a glow of life into the prince's cheeks, but his eyes remained closed. The mermaid kissed his fair and lofty brow, and stroked back the dripping hair; it seemed to her that he was like the marble statue in her little garden, she kissed him again and longed that he might live.

At last she saw dry land before her, high blue mountains on whose summits the white snow glistened as if a flock of swans had settled there; down by the shore were beautiful green woods, and in the foreground a church or temple, she did not quite know which, but it was a building of some sort. Lemon and orange trees grew in the garden and lofty palms stood by the gate. At this point the sea formed a little bay where the water was quite calm, but very deep, right up to the cliffs; at their foot was a strip of fine white sand to which she swam with the beautiful prince, and laid him down on it, taking great care that his head should rest high up in the warm sunshine.

The bells now began to ring in the great white building and a number of young maidens came into the garden. Then the little mermaid swam further off behind some high rocks and covered her hair and breast with foam, so that no one should see her little face, and then she watched to see who would discover the poor prince.

It was not long before one of the maidens came up to him, at first she seemed quite frightened, but only for a moment, and then she fetched several others, and the mermaid saw that the prince was coming to life, and that he smiled at all those around him, but he never smiled at her, you see he did not know that she had saved him; she felt so sad that when he was led away into the great building she dived sorrowfully into the water and made her way home to her father's Palace.

Always silent and thoughtful, she became more so now than ever. Her sisters often asked her what she had seen on her first visit to the surface, but she never would tell them anything.

Many an evening and many a morning she would rise to the place where she had left the prince. She saw the fruit in the garden ripen, and then gathered, she saw the snow melt on the mountain-tops, but she never saw the prince, so she always went home still sadder than before. At home her only consolation was to sit in her little garden with her arms twined round the handsome marble statue which reminded her of the prince. It was all in gloomy shade now, as she had ceased to tend her flowers and the garden had become a neglected wilderness of long stalks and leaves entangled with the branches of the tree.

At last she could not bear it any longer, so she told one of her sisters, and from her it soon spread to the others, but to no one else except to one or two other mermaids who only told their dearest friends. One of these knew all about the prince, she had also seen the festivities on the ship; she knew where he came from and where his kingdom was situated.

"Come, little sister!" said the other princesses, and, throwing their arms round each other's shoulders, they rose from the water in a long line, just in front of the prince's palace.

It was built of light yellow glistening stone, with great marble staircases, one of which led into the garden. Magnificent gilded cupolas rose above the roof, and the spaces between the columns which encircled the building were filled with life-like marble statues. Through the clear glass of the lofty windows you could see gorgeous halls adorned with costly silken hangings, and the pictures on the walls were a sight worth seeing. In the midst of the central hall a large fountain played, throwing its jets of spray upwards to a glass dome in the roof, through which the sunbeams lighted up the water and the beautiful plants which grew in the great basin.

She knew now where he lived and often used to go there in the evenings and by night over the water; she swam much nearer the land than any of the others dared, she even ventured right up the narrow channel under the splendid marble terrace which threw a long shadow over the water. She used to sit here looking at the young prince who thought he was quite alone.

She saw him many an evening sailing about in his beautiful boat, with flags waving and music playing, she used to peep through the green rushes, and if the wind happened to catch her long silvery veil and anyone saw it, they only thought it was a swan flapping its wings.

Many a night she heard the fishermen, who were fishing by torchlight, talking over the good deeds of the young prince; and she was happy to think that she had saved his life when he was drifting about on the waves, half dead, and she could not forget how closely his head had pressed her breast, and how passionately she had kissed him; but he knew nothing of all this, and never saw her even in his dreams.

She became fonder and fonder of mankind, and longed more and more to be able to live among them; their world seemed so infinitely bigger than hers; with their ships they could scour the ocean, they could ascend the mountains high above the clouds, and their wooded, grass-grown lands extended further than her eye could reach. There was so much that she wanted to know, but her sisters could not give an answer to all her questions, so she asked her old grandmother who knew the upper world well, and rightly called it the country above the sea.

"If men are not drowned," asked the little mermaid, "do they live for ever, do they not die as we do down here in the sea?"

"Yes," said the old lady, "they have to die too, and their life time is even shorter than ours. We may live here for three hundred years, but when we cease to exist, we become mere foam on the water and do not have so much as a grave among our dear ones. We have no immortal souls, we have no future life, we are just like the green sea-weed, which, once cut down, can never revive again! Men, on the other hand, have a soul which lives for ever, lives after the body has become dust; it rises through the clear air, up to the shining stars! Just as we rise from the water to see the land of mortals, so they rise up to unknown beautiful regions which we shall never see."

"Why have we no immortal souls?" asked the little mermaid sadly. "I would give all my three hundred years to be a human being for one day, and afterwards to have a share in the heavenly kingdom."

"You must not be thinking about that," said the grandmother; "we are much better off and happier than human beings."

"Then I shall have to die and to float as foam on the water, and never hear the music of the waves or see the beautiful flowers or the red sun! Is there nothing I can do to gain an immortal soul?"

"No," said the grandmother, "only if a human being so loved you, that you were more to him than father or mother, if all his thoughts and all his love were so centered in you that he would let the priest join your hands and would vow to be faithful to you here, and to all eternity; then your body would become infused with his soul. Thus and only thus, could you gain a share in the felicity of mankind. He would give you a soul while yet keeping his own. But that can never happen! That which is your greatest beauty in the sea, your fish's tail, is thought hideous up on earth, so little do they understand about it; to be pretty there you must have two clumsy supports which they call legs!"

Then the little mermaid sighed and looked sadly at her fish's tail.

"Let us be happy," said the grandmother, "we will hop and skip during our three hundred years of life, it is surely a long enough time, and after it is over, we shall rest all the better in our graves. There is to be a court ball tonight."

This was a much more splendid affair than we ever see on earth. The walls and the ceiling of the great ballroom were of thick but transparent glass. Several hundreds of colossal mussel shells, rose-red and grass-green, were ranged in order round the sides holding blue lights, which illuminated the whole room and shone through the walls, so that the sea outside was quite lit up. You could see countless fish, great and small, swimming towards the glass walls, some with shining scales of crimson hue, while others were golden and silvery. In the middle of the room was a broad stream of running water, and on this the mermaids and mermen danced to their own beautiful singing. No earthly beings have such lovely voices. The little mermaid sang more sweetly than any of them and they all applauded her. For a moment she felt glad at heart, for she knew that she had the finest voice either in the sea or on land. But she soon began to think again about the upper world, she could not forget the handsome prince and her sorrow in not possessing, like him, an immortal soul. Therefore she stole out of her father's palace, and while all within was joy and merriment, she sat sadly in her little garden. Suddenly she heard the sound of a horn through the water, and she thought, "Now he is out sailing up there; he whom I love more than father or mother, he to whom my thoughts cling and to whose hands I am ready to commit the happiness of my life. I will dare anything to win him and to gain an immortal soul! While my sisters are dancing in my father's palace, I will go to the sea witch of whom I have always been very much afraid, she will perhaps be able to advise and help me!"

Thereupon the little mermaid left the garden and went towards the roaring whirlpools at the back of which the witch lived. She had never been that way before; no flowers grew there, no seaweed, only the bare gray sands, stretched towards the whirlpools, which like rushing millwheels swirled round, dragging everything that came within reach down to the depths. She had to pass between these boiling eddies to reach the witches' domain, and for a long way the only path led over warm bubbling mud, which the witch called her "peat bog." Her house stood behind this in the midst of a weird forest. All the trees and bushes were polyps, half animal and half plant; they looked like hundred-headed snakes growing out of the sand, the branches were long slimy arms, with tentacles like wriggling worms, every joint of which from the root to the outermost tip was in constant motion. They wound themselves tightly round whatever they could lay hold of and never let it escape. The little mermaid standing outside was quite frightened, her heart beat fast with terror and she nearly turned back, but then she remembered the prince and the immortal soul of mankind and took courage. She bound her long flowing hair tightly round her head, so that the polyps should not seize her by it, folded her hands over her breast, and darted like a fish through the water, in between the hideous polyps which stretched out their sensitive arms and tentacles towards her. She could see that every one of them had something or other, which they had grasped with their hundred arms, and which they held as if in iron bands. The bleached bones of men who had perished at sea and sunk below peeped forth from the arms of some, while others clutched rudders and sea chests, or the skeleton of some land animal; and most horrible of all, a little mermaid whom they had caught and suffocated. Then she came to a large opening in the wood where the ground was all slimy, and where some huge fat water snakes were gamboling about. In the middle of this opening was a house built of the bones of the wrecked; there sat the witch, letting a toad eat out of her mouth, just as mortals let a little canary eat sugar. She called the hideous water snakes her little chickens, and allowed them to crawl about on her unsightly bosom.

"I know very well what you have come here for," said the witch. "It is very foolish of you! all the same you shall have your way, because it will lead you into misfortune, my fine princess. You want to get rid of your fish's tail, and instead to have two stumps to walk about upon like human beings, so that the young prince may fall in love with you, and that you may win him and an immortal soul." Saying this, she gave such a loud hideous laugh that the toad and snakes fell to the ground and wriggled about there.

"You are just in the nick of time," said the witch; "after sunrise tomorrow I should not be able to help you until another year had run its course. I will make you a potion, and before sunrise you must swim ashore with it, seat yourself on the beach and drink it; then your tail will divide and shrivel up to what men call beautiful legs, but it hurts, it is as if a sharp sword were running through you. All who see you will say that you are the most beautiful child of man they have ever seen. You will keep your gliding gait, no dancer will rival you, but every step you take will be as if you were treading upon sharp knives, so sharp as to draw blood. If you are willing to suffer all this I am ready to help you!"

"Yes!" said the little princess with a trembling voice, thinking of the prince and of winning an undying soul.

"But remember," said the witch, "when once you have received a human form, you can never be a mermaid again, you will never again be able to dive down through the water to your sisters and to your father's palace. And if you do not succeed in winning the prince's love, so that for your sake he will forget father and mother, cleave to you with his whole heart, let the priest join your hands and make you man and wife, you will gain no immortal soul! The first morning after his marriage with another your heart will break, and you will turn into foam of the sea."

"I will do it," said the little mermaid as pale as death.

"But you will have to pay me, too," said the witch, "and it is no trifle that I demand. You have the most beautiful voice of any at the bottom of the sea, and I daresay that you think you will fascinate him with it, but you must give me that voice, I will have the best you possess in return for my precious potion! I have to mingle my own blood with it so as to make it as sharp as a two-edged sword."

"But if you take my voice," said the little mermaid, "what have I left?"

"Your beautiful form," said the witch, "your gliding gait, and your speaking eyes, with these you ought surely to be able to bewitch a human heart. Well! have you lost courage? Put out your little tongue and I will cut it off in payment for the powerful draught."

"Let it be done," said the little mermaid, and the witch put on her cauldron to brew the magic potion. "There is nothing like cleanliness," said she, as she scoured the pot with a bundle of snakes; then she punctured her breast and let the black blood drop into the cauldron, and the steam took the most weird shape, enough to frighten anyone. Every moment the witch threw new ingredients into the pot, and when it boiled the bubbling was like the sound of crocodiles weeping. At last the potion was ready and it looked like the clearest water.

"There it is," said the witch, and thereupon she cut off the tongue of the little mermaid, who was dumb now and could neither sing nor speak.

"If the polyps should seize you, when you go back through my wood," said the witch, "just drop a single drop of this liquid on them, and their arms and fingers will burst into a thousand pieces." But the little mermaid had no need to do this, for at the mere sight of the bright liquid which sparkled in her hand like a shining star, they drew back in terror. So she soon got past the wood, the bog, and the eddying whirlpools.

She saw her father's palace, the lights were all out in the great ballroom, and no doubt all the household was asleep, but she did not dare to go in now that she was dumb and about to leave her home forever. She felt as if her heart would break with grief. She stole into the garden and plucked a flower from each of her sister's plots, wafted with her hand countless kisses towards the palace, and then rose up through the dark blue water.

The sun had not risen when she came in sight of the prince's palace and landed at the beautiful marble steps. The moon was shining bright and clear. The little mermaid drank the burning, stinging draught, and it was like a sharp, two-edged sword running through her tender frame; she fainted away and lay as if she were dead. When the sun rose on the sea she woke up and became conscious of a sharp pang, but just in front of her stood the handsome young prince, fixing his coal black eyes on her; she cast hers down and saw that her fish's tail was gone, and that she had the prettiest little white legs any maiden could desire, but she was quite naked, so she wrapped her long thick hair around her. The prince asked who she was and how she came there, she looked at him tenderly and with a sad expression in her dark blue eyes, but could not speak. Then he took her by the hand and led her into the palace. Every step she took was, as the witch had warned her beforehand, as if she were treading on sharp knives and spikes but she bore it gladly; led by the prince she moved as lightly as a bubble, and he and every one else marveled at her graceful gliding gait.

Clothed in the costliest silks and muslins she was the greatest beauty in the palace, but she was dumb and could neither sing nor speak. Beautiful slaves clad in silks and gold came forward and sang to the prince and his royal parents; one of them sang better than all the others, and the prince clapped his hands and smiled at her; that made the little mermaid very sad, for she knew that she used to sing far better herself. She thought, "Oh! if he only knew that for the sake of being with him I had given up my voice for ever!" Now the slaves began to dance, graceful undulating dances to enchanting music; thereupon the little mermaid lifting her beautiful white arms and raising herself on tiptoe glided on the floor with a grace which none of the other dancers had yet attained. With every motion her grace and beauty became more apparent, and her eyes appealed more deeply to the heart than the songs of the slaves. Everyone was delighted with it, especially the prince, who called her his foundling, and she danced on and on, notwithstanding that every time her foot touched the ground it was like treading on sharp knives. The prince said that she should always be near him, and she was allowed to sleep outside his door on a velvet cushion.

He had a man's dress made for her, so that she could ride about with him. They used to ride through scented woods, where the green branches brushed her shoulders, and little birds sang among the fresh leaves. She climbed up the highest mountains with the prince, and although her delicate feet bled so that others saw it, she only laughed and followed him until they saw the clouds sailing below them like a flock of birds, taking flight to distant lands.

At home in the prince's palace, when at night the others were asleep, she used to go out on to the marble steps; it cooled her burning feet to stand in the cold sea water, and at such times she used to think of those she had left in the deep.

One night her sisters came arm in arm; they sang so sorrowfully as they swam on the water that she beckoned to them and they recognized her, and told her how she had grieved them all. After that they visited her every night, and one night she saw, a long way out, her old grandmother (who for many years had not been above the water), and the Merman King with his crown on his head; they stretched out their hands toward her, but did not venture so close to land as her sisters.

Day by day she became dearer to the prince, he loved her as one loves a good sweet child, but it never entered his head to make her his queen; yet unless she became his wife she would never win an everlasting soul, but on his wedding morning would turn to sea foam.

"Am I not dearer to you than any of them?" the little mermaid's eyes seemed to say when he took her in his arms and kissed her beautiful brow.

"Yes, you are the dearest one to me," said the prince, "for you have the best heart of them all, and you are fondest of me; you are also like a young girl I once saw, but whom I never expect to see again. I was on board a ship which was wrecked, I was driven on shore by the waves close to a holy Temple where several young girls were ministering at a service; the youngest of them found me on the beach and saved my life; I saw her but twice. She was the only person I could love in this world, but you are like her, you almost drive her image out of my heart. She belongs to the holy Temple, and therefore by good fortune you have been sent to me, we will never part!"

"Alas! he does not know that it was I who saved his life," thought the little mermaid. "I bore him over the sea to the wood, where the Temple stands. I sat behind the foam and watched to see if anyone would come. I saw the pretty girl he loves better than me." And the mermaid heaved a bitter sigh, for she could not weep.

"The girl belongs to the holy Temple, he has said, she will never return to the world, they will never meet again, I am here with him, I see him every day. Yes! I will tend him, love him, and give up my life to him."

But now the rumor ran that the prince was to be married to the beautiful daughter of a neighboring king, and for that reason was fitting out a splendid ship. It was given out that the prince was going on a voyage to see the adjoining countries, but it was without doubt to see the king's daughter; he was to have a great suite with him, but the little mermaid shook her head and laughed; she knew the prince's intentions much better than any of the others. "I must take this voyage," he had said to her; "I must go and see the beautiful princess; my parents demand that, but they will never force me to bring her home as my bride; I can never love her! She will not be like the lovely girl in the Temple whom you resemble. If ever I had to choose a bride it would sooner be you with your speaking eyes, my sweet, dumb foundling!" And he kissed her rosy mouth, played with her long hair, and laid his head upon her heart, which already dreamt of human joys and an immortal soul.

"You are not frightened of the sea, I suppose, my dumb child?" he said, as they stood on the proud ship which was to carry them to the country of the neighboring king; and he told her about storms and calms, about curious fish in the deep, and the marvels seen by divers; and she smiled at his tales, for she knew all about the bottom of the sea much better than anyone else.

At night, in the moonlight, when all were asleep, except the steersman who stood at the helm, she sat at the side of the ship trying to pierce the clear water with her eyes, and fancied she saw her father's palace, and above it her old grandmother with her silver crown on her head, looking up through the cross currents towards the keel of the ship. Then her sisters rose above the water, they gazed sadly at her, wringing their white hands; she beckoned to them, smiled, and was about to tell them that all was going well and happily with her, when the cabin boy approached, and the sisters dived down, but he supposed that the white objects he had seen were nothing but flakes of foam.

The next morning the ship entered the harbor of the neighboring king's magnificent city. The church bells rang and trumpets were sounded from every lofty tower, while the soldiers paraded with flags flying and glittering bayonets. There was a fete every day, there was a succession of balls, and receptions followed one after the other, but the princess was not yet present, she was being brought up a long way off, in a holy Temple they said, and was learning all the royal virtues. At last she came. The little mermaid stood eager to see her beauty, and she was obliged to confess that a lovelier creature she had never beheld. Her complexion was exquisitely pure and delicate, and her trustful eyes of the deepest blue shone through their dark lashes.

"It is you," said the prince, "you who saved me when I lay almost lifeless on the beach?" and he clasped his blushing bride to his heart. "Oh! I am too happy!" he exclaimed to the little mermaid.

"A greater joy than I had dared to hope for has come to pass. You will rejoice at my joy, for you love me better than anyone." Then the little mermaid kissed his hand, and felt as if her heart were broken already.

His wedding morn would bring death to her and change her to foam.

All the church bells pealed and heralds rode through the town proclaiming the nuptials. Upon every altar throughout the land fragrant oil was burnt in costly silver lamps. Amidst the swinging of censers by the priests, the bride and bridegroom joined hands and received the bishop's blessing. The little mermaid dressed in silk and gold stood holding the bride's train, but her ears were deaf to the festal strains, her eyes saw nothing of the sacred ceremony, she was thinking of her coming death and of all that she had lost in this world.

That same evening the bride and bridegroom embarked, amidst the roar of cannon and the waving of banners. A royal tent of purple and gold softly cushioned was raised amidships where the bridal pair were to repose during the calm cool night.

The sails swelled in the wind and the ship skimmed lightly and almost without motion over the transparent sea.

At dusk lanterns of many colors were lighted and the sailors danced merrily on deck. The little mermaid could not help thinking of the first time she came up from the sea and saw the same splendor and gaiety; and she now threw herself among the dancers, whirling, as a swallow skims through the air when pursued. The onlookers cheered her in amazement, never had she danced so divinely; her delicate feet pained her as if they were cut with knives, but she did not feel it, for the pain at her heart was much sharper. She knew that it was the last night that she would breathe the same air as he, and would look upon the mighty deep, and the blue starry heavens; an endless night without thought and without dreams awaited her, who neither had a soul, nor could win one. The joy and revelry on board lasted till long past midnight, she went on laughing and dancing with the thought of death all the time in her heart. The prince caressed his lovely bride and she played with his raven locks, and with their arms entwined they retired to the gorgeous tent. All became hushed and still on board the ship, only the steersman stood at the helm, the little mermaid laid her white arms on the gunwale and looked eastwards for the pink tinted dawn; the first sunbeam, she knew would be her death. Then she saw her sisters rise from the water, they were as pale as she was, their beautiful long hair no longer floated on the breeze, for it had been cut off.

"We have given it to the witch to obtain her help, so that you may not die tonight! she has given us a knife, here it is, look how sharp it is! Before the sun rises, you must plunge it into the prince's heart, and when his warm blood sprinkles your feet they will join together and grow into a tail, and you will once more be a mermaid; you will be able to come down into the water to us, and to live out your three hundred years before you are turned into dead, salt, seafoam. Make haste! you or he must die before sunrise! Our old grandmother is so full of grief that her white hair has fallen off as ours fell under the witch's scissors. Slay the prince and come back to us! Quick! Quick! do you not see the rosy streak in the sky? In a few moments the sun will rise and then you must die!" saying this they heaved a wondrous deep sigh and sank among the waves.

The little mermaid drew aside the purple curtain from the tent and looked at the beautiful bride asleep with her head on the prince's breast; she bent over him and kissed his fair brow, looked at the sky where the dawn was spreading fast; looked at the sharp knife, and again fixed her eyes on the prince who, in his dream called his bride by name, yes she alone was in his thoughts!—For a moment the knife quivered in her grasp, then she threw it far out among the waves now rosy in the morning light and where it fell the water bubbled up like drops of blood.

Once more she looked at the prince, with her eyes already dimmed by death, then dashed overboard and fell, her body dissolving into foam.

Now the sun rose from the sea and with its kindly beams warmed the deadly cold foam, so that the little mermaid did not feel the chill of death. She saw the bright sun and above her floated hundreds of beauteous ethereal beings through which she could see the white ship and the rosy heavens, their voices were melodious but so spirit-like that no human ear could hear them, any·more than an earthly eye could see their forms. Light as bubbles they floated through the air without the aid of wings. The little mermaid perceived that she had a form like theirs, it gradually took shape out of the foam. "To whom am I coming?" said she, and her voice sounded like that of the other beings, so unearthly in its beauty that no music of ours could reproduce it.

"To the daughters of the air!" answered the others; "a mermaid has no undying soul, and can never gain one without winning the love of a human being. Her eternal life must depend upon an unknown power. Nor have the daughters of the air an everlasting soul, but by their own good deeds they may create one for themselves. We fly to the tropics where mankind is the victim of hot and pestilent winds, there we bring cooling breezes. We diffuse the scent of flowers all around, and bring refreshment and healing in our train. When, for three hundred years, we have labored to do all the good in our power we gain an undying soul and take a part in the everlasting joys of mankind. You, poor little mermaid, have with your whole heart, struggled for the same thing as we have struggled for. You have suffered and endured, raised yourself to the spirit world of the air; and now, by your own good deeds you may, in the course of three hundred years, work out for yourself an undying soul."

Then the little mermaid lifted her transparent arms towards God's sun, and for the first time shed tears.

On board ship all was again life and bustle, she saw the prince with his lovely bride searching for her, they looked sadly at the bubbling foam, as if they knew that she had thrown herself into the waves. Unseen she kissed the bride on her brow, smiled at the prince and rose aloft with the other spirits of the air to the rosy clouds which sailed above.

"In three hundred years we shall thus float into Paradise."

"We might reach it sooner," whispered one. "Unseen we flit into those homes of men where there are children, and for every day that we find a good child who gives pleasure to its parents and deserves their love, God shortens our time of probation. The child does not know when we fly through the room, and when we smile with pleasure at it, one year of our three hundred is taken away. But if we see a naughty or badly disposed child, we cannot help shedding tears of sorrow, and every tear adds a day to the time of our probation."

THE FIGHT IN THE FORETOP

James Boyd

WHEN LATE September gales were blowing, they raised the meager brown, green coasts of Scotland. For a month they had cruised in British waters; a dozen British merchantmen had lowered topsails to them; their orlop deck was crowded with three hundred British prisoners. Quite satisfied with what had been accomplished, the crew of the "Bonhomme Richard" figured out each man's prize money and grumbled in six different languages to be sent home; but every day the home port lay farther from the vessel's course and farther, too, it seemed, from Captain Jones' mind.

To Johnny Fraser, still working on the ship's accounts, spending the weeks at the wardroom table under the lean-faced purser's eye, the future had become a matter of indifference; there was nothing for him in gazing idly over the side while helpless merchantmen hove to and hauled down their colors; and even if it came to fighting, who ever heard of a purser's assistant in a naval battle? Most likely he would be put to passing water or carrying the wounded.

Seated one afternoon among his detested ledgers, he had just copied out an item in duplicate, or was it triplicate? His bored, bemused mind hardly knew; at all events, there it stood in all its futile imbecility:

June 9th, 1779, By 7bbl, best Norwegian turpentine,   £7, s.9, d.6.

The Captain's orderly entered, removed his cap, pasted an order on the wardroom wall. Johnny stared at him indifferently; he had long since ceased to look to orders of the day for interest, still less for excitement. Trivial in

from "Drums" by James Boyd. By permission of Charles Scribner's Sons.

themselves, they never by any chance had the remotest connection with a purser's assistant, who was, it appeared, a species outside the natural order as far as a ship's company was concerned.

The orderly having stuck the sheet of paper on the wall with two red wafers, turned and, fixing his eyes on the ceiling above Johnny's head, announced in sharp but lifeless tones, "You're in orders, sir." He put on his cap and marched from the room. Johnny stared at the bulkhead through which the man had disappeared.

" 'Seh'?" he said to himself. "Now why did that high-toned scoundrel call me 'Seh'? They ain't a man on the ship has done that except the niggers." He went to the order board and read the paper:

> On board the Bonhomme Richard Sept. 18th 1779
> Order No. 99
> From this date the following Altered Dispositions of
> Small Armed Parties will be observed in Action:
> Forecastle—Captain Richard Dale and American Marines
> Poop—Colonel Chamillard and French Marines
> Foretop—Midshipman Walters and twenty men
> Maintop—Lieutenant Fanning and thirty men
> Mizzentop—Ensign Crouch and twenty men
> Vice-Captains of the tops.
> Foretop—Mr. Fraser
> Main top——

Johnny Fraser was fumbling under the table. Where in the nation was his hat? There it was—the fine new French cocked hat of naval cut. He clapped it proudly on his spinning head and ran up to the deck. There, all was strangely quiet, orderly, unmoved by the stupendous event. The deck watch lay stretched in the feeble sunlight under the weather bulwarks, the lookout peered stolidly over the foretop's canvas screen; astern, the quartermaster lowered his eyes to the binnacle and touched the great mahogany wheel; on the quarterdeck, the watch-lieutenant paced slowly to and fro on the weather side; alone by the lee rail stood the short, square figure in dark blue just as it had always stood, it seemed, unchanged, immovable, unsleeping, since the first day they had left port. His eyes fixed aloft, he watched minutely how the canvas filled to the blustering, mist-laden wind.

Johnny Fraser gazed at Captain Jones with longing. He would give a hundred pounds to rush up on the quarterdeck, blurt out his thanks and devise, without a moment's delay, grand schemes by which the foretop should be fought. But he had long since learned that however much back-clapping, handshaking and convivial laughter there might be to Captain Jones when that commander was seeking to raise a crew on shore, at sea no man so much as spoke to him without authority. Spoke to him? By Zooks, it was worth a man's neck to look at him as Johnny was doing now! He glanced hastily away; he had best let the raw wind cool his burning cheeks until he could compose his mind, then confer in a quiet, steady manner with Midshipman Walters, an ancient, long-nosed seaman, raised temporarily, and much to his own discomfiture, to commissioned rank.

"Fraser!" The little man's great voice boomed up through the wind; the Captain was beckoning him.

"Ye've seen the orders?" Captain Jones asked as Johnny gained the quarterdeck.

"Yes, seh, and I certainly am obliged to you."

"Ye should be," said Captain Jones with a comfortable grin. "I'm over tender, I fear. When a man wishes to risk his life I've never the heart to deny him."

Johnny Fraser laughed, laughed on the quarterdeck where few men dared to smile. "Yes, that's so, but I'm obliged just the same."

"Aweel," said Captain Jones with a friendly jerk of his head toward Johnny, " 'tis no more than your due; ye've stuck by me; ye've done the dirty work and now ye shall have your share of glory."

"I'll try to make out all right, seh," said Johnny modestly.

"Ye'll make out, I've no doubt; jest ye remember this: to lead men in a fight, the great thing is this—to show them the way yourself and yet to keep your wits and eyes about ye and observe how matters stand." He whistled between his teeth. "It's naught but a question," he added, "of doing two things, neither of them easy, at the same time."

"Yes, seh," said Johnny, "I hope I'll have the chance to try."

Captain Jones leaned over the rail and gazed astern where the vessel's long white wake writhed and heaved across the tumbling seas.

"Nine knots," he observed. "We're logging nine knots toward as fine a chance to fight as ye'll ever wish for, boy."

"Yes, seh," said Johnny without conviction. "That's good. They's been nothing much to this picking up of merchantmen," he added superciliously.

For an instant Captain Jones seemed angry, then he smiled.

"Ye're an arrogant young cock," he observed. "But not so fast. There's more to it perhaps than ye guess. We've made prisoners and we'll exchange them and save just that many Americans from dying in the British hulks."

"Yes, seh," said Johnny more humbly. "I hadn't thought of that."

"Nor of what our raiding has done to the British navy, I dare say. They're scouring the Atlantic for us, which gives us a chance i' the Channel."

"My lord, seh!" Johnny muttered. "Are we bound fo' the Channel?"

"The same." He eyed Johnny keenly. "Have ye enough Scots blood to close your mouth? Well, then, since ye think there's naught to sinking merchantmen, I'll just tell ye what we're up to. We're off to take the Baltic Fleet."

"The Baltic Fleet!" Johnny pursed his lips to whistle. He had heard of that cloud of British merchantmen flanked by British men-of-war.

"Aye. We'll engage their men o' war and leave the convoy to be picked up by the lousy French sloops that are supposed to be our consorts." He drew himself up. "And that's the sort of skipper I am, my gay young fire-eater, so I hope ye're satisfied." He stared complacently into Johnny's awestruck eyes. "They gave me a medal for my last cruise." He gazed out over the sea. "But they'll be put to it to do me proper honor for this." Squaring off to the breeze he whistled gratingly. "Now mind ye. Not a word o' this; these men o' mine would rise against me if they knew where I was fetchin' 'em. Good luck." He nodded brusquely.

As Johnny went down the companionway, the Captain's voice descended after him. "Make the men take aim; it's i' the tops we'll beat 'em." Johnny turned; the ruddy blue-jowled face peered down at him. "I'll be watchin' the foretop for a nice, brisk fire," he favored Johnny with a grin, sardonic, cheerful and inspiring, "as long as there's a man o' ye alive."

On the fifth day they hove to and waited. They lay in a great bay whose circling shore reached round them to the north and ended in a brown, low-lying headland. The wind had fallen to a light air; all round the ship, the soft autumnal sunlight sank deep into the slowly heaving sea; beyond, it glanced and shone from shifting planes of water and, farther still, lay level on the surface of cold shallow green.

The men gathered at the rail and whispered; the coast they saw, the old hands said, was England, Flamborough Head; they knew the "Bonhomme Richard" would not lay to in sight of it without a purpose. There was wagging of whiskered chins amongst the old sea-dogs, rolling of eyes among the negroes and violent, whispered monkey chatter amongst the Malays and Portuguese.

The two bells marking one o'clock had scarcely died away when the lookout sang out sharply.

"A sail four points off the port quarter!" Silence fell; a young lieutenant with his glass under his arm ran along the gangway overhead and climbed up to the foretop. He had scarcely put his glass to his eye before the quarter-deck hailed him impatiently.

"Weel, Mr. Fanning, what do ye make out?"

"I make out nearly forty sail, sir," the lieutenant answered slowly, "in convoy; their course is South by East."

Johnny Fraser gripped the hammock nettings and peered at the horizon. "The Baltic Fleet!" he whispered to himself.

The boatswain's whistle sounded, the yards were squared away, sails filled, water murmured; the "Bonhomme Richard" stood out to meet the enemy.

By three o'clock the fleet, a long low cloud of canvas, could be seen from the deck where Johnny stood.

Now their own ship had been sighted. Within three minutes forty topsails were let fly, forty main courses fluttered distractedly in the breeze, the Baltic Fleet of merchantmen turned and fled for cover. The leading ship, however, stood on her course, the "Bonhomme Richard" still held hers. Drifting slowly in the light breeze, the two drew together until along the stranger's yellow side they could see the gun-ports of a British man-of-war. Her gilded figurehead shone, her bright blue upper works, fresh-painted, showed clear against the bright green sea. In the soft airs the red ensign at her staff, the pennant at her mast-head, formed graceful, slow-dissolving scrolls of color. Winking points of light across her poop marked where her company of marines paraded. Her new, varnished hull glowed softly in the green reflected light.

On board the "Richard" the boatswain's whistle sounded "Clear for action"; the groups that had been standing by the rail turned and ran for their stations. Fighting his way through the melee, Johnny Fraser gained the forecastle and climbed the ratlines to the top. The foretop crew were at his heels; in quick succession, their faces, keen, leathery, American, popped up above the foretop flooring.

"Stand by to hoist up arms and ammunition!" said Johnny. "Here comes the Captain of the top." Midshipman Walters crawled painfully through the opening; gasping for breath, he wiped his long, thin nose on the back of his wrist.

"You scurvy lime juicers!" he panted, "what the bloody blazes—! Lower away with that rope!" He peered down at the teeming deck. "Ahoy, you below, stand by with them there sandbags!" He turned back to the crew. "Now haul away! Snatch it, you bob-tailed parrots, snatch it!"

The sandbags were hoisted to the top and lashed to form a breastwork; tubs of water, kegs of powder, cases of hand grenades and twenty old French muskets followed. "Now, then, Mister," Walters turned to Johnny, "look at them muskets and see that the flints is right!"

"What if they is?" a tall Vermonter muttered gloomily. "You couldn't hit a man with one of these consarned waffle-irons 'less'n he was to lean his butt against the muzzle."

"Dot's so it iss," a stocky Pennsylvania Dutchman nodded his head with cheerful vigor. "And den efen, by Gott, bullet maybe come out de wrong end." He snapped the lock of his musket disconsolately. "Ach my, for vy ve haven't Deckhardt rifle, eh?"

"Oh, I dun't know," the Vermonter broke in. "Up to Varmount folks dun't set so much by Deckhardts; but there's a feller in Deerfield makes a gun——"

A red haired Georgian turned on the Vermonter. "God in the Mountain, Yankee, talk like you had sense. You know they's nothing to touch a Deckhardt."

"Darned if that ain't so," one said.

"Deckhardts, though," another answered, "ain't what they used to be."

The rest took up the argument. They closed in, disputing earnestly, wagged fingers, clutched each other's sleeves.

Down on the decks, match tubs were being set out behind the batteries, guns run back, tompions drawn, ram-rods, spongers, match sticks unshipped for action. On the forecastle the voice of the sergeant-major of Marines was calling the roll. The butts of their muskets thumped smartly on the deck.

Oblivious of the deck below, the foretop crew grew violent in dispute, they shouted each other down, denied and assented with powerful oaths, shook the despised French muskets in each other's faces.

"Sure she throws to the right—they all do."

"But she bears up her ball—you can draw fine up till sixty."

"But it was only half a charge, I tell ye."

"Yes, sir, a good two hundred yards or I'm an old bitch!"

"Bobcat hell! I bet it was a gray squirrel."

Enthralled by their aimless, incoherent tumult they grudged the second which it took to spit perfunctorily over the side; and as for the British ship, they did not waste a glance on her.

She, however, drew slowly nearer. Johnny could now make out the small blue and white figures of her officers on the quarterdeck. He could hear the faint piping of her bosun's whistle and see the pipe-clayed cross-belts of the British Marines.

The foretop argument having spent its first fury settled down to anecdote and retrospection. Leaning on the muzzles of their muskets, their heads cocked attentively, they rehearsed to each other the merits of all makes of rifles, recalled all known and many fictitious instances of marksmanship, girded themselves up sturdily to cover, re-cover and utterly exhaust the whole grand subject of the rifle.

The bosun's whistle sounded. Reluctantly they took their stations.

"By Zooks!" said Johnny, peering under the topsails. "She's nearly on us!" As he watched her, the Britisher came slowly about; the tall, yellow ship filled away, her port-side gun-port lids swung up, the muzzles of her guns peered from her depths. Immediately the "Bonhomme Richard" tacked ship and, paying off before the failing wind, drew slowly closer to her enemy. Below decks, Johnny heard the rumble of the carriages as the "Richard's" guns were run out to starboard.

Slowly, softly, they drifted together. The sunset light was waning but Johnny Fraser could now make out the English gun crews stripping off their singlets and the tall English captain with his blue coat, white breeches, cocked hat, sword and cane, standing by the rail, watching them through his glass, raising his speaking trumpet.

Across the shadowy, still water an English voice hailed them. "What ship is that?"

Captain Jones did not reply. With his eye aloft he turned the wheel himself, seeking some last advantage from the wind; forming a funnel of his hands, he went to the side.

"I can't hear what ye say!" he shouted. He brought his hands down with a chuckle.

For answer, a flame-pierced cloud of smoke burst from the English vessel's side; a dull roar followed, and the thump of round shot against the "Richard's" hull. Splinters leapt spinning through the air, a topsail ripped, a man cried out. Before Johnny could catch his breath, the foremast shuddered with the recoil of the "Richard's" broadside. "Huzzah!" he thought. "We're after them." He looked triumphantly below. But something had gone wrong; flame leapt from the hatchways; from the started deck seams long lines of smoke curled up in the still air. An endless moment's silence, then deep down in the ship, cries, hoarse, muffled, inarticulate, like the cries of wounded beasts.

Old Walters was beside him; his corded hand trembled on the sandbags. "Good Christ!" he muttered. "Them guns has burst. We're beat before we've started, boy." As he spoke a blackened figure with long red streamers trailing about its knees crawled from a belching hatchway, kicked slowly and lay still. Johnny Fraser looked away, a cold sweat broke out on his brow, crept down to his belly. His throat turned hard, his eyes swam, he felt the slobber running down his chin. By Zooks, he must not faint; he must not! What would his mother say? He rubbed his sleeve across his mouth and took a breath of air. Far off a voice was saying, "Steady, you men, stand by to open fire!" He blinked his eyes, stood up straight. The voice was his.

As they cocked their rifles, a second broadside from the enemy struck them. They fired blindly into the smoke. Before it cleared another broadside followed. Johnny peered down from the top and listened. At last he heard a feeble reply from the few remaining guns.

The two ships closed in. The English salvos began again while the "Richard" could only shiver, helpless, beneath the iron blows.

"Tell 'em to hold their fire," Walters said, "till she gits in range."

The foretop crew crouched down behind their sandbags and watched the British ship appear each time a little nearer through her cloud of broadside smoke.

"Cap'n," said the Georgian in a low voice, "let me have a shot."

"Aye, try it," Walters answered. "But only you, it's too fur yet." The Georgian pressed his lean chin against the stock and fired; the bullet struck half-way down the mast.

"Next time the smoke clears," Johnny said, "she'll be in range."

Walters tugged at his sleeve. "You tell 'em how to shoot, boy, that's out o' my line."

"Fire at their foretop," Johnny said, "and hold about three feet above their heads; lay right dead on 'em, they's no wind now." Another round from the Englishman's main batteries crashed along the "Richard's" littered deck. Then from behind the hovering smoke, the enemy's foretop came slowly into view. "Ready," said Johnny, "take aim, boys. Now let's see something drop. Fire!" The muskets rattled. Except for a few small splinters, the other foretop showed no damage. "My Lord!" thought Johnny, "we missed 'em; curse these muskets!" But now in the English foretop, a red-coated marine rose up slowly, stretched out his arms like a sleeper waking, turned slowly rigid, toppled, plunged to the deck below. "Come on, you boys!" shouted Johnny. "Load! Load! We reached 'em that time!"

From both ships he heard the crackle of small arms now; a spurt of sand flew in his mouth, he spit it out and grinned; he raised his rifle and fired at a figure crouching by the foremast; the man went down.

"You shoot goot," the little Dutchman nodded at him cheerfully over his swiftly sliding ramrod.

"We're bound to clean out their foretop," Johnny answered. "Hold on ther', brother, that's only half a charge." He took a powder-horn and charger from a seaman's hands, filled the charger neatly and poured it down the muzzle. "Take your time!" He crawled on hands and knees behind the crouching ring. "Aim steady at that foretop; we're gwine to burn 'em up!"

Now one thunder cloud enveloped both the ships; the foretop crew were forced to wait and fire at a shrouded flash or through rifts in the smoke; the Englishman, a faster sailer, drew slowly ahead. Shifting to the forward edge of the foretop, they followed her as best they could with their fire. Then she dropped back alongside, hung there just out of reach and pounded the "Richard" to pieces with her heavy guns.

"We ought to grapple," Johnny shouted in Walters' ear, "oughtn't we?"

"Grapple? Aye, but where's our wind?"

The wind indeed had fallen; the "Bonhomme Richard," her deserted decks a ruin, shuddered and wallowed on the oily sea. She answered the British broadsides with a scattered fire from three light guns.

"Whistle for a wind, boys!" Walters roared through the din, "if you want to save your skins. We've got to close with her!" Loading and firing their muskets, the men began to whistle. The only answer to their sailors' prayer was a blast of rifle fire from the enemy. Sand spurted, patches of sacking flew, the little Dutchman, his lips still pursed in a whistle, slid backward across Johnny's legs with a red hole in his forehead.

Unending minutes passed and still she lay becalmed, her big black hulk in splinters, her decks aflame.

"Oh, God," said Johnny, "send us a little breeze. Amen!" Peering over the port-side bags, he saw through a rift in the smoke, the littered deck, deserted except where under the pent house the helmsman still held his post and, beside him, Captain Jones stared up at the flapping topsails with a face to break a man's heart.

While Johnny looked at the smoke-rift it seemed to widen; over the water crept a small breath of air. He looked aloft. By Zooks, the topsails filled! He looked below, the water was slowly curdling along her strakes; she gathered way. The blunt, quick figure at the wheelhouse sprang to the wheel and spun it. The old ship answered, squared away, slid athwart the enemy's bows. The Englishman's bowsprit crackled amongst her rigging; a dozen men sprang up and lashed it fast; another breathless instant, and the two ships hung together, stem to stem.

From decks and tops burst out the frantic rattle of small arms. Old Walters squinted through a crack between two sandbags.

"We're just athwart their mizzentop," he said. "Let's clear it. When I say 'three,' we'll pop up our heads and give 'em a volley." At the word three, they poured a volley into the mizzentop; pale, smoke-veiled faces withered away before it, but a volley answered them, two men fell backward moaning, they dragged them aside, loaded and fired again.

A ponderous smothered grunt from beneath the enemy's deck made the foretop tremble; the heavy English guns were firing through their own port lids into the "Bonhomme Richard's" side. They could hear the muffled shouting of the British gun-crews and the heavy trundle of the guns as one by one, deep down, close to the waterline, they coughed and smote her—smote her with measured strokes, beat against her sides, against her desperate seamen's brains, like the drumming of a doom—unhurried yet inexorable. Johnny Fraser cast an anxious glance down through the floor of the foretop.

"Never mind that there below," Walters admonished. "Stick to their mizzentop!" They fired their volley again; the answering fire was weak and scattering.

"We've got 'em!" Johnny whispered. "Let this red-headed fellow and four more keep 'em down with muskets; we'll give 'em the hand-grenades!" Walters nodded and passed out the grenades; they rose together; two of them went down before they could let fly, the others hurled their iron bombs at the English mizzentop; it vanished in a burst of flame and smoke. They crouched again and waited till it came in view. They saw three solitary figures drop from the far side of the top and scramble down the ratlines for the deck. The Georgian was loading like mad, his charge was in, the patch and the bullet were at the muzzle, the ram-rod shot them home. Before the last of the three was half way down he raised his rifle. He fired; the man clutched the ratlines frantically, his head rolled back, his eyes stared fixedly at the sky; slowly his hands relaxed, he fell, slowly tumbling, into the sea. The foretop crew stood up, grinned, stretched themselves, then turned to the white-lipped wounded on the floor.

"We've done a good job," thought Johnny to himself as he tied a black silk handkerchief around a hairy arm. "A mighty good job."

"Come on now, mister," said Walters, "we got to clear her upper decks."

"All right, Cap'n, but we can't see a doggone thing from here."

"See it from their top, though. Come on! The whole passel of ye!" Old Walters swung out over the sandbags and worked his way along the yardarm to where the English yardarm fouled it.

"That's something I don't like," thought Johnny, as he watched the old man, spry but unhurried, sliding along the foot lines. He saw him pause in mid air, turn his long-nosed face over his shoulder in a glance of interrogation; slinging his musket on his back, Johnny followed him. He seemed to spend an age swinging alone and naked through dizzy chaos, the roar of guns beneath his feet, the moan of bullets in his ears, his musket flopping against his trembling thighs. Then Walters' hand seized his, he tumbled into the British mizzentop and fell on a heap of British dead. One by one the others followed; they cleared a space among the bodies and opened fire on the deck below them.

But now the ship which they had left burst into flame; all down her starboard side a glowing sheet leapt up, ran up the rigging in sputtering lines, gnawed at the topsails. Below them, too, broad flames climbed from the English hatchways; all firing ceased, on both ships scorched, half-naked seamen with waterbuckets ran stumbling across the ruined decks. Aloft, the top-men squirmed out on the yards, clapped their jackets around the blazing shrouds. The locked enemies lay silent except for the running feet along the decks and the fire's low malignant hum. The flames on board the Englishman died out at last, but the "Richard's" rotten timbers burned fiercer still. In the ruddy light, a frantic seaman ran to the "Richard's" quarterdeck.

"Quarter! Quarter!" he screamed out brokenly. His arms flew wide as he went down under the butt of Captain Jones' pistol. The English Captain had heard the cry.

"Have you struck?" His voice was proud and sharp. On both ships every man stood fast, turned anxious eyes to the "Richard's" smoke-veiled quarter-rail. The foretop crew crouched against the shrouds, listening. There was no sound except the seething of the flames. Then the little man's great voice came booming through the tops.

"Struck?" A cheerful, terrier grin was in the very tone. "Why, sir, I've not begun to fight!" Silence again. Then high aloft from the "Richard's" crosstrees they heard a sailor's long sardonic laughter. Cheering hoarsely, they stood up on the dead and opened fire. From behind a cloud rose a bloody harvest moon.

It had seemed after that as though the cloud and the bloody moon had settled down on them, enveloped them. Adrift in a sea of smoke—of blood—of fire—they swam, they sank, came up for air, swam on again. They made a bulwark of dead against the English fire, cursing the stiff, unwieldy bodies for their awkwardness. For uncounted ages they crouched among the corpses, winking their deep-sunk, burning eyes, sighting their red-hot muskets at puffs of smoke, at running figures, at desperate straining faces. And ever and again from high aloft, whirling, hanging, dropping from spar to spar, a dead man plunged slowly through their limbo to the pit where lost souls, black and naked, struck at each other with pikes and cutlasses across the hammock nettings.

And now Johnny Fraser, alone in a ruined blazing universe, was treading the airy footways; a heavy sack hung on his shoulder, clung to him, tried to bear him down.   Three blank-eyed ghosts reached out hands to him, seized the sack ravenously, clutched him to themselves.   Then the four of them were raining down hand-grenades.   The deck on which they fell was a blackened waste; great guns, however, still rumbled somewhere below; a feeble light showed in a hatchway.   Johnny Fraser waggled his stiff, thick tongue.

"Throw down the hatchway!" he muttered over and over again.   It was hard to do; the hatchway bobbed and swam across his eyes; the thing, he told himself, was to catch it at the turn where it always hung before swimming slowly back again.   He tried to tell the others, but his tongue had turned rigid, which made him cry.   Now their grenades, too, were bursting on the coamings.

A cone of flame shot from the hatchway, shot higher than the tops; it dropped to a steady blaze which showed the deck fresh-strewn with stripped dead bodies. The English mainmast, eaten half through by the gnawing of a single, distant gun, swayed slowly, plunged over the side.

In the silence which followed, a tall, solitary gentleman in blue coat and white knee-breeches appeared on the deck where no one else dared venture. He climbed to the quarterdeck, climbed to the poop.   Looking neither right nor left, he reached the great red ensign at the stern.   The British flag dropped down.

Old Walters struggled to his feet.   He clapped a bloody hand on Johnny's shoulder.   "She's struck, boy!"   A man among the heap of bodies gave a gurgling cheer; a great red bubble formed around his lips, burst with a tiny smack. "Go fetch a surgeon's mate," said Walters.

"Yes, seh . . . I will . . . yes, seh!"   Johnny Fraser's voice trailed off; he felt a warm stream dripping in his palm.   The harvest moon dove down at him and struck him to the ground.

All next day the hollow-eyed survivors worked unceasingly, they cut the sinking "Bonhomme Richard" free, they moved the wounded and what stores they could to the captured English frigate—the "Serapis," a new-built, fifty-four-gun ship of the line, on her first commission.

Lying on a chest in the cabin of the "Serapis," Johnny Fraser turned his face away from the odor of rum and vinegar, from the rows of wounded huddled on the floor and looked out the cabin window.   The sun was far down in the west; across its burnished wake lay the silhouette of the "Bonhomme Richard." Her deserted hulk lurched heavily as she drifted slowly astern, the sunlight glinted through her riddled sides, her head was buried under each light swell. He watched her steadily; the sun was sinking and she, too, was going down. Her decks were now awash, still she hung on—seemed to hang on blindly, sullenly, as if she did not know the fight was over. The end was near; a swell washed clear across her; her head went under, her dripping stern swung up, poised high in air, shone in the sunset light. She shot down out of sight so smoothly, the waters closed over her so smoothly, that Johnny Fraser wondered whether he could really have seen her there at all. And yet he must; for among the American seamen on the deck above him he heard a long-drawn whisper, half a groan, half a hushed cheer.

Three days later they dropped anchor in a broad, calm harbor flanked by salt meadows where belted cattle grazed and windmills made their grotesque gestures against the sky; up the harbor lay high-pitched roofs and brick gable-ends in fanciful designs. Round-faced Dutchmen in baggy pantaloons paddled out to them, pulled short pipes from mouths, grunted their admiration and surprise.

That night the Captain sent for Johnny. Nursing his bandaged arm, he climbed unsteadily to the quarterdeck. The light of the binnacle fell on Captain Jones' face and on a paper which he held in his hand. He nodded to Johnny briefly.

"Ye're good at figures, Fraser, so just tell me the answer to this!" He whistled between his teeth. "I've lost near half my men, I've seven hundred prisoners below decks, and I've got to work this ship to France."

"Well, seh," said Johnny with a white smile, "I reckon you can make the prisoners work—you made 'em fight."

"The answer is correct," said Captain Jones. "And that's the last bit of figurin' I'll ask from ye. The wounded are to be put ashore here, and that means you, I see."

"Yes, seh," said Johnny. "I'm sorry I can't be of more he'p."

"Hoots toots!" said Captain Jones brusquely. "Ye helped when ye were wanted, didn't ye? But here's what I sent for ye about. There's a Dutch brig in port makin' ready to sail for America. I've told them to hold a cabin for ye."

The color flowed into Johnny's face. "Home!" he murmured. "Yes, seh, thank you, thank you!"

"No thanks are due me. It's what I promised, and, on land or sea, I never do less than I promise, but, as a' the world knows, I sometimes do more." He drew himself up and gazed with grim arrogance across the star-strewn waters as if they were his own.

"Yes, seh!" said Johnny.

The inadequacy of this reply seemed to bring Captain Jones to himself; his brusque glance fell on Johnny.

"Have ye the money for your passage?"

"No, seh," said Johnny, "not much."

"Awell," said Captain Jones comfortably, "your friends can just pay your passage on the other side—and now good luck." He held out his hand, then made Johnny a naval salute. "And if anyone home should ask ye, ye can just say for me, that there was a real brisk fire from the foretop."

COLLISION AT SEA

Frank T. Bullen

No SOONER had the ship got to sea than the skipper arranged a three-watch system, whereby Frank had the first watch from 8 P.M. till midnight, Mr. Wilson the middle watch, and the mate from 4 A.M. to 8 A.M., thus giving each of the officers a long spell of rest and recreation, as well as a chance to feel their power of independent command. And as the captain invariably rose about 4 A.M., he was able to keep his eye upon the mate and see that he did nothing wrong, but he never actively interfered. What he said to the mate in the privacy of his cabin no one but themselves ever knew, but it was doubtless something very stern and searching. Yet it had no effect whatever.

The man was hopelessly incompetent and growing worse, not better, every day. So that when at noon all the officers were grouped on the poop with their sextants, getting the sun's meridian altitude, he was always the one to be out at even this, the simplest of all marine operations. For when you have, by moving the vernier on the arc of the instrument, brought the sun's lower limb in contact with the horizon and clamped it, you have only to turn the tangent screw gently as the sun rises until it rises no more, a sign that it is at its highest point or meridian for the day—it is noon at that particular spot. It is so simple, so easy, that any schoolboy could perform the operation with just a few minutes' tuition; but this poor bungler seldom if ever got a correct meridian altitude. And at the working up of the ship's noon position, while the agreement between the captain and Mr. Wilson and Frank was scarcely ever out more than a mile, it was the rarest thing for Mr. Carter to be within five miles of the correct position.

from "Frank Brown, Sea Apprentice" by Frank T. Bullen

Still, as I said, this matter did not affect the general comfort of the ship or the happiness of the two junior officers, who both made splendid progress, the captain saying one day to Frank, "What a pity it is you weren't either a *Worcester* or a *Conway* boy, or would have been able to come as second mate next voyage. As it is, you'll have to make another trip as third before you can go up for your ticket."

"Then all I hope and pray is, Captain Sharpe," brightly responded Frank, "that it will be with you. I don't care a bit about the position as long as I am treated as you treat me; I am happier than I have ever been in my life before."

"That's all right, my lad, you deserve all you're getting," answered the captain. "I am always very pleased with you."

At which Frank turned away, his heart too full for utterance, and yet with a sense of shame that he should have allowed the transient evil of being under Captain Forrest to have almost made him hate the noble profession. In which I do not at all agree with him, knowing as I so well do what a hell of misery a bad captain can make of a ship.

So the *Thurifer* fared homeward, happily, uneventfully, her crew all now thoroughly trained and ready for any eventuality, a ship where there were no quarrels or discontents, where the work went as goes well-oiled machinery, dominated by the splendid personality of one man. Shall I be believed when I say Frank actually dreaded the arrival of the ship at her destination? I am afraid not, yet such was really the case. As each day saw her drawing nearer home, he had hard work to keep from feeling downhearted with the prospect of another ship or another skipper in view; he felt so fit and so happy, that the idea of again being bullied and worried as he had been on the passage out almost terrified him. So that in very truth he was what the old salts used to say the perfect sailor must be, wedded to his ship. Indeed he grew to love her more and more every day, as the perfect weather they were having allowed them to paint, polish, varnish, and beautify her generally, even to the extent of granting a calm for two days, without more than an incipient swell, just to the southward of the Western Islands, so that they were able to paint her round outside quite close to the water's edge. Oh but they were proud men on board that ship, feeling that never did a homeward bound Sou'spanier come into port looking as their ship would look.

Nearer and nearer home they drew, still favored by fortune with the brightest and best of weather, until they were met in the chops of the Channel by a

heavy easterly wind, hardly a gale, but necessitating a good deal of stern carrying on in order to hold their own, since the bottom of the ship was of necessity foul, affecting her weatherly qualities very much.   Now it so happened
that just about this time Captain Sharpe was not at all well, not ill enough to
lay up entirely, but compelled to take all the rest he could.   And so he was not
able to be with Mr. Carter in taking over the "gravy-eye" watch, as it is called
—4 A.M.—when the tides of life run lowest, and some men find it positive
agony to keep awake.   There is little doubt that owing to the captain's constant supervision of him the mate had become utterly careless, so much so, that
even the fact that he was left to himself to watch over the lives of thirty-four
of his shipmates had no power to make him vigilant.   At least that is the only
construction I can put upon his behavior upon this terrific occasion, the account of which I am now about to give.

It was about 4.15 A.M., with a moderate gale blowing and the fine ship under
topgallant sails, a tremendous press of canvas for the weight of wind, was standing across the mouth of the Channel on the starboard tack.   As always with an
easterly wind up there the weather was clear, but there being no moon it was
fairly dark.   Still there was ample range of sight for a sailor.

Suddenly a shout was heard from the forecastle, "A green light on the port
bow, sir."

The mate emitted a sleepy roar in reply, but actually for several minutes did
not trouble himself to go to leeward and look, although he must have known
that by the rule of the road at sea it was his duty to give away to the other
vessel in the event of their approaching too closely to each other, and at night
it is impossible to be too careful with ships crossing.   When he did go over
and look, the crossing vessel seemed to leap out of the dark at him, she was so
close.

Panic-stricken, he ordered the helm hard up, but as the *Thurifer* swung
slowly off the wind, the officer in charge of the crossing ship having waited
in agony for some sign that the other vessel was going to do the right thing
and give way, until he could bear it no longer, hove his helm hard up also.
The result was that the two ships, which might have gone clear had both kept
their course, rushed at each other end on, and when the stranger hauled his
wind again, it was too late, he had only time to present his broadside to the
immense shock of the *Thurifer's* 4000 tons coming on at the rate of about
eight miles an hour.   There was an awful moment of suspense as men's hearts

stood still, a tremendous crash, and the huge steel wedge of the *Thurifer's* bow shore its relentless way right through the strange vessel's middle, amid a gigantic chorus of crashing masts, rending metal, and human yells of terror.

There are, I think, few more terrible and majestic spectacles to be witnessed than a collision at sea between two large ships, and especially between two large sailing-ships. The moment before the shock the immense cobweb-like entanglement of masts, yards, sails and rigging is towering skyward in all its graceful beauty and scientific arrangement, making the uninstructed beholder marvel, not merely how it can support the tremendous stress put upon it by the vast sail area acted upon by the wind, but how it is held in its place at all against the incessant pitching and rolling of the hull upon which it is reared.

But when two vessels like that come crashing into one another with an impact of several thousands of tons, and the mighty top-hamper comes hurtling down in ghastly entanglement of ruin, the scene is even more terrifying than that of some gigantic forest-tree with wide-spreading branches being struck by lightning and falling in an avalanche of riven fragments of timber. It is, however, a sight that is seldom seen by an outsider, and as, moreover, it usually occurs at night, few indeed are the people who have even had the momentary glimpse of its terrors caught by the crew of either vessel in their agony.

In the impact of the *Thurifer* upon the stranger, not one of the usual horrors was wanting. In the first place the *Thurifer* appeared to rebound as if aghast at the deed she had done, but her impetus carried her on again, rending and tearing her gigantic way through the hull of her victim, which was literally cut in twain, and heeling away from her, settled down as the *Thurifer* passed through her.

Amid all the horror of the scene, two figures in fluttering white were noticed on the top of the forward house of the doomed ship as it came abreast of the main rigging of the *Thurifer*.

Some instinct, I suppose, prompted Mr. Wilson to leap with a rope from the *Thurifer's* rail on the house of the other ship, shouting as he did so, "Come on, Frank—women!"

Frank was close behind him at the time, and in a very tempest of energy the two succeeded in saving the two unfortunates, who were indeed the wife and daughter of the captain of the sinking vessel. And as they were hauled into the rigging of the *Thurifer* they sent up shriek after shriek for "husband" and "father" in Italian, and had to be forcibly restrained from leaping back into the whirling blackness of sea and wreck through which the *Thurifer* was relentlessly ploughing her way. At last, that is after two or three minutes of eternity, the *Thurifer* dragged clear, her upper gear a mass of entanglement, ropes, sails, and masts carried away and dangling most dangerously overhead, while beneath her keel the mass of ruin which had so recently been a splendid ship settled quietly down to a final resting-place on the sea-bed.

Now here was a case where the most superb seamanship was absolutely of no avail for any attempt to save life. The ship could not be handled, for her braces and running gear generally were in an apparently inextricable confusion, no one knew the extent of the damage done to the hull, although the carpenter, true to the instinct of that most valuable class of seafarer, regardless of the falling and dangling gear overhead, ran and sounded the well, finding that she was as yet making no water. The boats were mostly destroyed, and in any case the falling wreckage had made it an impossibility to get at them even had they remained intact. So Captain Sharpe did the only thing possible, called all hands aft to see if any were injured or lost, and found to his delight that every man answered to his name.

But Mr. Carter was missing! Is missing still. Whether in horror at the deed he had done he had jumped overboard, or whether he had been knocked overboard by a falling spar, no one will ever know; he was gone, and, if the truth must be told, no one could regret him very much. The unanimous opinion was, "Well, poor chap, if he made a mistake, and there isn't much doubt that he did, he's paid for it with all that man has to give, and may God have mercy upon his soul."

Now, while Captain Sharpe was outlining his plan of work to the men, who were all recovered from their fright and confident in the safety of the ship, one of the boys came up to him with the startling news that two men had just crept into their house looking like lunatics, as indeed they were temporarily. How they got there they could not explain, but the supposition is that when the *Thurifer* passed through their ship, they, feeling only the blind desire to save themselves, had sprung at the black side of their destroyer, had caught some gear hanging outboard, or perhaps the chain plates, as the iron bars to which the standing rigging is secured and which are bolted on the outside of the ship are called, and had climbed on board, hiding in some corner until their paroxysm of fear had passed away, when they had emerged and entered the first open door they saw, which happened to be that of the boys' house. But they completed the tale of the rescued, four in all, the other two being the late captain's wife and daughter, whom the steward was vainly trying to comfort in the captain's cabin.

Daylight was now beginning to struggle through the mist on the horizon, and the wind was falling fast. So that after giving a few general orders as to the clearing away of the gear aloft in order to enable the ship to be handled, and men to move about the decks without the imminent danger to life and limb of spars falling upon their heads, the captain and carpenter went forward to survey the damage done to the bows. In truth it was a grim spectacle. The ministering priest, torn from his beautiful attitude of blessing, hung dolefully head downward, battered out of all recognition and only held by a few wrenched and twisted bolts whose tenacity would not be denied, and the thurible, that emblem of beatific aspersion, was gone.

The huge bar of iron which held down the bowsprit, the bobstay, was still in place though bent and curiously twisted, and so was the sturdy steel bowsprit itself. The jibboom with its great complication of stays, guys, footropes, sails, and downhaul was like a scene I witnessed once, where a man fishing from the end of a pier caught a conger-eel which he flung into the midst of his line by mistake and then attacked with his umbrella. It was just hideously hopeless, the sort of thing you want to cut off and let drift away as beyond the wit or skill of man to get disentangled.

The anchors, snugly stowed and firmly lashed to their respective bolts by the cat-tails, were all right but useless, for the hawse-pipes through which the cables should have led to secure the ship to them while they bit into the ground were torn and twisted beyond locating or use. And the stem, that splendid curvilinear girder of steel which had cleft the waves so proudly, it reminded now only of the battered, inhuman visage of an old prizefighter, so curiously bent and broken did it appear. Lastly, and most serious of all, the two sides of the bows were stove in, two huge rents appeared there, into either of which you might have driven a cart, and into which the unresisted sea flowed gaily, resurging discolored with coal-dust and laden with curious fragments, for the forepeak, as that part of a ship is called, was now getting such a scouring as it had never received since she was built.

But it will be asked, why did this fine ship not sink with such a tremendous wound in her most vulnerable part?   Only because of that invaluable invention, the water-tight bulkhead.   At a distance of some twenty feet from the stem or cutwater there is built into all such ships a barrier of steel plates at right angles to the line of the ship's keel, or right across the ship.   And the general practice was to build them without any door, so that neglect could not vitiate the safety they promised.   They were built quite perpendicular and flat, which I have always thought a mistake, a slight curve or angle from each side pointing forward would have made them so much safer when resisting the inrush of the water when the ship was head-reaching with a hole in her bows.

Now with the exception of any possible damage done to the bottom plates of the ship by the wreck as she bumped over it, the extent of the structural damage to the ship was fairly well defined, and as the bulkhead which kept the water out of the main hold was well shored up behind by the well-packed cargo of jute, and consequently there was little or no danger of its giving way under pressure of the head sea, Captain Sharpe's mind as far as the ship's safety was concerned was quite easy.

What, however, he could not rid himself of was the fear which all shipmasters must have when any accident to the vessel under their command occurs—would he be brought in as being to blame?   It is here that so much injustice is done to the men of the sea.   No allowance is made for possible accidents over which a man has no control; could have none, in the nature of the case, be he as careful and vigilant as a man may be, there being no discharge in this war.   And if he be brought in to blame, in most cases he falls, like Lucifer, never to rise again.   Too old for service as a junior officer in a tramp, he may get a precarious position in a line whose directors, trading upon their fellow-creatures' misfortunes, get skippers upon whom disgrace has come to command their vessels at a miserably inadequate salary, and keep them in terror of instant dismissal, making an immense merit of employing them at all.   Pah! the whole business is vile, it should stink in the nostrils of all honest men.

However, Captain Sharpe was not the man to allow his work to be hindered by any premonition of coming disaster to himself, so he proceeded as vigorously as he possibly could, aided to the utmost by his good crew, in the work of getting his ship so far repaired aloft as to be manageable.   This enormous task was made somewhat easier by the wind falling away to an almost perfect calm, during which many an anxious glance was cast around in the hope of espying some sign of life upon the floating wreckage. But never a glimpse did they see, and consequently, the work being unhindered by the arduous job of getting boats out, by nightfall they had her again well under control.

True, she looked ragged and unkempt aloft, a sad, strange contrast to the beautifully-rigged and splendidly-kept ship she was before the collision, but the great thing, getting her dirigible again, was accomplished by sunset. In this work the two rescued men took active part, albeit they had to be spoken to in sign language almost exclusively. But all sailors know that at sea this disability is no bar to the employment of fereigners, it being no uncommon thing for an officer to find himself commanding a whole crew, none of the members of which can speak more than two or three words of English, and some no word at all.

When at last the *Thurifer* was moving through the water again to a light south-westerly breeze, Captain Sharpe went below, and calling the steward, inquired after the well-being of his two unhappy and unwilling passengers. He was informed that they were now quite calm, and had taken a little food. So the good man went to their state-room and introduced himself to them, finding that the young woman spoke sufficient English to make herself understood. From her he learned that the sunken ship was the *Due Fratelli* of Genoa, bound from Peru to London with nitrate of soda, and that she had been one hundred and thirty days out when the calamity occurred.

More than that he could not ascertain, partly because the poor ladies were so overcome at the thought of all their woes and the anticipation of destitution in the future that they speedily became inarticulate with lamentation and sobbing, and such poor consolation as the captain was able to offer them was entirely unheeded. Moreover, he somehow could not help feeling that in a great measure they looked upon him as the author, or at least the proximate cause, of all their suffering. So after assuring them that every possible care should be taken of them, and that they should be landed as soon as possible, he left them to each other's sad company.

The vessel was now headed for Falmouth, and going at a fairly good rate, remembering her crippled condition, before the fresh breeze which had now sprung up. But the captain's mind was full of anxiety, knowing as he did that the bulkhead, which alone stood between them and foundering, was quite

weak in itself; indeed, but for the backing of the close-packed jute it would
not have been possible to sail the ship at all, for the sea rushing through those
two enormous holes in the bows would have soon crushed it in. And nothing
could be done to block those holes in any way, because of the great area of
open, ragged ironwork they presented to the incoming sea. However, the
distance being small, only some forty miles, and the wind as yet light, he hoped
for the best, and carried all the available sail, which drove her heavily along at
about four knots. Meanwhile every precaution was taken, in case of a sudden bursting-in of the saving bulkhead, to have the boats ready to get out at a
minute's notice, and all the equipment they required or could carry put into
them. And so that long, anxious night wore through, during which every
man who slept did so ready to jump for his life at the call.

Fortunately the weather held good throughout the night, and at the first
premonition of dawn the captain, sending Frank up on the main-topsail yard
to have a keen look around, was intensely relieved to hear him shout, "Land
right ahead, sir!" a shout that brought all hands on deck with a rush to realize
the good news. Shortly afterwards they were spoken by a tailor's boat, the
skipper of which, hearing the news, piled on all canvas he could carry for
Falmouth, in order to warn a tug-boat of the job that awaited them. The day
strengthened into beauty, and the great sun came out in all its autumn glory,
flooding the heavens with gold, as the once splendid *Thurifer*, like some gallant warrior wounded, his armor dented and broken, his proud plumes drooping and bedabbled with blood, dragging himself wearily homeward from a
stricken field, crept heavily towards the lovely entrance to Falmouth harbor.

The wind died away to a calm, the exquisite beauty of the shores, in all the
splendor of their autumn tints, lay basking in the sun, under a cloudless sky;
but most glorious sight of all to those hardly bestead ones was a grimy, fussy,
gasping tug heading straight for them. So she came panting up alongside, full
of importance, and lowering a boat put the pilot on board. There was no
bargain, only a warning word from Captain Sharpe that his ship was in no
danger, and that this towage was quite ordinary, having nothing in the nature
of salvage about it.

Then the tug's hawser was passed, and the *Thurifer* began to move gently
in towards the beautiful harbor of Falmouth. The sails were all furled as
neatly as possible under the circumstances, and presently, under the eyes of the
crews of the great crowd of shipping in the harbor (for Falmouth in those

days had an immense vogue as a port for orders), the crippled but gallant
Thurifer was towed to a berth alongside the wharf, where her arrival was
greeted with thunderous cheers by the great crowd which had assembled to
greet her on her triumphant emergence from one of the most terrible dangers
of the sea.   Then as soon as the shore warps were properly fast and the decks
cleared up, the very welcome word was given, "That will do, men," and
everybody retired to their respective portions of the ship's accommodation to
rest and think over their wonderful escape.

THE VOYAGE OF 1492

Christopher Columbus

BECAUSE, O most Christian, and very high, very excellent and puissant Princes, King and Queen of the Spains and of the islands of the Sea, our Lords, in this present year of 1492, acting on the information that I had given to your Highnesses touching the lands of India, resolved to send me, Cristobal Colon, to the said parts of India, and ordered that I should not go by land to the eastward, but by way of the west, whither up to this day we do not know for certain that anyone has gone.

Thus, in the month of January, your Highnesses gave orders to me that with a sufficient fleet I should go to the said parts of India, and for this they made great concessions to me, and ennobled me, so that henceforward I should be called Don, and should be chief Admiral of the Ocean Sea, perpetual Viceroy and Governor of all the islands and continents that I should discover and gain, and that I might hereafter discover and gain in the Ocean Sea, and that my eldest son should succeed, and so on from generation to generation for ever.

I left the city of Granada on the 12th of May, in the same year of 1492, being Saturday, and came to the town of Palos which is a seaport; where I equipped three vessels well suited for such service; and departed from that port, well supplied with provisions and with many sailors, on the 3rd day of August of the same year, being Friday, half an hour before sunrise, taking the route to the islands of Canaria, belonging to your Highnesses, which are in the said Ocean Sea, that I might thence take my departure for navigating until I should arrive at the Indies. As part of my duty I thought it well to write an account of all the voyage very punctually, noting from day to day all that I

from "The Journal of Christopher Columbus"

should do and see, that should happen, as will be seen further on. Also, Lords Princes, I resolved to describe each night what passed in the day, and to note each day how I navigated at night. I propose to construct a new chart for navigating, on which I shall delineate all the sea and lands of the Ocean in their proper positions under their bearings; and further, I propose to prepare a book, and to put down all as it were in a picture, by latitude from the equator, and western longitude. Above all, I shall have accomplished much, for I shall forget sleep, and shall work at the business of navigation, that so the service may be performed; all which will entail great labor.

Friday, 3rd of August. We departed on Friday, the 3rd of August, in the year 1492, from the bar at Saltes, at 8 o'clock, and proceeded with a strong sea breeze until sunset, towards the south, for 60 miles, equal to 15 leagues; afterwards S.W. and W.S.W., which was the course for the Canaries.

Saturday, 4th of August. They steered S.W. ¼ S.

Sunday, 5th of August. They continued their course day and night more than 40 leagues.

Monday, 6th of August. The rudder of the caravel *Pinta* became unshipped, and Martin Alonso Pinzon, who was in command, believed or suspected that it was by contrivance of Gomes Rascon and Cristobal Quintero, to whom the caravel belonged, for they dreaded to go on that voyage. The Admiral says that before they sailed, these men had been displaying a certain backwardness, so to speak. The Admiral was much disturbed at not being able to help the said caravel without danger, and he says that he was eased of some anxiety when he reflected that Martin Alonso Pinzon was a man of energy and ingenuity. They made, during the day and night, 29 leagues.

Tuesday, 7th of August. The rudder of the *Pinta* was shipped and secured, and they proceeded on a course for the island of Lanzarote, one of the Canaries. They made, during the day and night, 25 leagues.

Wednesday, 8th of August. Opinions respecting their position varied among the pilots of the three caravels; but that of the Admiral proved to be nearer the truth. He wished to go to Gran Canaria, to leave the caravel *Pinta,* because she was disabled by the faulty hanging of her rudder, and was making water. He intended to obtain another there if one could be found. They could not reach the place that day.

Thursday, 9th of August. The Admiral was not able to reach Gomera until the night of Sunday, while Martin Alonso remained on that coast of Gran

Canaria by order of the Admiral, because his vessel could not be navigated. Afterwards the Admiral took her to Canaria, and they repaired the *Pinta* very thoroughly through the pains and labor of the Admiral of Martin Alonso and the rest. Finally they came to Gomera. They saw a great fire issue from the mountain of the island of Tenerife, which is of great height. They rigged the *Pinta* with square sails, for she was lateen rigged; and the Admiral reached Gomera on Sunday the 2nd of September, with the *Pinta* repaired.

The Admiral says that many honorable Spanish gentlemen who were at Gomera with Doña Ines Peraza, mother of Guillen Peraza (who was afterwards the first Count of Gomera), and who were natives of the island of Hierro, declared that every year they saw land to the west of the Canaries; and others, natives of Gomera, affirmed the same on oath. The Admiral here says that he remembers, when in Portugal in the year 1484, a man came to the King from the island of Madeira, to beg for a caravel to go to this land that was seen, who swore that it could be seen every year, and always in the same way. He also says that he recollects the same thing being affirmed in the islands of the Azores; and all these lands were described as in the same direction, and as being like each other, and of the same size. Having taken in water, wood, and meat, and all else that the men had who were left at Gomera by the Admiral when he went to the island of Canaria to repair the caravel *Pinta*, he finally made sail from the said island of Gomera, with his three caravels, on Thursday the 6th day of September.

Thursday, 6th of September. He departed on that day from the port of Gomera in the morning, and shaped a course to go on his voyage; having received tidings from a caravel that came from the island of Hierro that three Portuguese caravels were off that island with the object of taking him. There was a calm all that day and night, and in the morning he found himself between Gomera and Tenerife.

Friday, 7th of September. The calm continued all Friday and Saturday, until the third hour of the night.

Saturday, 8th of September. At the third hour of Saturday night it began to blow from the N.E., and the Admiral shaped a course to the west. He took in much sea over the bows, which retarded progress, and 9 leagues were made in that day and night.

Sunday, 9th of September. This day the Admiral made 19 leagues, and he arranged to reckon less than the number run, because if the voyage were of long duration, the people would not be so terrified and disheartened. In the night he made 120 miles, at the rate of 12 miles an hour, which are 30 leagues. The sailors steered badly, letting the ship fall off to N.E., and even more, respecting which the Admiral complained many times.

Monday, 10th of September. In this day and night he made 60 leagues, at the rate of 10 miles an hour, which are 2½ leagues; but he only counted 48 leagues, that the people might not be alarmed if the voyage should be long.

Tuesday, 11th of September. That day they sailed on their course, which was west, and made 20 leagues and more. They saw a large piece of the mast of a ship of 120 tons, but were unable to get it. In the night they made nearly 20 leagues, but only counted 16, for the reason already given.

Wednesday, 12th of September. That day, steering their course, they made 33 leagues during the day and night, counting less.

Thursday, 13th of September. That day and night, steering their course, which was west, they made 33 leagues, counting 3 or 4 less. The currents were against them. On this day, at the commencement of the night, the needles turned a half point to north-west, and in the morning they turned somewhat more north-west.

Friday, 14th of September. That day they navigated, on their westerly course, day and night, 20 leagues, counting a little less. Here those of the caravel *Niña* reported that they had seen a tern and a boatswain bird, and these birds never go more than 25 leagues from the land.

Saturday, 15th of September. That day and night they made 27 leagues and rather more on their west course; and in the early part of the night there fell from heaven into the sea a marvelous flame of fire, at a distance of about 4 or 5 leagues from them.

Sunday, 16th of September. That day and night they steered their course west, making 39 leagues, but the Admiral only counted 36. There were some clouds and small rain. The Admiral says that on that day, and ever afterwards, they met with very temperate breezes, so that there was great pleasure in enjoying the mornings, nothing being wanted but the song of nightingales. He says that the weather was like April in Andalusia. Here they began to see many tufts of grass which were very green, and appeared to have been quite recently torn from the land. From this they judged that they were near some island, but not the main land, according to the Admiral, "because," as he says, "I make the main land to be more distant."

Monday, 17th of September. They proceeded on their west course, and made over 50 leagues in the day and night, but the Admiral only counted 47. They were aided by the current. They saw much very fine grass and herbs from rocks, which came from the west. They, therefore, considered that they were near land. The pilots observed the north point, and found that the needles turned a full point to the west of north. So the mariners were alarmed and dejected, and did not give their reason. But the Admiral knew, and ordered that the north should be again observed at dawn. They then found that the needles were true. The cause was that the star makes the movement, and not the needles. At dawn, on that Monday, they saw much more weed appearing, like herbs from rivers, in which they found a live crab, which the Admiral kept. He says that these crabs are certain signs of land. The sea-water was found to be less salt than it had been since leaving the Canaries. The breezes were always soft. Everyone was pleased, and the best sailers went ahead to sight the first land. They saw many tunny fish, and the crew of the *Niña* killed one. The Admiral here says that these signs of land came from the west, "in which direction I trust in that high God in whose hands are all victories that very soon we shall sight land." In that morning he says that a white bird was seen which has not the habit of sleeping on the sea, called *rabo de junco* (boatswain-bird).

Tuesday, 18th of September. This day and night they made over 55 leagues, the Admiral only counting 48. In all these days the sea was very smooth, like the river at Seville. This day Martin Alonso, with the *Pinta*, which was a fast sailer, did not wait, for he said to the Admiral, from his caravel, that he had seen a great multitude of birds flying westward, that he hoped to see land that night, and that he therefore pressed onward. A great cloud appeared in the north, which is a sign of the proximity of land.

Wednesday, 19th of September. The Admiral continued on his course, and during the day and night he made but 25 leagues because it was calm. He counted 22. This day, at 10 o'clock, a booby came to the ship, and in the afternoon another arrived, these birds not generally going more than 20 leagues from the land. There was also some drizzling rain without wind, which is a sure sign of land. The Admiral did not wish to cause delay by beating to windward to ascertain whether land was near, but he considered it certain that there were islands both to the north and south of his position. For his desire was to press onwards to the Indies, the weather being fine. For on his return, God willing, he could see all. These are his own words. Here the pilots found their positions. He of the *Niña* made the Canaries 440 leagues distant, the *Pinta* 420. The pilot of the Admiral's ship made the distance exactly 400 leagues.

Thursday, 20th of September. This day the course was W.b.N., and as her head was all round the compass owing to the calm that prevailed, the ships made only 7 or 8 leagues. Two boobies came to the ship, and afterwards another, a sign of the proximity of land. They saw much weed, although none was seen on the previous day. They caught a bird with the hand, which was like a tern. But it was a river-bird, not a sea-bird, the feet being like those of a gull. At dawn two or three land-birds came singing to the ship, and they disappeared before sunset. Afterwards a booby came from W.N.W., and flew to the S.W., which was a sign that it left land in the W.N.W.; for these birds sleep on shore, and go to sea in the mornings in search of food, not extending their flight more than 20 leagues from the land.

Friday, 21st of September. Most of the day it was calm, and later there was a little wind. During the day and night they did not make good more than 13 leagues. At dawn they saw so much weed that the sea appeared to be covered with it, and it came from the west. A booby was seen. The sea was very smooth, like a river, and the air the best in the world. They saw a whale, which is a sign that they were near land, because they always keep near the shore.

Saturday, 22nd of September. They shaped a course W.N.W. more or less, her head turning from one to the other point, and made 30 leagues. Scarcely any weed was seen. They saw some sandpipers and another bird. Here the Admiral says: "This contrary wind was very necessary for me, because my people were much excited at the thought that in these seas no wind ever blew in the direction of Spain." Part of the day there was no weed, and later it was very thick.

Sunday, 23rd of September. They shaped a course N.W., and at times more northerly; occasionally they were on their course, which was west, and they made about 22 leagues. They saw a dove and a booby, another river-bird, and some white birds. There was a great deal of weed, and they found crabs in it. The sea being smooth and calm, the crew began to murmur, saying that here there was no great sea, and that the wind would never blow so that they could return to Spain. Afterwards the sea rose very much, without wind, which astonished them. The Admiral here says: "Thus the high sea was very necessary to me, such as had not appeared but in the time of the Jews when they went out of Egypt and murmured against Moses, who delivered them out of captivity."

Monday, 24th of September. The Admiral went on his west course all day and night, making 14 leagues. He counted 12. A booby came to the ship, and many sandpipers.

Tuesday, 25th of September. This day began with a calm, and afterwards there was wind. They were on their west course until night. The Admiral conversed with Martin Alonso Pinzon, captain of the other caravel *Pinta*, respecting a chart which he had sent to the caravel three days before, on which, as it would appear, the Admiral had certain islands depicted in that sea. Martin Alonso said that the ships were in the position on which the islands were placed, and the Admiral replied that so it appeared to him; but it might be that they had not fallen in with them, owing to the currents which had always set the ships to the N.E., and that they had not made so much as the pilots reported. The Admiral then asked for the chart to be returned, and it was sent back on a line. The Admiral then began to plot the position on it, with the pilot and mariners. At sunset Martin Alonso went up on the poop of his ship, and with much joy called to the Admiral, claiming the reward as he had sighted land. When the Admiral heard this positively declared, he says that he gave thanks to the Lord on his knees, while Martin Alonso said the *Gloria in excelsis* with his people. The Admiral's crew did the same. Those of the *Niña* all went up on the mast and into the rigging, and declared that it was land. It so seemed to the Admiral, and that it was distant 25 leagues. They all continued to declare it was land until night. The Admiral ordered the course to be altered from W. to S.W., in which direction the land had appeared. That day they made 4 leagues on a west course, and 17 S.W. during the night, in all 21; but the people were told that 13 was the distance made good; for it was always feigned to them that the distances were less, so that the voyage might not appear so long. Thus two reckonings were kept on this voyage, the shorter being feigned, and the longer being the true one. The sea was very smooth, so that many sailors bathed alongside. They saw many *dorados* and other fish.

Wednesday, 26th of September. The Admiral continued on the west course until after noon. Then he altered course to S.W., until he made out that what had been said to be land was only clouds. Day and night they made 31 leagues, counting 24 for the people. The sea was like a river, the air pleasant and very mild.

Thursday, 27th of September. The course west, and distance made good during day and night 24 leagues, 20 being counted for the people. Many *dorados* came. One was killed. A boatswain bird came.

Friday, 28th of September. The course was west, and the distance, owing to calms, only 14 leagues in day and night, 13 leagues being counted. They met with little weed; but caught two *dorados*, and more in the other ships.

Saturday, 29th of September. The course was west, and they made 24 leagues, counting 21 for the people. Owing to calms, the distance made good during day and night was not much. They saw a bird called *rabiforcado* (man-o'-war bird), which makes the boobies vomit what they have swallowed, and eats it, maintaining itself on nothing else. It is a sea-bird, but does not sleep on the sea, and does not go more than 20 leagues from the land. There are many of them at the Cape Verde Islands. Afterwards they saw two boobies. The air was very mild and agreeable, and the Admiral says that nothing was wanting but to hear the nightingale. The sea smooth as a river. Later, three boobies and a man-o'-war bird were seen three times. There was much weed.

Sunday, 30th of September. The western course was steered, and during the day and night, owing to calms, only 14 leagues were made, 11 being counted. Four boatswain-birds came to the ship, which is a great sign of land, for so many birds of this kind together is a sign that they are not straying or lost. They also twice saw four boobies. There was much weed. *Note* that the stars which are called *las guardias* (the Pointers), when night comes on, are near the western point, and when dawn breaks they are near the N.E. point; so that, during the whole night, they do not appear to move more than three lines or 9 hours, and this on each night. The Admiral says this, and also that at nightfall the needles vary a point westerly, while at dawn they agree exactly with the star. From this it would appear that the north star has a movement like the other stars, while the needles always point correctly.

Monday, 1st of October. Course west, and 25 leagues made good, counted for the crew as 20 leagues. There was a heavy shower of rain. At dawn the Admiral's pilot made the distance from Hierro 578 leagues to the west. The reduced reckoning which the Admiral showed to the crew made it 584 leagues; but the truth which the Admiral observed and kept secret was 707.

Tuesday, 2nd of October. Course west, and during the day and night 39 leagues were made good, counted for the crew as 30. The sea always smooth. Many thanks be given to God, says the Admiral, that the wind is coming from east to west, contrary to its usual course. Many fish were seen, and one was killed. A white bird was also seen that appeared to be a gull.

Wednesday, 3rd of October. They navigated on the usual course, and made good 47 leagues, counted as 40. Sandpipers appeared, and much weed, some of it very old and some quite fresh and having fruit. They saw no birds. The Admiral, therefore, thought that they had left the islands behind them which were depicted on the charts. The Admiral here says that he did not wish to keep the ships beating about during the last week, and in the last few days when there were so many signs of land, although he had information of certain islands in this region. For he wished to avoid delay, his object being to reach the Indies. He says that to delay would not be wise.

Thursday, 4th of October. Course west, and 63 leagues made good during the day and night, counted as 46. More than forty sandpipers came to the ship in a flock, and two boobies, and a ship's boy hit one with a stone. There also came a man-o'-war bird, and a white bird like a gull.

Friday, 5th of October. The Admiral steered his course, going 11 miles an hour, and during the day and night they made good 57 leagues, as the wind increased somewhat during the night: 45 were counted. The sea was smooth and quiet. "To God," he says, "be many thanks given, the air being pleasant and temperate, with no weed, many sandpipers, and flying-fish coming on the deck in numbers."

Saturday, 6th of October. The Admiral continued his west course, and during day and night they made good 40 leagues, 33 being counted. This night Martin Alonso said that it would be well to steer south of west, and it appeared to the Admiral that Martin Alonso did not say this with respect to the island of Cipango. He saw that if an error was made the land would not be reached so quickly, and that consequently it would be better to go at once to the continent and afterwards to the islands.

Sunday, 7th of October. The west course was continued; for two hours they went at the rate of 12 miles an hour, and afterwards 8 miles an hour. They made good 23 leagues, counting 18 for the people. This day, at sunrise, the caravel *Niña*, which went ahead, being the best sailer, and pushed forward as much as possible to sight the land first, so as to enjoy the reward which the Sovereigns had promised to whoever should see it first, hoisted a flag at the mast-head and fired a gun, as a signal that she had sighted land, for such was the Admiral's order. He had also ordered that, at sunrise and sunset, all the ships should join him; because those two times are most proper for seeing the greatest distance, the haze clearing away. No land was seen during the afternoon, as reported by the caravel *Niña,* and they passed a great number of birds flying from N. to S.W. This gave rise to the belief that the birds were either going to sleep on land, or were flying from the winter which might be supposed to be near in the land whence they were coming. The Admiral was aware that most of the islands held by the Portuguese were discovered by the flight of birds. For this reason he resolved to give up the west course, and to shape a course W.S.W. for the two following days. He began the new course one hour before sunset. They made good, during the night about 5 leagues, and 23 in the day, altogether 28 leagues.

Monday, 8th of October. The course was W.S.W., and 11½ or 12 leagues were made good in the day and night; and at times it appears that they went at the rate of 15 miles an hour during the night (if the handwriting be not deceptive). The sea was like the river at Seville. "Thanks be to God," says the Admiral, "the air is very soft like the April at Seville; and it is a pleasure to be here, so balmy are the breezes." The weed seemed to be very fresh. There were many land-birds, and they took one that was flying to the S.W. Terns, ducks, and a booby were also seen.

Tuesday, 9th of October. The course was S.W., and they made 5 leagues. The wind then changed, and the Admiral steered W. by N. 4 leagues. Altogether, in day and night, they made 11 leagues by day and 20½ by night; counted as 17 leagues altogether. Throughout the night birds were heard passing.

Wednesday, 10th of October. The course was W.S.W., and they went at the rate of 10 miles an hour, occasionally 12 miles, and sometimes 7. During the day and night they made 59 leagues, counted as no more than 44. Here the people could endure no longer. They complained of the length of the voyage. But the Admiral cheered them up in the best way he could, giving them good hopes of the advantages they might gain from it. He added that, however much they might complain, he had to go to the Indies, and that he would go on until he found them, with the help of the Lord.

Thursday, 11th of October.   The course was W.S.W. and there was more sea than there had been during the whole of the voyage.   They saw sandpipers, and a green reed near the ship.   Those of the caravel *Pinta* saw a cane and a pole, and they took up another small pole which appeared to have been worked with iron; also another bit of cane, a land-plant, and a small board. The crew of the caravel *Niña* also saw signs of land, and a small branch covered with berries.   Everyone breathed afresh and rejoiced at these signs.   The run until sunset was 26 leagues.

After sunset the Admiral returned to his original west course and they went along at the rate of 12 miles an hour.   Up to two hours after midnight they had gone 90 miles, equal to 22½ leagues.   As the caravel *Pinta* was a better sailer, and went ahead of the Admiral, she found the land, and made the signals ordered by the Admiral.   The land was first seen by a sailor named Rodrigo de Triana.   But the Admiral, at ten in the previous night, being on the castle of the poop, saw a light, though it was so uncertain that he could not affirm it was land.   He called Pero Gutierrez, a gentleman of the King's bedchamber, and said that there seemed to be a light, and that he should look at it.   He did so, and saw it.   The Admiral said the same to Rodrigo Sanchez of Segovia, whom the King and Queen had sent with the fleet as inspector, but he could see nothing because he was not in a place whence anything could be seen.   After the Admiral had spoken he saw the light once or twice, and it was like a wax candle rising and falling.   It seemed to few to be an indication of land; but the Admiral made certain that land was close. When they said the *Salve*, which all the sailors were accustomed to sing in their way, the Admiral asked and admonished the men to keep a good lookout on the forecastle, and to watch well for land; and to him who should first cry out that he saw land, he would give a silk doublet, besides the rewards promised by the Sovereigns, which were 10,000 maravedis to him who should first see it.   At two hours after midnight the land was sighted at a distance of two leagues.   The shortened sail, and lay under the mainsail without the bonnets.   The vessels were hove to, waiting for daylight; and on Friday they arrived at a small island of the Lucayos, called, in the language of the Indians, *Guanahani*.   Presently they saw naked people.   The Admiral went on shore in the armed boat, and Martin Alonso Pinzon, and Vicente Yañez, his brother, who was captain of the *Niña*.   The Admiral took the royal standard, and the captains went with two banners of the green cross, which the Admiral took in all the ships as a sign, with an F and a Y and a crown over each letter, one on one side of the cross and the other on the other. Having landed, they saw trees very green, and much water, and fruits of diverse kinds. The Admiral called to the two captains and to the others who leaped on shore, and to Rodrigo Escovedo, secretary of the whole fleet, and to Rodrigo Sanchez of Segovia, and said that they should bear faithful testimony that he, in presence of all, had taken, as he now took, possession of the said island for the King and for the Queen, his Lords.

THE WRECK
OF THE ROYAL CAROLINE

James Fenimore Cooper

O UR WATCHFUL adventurer was not blind to these sinister omens. No sooner did the peculiar atmosphere by which the mysterious image that he so often examined was suddenly surrounded, catch his eye, than his voice was raised in the clear, powerful, and exciting notes of warning.

"Stand by," he called aloud, "to in-all-studding-sails! Down with them!" he added, scarcely giving his former words time to reach the ears of his subordinates. "Down with every rag of them, fore and aft the ship! Man the top-gallant clew-lines, Mr. Earing. Clew up, and clew down! In with everything, cheerily, men!—In!"

This was a language to which the crew of the *Caroline* were no strangers, and it was doubly welcome, since the meanest seaman amongst them had long thought that his unknown commander had been heedlessly trifling with the safety of the vessel, by the hardy manner in which he disregarded the wild symptoms of the weather. But they undervalued the keen-eyed vigilance of Wilder. He had certainly driven the Bristol trader through the water at a rate she had never been known to go before; but, thus far, the facts themselves gave evidence in his favor, since no injury was the consequence of what they deemed temerity. At the quick sudden order just given, however, the whole ship was in an uproar. A dozen seamen called to each other, from different parts of the vessel, each striving to lift his voice above the roaring ocean; and there was every appearance of a general and inextricable confusion; but the same authority which had so unexpectedly aroused them into

from "The Red Rover" by James Fenimore Cooper

activity, produced order from their ill-directed though vigorous efforts.

Wilder had spoken, to awaken the drowsy and to excite the torpid. The instant he found each man on the alert, he resumed his orders with a calmness that gave a direction to the powers of all, and yet with an energy that he well knew was called for by the occasion. The enormous sheets of duck, which had looked like so many light clouds in the murky and threatening heavens, were soon seen fluttering wildly, as they descended from their high places, and, in a few minutes, the ship was reduced to the action of her more secure and heavier canvass. To effect this object, every man in the ship exerted his powers to the utmost, under the guidance of the steady but rapid mandates of their commander. Then followed a short and apprehensive pause. All eyes were turned towards the quarter where the ominous signs had been discovered; and each individual endeavored to read their import, with an intelligence correspondent to the degree of skill he might have acquired, during his particular period of service on that treacherous element which was now his home.

The dim tracery of the stranger's form had been swallowed by the flood of misty light, which, by this time, rolled along the sea like drifting vapor, semipellucid, preternatural, and seemingly tangible. The ocean itself appeared admonished that a quick and violent change was nigh. The waves ceased to break in their former foaming and brilliant crests, and black masses of the water lifted their surly summits against the eastern horizon, no longer shedding their own peculiar and lucid atmosphere around them. The breeze which had been so fresh, and which had even blown with a force that nearly amounted to a gale, was lulling and becoming uncertain, as it might be awed by the more violent power that was gathering along the borders of the sea, in the direction of the neighboring continent. Each moment, the eastern puffs of air lost their strength, becoming more and more feeble, until, in an incredibly short period, the heavy sails were heard flapping against the masts. A frightful and ominous calm succeeded. At this instant, a gleam flashed from the fearful obscurity of the ocean, and a roar, like that of a sudden burst of thunder, bellowed along the waters. The seamen turned their startled looks on each other, standing aghast, as if a warning of what was to follow had come out of the heavens themselves. But their calm and more sagacious commander put a different construction on the signal. His lip curled, in high professional pride, and he muttered with scorn,——

"Does he imagine that we sleep? Ay, he has got it himself, and would open our eyes to what is coming! What does he conjecture we have been about, since the middle watch was set?"

Wilder made a swift turn or two on the quarter-deck, turning his quick glances from one quarter of the heavens to another; from the black and lulling water on which his vessel was rolling, to the sails; and from his silent and profoundly expectant crew, to the dim lines of spars that were waving above his head, like so many pencils tracing their curvilinear and wanton images over the murky volumes of the superincumbent clouds.

"Lay the after-yards square!" he said, in a voice which was heard by every man on deck, though his words were apparently spoken but little above his breath. The creaking of the blocks, as the spars came slowly and heavily round to the indicated position, contributed to the imposing character of the moment, sounding like notes of fearful preparation.

"Haul up the courses!" resumed Wilder with the same eloquent calmness of manner. Then, taking another glance at the threatening horizon, he added slowly but with emphasis, "Furl them—furl them both. Away aloft, and hand your courses!" he continued in a shout; "roll them up, cheerily; in with them, boys, cheerily; in!"

The conscious seamen took their impulses from the tones of their commander. In a moment, twenty dark forms were leaping up the rigging, with the alacrity of so many quadrupeds. In another minute, the vast and powerful sheets of canvas were effectually rendered harmless, by securing them in tight rolls to their respective spars. The men descended as swiftly as they had mounted to the yards; and then succeeded another breathing pause. At this appalling moment, a candle would have sent its flame perpendicularly towards the heavens. The ship, missing the steadying power of the wind, rolled heavily in the troughs of the seas, which began to lessen at each instant, as if the startled element was recalling into the security of its own vast bosom that portion of its particles which had so lately been permitted to gambol madly over its surface. The water washed sullenly along the side of the ship, or, as she laboring rose from one of her frequent falls into the hollows of the waves, it shot back into the ocean from her decks in glittering cascades. Every hue of the heavens, every sound of the element, and each dusky and anxious countenance, helped to proclaim the intense interest of the moment. In this brief interval of expectation and inactivity, the mates again approached their commander.

"It is an awful night, Captain Wilder!" said Earing, presuming on his rank to be the first to speak.

"I have known far less notice given of a shift of wind," was the answer.

"We have had time to gather in our kites, 'tis true, sir; but there are signs and warnings that come with this change which the oldest seaman must dread!"

"Yes," continued Knighthead, in a voice that sounded hoarse and powerful, even amid the fearful accessories of that scene; "yes, it is no trifling commission that can call people that I shall not name out upon the water in such a night as this. It was in just such weather that I saw the *Vesuvius* ketch go to a place so deep, that her own mortar would not have been able to have sent a bomb into the open air, had hands and fire been there fit to let it off!"

"Aye; and it was in such a time that the *Greenlandman* was cast upon the Orkneys, in as flat a calm as ever lay on the sea."

"Gentlemen," said Wilder, with a peculiar and perhaps an ironical emphasis on the word, "what would ye have? There is not a breath of air stirring, and the ship is naked to her top-sails!"

It would have been difficult for either of the two malcontents to give a very satisfactory answer to this question. Both were secretly goaded by mysterious and superstitious apprehensions, that were powerfully aided by the more real and intelligible aspect of the night; but neither had so far forgotten his manhood, and his professional pride, as to lay bare the full extent of his own weakness, at a moment when he was liable to be called upon for the exhibition of qualities of a more positive and determined character. The feeling that was uppermost betrayed itself in the reply of Earing, though in an indirect and covert manner.

"Yes, the vessel is snug enough now," he said, "though eyesight has shown us it is no easy matter to drive a freighted ship through the water as fast as one of those flying craft aboard which no man can say who stands at the helm, by what compass she steers, or what is her draught!"

"Aye," resumed Knighthead, "I call the *Caroline* fast for an honest trader. There are few square-rigged boats who do not wear the pennants of the king, that can eat her out of the wind on a bowline, or bring her into their wake with studding-sails set. But this is a time and an hour to make a seaman think. Look at yon hazy light, here in with the land, that is coming so fast down upon us, and then tell me whether it comes from the coast of America, or whether it comes from out of the stranger who has been so long running under our lee, but who has got, or is fast getting, the wind of us at last, while none here can say how, or why. I have just this much, and no more, to say: give me for consort a craft whose captain I know, or give me none!"

"Such is your taste, Mr. Knighthead," said Wilder, coldly; "mine may, by some accident, be different."

"Yes, yes," observed the more cautious and prudent Earing, "in time of war, and with letters of marque aboard, a man may honestly hope the sail he sees should have a stranger for her master; or otherwise he would never fall in with an enemy. But, though an Englishman born myself, I should rather give the ship in that mist a clear sea, seeing that I neither know her nation nor her cruise. Ah, Captain Wilder, this is an awful sight for the morning watch! Often and often have I seen the sun rise in the east, and no harm done; but little good can come of a day when the light first breaks in the west. Cheerfully would I give the owners the last month's pay, hard as it has been earned, did I but know under what flag the stranger sails."

"Frenchman, Don, or Devil, yonder he comes!" cried Wilder. Then, turning towards the attentive crew, he shouted, in a voice that was appalling by its vehemence and warning, "Let run the after-halyards! round with the fore-yard; round with it, men, with a will!"

These were cries that the startled crew but too well understood. Every nerve and muscle were exerted to execute the orders, to be in readiness for the tempest. No man spoke; but each expended the utmost of his power and skill in direct and manly efforts. Nor was there, in verity, a moment to lose, or a particle of human strength expended here, without a sufficient object.

The lurid and fearful-looking mist, which, for the last quarter of an hour, had been gathering in the northwest, was driving down upon them with the speed of a race horse. The air had already lost the damp and peculiar feeling of an easterly breeze; and little eddies were beginning to flutter among the masts—precursors of the coming squall. Then, a rushing, roaring sound was heard moaning along the ocean, whose surface was first dimpled, next ruffled, and finally covered with a sheet of clear, white, and spotless foam. At the next moment, the power of the wind fell upon the inert and laboring Bristol trader.

While the gust was approaching, Wilder had seized the slight opportunity afforded by the changeful puffs of air to get the ship as much as possible before the wind; but the sluggish movement of the vessel met neither the wishes of his own impatience nor the exigencies of the moment. Her bows slowly and heavily fell off from the north, leaving her precisely in a situation to receive the first shock on her broadside. Happy it was, for all who had life at risk in that defenseless vessel, that she was not fated to receive the whole weight of the tempest at a blow. The sails fluttered and trembled on their massive yards, bellying and collapsing alternately for a minute, and then the rushing wind swept over them in a hurricane.

The *Caroline* received the blast like a stout and buoyant ship as she was, yielding to its impulse until her side lay nearly incumbent on the element; and then, as if the fearful fabric were conscious of its jeopardy, it seemed to lift its reclining masts again, struggling to work its way through the water.

"Keep the helm-a-weather! Jam it a-weather, for your life!" shouted Wilder, amid the roar of the gust.

The veteran seaman at the wheel obeyed the order with steadiness, but in vain did he keep his eyes on the margin of his head sail, to watch the manner in which the ship would obey its power. Twice more, in as many moments, the giddy masts fell towards the horizon, waving as often gracefully upward, and then they yielded to the mighty pressure of the wind, until the whole machine lay prostrate on the water.

"Be cool!" said Wilder, seizing the bewildered Earing by the arm, as the latter rushed madly up the steep of the deck; "it is our duty to be calm: bring hither an ax."

Quick as the thought which gave the order, the admonished mate complied, jumping into the mizzen-channels of the ship, to execute with his own hands the mandate that he knew must follow.

"Shall I cut?" he demanded, with uplifted arms, and in a voice that atoned for his momentary confusion, by its steadiness and force.

"Hold!—Does the ship mind her helm at all?"

"Not an inch, sir."

"Then cut," Wilder clearly and calmly added.

A single blow sufficed for the discharge of this important duty. Extended to the utmost powers of endurance, by the vast weight it upheld, the lanyard struck by Earing no sooner parted, than each of its fellows snapped in succession, leaving the mast dependent on its wood for the support of all the ponderous and complicated hamper it upheld. The cracking of the spar came next; and the whole fell, like a tree that had been snapped at its foundation.

"Does she fall off?" called Wilder, to the observant seaman at the wheel.

"She yielded a little, sir; but this new squall is bringing her up again."

"Shall I cut?" shouted Earing from the main-rigging, whither he had leaped, like a tiger who had bounded on his prey.

"Cut."

A louder and more imposing crash succeeded this order, though not before several heavy blows had been struck into the massive mast itself. As before, the sea received the tumbling maze of spars, rigging, and sails; the vessel surging, at the same instant, from its recumbent position, and rolling far and heavily to windward.

"She rights! she rights!" exclaimed twenty voices which had been mute, in a suspense that involved life and death.

"Keep her dead away!" added the calm but authoritative voice of the young commander. "Stand by to furl the fore-top-sail—let it hang a moment to drag the ship clear of the wreck—cut, cut—cheerily, men—hatchets and knives—cut with all, and cut off all!"

As the men now worked with the vigor of hope, the ropes that still confined the fallen spars to the vessel were quickly severed; and the *Caroline*, by this time dead before the gale, appeared barely to touch the foam that covered the sea. The wind came over the waste in gusts that rumbled like distant thunder, and with a power that seemed to threaten to lift the ship from its proper element. As a prudent and sagacious seaman had let fly the halyards of the solitary sail that remained, at the moment the squall approached, the loosened but lowered topsail was now distended in a manner that threatened to drag after it the only mast which still stood. Wilder saw the necessity of getting rid of the sail, and he also saw the utter impossibility of securing it. Calling Earing to his side, he pointed out the danger, and gave the necessary order.

"The spar cannot stand such shocks much longer," he concluded; "should it go over the bows, some fatal blow might be given to the ship at the rate she is moving. A man or two must be sent aloft to cut the sail from the yards."

"The stick is bending like a willow whip," returned the mate, "and the lower mast itself is sprung. There would be great danger in trusting a hand in that top, while these wild squalls are breathing around us."

"You may be right," returned Wilder, with a sudden conviction of the truth of what the other had said. "Stay you then here; if anything befall me, try to get the vessel into port as far north as the Capes of Virginia, at least;—on no account attempt Hatteras, in the present condition of——"

"What would you do, Captain Wilder?" interrupted the mate, laying his hand on the shoulder of his commander, who had already thrown his sea-cap on the deck, and was preparing to divest himself of some of his outer garments.

"I go aloft to ease the mast of that topsail, without which we lose the spar, and possibly the ship."

"I see that plain enough, sir; but, shall it be said that another did the duty of Edward Earing? It is your business to carry the vessel into the Capes of Virginia, and mine to cut the topsail adrift. If harm comes to me, why, put it in the log, with a word or two about the manner in which I played my part. That is the most proper epitaph for a sailor."

Wilder made no resistance. He resumed his watchful and reflecting attitude, with the simplicity of one who had been too long trained to the discharge of certain obligations himself, to manifest surprise that another should acknowledge their imperative character. In the meantime, Earing proceeded steadily to perform what he had just promised. Passing into the waist of the ship, he provided himself with a suitable hatchet, and then, without speaking a syllable to any of the mute but attentive seamen, he sprang into the fore-rigging, every strand and rope-yarn of which was tightened by the strain nearly to snapping. The understanding eyes of his observers comprehended his intention; and with precisely the same pride of station as had urged him to the dangerous undertaking, four or five of the oldest mariners jumped upon the rattlings, to mount into an air that apparently teemed with a hundred hurricanes.

"Lie down out of that fore-rigging," shouted Wilder, through a deck trumpet; "lie down; all, but the mate, lie down!" His words were borne past the inattentive ears of the excited and mortified followers of Earing, but for once they failed of their effect. Each man was too earnestly bent on his purpose to listen to the sounds of recall. In less than a minute, the whole were scattered along the yards, prepared to obey the signal of their officer. The mate cast a look about him; perceiving that the time was comparatively favorable, he struck a blow upon the large rope that confined one of the lower angles of the distended and bursting sail to the yard. The effect was much the same as would be produced by knocking away the key-stone of an ill-cemented arch. The canvas broke from its fastenings with a loud explosion, and, for an instant, it was seen sailing in the air ahead of the ship, as if it were sustained on wings. The vessel rose on a sluggish wave—the lingering remains of the former breeze —and settled heavily over the rolling surge, borne down alike by its own weight and the renewed violence of the gusts. At this critical instant, while the seamen aloft were still gazing in the direction in which the little cloud of canvas had disappeared, a lanyard of the lower rigging parted, with a crack that reached the ears of Wilder.

"Lie down!" he shouted wildly through his trumpet; "down by the back-stays; down for your lives; every man of you, down!"

A solitary individual profited by the warning, gliding to the deck with the velocity of the wind. But rope parted after rope, and the fatal snapping of the wood followed. For a moment, the towering maze tottered, seeming to wave towards every quarter of the heavens; and then, yielding to the movement of the hull, the whole fell, with a heavy crash, into the sea. Cord, lanyard, and stay snapped like thread, as each received in succession the strain of the ship, leaving the naked and despoiled hull of the *Caroline* to drive before the tempest, as if nothing had occurred to impede its progress.

A mute and eloquent pause succeeded the disaster. It seemed as if the elements themselves were appeased by their work, and something like a momentary lull in the awful rushing of the winds might have been fancied. Wilder sprang to the side of the vessel, and distinctly beheld the victims, who still clung to their frail support. He even saw Earing waving his hand in adieu with a seaman's heart, like a man who not only felt how desperate was his situation, but who knows how to meet it with resignation. Then the wreck of spars, with all who clung to it, was swallowed up in the body of the frightful, preternatural-looking mist which extended on every side of them, from the ocean to the clouds.

"Stand by, to clear away a boat!" shouted Wilder, without pausing to think of the impossibility of one's swimming, or of effecting the least good, in so violent a tornado.

He struck a blow upon the large rope that confined one of the lower angles of the sail to the yard.

But the amazed and confounded seamen who remained needed no instruction in this matter. Not a man moved, nor was the smallest symptom of obedience given. The mariners looked wildly around them, each endeavoring to trace in the dusky countenance of some shipmate his opinion of the extent of the evil; but not a mouth opened among them all.

"It is too late—it is too late!" murmured Wilder; "human skill and human efforts could not save them!"

"Sail, ho!" Knighthead shouted in a voice that was teeming with superstitious awe.

"Let him come on," returned his young commander, bitterly; "the mischief is ready done to his hands!"

"Should this be a true ship, it is our duty to the owners and the passengers to speak her, if a man can make his voice heard in this tempest," the second mate continued, pointing, through the haze, at the dim object that was certainly at hand.

"Speak her!—passengers!" muttered Wilder, involuntarily repeating his words. "No; anything is better than speaking her. Do you see the vessel that is driving down upon us so fast?" he sternly demanded of the watchful seaman who still clung to the wheel of the *Caroline*.

"Ay, ay, sir."

"Give her a berth—sheer away hard to port—perhaps he may pass us in the gloom, now we are no higher than our decks. Give the ship a broad sheer, I say, sir."

The usual laconic answer was given; and, for a few moments, the Bristol trader was seen diverging a little from the line in which the other approached; but a second glance assured Wilder that the attempt was useless. The strange ship (every man on board felt certain it was the same that had so long been seen hanging in the northwestern horizon) came on through the mist, with a swiftness that nearly equaled the velocity of the tempestuous winds themselves. Not a thread of canvas was seen on board her. Each line of spars, even to the tapering and delicate top-gallant masts, was in its place, preserving the beauty and symmetry of the whole fabric; but nowhere was there the smallest fragment of a sail opened to the gale. Under her bows rolled a volume of foam that was even discernible amid the universal agitation of the ocean; and, as she came within sound, the sullen roar of the water might have been likened to the noise of a cascade. At first, the spectators on the decks of the *Caroline* believed they were not seen, and some of the men called madly for lights, in order that the disasters of the night might not terminate in an encounter.

"Too many see us there already!" said Wilder.

"No, no," muttered Knighthead; "no fear but we are seen; and by such eyes, too, as never yet looked out of mortal head!"

The seamen paused. In another instant, the long-seen and mysterious ship was within a hundred feet of them. The very power of that wind, which was wont usually to raise the billows, now pressed the element, with the weight of mountains, into its bed. The sea was everywhere a sheet of froth, but the water did not rise above the level of the surface. The instant a wave lifted itself from the security of the vast depths, the fluid was borne away before the tornado in glittering spray. Along this frothy but comparatively motionless surface, then, the stranger came booming with the steadiness and grandeur with which a cloud is seen sailing in the hurricane. No sign of life was discovered about her. If men looked out from their secret places, upon the straitened and discomfited wreck of the Bristol trader, it was covertly, and as darkly as the tempest before which they drove. Wilder held his breath, for the moment the stranger was nighest, in the very excess of suspense; but, as he saw no signal of recognition, no human form, nor any intention to arrest, if possible, the furious career of the other, a smile gleamed across his countenance, and his lips moved rapidly, as if he found pleasure in being abandoned to his distress. The stranger drove by, like a dark vision; and, ere another minute, her form was beginning to grow less distinct, in the body of spray to leeward.

"She is going out of sight in the mist!" exclaimed Wilder, when he drew his breath, after the fearful suspense of the few last moments.

"Ay, in mist or clouds," responded Knighthead, who now kept obstinately at his elbow, watching, with the most jealous distrust, the smallest movement of his unknown commander.

"In the heavens, or in the sea, I care not, provided he be gone."

"Most seamen would rejoice to see a strange sail, from the hull of a vessel shaved to the deck like this."

"Men often court their destruction, from ignorance of their own interests. Let him drive on, say I, and pray I! He goes four feet to our one; and I ask no better favor than that this hurricane may blow until the sun shall rise."

Knighthead started, and cast an oblique glance, which resembled denunciation, at his companion. To his superstitious mind, there was profanity in thus invoking the tempest, at a moment when the winds seemed already to be pouring out their utmost wrath.

"This is a heavy squall, I will allow," he said, "and such a one as many mariners pass whole lives without seeing; but he knows little of the sea who thinks there is not more wind where this comes from."

"Let it blow!" cried the other, striking his hands together a little wildly; "I pray for wind!"

All the doubts of Knighthead, as to the character of the young stranger who had so unaccountably got possession of the office of Nicholas Nichols, if any remained, were now removed. He walked forward among the silent and thoughtful crew, with the air of a man whose opinion was settled. Wilder, however, paid no attention to the movements of his subordinate, but continued pacing the deck for hours; now casting his eyes at the heavens, and now sending frequent and anxious glances around the limited horizon, while the *Royal Caroline* still continued drifting before the wind a shorn and naked wreck.

DEATH AT SEA

Richard Henry Dana, Jr.

MONDAY, NOV. 19TH. This was a black day in our calendar. At seven o'clock in the morning, it being our watch below, we were aroused from a sound sleep by the cry of "All hands ahoy! a man overboard!" This unwonted cry sent a thrill through the heart of everyone, and hurrying on deck we found the vessel hove flat aback, with all her studding-sails set; for the boy who was at the helm left it to throw something overboard, and the carpenter, who was an old sailor, knowing that the wind was light, put the helm down and hove her aback. The watch on deck were lowering away the quarter-boat, and I got on deck just in time to heave myself into her as she was leaving the side; but it was not until out upon the wide Pacific, in our little boat, that I knew whom we had lost. It was George Ballmer, a young English sailor, who was prized by the officers as an active and willing seaman, and by the crew as a lively, hearty fellow, and a good shipmate. He was going aloft to fit a strap round the main top-mast-head, for ringtail halyards, and had the strap and block, a coil of halyards, and a marline-spike about his neck. He fell from the starboard futtock shrouds, and not knowing how to swim, and being heavily dressed, with all those things round his neck, he probably sank immediately. We pulled astern, in the direction in which he fell, and though we knew that there was no hope of saving him, yet no one wished to speak of returning, and we rowed about for nearly an hour, without the hope of doing anything, but unwilling to acknowledge to ourselves that we must give him up. At length we turned the boat's head and made towards the vessel.

from "Two Years Before the Mast" by Richard Henry Dana, Jr.

Death is at all times solemn, but never so much so as at sea. A man dies on shore; his body remains with his friends, and "the mourners go about the streets;" but when a man falls overboard at sea and is lost, there is a suddenness in the event, and a difficulty in realizing it, which give to it an air of awful mystery. A man dies on shore—you follow his body to the grave, and a stone marks the spot. You are often prepared for the event. There is always something which helps you to realize it when it happens, and to recall it when it has passed. A man is shot down by your side in battle, and the mangled body remains an *object*, and a *real evidence;* but at sea, the man is near you—at your side—you hear his voice, and in an instant he is gone, and nothing but a *vacancy* shows his loss. Then, too, at sea—to use a homely but expressive phrase—you *miss* a man so much. A dozen men are shut up together in a little bark, upon the wide, wide sea, and for months and months see no forms and hear no voices but their own, and one is taken suddenly from among them, and they miss him at every turn. It is like losing a limb. There are no new faces or new scenes to fill up the gap. There is always an empty berth in the forecastle, and one man wanting when the small night watch is mustered. There is one less to take the wheel, and one less to lay out with you upon the yard. You miss his form, and the sound of his voice, for habit had made them almost necessary to you, and each of your senses feels the loss.

All these things make such a death peculiarly solemn, and the effect of it remains upon the crew for some time. There is more kindness shown by the officers to the crew, and by the crew to one another. There is more quietness and seriousness. The oath and the loud laugh are gone. The officers are more watchful, and the crew go more carefully aloft. The lost man is seldom mentioned, or is dismissed with a sailor's rude eulogy—"Well, poor George is gone! His cruise is up soon! He knew his work, and did his duty, and was a good shipmate." Then usually follows some allusion to another world, for sailors are almost all believers; but their notions and opinions are unfixed and at loose ends. They say,—"God won't be hard upon the poor fellow," and seldom get beyond the common phrase which seems to imply that their sufferings and hard treatment here will excuse them hereafter,—"*To work hard, live hard, die hard, and go to hell after all, would be hard indeed!*" Our cook, a simple-hearted old African, who had been through a good deal in his day, and was rather seriously inclined, always going to church twice a day when on shore, and reading his Bible on a Sunday in the galley, talked to the crew about spending their Sabbaths badly, and told them that they might go as suddenly as George had, and be as little prepared.

Yet a sailor's life is at best but a mixture of a little good with much evil, and a little pleasure with much pain. The beautiful is linked with the revolting the sublime with the commonplace, and the solemn with the ludicrous.

We had hardly returned on board with our sad report, before an auction was held of the poor man's clothes. The captain had first, however, called all hands aft and asked them if they were satisfied that everything had been done to save the man, and if they thought there was any use in remaining there longer. The crew all said that it was in vain, for the man did not know how to swim, and was very heavily dressed. So we then filled away and kept her off to her course.

The laws regulating navigation make the captain answerable for the effects of a sailor who dies during the voyage, and it is either a law or a universal custom, established for convenience, that the captain should immediately hold an auction of his things, in which they are bid off by the sailors, and the sums which they give are deducted from their wages at the end of the voyage. In this way the trouble and risk of keeping his things through the voyage are avoided, and the clothes are usually sold for more than they would be worth on shore. Accordingly, we had no sooner got the ship before the wind, than his chest was brought up upon the forecastle, and the sale began. The jackets and trousers in which we had seen him dressed but a few days before, were exposed and bid off while the life was hardly out of his body, and his chest was taken aft and used as a store-chest, so that there was nothing left which could be called *his*. Sailors have an unwillingness to wear a dead man's clothes during the same voyage, and they seldom do so unless they are in absolute want.

As is usual after a death, many stories were told about George. Some had heard him say that he repented never having learned to swim, and that he knew that he should meet his death by drowning. Another said that he never knew any good to come of a voyage made against the will, and the deceased man shipped and spent his advance and was afterwards very unwilling to go, but not being able to refund, was obliged to sail with us. A boy, too, who had become quite attached to him, said that George talked to him during most of the watch on the night before, about his mother and family at home, and this was the first time that he had mentioned the subject during the voyage.

NORTH-WESTER

Richard Henry Dana, Jr.

SATURDAY, NOV. 14TH. This day we got under weigh, with the agent and several Spaniards of note, as passengers, bound up to Monterey. We went ashore in the gig to bring them off with their baggage, and found them waiting on the beach, and a little afraid about going off, as the surf was running very high. This was nuts to us; for we liked to have a Spaniard wet with salt water; and then the agent was very much disliked by the crew, one and all; and we hoped, as there was no officer in the boat, to have a chance to duck them; for we knew that they were such "marines" that they would not know whether it was our fault or not. Accordingly, we kept the boat so far from shore as to oblige them to wet their feet in getting into her; and then waited for a good high comber, and letting the head slue a little round, sent the whole force of the sea into the stern-sheets, drenching them from head to feet. The Spaniards sprang out of the boat, swore, and shook themselves, and protested against trying it again; and it was with the greatest difficulty that the agent could prevail upon them to make another attempt. The next time we took care, and went off easily enough, and pulled aboard. The crew came to the side to hoist in their baggage, and we gave them the wink, and they heartily enjoyed the half-drowned looks of the company.

Everything being now ready, and the passengers aboard, we ran up the ensign and broad pennant (for there was no man-of-war, and we were the largest vessel on the coast), and the other vessels ran up their ensigns. Having hove short, cast off the gaskets, and made the bunt of each sail fast by the jigger, with a man on each yard; at the word, the whole canvas of the ship was loosed,

from "Two Years Before the Mast" by Richard Henry Dana, Jr.

and with the greatest rapidity possible, everything was sheeted home and hoisted up, the anchor tripped and catheaded, and the ship under headway. We were determined to show the "spouter" how things could be done in a smart ship, with a good crew, though not more than half their number. The royal yards were all crossed at once, and royals and skysails set, and, as we had the wind free, the booms were run out, and every one was aloft, active as cats, laying out on the yards and booms, reeving the studding-sail gear; and sail after sail the captain piled upon her, until she was covered with canvas, her sails looking like a great white cloud resting upon a black speck. Before we doubled the point, we were going at a dashing rate, and leaving the shipping far astern. We had a fine breeze to take us through the Canal, as they call this bay of forty miles long by ten wide. The breeze died away at night, and we were becalmed all day on Sunday, about halfway between Santa Barbara and Point Conception. Sunday night we had a light, fair wind, which set us up again; and having a fine sea-breeze on the first part of Monday, we had the prospect of passing, without any trouble, Point Conception,—the Cape Horn of California, where it begins to blow the first of January, and blows all the year round. Toward the latter part of the afternoon, however, the regular north-west wind, as usual, set in, which brought in our studding-sails, and gave us the chance of beating round the Point, which we were now just abreast of, and which stretched off into the Pacific, high, rocky and barren, forming the central point of the coast for hundreds of miles north and south. A cap-full of wind will be a bag-full here, and before night our royals were furled, and the ship was laboring hard under her top-gallant-sails. At eight bells our watch went below, leaving her with as much sail as she could stagger under, the water flying over the forecastle at every plunge. It was evidently blowing harder, but then there was not a cloud in the sky, and the sun had gone down bright.

We had been below but a short time, before we had the usual promonitions of a coming gale: seas washing over the whole forward part of the vessel, and her bows beating against them with a force and sound like the driving of piles. The watch, too, seemed very busy trampling about decks, and singing out at the ropes. A sailor can always tell, by the sound, what sail is coming in, and, in a short time, we heard the top-gallant-sails come in, one after another, and then the flying jib. This seemed to ease her a good deal, and we were fast going off to the land of Nod, when—bang, bang, bang—on the scuttle, and "All hands, reef topsails, ahoy!" started us out of our berths; and, it not being very cold weather, we had nothing extra to put on, and were soon on deck. I shall never forget the fineness of the sight. It was a clear, and rather a chilly night; the stars were twinkling with an intense brightness, and as far as the eye could reach, there was not a cloud to be seen. The horizon met the sea in a defined line. A painter could not have painted so clear a sky. There was not a speck upon it. Yet it was blowing great guns from the north-west. When you can see a cloud to windward, you feel that there is a place for the wind to come from; but here, it seemed to come from nowhere. No person could have told, from the heavens, by their eyesight alone, that it was not a still summer's night. One reef after another, we took in the topsails, and before we could get them hoisted up, we heard a sound like a short, quick rattling of thunder, and the jib was blown to atoms out of the bolt-rope. We got the topsails set, and the fragments of the jib stowed away, and the fore top-mast stay-sail set in its place, when the great mainsail gaped open, and the sail ripped from head to foot. "Lay up on that main-yard and furl the sail, before it blows to tatters!" shouted the captain; and in a moment, we were up, gathering the remains of it upon the yard. We got it wrapped round the yard, and passed gaskets over it as snugly as possible, and were just on deck again, when, with another loud rent, which was heard throughout the ship, the fore topsail, which had been double-reefed, split in two, athwartships, just below the reef-band, from earing to earing. Here again it was down yard, haul out reef-tackles, and lay out upon the yard for reefing. By hauling the reef-tackles chock-a-block, we took the strain from the other earings, and passing the close-reef earing, and knotting the points carefully, we succeeded in setting the sail, close-reefed.

We had but just got the rigging coiled up, and were waiting to hear "go below the watch!" when the main royal worked loose from the gaskets, and blew directly out to leeward, flapping, and shaking the mast like a wand. Here was a job for somebody. The royal must come in or be cut adrift, or the mast would be snapped short off. All the light hands in the starboard watch were sent up, one after another, but they could do nothing with it. At length, John, the tall Frenchman, the head of the starboard watch (and a better sailor never stepped upon a deck), sprang aloft, and, by the help of his long arms and legs, succeeded, after a hard struggle,—the sail blowing over the yard-arm to leeward, and the skysail blowing directly over his head,—in smothering it, and frapping it with long pieces of sinnet. He came very near being blown or shaken from the yard, several times, but he was a true sailor, every finger a fish-hook. Having made the sail snug, he prepared to send the yard down, which was a long and difficult job; for, frequently, he was obliged to stop and hold on with all his might, for several minutes, the ship pitching so as to make it impossible to do anything else at that height. The yard at length came down safe, and after it, the fore and mizen royal-yards were sent down. All hands were then sent aloft, and for an hour or two we were hard at work, making the booms well fast; unreeving the studding-sail and royal and skysail gear; getting rolling-ropes on the yards; setting up the weather breast-backstays; and making other preparations for a storm. It was a fine night for a gale; just cool and bracing enough for quick work, without being cold, and as bright as day. It was sport to have a gale in such weather as this. Yet it blew like a hurricane. The wind seemed to come with a spite, an edge to it, which threatened to scrape us off the yards. The mere force of the wind was greater than I had ever seen it before; but darkness, cold, and wet are the worst parts of a storm, to a sailor.

Having got on deck again, we looked round to see what time of night it was, and whose watch. In a few minutes the man at the wheel struck four bells, and we found that the other watch was out, and our own half out. Accordingly, the starboard watch went below, and left the ship to us for a couple of hours, yet with orders to stand by for a call.

Hardly had they got below, before away went the fore top-mast stay-sail, blown to ribands. This was a small sail, which we could manage in the watch, so that we were not obliged to call up the other watch. We laid out upon the bowsprit, where we were under water half the time, and took in the fragments of the sail, and as she must have some head sail on her, prepared to bend another stay-sail. We got the new one out, into the nettings; seized on the tack, sheets, and halyards, and the hanks; manned the halyards, cut adrift the frapping lines, and hoisted away; but before it was halfway up the stay, it was blown all to pieces. When we belayed the halyards, there was nothing left but the bolt-rope. Now large eyes began to show themselves in the foresail, and knowing that it must soon go, the mate ordered us upon the yard to furl it. Being unwilling to call up the watch who had been on deck all night, he roused out the carpenter, sailmaker, cook, steward, and other idlers, and, with their help, we manned the fore-yard, and, after nearly half an hour's struggle, mastered the sail, and got it well furled round the yard. The force of the wind had never been greater than at this moment. In going up the rigging, it seemed ab-

solutely to pin us down to the shrouds; and on the yard, there was no such
thing as turning a face to windward. Yet here was no driving sleet, and darkness, and wet, and cold, as off Cape Horn; and instead of a stiff oil-cloth suit,
southwester caps, and thick boots, we had on hats, round jackets, duck trousers, light shoes, and everything light and easy. All these things make a great
difference to a sailor. When we got on deck, the man at the wheel struck eight
bells (four o'clock in the morning), and "All starbowlines, ahoy!" brought the
other watch up. But there was no going below for us. The gale was now at its
height, "blowing like scissors and thumb-screws;" the captain was on deck; the
ship, which was light, rolling and pitching as though she would shake the long
sticks out of her; and the sails gaping open and splitting, in every direction.
The mizen topsail, which was a comparatively new sail, and close-reefed, split,
from head to foot, in the bunt; the fore topsail went, in one rent, from clew to
earing, and was blowing to tatters; one of the chain bobstays parted; the sprit-
sail yard sprung in the slings; the martingale had slued away off to leeward;
and, owing to the long dry weather, the lee rigging hung in large bights, at
every lurch. One of the main top-gallant shrouds had parted; and, to crown
all, the galley had got adrift, and gone over to leeward, and the anchor on the
lee bow had worked loose, and was thumping the side. Here was work enough
for all hands for half a day. Our gang laid out on the mizen topsail yard, and
after more than half an hour's hard work, furled the sail, though it bellied out
over our heads, and again, by a slat of the wind, blew in under the yard, with a
fearful jerk, and almost threw us off from the foot-ropes.

Double gaskets were passed round the yards, rolling tackles and other gear
bowsed taught, and everything made as secure as could be. Coming down, we
found the rest of the crew just laying down the fore rigging, having furled
the tattered topsail, or, rather, swathed it round the yard, which looked like a
broken limb, bandaged. There was no sail now on the ship but the spanker
and the close-reefed main topsail, which still held good. But this was too much
after sail; and order was given to furl the spanker. The brails were hauled up,
and all the light hands in the starboard watch sent out on the gaff to pass the
gaskets; but they could do nothing with it. The second mate swore at them
for a parcel of "sogers," and sent up a couple of the best men; but they could
do no better, and the gaff was lowered down. All hands were now employed
in setting up the lee rigging, fishing the sprit-sail yard, lashing the galley, and
getting tackles upon the martingale, to bowse it to windward. Being in the

larboard watch, my duty was forward, to assist in setting up the martingale, Three of us were out on the martingale guys and back-ropes for more than half an hour, carrying out, hooking and unhooking the tackles, several times buried in the seas, until the mate ordered us in, from fear of our being washed off. The anchors were then to be taken up on the rail, which kept all hands on the forecastle for an hour, though every now and then the seas broke over it, washing the rigging off to leeward, filling the lee scuppers breast high, and washing chock aft to the taffrail.

Having got everything secure again, we were promising ourselves some breakfast, for it was now nearly nine o'clock in the forenoon, when the main topsail showed evident signs of giving way. Some sail must be kept on the ship, and the captain ordered the fore and main spencer gaffs to be lowered down, and the two spencers (which were storm sails, brand new, small, and made of the strongest canvas) to be got up and bent; leaving the main topsail to blow away, with a blessing on it, if it would only last until we could set the spencers. These we bent on very carefully, with strong robands and seizings, and making tackles fast to the clues, bowsed them down to the water-ways. By this time the main topsail was among the things that have been, and we went aloft to stow away the remnant of the last sail of all those which were on the ship twenty-four hours before. The spencers were now the only whole sails on the ship, and being strong and small, and near the deck, presenting but little surface to the wind above the rail, promised to hold out well. Hove-to under these, and eased by having no sail above the tops, the ship rose and fell, and drifted off to leeward like a line-of-battle ship.

It was now eleven o'clock, and the watch was sent below to get breakfast, and at eight bells (noon), as everything was snug, although the gale had not in the least abated, the watch was set, and the other watch and idlers sent below. For three days and three nights, the gale continued with unabated fury, and with singular regularity. There were no lulls, and very little variation in its fierceness. Our ship, being light, rolled so as almost to send the fore yard-arm under water, and drifted off bodily, to leeward. All this time there was not a cloud to be seen in the sky, day or night;—no, not so large as a man's hand. Every morning the sun rose cloudless from the sea, and set again at night, in the sea, in a flood of light. The stars, too, came out of the blue, one after another, night after night, unobscured, and twinkled as clear as on a still frosty night at home, until the day came upon them. All this time, the sea was rolling in immense surges, white with foam, as far as the eye could reach, on every side, for we were now leagues and leagues from shore.

The between-decks being empty, several of us slept there in hammocks, which are the best things in the world to sleep in during a storm; it not being true of them, as it is of another kind of bed, "when the wind blows, the cradle will rock"; for it is the ship that rocks, while they always hang vertically from the beams. During these seventy-two hours we had nothing to do, but to turn in and out, four hours on deck, and four below, eat, sleep, and keep watch. The watches were only varied by taking the helm in turn, and now and then, by one of the sails, which were furled, blowing out of the gaskets, and getting adrift, which sent us up on the yards; and by getting tackles on different parts of the rigging, which were slack. Once, the wheel-rope parted, which might have been fatal to us, had not the chief mate sprung instantly with a relieving tackle to windward, and kept the tiller up, till a new one could be rove. On the morning of the twentieth, at daybreak, the gale had evidently done its worst, and had somewhat abated; so much so, that all hands were called to bend new sails, although it was still blowing as hard as two common gales. One at a time, and with great difficulty and labor, the old sails were unbent and sent down by the buntlines, and three new topsails, made for the homeward passage round Cape Horn, and which had never been bent, were got up from the sail-room, and, under the care of the sailmaker, were fitted for bending, and sent up by the halyards into the tops, and, with stops and frapping lines, were bent to the yards, close-reefed, sheeted home, and hoisted. These were done one at a time, and with the greatest care and difficulty. Two spare courses were then got up and bent in the same manner and furled, and a storm-jib, with the bonnet off, bent and furled to the boom. It was twelve o'clock before we got through; and five hours of more exhausting labor I never experienced; and no one of that ship's crew, I will venture to say, will ever desire again to unbend and bend five large sails, in the teeth of a tremendous north-wester. Towards night, a few clouds appeared in the horizon, and as the gale moderated, the usual appearance of driving clouds relieved the face of the sky. The fifth day after the commencement of the storm, we shook a reef out of each topsail, and set the reefed fore-sail, jib and spanker; but it was not until after eight days of reefed topsails that we had a whole sail on the ship; and then it was quite soon enough, for the captain was anxious to make up for leeway, the gale having blown us half the distance to the Sandwich Islands.

Inch by inch, as fast as the gale would permit, we made sail on the ship, for the wind still continued a-head, and we had many days' sailing to get back to the longitude we were in when the storm took us. For eight days more we beat to windward under a stiff top-gallant breeze, when the wind shifted and became variable. A light south-easter, to which we could carry a reefed top-mast studding-sail, did wonders for our dead reckoning.

Friday, December 4th, after a passage of twenty days, we arrived at the mouth of the bay of San Francisco.

THREE ADVENTURES OF
ROBINSON CRUSOE

Daniel Defoe

A Perilous Voyage

THE CHIEF things I was employed in, besides my yearly labor of planting my barley and rice, and curing my raisins, of both which I always kept up just enough to have sufficient stock of one year's provisions beforehand— and my daily labor of going out with my gun, I had one labor, to make me a canoe, which at last I finished; so that by digging a canal to it of six feet wide, and four feet deep, I brought it into the creek, almost half a mile. As for the first, which was so vastly big, as I made it without considering beforehand, as I ought to do, how I should be able to launch it; so, never being able to bring it to the water, or bring the water to it, I was obliged to let it lie where it was, as a memorandum to teach me to be wiser next time. Indeed, the next time, though I could not get a tree proper for it, and in a place where I could not get the water to it at any less distance than, as I have said, near half a mile, yet as I saw it was practicable at last, I never gave it over; and though I was near two years about it, yet I never grudged my labor, in hopes of having a boat to go off to sea at last.

However, though my little *periagua* was finished, yet the size of it was not at all answerable to the design which I had in view when I made the first; I mean, of venturing over to the *terra firma*, where it was above forty miles broad. Accordingly, the smallness of my boat assisted to put an end to that design, and now I thought no more of it. But as I had a boat, my next design

from "Robinson Crusoe" by Daniel Defoe

was to make a tour round the island; for as I had been on the other side in one place, crossing, as I have already described it, over the land, so the discoveries I made in that little journey made me very eager to see other parts of the coast; and now I had a boat, I thought of nothing but sailing round the island.

For this purpose, that I might do everything with discretion and consideration, I fitted up a little mast to my boat, and made a sail to it out of some of the piece of the ship's sail, which lay in store, and of which I had a great stock.

Having fitted my mast and sail, and tried the boat, I found she would sail very well. Then I made little lockers, or boxes, at either end of my boat, to put provisions, necessaries, and ammunition, etc., into, to be kept dry, either from rain or the spray of the sea; and a little long hollow place I cut in the inside of the boat, where I could lay my gun, making a flap to hang down over it to keep it dry.

I fixed my umbrella also in a step at the stern, like a mast, to stand over my head, and keep the heat of the sun off of me, like an awning; and thus I every now and then took a little voyage upon the sea, but never went far out, nor far from the little creek. But at last, being eager to view the circumference of my little kingdom, I resolved upon my tour; and accordingly I victualled my ship for the voyage, putting in two dozen of my loaves (cakes I should rather call them) of barley bread, an earthen pot full of parched rice, a food I ate a great deal of, a little bottle of rum, half a goat, and powder and shot for killing more, and two large watch-coats, of those which, as I mentioned before, I had saved out of the seamen's chests; these I took, one to lie upon, and the other to cover me in the night.

It was the 6th of November, in the sixth year of my reign, or my captivity, which you please, that I set out on this voyage, and I found it much longer than I expected; for though the island itself was not very large, yet when I came to the east side of it I found a great ledge of rocks lie out about two leagues into the sea, some above water, some under it, and beyond that a shoal of sand, lying dry half a league more; so that I was obliged to go a great way out to sea to double the point.

When first I discovered them, I was going to give over my enterprise, and come back again, not knowing how far it might oblige me to go out to sea, and, above all, doubting how I should get back again, so I came to an anchor; for I had made me a kind of anchor with a piece of a broken grappling which I got out of the ship.

Having secured my boat, I took my gun and went on shore, climbing up upon a hill, which seemed to overlook that point, where I saw the full extent of it, and resolved to venture.

In my viewing the sea from that hill, where I stood, I perceived a strong, and indeed a most furious current, which ran to the east, and even came close to the point; and I took the more notice of it, because I saw there might be some danger that when I came into it I might be carried out to sea by the strength of it, and not be able to make the island again. And indeed, had I not gotten first up upon this hill, I believe it would have been so; for there was the same current on the other side of the island, only that it set off at a farther distance; and I saw there was a strong eddy under the shore; so I had nothing to do but to get in out of the first current, and I should presently be in an eddy.

I lay here, however, two days; because the wind, blowing pretty fresh at E.S.E., and that being just contrary to the said current, made a great breach of the sea upon the point; so that it was not safe for me to keep too close to the shore for the breach, nor to go too far off because of the stream.

The third day, in the morning, the wind having abated overnight, the sea was calm, and I ventured. But I am a warning-piece again to all rash and ignorant pilots; for no sooner was I come to the point, when even I was not my boat's length from the shore, but I found myself in a great depth of water, and a current like the sluice of a mill. It carried my boat along with it with such violence, that all I could do could not keep her so much as on the edge of it, but I found it hurried me farther and farther out from the eddy, which was on my left hand. There was no wind stirring to help me, and all I could do with my paddlers signified nothing. And now I began to give myself over for lost; for, as the current was on both sides the island, I knew in a few leagues' distance they must join again, and then I was irrevocably gone. Nor did I see any possibility of avoiding it; so that I had no prospect before me but of perishing; not by the sea, for that was calm enough, but of starving for hunger. I had indeed found a tortoise on the shore, as big almost as I could lift, and had tossed it into the boat; and I had a great jar of fresh water, that is to say, one of my earthen pots; but what was all this to being driven into the vast ocean, where, to be sure, there was no shore, no mainland or island, for a thousand leagues at least.

And now I saw how easy it was for the providence of God to make the most miserable condition mankind could be in worse. Now I looked back upon my

I took my gun and went on shore, climbing up a hill, which overlooked that point where I resolved to venture.

desolate solitary island as the most pleasant place in the world, and all the happiness my heart could wish for was to be but there again. I stretched out my hands to it, with eager wishes. "O happy desert!" said I, "I shall never see thee more. O miserable creature," said I, "whither am I going?" Then I reproached myself with my unthankful temper, and how I had repined at my solitary condition; and now what would I give to be on shore there again. Thus we never see the true state of our condition till it is illustrated to us by its contraries; nor know how to value what we enjoy, but by the want of it. It is scarce possible to imagine the consternation I was now in, being driven from my beloved island (for so it appeared to me now to be) into the wide ocean, almost two leagues, and in the utmost despair of ever recovering it again. However, I worked hard, till indeed my strength was almost exhausted, and kept my boat as much to the northward, that is, towards the side of the current which the eddy lay on, as possibly I could; when about noon, as the sun passed the meridian, I thought I felt a little breeze of wind in my face, springing up from the S.S.E. This cheered my heart a little, and especially when, in about half an hour more, it blew a pretty small gentle gale. By this time I was gotten at a frightful distance from the island; and had the least cloud or hazy weather intervened, I had been undone another way too; for I had no compass on board, and should never have known how to have steered towards the island if I had but once lost sight of it. But the weather continuing clear, I applied myself to get up my mast again, and spread my sail, standing away to the north as much as possible, to get out of the current.

Just as I had set my mast and sail, and the boat began to stretch away, I saw even by the clearness of the water some alteration of the current was near; for where the current was so strong, the water was foul. But perceiving the water clear, I found the current abate, and presently I found to the east, at about half a mile, a breach of the sea upon some rocks. These rocks I found caused the current to part again; and as the main stress of it ran away more southerly, leaving the rocks to the north-east, so the other returned by the repulse of the rocks, and made a strong eddy, which ran back again to the north-west with a very sharp stream.

They who know what it is to have a reprieve brought to them upon the ladder, or to be rescued from thieves just going to murder them, or who have been in such like extremities, may guess what my present surprise of joy was, and how gladly I put my boat into the stream of this eddy; and the wind also freshening, how gladly I spread my sail to it, running cheerfully before the wind, and with a strong tide or eddy under foot.

This eddy carried me about a league in my way back again, directly towards the island, but about two leagues more to the northward than the current which carried me away at first; so that when I came near the island, I found myself open to the northern shore of it, that is to say, the outer end of the island, opposite to that which I went out from.

When I had made something more than a league of way by the help of this current or eddy, I found it was spent, and served me no farther. However, I found that being between the two great currents, viz., that on the south side, which had hurried me away, and that on the north, which lay about a league on the other side; I say, between these two, in the wake of the island, I found the water at least still, and running no way; and having still a breeze of wind fair for me, I kept on steering directly for the island, though not making such fresh way as I did before.

About four o'clock in the evening, being then within about a league of the island, I found the point of the rocks which occasioned this disaster stretching out, as is described before, to the southward, and casting off the current more southwardly had, of course, made another eddy to the north, and this I found very strong, but not directly setting the way my course lay, which was due west, but almost full north. However, having a fresh gale, I stretched across this eddy, slanting north-west; and in about an hour came within about a mile of the shore, where, it being smooth water, I soon got to land.

When I was on shore, I fell on my knees, and gave God thanks for my deliverance, resolving to lay aside all thoughts of my deliverance by my boat; and refreshing myself with such things as I had, I brought my boat close to the shore, in a little cove that I had spied under some trees, and laid me down to sleep, being quite spent with the labor and fatigue of the voyage.

The Very Print of a Foot

IT HAPPENED one day, about noon, going towards my boat, I was exceedingly surprised with the print of a man's naked foot on the shore, which
was very plain to be seen in the sand. I stood like one thunderstruck, or as if
I had seen an apparition. I listened, I looked round me, I could hear nothing,
nor see anything. I went up to a rising ground, to look farther. I went up
the shore, and down the shore, but it was all one; I could see no other impression but that one.

I went to it again to see if there were any more, and to observe if it might
not be my fancy; but there was no room for that, for there was exactly the
very print of a foot—toes, heel, and every part of a foot. How it came thither
I knew not, nor could in the least imagine. But after innumerable fluttering
thoughts, like a man perfectly confused and out of myself, I came home to my
fortification, not feeling, as we say, the ground I went on, but terrified to the
last degree, looking behind me at every two or three steps, mistaking every
bush and tree, and fancying every stump at a distance to be a man; nor is it
possible to describe how many various shapes affrighted imagination represented things to me in, how many wild ideas were found every moment in my
fancy, and what strange, unaccountable whimsies came into my thoughts by
the way.

When I came to my castle, for so I think I called it ever after this, I fled
into it like one pursued. Whether I went over by the ladder, as first contrived, or went in at the hole in the rock, which I called a door, I cannot
remember; no, nor could I remember the next morning, for never frightened
hare fled to cover, or fox to earth, with more terror of mind than I to this
retreat.

I slept none that night. The farther I was from the occasion of my fright,
the greater my apprehensions were; which is something contrary to the nature
of such things, and especially to the usual practice of all creatures in fear.
But I was so embarrassed with my own frightful ideas of the thing, that I

formed nothing but dismal imaginations to myself, even though I was now a great way off it. Sometimes I fancied it must be the devil, and reason joined in with me upon this supposition; for how should any other thing in human shape come into the place? Where was the vessel that brought them? What marks were there of any other footsteps? And how was it possible a man should come there? But then to think that Satan should take human shape upon him in such a place, where there could be no manner of occasion for it, but to leave the print of his foot behind him, and that even for no purpose too, for he could not be sure I should see it; this was an amusement the other way. I considered that the devil might have found out abundance of other ways to have terrified me than this of the single print of a foot; that as I lived quite on the other side of the island, he would never have been so simple to leave a mark in a place where it was ten thousand to one whether I should ever see it or not, and in the sand too, which the first surge of the sea, upon a high wind, would have defaced entirely. All this seemed inconsistent with the thing itself, and with all the notions we usually entertain of the subtility of the devil.

Abundance of such things as these assisted to argue me out of all apprehensions of its being the devil; and I presently concluded then, that it must be some more dangerous creature, viz., that it must be some of the savages of the mainland over against me, who had wandered out to sea in their canoes, and, either driven by the currents or by contrary winds, had made the island, and had been on shore, but were gone away again to sea, being as loth, perhaps, to have stayed in this desolate island as I would have been to have had them.

While these reflections were rolling upon my mind, I was very thankful in my thoughts that I was so happy as not to be thereabouts at that time, or that they did not see my boat, by which they would have concluded that some inhabitants had been in the place, and perhaps have searched farther for me. Then terrible thoughts racked my imagination about their having found my boat, and that there were people here; and that if so, I should certainly have them come again in greater numbers, and devour me; and if it should happen so that they should not find me, yet they would find my enclosure, destroy all my corn, carry away all my flock of tame goats, and I should perish at last for mere want.

Thus my fear banished all my religious hope. All that former confidence in God, which was founded upon such wonderful experience as I had had of

His goodness, now vanished, as if He that had fed me by miracle hitherto could not preserve, by His power, the provision which He had made for me by His goodness. I reproached myself with my easiness, that would not sow any more corn one year than would just serve me till the next season, as if no accident could intervene to prevent my enjoying the crop that was upon the ground. And this I thought so just a reproof, that I resolved for the future to have two or three years' corn beforehand, so that, whatever might come, I might not perish for want of bread.

How strange a checker-work of Providence is the life of man! and by what secret differing springs are the affections hurried about as differing circumstances present! Today we love what tomorrow we hate; today we seek what tomorrow we shun; today we desire what tomorrow we fear; nay, even tremble at the apprehensions of. This was exemplified in me, at this time, in the most lively manner imaginable; for I, whose only affliction was that I seemed banished from human society, that I was alone, circumscribed by the boundless ocean, cut off from mankind, and condemned to what I called silent life; that I was as one whom Heaven thought not worthy to be numbered among the living, or to appear among the rest of His creatures; that to have seen one of my own species would have seemed to me a raising me from death to life, and the greatest blessing that Heaven itself, next to the supreme blessing of salvation, could bestow; I say, that I should now tremble at the very apprehensions of seeing a man, and was ready to sink into the ground at but the shadow or silent appearance of a man's having set his foot in the island!

Visit to a Shipwreck

IT WAS in the middle of May, on the sixteenth day, I think, as well as my poor wooden calendar would reckon, for I marked all upon the post still: I say, it was the sixteenth of May that it blew a very great storm of wind all day, with a great deal of lightning and thunder, and a very foul night it was after it. I know not what was the particular occasion of it, but as I was reading in the Bible, and taken up with very serious thoughts about my present condition, I was surprised with a noise of a gun, as I thought, fired at sea.

This was, to be sure, a surprise of a quite different nature from any I had met with before; for the notions this put into my thoughts were quite of another kind. I started up in the greatest haste imaginable, and, in a trice, clapped my ladder to the middle place of the rock, and pulled it after me; and mounting it the second time, got to the top of the hill the very moment that flash of fire bid me listen for a second gun, which accordingly, in about half a minute, I heard; and, by the sound, knew that it was from that part of the sea where I was driven down the current in my boat.

I immediately considered that this must be some ship in distress, and that they had some comrade, or some other ship in company, and fired these guns for signals of distress, and to obtain help. I had this presence of mind, at that minute, as to think that though I could not help them, it may be they might help me; so I brought together all the dry wood I could get at hand, and, making a good handsome pile, I set it on fire upon the hill. The wood was dry, and blazed freely; and though the wind blew very hard, yet it burnt fairly out; so that I was certain, if there was any such thing as a ship, they must needs see it, and no doubt they did; for as soon as ever my fire blazed up I heard another gun, and after that several others, all from the same quarter. I plied my fire all night long till day broke; and when it was broad day, and the air cleared up, I saw something at a great distance at sea, full east of the island, whether a sail or a hull I could not distinguish, no, not with my glasses, the distance was so great, and the weather still something hazy also; at least it was so out at sea.

I looked frequently at it all that day, and soon perceived that it did not move; so I presently concluded that it was a ship at an anchor. And being eager, you may be sure, to be satisfied, I took my gun in my hand and ran toward the south side of the island, to the rocks where I had formerly been carried away with the current; and getting up there, the weather by this time being perfectly clear, I could plainly see, to my great sorrow, the wreck of a ship, cast away in the night upon those concealed rocks which I found when I was out in my boat; and which rocks, as they checked the violence of the stream, and made a kind of counter-stream or eddy, were the occasion of my recovering from the most desperate, hopeless condition that ever I had been in in all my life.

Thus, what is one man's safety is another man's destruction; for it seems these men, whoever they were, being out of their knowledge, and the rocks being wholly under water, had been driven upon them in the night, the wind blowing hard at E. and E.N.E. Had they seen the island, as I must necessarily suppose they did not, they must, as I thought, have endeavored to have saved themselves on shore by the help of their boat; but their firing of guns for help, especially when they saw, as I imagined, my fire, filled me with many thoughts. First, I imagined that upon seeing my light, they might have put themselves into their boat, and have endeavored to make the shore; but that the sea going very high, they might have been cast away. Other times I imagined that they might have lost their boat before, as might be the case many ways; as, particularly, by the breaking of the sea upon their ship, which many times obliges men to stave, or take in pieces their boat, and sometimes to throw it overboard with their own hands.

Other times I imagined they had some other ship or ships in company, who, upon the signals of distress they had made, had taken them up and carried them off. Other times I fancied they were all gone off to sea in their boat, and being hurried away by the current that I had been formerly in, were carried out into the great ocean, where there was nothing but misery and perishing; and that, perhaps, they might by this time think of starving, and of being in a condition to eat one another.

As all these were but conjectures at best, so, in the condition I was in, I could do no more than look on upon the misery of the poor men, and pity them; which had still this good effect on my side, that it gave me more and more cause to give thanks to God, who had so happily and comfortably provided for me in my desolate condition; and that of two ships' companies who were now cast away upon this part of the world, not one life should be spared but mine. I learned here again to observe, that it is very rare that the providence of God casts us into any condition of life so low, or any misery so great, but we may see something or other to be thankful for, and may see others in worse circumstances than our own.

Such certainly was the case of these men, of whom I could not so much as see room to suppose any of them were saved. Nothing could make it rational so much as to wish or expect that they did not all perish there, except the possibility only of their being taken up by another ship in company; and this was but mere possibility indeed, for I saw not the least sign or appearance of any such thing.

I cannot explain, by any possible energy of words, what a strange longing or hankering of desires I felt in my soul upon this sight, breaking out some-times thus: "Oh that there had been but one or two, nay, or but one soul, saved out of this ship, to have escaped to me, that I might but have had one companion, one fellow-creature, to have spoken to me, and to have conversed with!" In all the time of my solitary life, I never felt so earnest, so strong a desire after the society of my fellow-creatures, or so deep a regret at the want of it.

There are some secret moving springs in the affections which, when they are set agoing by some object in view, or be it some object, though not in view, yet rendered present to the mind by the power of imagination, that motion carries out the soul by its impetuosity to such violent, eager embrac-ings of the object, that the absence of it is insupportable.

Such were these earnest wishings that but one man had been saved! "Oh that it had been but one!" I believe I repeated the words a thousand times; and the desires were so moved by it, that when I spoke the words my hands would clinch together, and my fingers press the palms of my hands, that if I had had any soft thing in my hand, it would have crushed it involuntarily; and my teeth in my head would strike together, and set against one another so strong, that for some time I could not part them again.

Let the naturalists explain these things, and the reason and manner of them. All I can say to them is to describe the fact, which was even surprising to me when I found it, though I knew not from what it should proceed. It was doubtless the effect of ardent wishes, and of strong ideas formed in my mind, realizing the comfort which the conversation of one of my fellow-Christians would have been to me.

But it was not to be. Either their fate or mine, or both, forbid it; for, till the last year of my being on this island, I never knew whether any were saved out of that ship or no; and had only the affliction, some days after, to see the corpse of a drowned boy come on shore at the end of the island which was next the shipwreck. He had on no clothes but a seaman's waistcoat, a pair of open-kneed linen drawers, and a blue linen shirt; but nothing to direct me so much as to guess what nation he was of. He had nothing in his pocket but two pieces of eight and a tobacco-pipe. The last was to me of ten times more value than the first.

It was now calm, and I had a great mind to venture out in my boat to this wreck, not doubting but I might find something on board that might be useful to me. But that did not altogether press me so much as the possibility that there might be yet some living creature on board, whose life I might not only save, but might, by saving that life, comfort my own to the last degree. And this thought clung so to my heart, that I could not be quiet night nor day, but I must venture out in my boat on board this wreck; and committing the rest to God's providence, I thought, the impression was so strong upon my mind that it could not be resisted, that it must come from some invisible direction, and that I should be wanting to myself if I did not go.

Under the power of this impression, I hastened back to my castle, prepared everything for my voyage, took a quantity of bread, a great pot of fresh water, a compass to steer by, a bottle of rum (for I had still a great deal of that left), a basket full of raisins. And thus, loading myself with everything neces-sary, I went down to my boat, got the water out of her, and got her afloat, loaded all my cargo in her, and then went home again for more. My second cargo was a great bag full of rice, the umbrella to set up over my head for shade, another large pot full of fresh water, and about two dozen of my small loaves, or barley-cakes, more than before, with a bottle of goat's milk and a cheese; all of which, with great labor and sweat, I brought to my boat. And praying to God to direct my voyage, I put out; and rowing, or paddling, the canoe along the shore, I came at last to the utmost point of the island on that side, viz., N.E. And now I was to launch out into the ocean, and either to venture or not to venture. I looked on the rapid currents which ran con-stantly on both sides of the island at a distance, and which were very terrible to me, from the remembrance of the hazard I had been in before, and my heart began to fail me; for I foresaw that if I was driven into either of those currents, I should be carried a vast way out to sea, and perhaps out of my reach, or sight of the island again; and that then, as my boat was but small, if any little gale of wind should rise, I should be inevitably lost.

These thoughts so oppressed my mind, that I began to give over my enter-prise; and having hauled my boat into a little creek on the shore, I stepped out, and sat me down upon a little rising bit of ground, very pensive and anxious, between fear and desire, about my voyage; when, as I was musing, I could perceive that the tide was turned, and the flood come on; upon which my going was for so many hours impracticable. Upon this, presently it occurred to me that I should go up to the highest piece of ground I could find and

observe, if I could, how the sets of the tide or currents, lay when the flood
came in, that I might judge whether, if I was driven one way out, I might not
expect to be driven another way home, with the same rapidness of the currents. This thought was no sooner in my head but I cast my eye upon a little
hill, which sufficiently overlooked the sea both ways, and from whence I had
a clear view of the currents, or sets of the tide, and which way I was to guide
myself in my return. Here I found, that as the current of the ebb set out close
by the south point of the island, so the current of the flood set in close by the
shore of the north side; and that I had nothing to do but to keep to the north
of the island in my return, and I should do well enough.

Encouraged with this observation, I resolved the next morning to set out
with the first of the tide, and reposing myself for the night in the canoe, under
the great watch-coat I mention, I launched out. I made first a little out to
sea, full north, till I began to feel the benefit of the current which set eastward,
and which carried me at a great rate; and yet did not so hurry me as the southern side current had done before, and so as to take from me all government of
the boat; but having a strong steerage with my paddle, I went at a great rate
directly for the wreck, and in less than two hours I came up to it.

It was a dismal sight to look at. The ship, which, by its building, was
Spanish, stuck fast, jammed in between two rocks. All the stern and quarter
of her was beaten to pieces with the sea; and as her forecastle, which stuck in
the rocks, had run on with great violence, her mainmast and foremast were
brought by the board; that is to say, broken short off; but her bowsprit was
sound, and the head and bow appeared firm. When I came close to her a dog
appeared upon her, who, seeing me coming, yelped and cried; and as soon as I
called him, jumped into the sea to come to me, and I took him into the boat,
but found him almost dead for hunger and thirst. I gave him a cake of my
bread, and he ate it like a ravenous wolf that had been starving a fortnight
in the snow. I then gave the poor creature some fresh water, with which, if
I would have let him, he would have burst himself.

After this I went on board; but the first sight I met with was two men
drowned in the cook-room, or forecastle of the ship, with their arms fast
about one another. I concluded, as is indeed probable, that when the ship
struck, it being in a storm, the sea broke so high, and so continually over her,
that the men were not able to bear it, and were strangled with the constant
rushing in of the water, as much as if they had been under water. Besides the

dog, there was nothing left in the ship that had life; nor any goods that I could see, but what were spoiled by the water. There were some casks of liquor, whether wine or brandy I knew not, which lay lower in the hold, and which, the water being ebbed out, I could see; but they were too big to meddle with. I saw several chests which I believed belonged to some of the seamen; and I got two of them into the boat, without examining what was in them.

Had the stern of the ship been fixed, and the forepart broken off, I am persuaded I might have made a good voyage; for by what I found in these two chests, I had room to suppose the ship had a great deal of wealth on board; and if I may guess by the course she steered, she must have been bound from the Buenos Ayres, or the Rio de la Plata, in the south part of America, beyond the Brazils, to Havana, in the Gulf of Mexico, and so perhaps to Spain. She had, no doubt, a great treasure in her, but of no use, at that time, to anybody; and what became of the rest of her people, I then knew not.

I found, besides these chests, a little cask full of liquor, of about twenty gallons, which I got into my boat with much difficulty. There were several muskets in a cabin, and a great powder-horn, with about four pounds of powder in it. As for the muskets, I had no occasion for them, so I left them, but took the powder-horn. I took a fire-shovel and tongs, which I wanted extremely; as also two little brass kettles, a copper pot to make chocolate, and a gridiron. And with this cargo, and the dog, I came away, the tide beginning to make home again; and the same evening, about an hour within night, I reached the island again, weary and fatigued to the last degree.

DANTÈS' ESCAPE
FROM THE CHÂTEAU D'IF

Alexander Dumas

ON THE bed, at full length, faintly lighted by a dim ray that entered through the window, Dantès saw a sack of coarse cloth, under the ample folds of which he could distinctly discern a long, stiff form: it was Faria's shroud. All was over then. Dantès was separated from his old friend. Faria, the helpful, kind companion, to whom he had become so attached, to whom he owed so much, existed now but in his memory. He sat on the edge of the bed and became a prey to deep and bitter melancholy.

Alone! He was quite alone once more! Alone! No longer to see, to hear the voice of, the only human being that attached him to life! Would it not be better to seek his Maker, as Faria had done, to learn the mystery of life even at the risk of passing through the dismal gates of suffering?

The idea of suicide which had been dispelled by his friend and which he himself had forgotten in his presence, rose again before him like a phantom beside Faria's corpse.

"If I could only die," he said, "I should go where he has gone. But how am I to die? It is quite simple," said he with a smile. "I will stay here, throw myself on the first one who enters, strangle him and then I shall be guillotined."

Dantès, however, recoiled from such an infamous death, and swiftly passed from despair to an ardent desire for life and liberty. "Die? Oh, no!" he cried out, "it would hardly have been worth while to live, to suffer so much and then to die now. No, I desire to live, to fight to the end. I wish to re-

from "The Count of Monte Cristo" by Alexander Dumas

conquer the happiness that has been taken from me. Before I die, I have my executioners to punish, and possibly also some friends to recompense. Yet they will forget me here and I shall only leave this dungeon in the same way that Faria has done."

As he uttered these words, Edmond stood stock-still, with eyes fixed like a man struck by a sudden and terrifying idea.

"Oh, who has given me this thought?" he murmured. "My God, comes this from Thee? Since it is only the dead who go free from here, I must take the place of the dead!"

Without giving himself time to reconsider his decision, and as though he would not give reflection time to destroy his desperate resolution, he leaned over the hideous sack, slit it open with the knife Faria had made, took the dead body out, carried it to his own cell, and placed it on his bed, put round the head the piece of rag he always wore, covered it with the bed-clothes, kissed for the last time the ice-cold forehead, endeavored to shut the rebellious eyes, which were still open, and stared so horribly, and turned the head to the wall so that, when the jailer brought his evening meal, he would think he had gone to bed as he often did. Then he returned to the other cell, took the needle and thread from the cupboard, flung off his rags that the men might feel naked flesh under the sacking, slipped into the sack, placed himself in the same position as the corpse, and sewed the sack up again from the inside. If, by any chance, the jailers had entered then, they would have heard the beating of his heart.

Now this is what Dantès intended doing. If the grave-diggers discovered that they were carrying a live body instead of a dead one, he would give them no time for thought. He would slit the sack open with his knife from top to bottom, jump out, and, taking advantage of their terror, escape; if they tried to stop him, he would use his knife. If they took him to the cemetery and placed him in a grave, he would allow himself to be covered with earth; then, as it was night, as soon as the grave-diggers had turned their backs, he would cut his way through the soft earth and escape; he hoped the weight would not be too heavy for him to raise.

He had eaten nothing since the previous evening, but he had not thought of his hunger in the morning, neither did he think of it now. His position was much too precarious to allow him time for any thought but that of flight.

At last, toward the time appointed by the governor, he heard footsteps on the staircase. He realized that the moment had come, he summoned all his courage and held his breath.

The door was opened, a subdued light reached his eyes. Through the sacking that covered him he saw two shadows approach the bed. There was a third one at the door holding a lantern in his hand. Each of the two men who had approached the bed took the sack by one of its two extremities.

"He is very heavy for such a thin old man," said one of them as he raised the head.

"They say that each year adds half a pound to the weight of one's bones," said the other, taking the feet.

They carried away the sham corpse on the bier. Edmond made himself rigid. The procession, lighted by the man with the lantern, descended the stairs. All at once Dantès felt the cold, fresh night air and the sharp northwest wind, and the sensation filled him at once with joy and with anguish.

The men went about twenty yards, then stopped and dropped the bier on to the ground. One of them went away, and Dantès heard his footsteps on the stones.

"Where am I?" he asked himself.

"He is by no means a light load, you know," said the man who had remained behind, seating himself on the edge of the bier.

Dantès' impulse was to make his escape, but, fortunately, he did not attempt it. He heard one of the men draw near and drop a heavy object on the ground; at the same moment a cord was tied round his feet, cutting into his flesh.

"Well, have you made the knot?" one of the men asked.

"Yes, and it is well made. I can answer for that."

"Let's on, then."

The bier was lifted once more, and the procession proceeded. The noise of the waves breaking against the rocks on which the Château is built sounded more distinctly to Dantès with each step they took.

"Wretched weather!" said one of the men, "the sea will not be very inviting tonight."

"Yes, the abbé runs a great risk of getting wet," said the other, and they burst out laughing.

Dantès could not understand the jest, nevertheless his hair began to stand on end.

"Here we are at last!"

"No, farther on, farther on! You know the last one was dashed on the rocks and the next day the governor called us a couple of lazy rascals."

They went another five yards, and then Dantès felt them take him by the head and feet and swing him to and fro.

"One! Two! Three!"

With the last word, Dantès felt himself flung into space. He passed through the air like a wounded bird falling, falling, ever falling with a rapidity which turned his heart to ice. At last—though it seemed to him like an eternity of time—there came a terrific splash; and as he dropped like an arrow into the icy cold water he uttered a scream which was immediately choked by his immersion.

Dantès had been flung into the sea, into whose depths he was being dragged down by a cannon-ball tied to his feet.

The sea is the cemetery of the Château d'If.

Though stunned and almost suffocated, Dantès had yet the presence of mind to hold his breath and, as he grasped the open knife in his right hand ready for any emergency, he rapidly ripped open the sack, extricated his arm and then his head; but in spite of his efforts to raise the cannon ball, he still felt himself being dragged down and down. He bent his back into an arch in his endeavor to reach the cord that bound his legs, and, after a desperate struggle, he severed it at the very moment when he felt that suffocation was getting the upper hand of him. He kicked out vigorously and rose unhampered to the surface, while the cannon ball dragged to the unknown depths the sacking which had so nearly become his shroud.

Dantès merely paused to take a deep breath and then he dived again to avoid being seen. When he rose the second time, he was already fifty yards from the spot where he had been thrown into the sea. He saw above him a black and tempestuous sky; before him was the vast expanse of dark, surging waters; while behind him, more gloomy than the sea and more somber than the sky, rose the granite giant like some menacing phantom, whose dark summit appeared to Dantès like an arm stretched out to seize its prey. He had always been reckoned the best swimmer in Marseilles, and he was now anxious to rise to the surface to try his strength against the waves. To his joy he found that

He bent his back into an arch in his endeavor to reach the cord that bound his legs.

his enforced inaction had not in any way impaired his strength and agility, and he felt he could still master the element in which he had so often sported when a boy.

An hour passed. Exalted by the feeling of liberty, Dantès continued to cleave the waves in what he reckoned should be a direct line for the Isle of Tiboulen. Suddenly it seemed to him that the sky, which was already black, was becoming blacker than ever, and that a thick, heavy cloud was rolling down on him. At the same time he felt a violent pain in his knee. With the incalculable rapidity of imagination, he thought it was a shot that had struck him, and he expected every moment to hear the report. But there was no sound. He stretched out his hand and encountered an obstacle; he drew his leg up and felt land; he then saw what it was he had mistaken for a cloud. Twenty yards from him rose a mass of strangely formed rocks looking like an immense fire petrified at the moment of its most violent combustion: it was the Isle of Tiboulen.

Dantès rose, advanced a few steps and with a prayer of gratitude on his lips, stretched himself out on the jagged rocks which seemed to him more restful and comfortable than the softest bed he had ever slept on. Then, in spite of the wind and storm, in spite of the rain that began to fall, worn out with fatigue as he was, he fell into the delicious sleep of a man whose body becomes torpid but whose mind remains alert in the consciousness of unexpected happiness.

For an hour he slept thus, and was awakened by the roar of a tremendous clap of thunder. A flash of lightning that seemed to open the heavens to the very throne of God, illuminated all around, and by its light he saw about a quarter of a mile away, between the Isle of Lemaire and Cap Croisille, a small fishing boat borne along by the wind, and riding like a phantom on the top of a wave only to disappear in the abyss below. A second later it appeared on the crest of another wave advancing with terrifying rapidity. By the light of another flash, he saw four men clinging to the masts and rigging; a fifth was clinging to the broken rudder. Then he heard a terrific crash followed by agonizing cries. As he clung to his rock like a limpet, another flash revealed to him the little boat smashed to pieces and, amongst the wreckage, heads with despairing faces, and arms stretched heavenward. Then all was dark again. There was nothing left but tempest.

By degrees the wind abated; the huge gray clouds rolled toward the west.

Shortly afterward a long, reddish streak was seen along the horizon; the waves leaped and frolicked, and a sudden light played on their foamy crests, turning them into golden plumes. Daylight had come.

It must have been five o'clock in the morning; the sea continued to grow calm. "In two or three hours," Dantès said to himself, "the turnkeys will enter my cell, find the dead body of my poor friend, recognize him, seek me in vain, and give the alarm. Then they will find the aperture and the passage; they will question the men who flung me into the sea and who must have heard the cry I uttered. Boats filled with armed soldiers will immediately give chase to the wretched fugitive who, they know, cannot be far off. The cannon will warn the whole coast that no one shall give shelter to a naked, famished wanderer. The spies and police of Marseilles will be notified, and they will beat the coast while the Governor of the Château d'If beats the sea. And what will become of me pursued by land and by sea? I am hungry and cold and have even lost my knife. I am at the mercy of the first peasant who cares to hand me over to the police for the reward of twenty francs. Oh God! my God! Thou knowest I have suffered to excess; help me now that I cannot help myself!"

As Dantès finished this fervent prayer that was torn from his exhausted and anguished heart, he saw appearing on the horizon what he recognized as a Genoese *tartan* coming from Marseilles.

"To think that I could join this vessel in half an hour if it were not for the fear of being questioned, recognized as a fugitive, and taken back to Marseilles," said Dantès to himself. "What am I to do? What can I say? What story can I invent which might sound credible? I might pass as one of the sailors wrecked last night." So saying he turned his gaze toward the wreck and gave a sudden start. There, caught on a point of rock, he perceived the cap of one of the shipwrecked sailors, and close by still floated some of the planks of the unfortunate vessel.

Dantès soon thought out a plan and as quickly put it into action. He dived into the sea, swam toward the cap, placed it on his head, seized one of the timbers, and turning back, struck out in a direction which would cut the course the vessel must take.

The boat changed her course, steering toward him, and Dantès saw that they made ready to lower a boat. He summoned all his strength to swim toward it, but his arms began to stiffen, his legs lost their flexibility, and his movements became heavy and difficult. Breath was failing him. A wave that he had not the strength to surmount, passed over his head, covering him with foam. Then he saw and heard nothing more.

When he opened his eyes again, Dantès found himself on the deck of the *tartan;* a sailor was rubbing his limbs with a woolen cloth, another was holding a gourd to his mouth, and a third, who was the master of the vessel, was looking at him with that feeling of pity which is uppermost in the hearts of most people when face to face with a misfortune which they escaped yesterday, and of which they may be the victim tomorrow.

"Who are you?" the skipper asked in bad French.

"I am a Maltese sailor," replied Dantès in equally bad Italian. "We were coming from Syracuse laden with wine and grain. We were caught in a storm last night off Cape Morgion, and we were wrecked on the rocks you see yonder."

"Where have you come from?"

"From those rocks over there. Fortunately for me I was able to cling to them, but our poor captain and my three companions were drowned. I believe I am the sole survivor. I saw your ship, and I risked swimming towards you. Thank you," he continued, "you have saved my life. I was lost when one of your sailors caught hold of my hair."

"It was I," said a sailor with a frank and open face, encircled by long black whiskers. "It was time, too, for you were sinking."

"Yes," said Dantès, holding out his hand to him. "I know, and I thank you once more."

"Lord! but you nearly frightened me," the sailor replied. "You looked more like a brigand than an honest man with your beard six inches long and your hair a foot in length."

Dantès suddenly recollected that neither his hair nor his beard had been cut all the time that he had been at the Château d'If.

"Once when I was in danger," he said, "I made a vow to the Madonna of Piedigrotta not to cut my hair or beard for ten years. The time is up this very day, and I nearly celebrated the event by being drowned."

"Now, what are we going to do with you?" asked the skipper.

"Alas! do with me what you will," replied Dantès. "The bark I sailed in is lost, my captain is dead, and I nearly shared the same fate. Fortunately I am a good sailor. Leave me at the first port you touch at, and I shall be sure to find employment in some merchantman."

"Take the helm and let us see how you frame."

The young man did as he was bid. Ascertaining by a slight pressure that the vessel answered to the rudder, he saw that, without being a first-rate sailer, she was yet tolerably obedient.

"Man the lee-braces," he cried.

The four seamen, who composed the crew, obeyed, whilst the skipper looked on.

"Haul away!"

They obeyed.

"Belay!"

This order was also executed, and, instead of tacking about, the vessel made straight for the Isle of Rion, leaving it about twenty fathoms to starboard.

"Bravo!" said the captain.

"Bravo!" repeated the sailors.

And they all regarded with astonishment this man whose eye had recovered an intelligence and his body a vigor they were far from suspecting him to possess.

"You see," said Dantès, handing over the tiller to the helmsman, "I shall be of some use to you, at any rate during the voyage. If you do not want me at Leghorn, you can leave me there and with the first wages I earn, I will pay you for my food and for the clothes you lend me."

"Very well," said the captain. "We can fix things up if you are not too exacting."

"Give me what you give the others," returned Dantès.

"Hallo! What's the matter at the Château d'If?" exclaimed the captain.

A small white cloud crowned the summit of the bastion of the Château d'If. At the same moment, the faint report of a gun was heard. The sailors all looked at one another.

"A prisoner has escaped from the Château d'If, and they are firing the alarm gun," said Dantès calmly.

"What is the day of the month?" he presently asked of Jacopo, the sailor who had saved him and who now sat beside him.

"The twenty-eighth of February."

"What year?"

"Have you forgotten that you ask such a question?"

"I was so frightened last night," replied Dantès, with a smile, "that I have almost lost my memory. What year is it?"

"The year eighteen-twenty-nine," returned Jacopo.

It was fourteen years to the very day since Dantès' arrest. He was nineteen when he entered the Château d'If; he was thirty-three when he escaped.

THE SPECKSIONEER

Elizabeth Gaskell

F ARMER ROBSON left Haytersbank betimes on a longish day's journey, to purchase a horse. Sylvia and her mother were busied with a hundred household things, and the early winter's evening closed in upon them almost before they were aware. The consequences of darkness in the country even now are to gather the members of a family together into one room, and to make them settle to some sedentary employment; and it was much more the case at the period of my story when candles were far dearer than they are at present, and when one was often made to suffice for a large family.

The mother and daughter hardly spoke at all when they sat down at last. The cheerful click of the knitting-needles made a pleasant home-sound; and in the occasional snatches of slumber that overcame her mother, Sylvia could hear the long-rushing boom of the waves, down below the rocks, for the Haytersbank gully allowed the sullen roar to come up so far inland. It might have been about eight o'clock—though from the monotonous course of the evening it seemed much later—when Sylvia heard her father's heavy step cranching down the pebbly path. More unusual, she heard his voice talking to some companion.

Curious to see who it could be, with a lively instinctive advance towards any event which might break the monotony she had begun to find somewhat dull, she sprang up to open the door. Half a glance into the gray darkness outside made her suddenly timid, and she drew back behind the door, as she opened it wide to admit her father and Kinraid.

Daniel Robson came in bright and boisterous. He was pleased with his

from "Sylvia's Lovers" by Elizabeth Gaskell

purchase, and had had some drink to celebrate his bargain. He had ridden the new mare into Monkshaven, and left her at the smithy there until morning, to have her feet looked at, and to be new shod. On his way from the town he had met Kinraid wandering about in search of Haytersbank Farm itself, so he had just brought him along with him; and here they were, ready for bread and cheese, and aught else the mistress would set before them.

To Sylvia the sudden change into brightness and bustle occasioned by the entrance of her father and the specksioneer was like that which you may effect any winter's night, when you come into a room where a great lump of coal lies hot and slumbering on the fire; just break it up with a judicious blow from the poker, and the room, late so dark, and dusk, and lone, is full of life, and light, and warmth.

She moved about with pretty household briskness attending to all her father's wants. Kinraid's eye watched her as she went backwards and forwards, to and fro, into the pantry, the back-kitchen, out of light into shade, out of the shadow into the broad firelight where he could see and note her appearance. She wore the high-crowned linen cap of that day, surmounting her lovely masses of golden-brown hair, rather than concealing them, and tied firm to her head by a broad blue ribbon. A long curl hung down on each side of her neck—her throat rather, for her neck was concealed by a little spotted handkerchief carefully pinned across, at the waist of her brown stuff gown.

How well it was, thought the young girl, that she had doffed her bed-gown, and linsey-woolsey petticoat, her working-dress, and made herself smart in her stuff gown, when she sat down to work with her mother.

By the time she could sit down again, her father and Kinraid had their glasses filled, and were talking of the relative merits of various kinds of spirits; that led on to tales of smuggling, and the different contrivances by which they or their friends had eluded the preventive service; the nightly relays of men to carry the goods inland; the kegs of brandy found by certain farmers whose horses had gone so far in the night that they could do no work the next day; the clever way in which certain women managed to bring in prohibited goods; in fact, that when a woman did give her mind to smuggling, she was more full of resources, and tricks, and impudence, and energy, than any man. There was no question of the morality of the affair; one of the greatest signs of the real progress we have made since those times seems to be that our daily concerns of buying and selling, eating and drinking, whatsoever we do, are more tested by the real practical standard of our religion than they were in the days of our grandfathers. Neither Sylvia nor her mother was in advance of their age. Both listened with admiration to the ingenious devices, and acted as well as spoken lies, that were talked about as fine and spirited things. Yet if Sylvia had attempted one tithe of this deceit in her everyday life, it would have half broken her mother's heart. But when the duty on salt was strictly and cruelly enforced, making it penal to pick up rough dirty lumps containing small quantities that might be thrown out with the ashes of the brine-houses on the highroads; when the price of this necessary was so increased by the tax upon it as to make it an expensive, sometimes an unattainable, luxury to the working man, government did more to demoralize the popular sense of rectitude and uprightness, than heaps of sermons could undo. And the same, though in smaller measure, was the consequence of many other taxes. It may seem curious to trace up the popular standard of truth to taxation; but I do not think the idea would be so very far-fetched.

From smuggling adventures, it was easy to pass on to stories of what had happened to Robson, in his youth a sailor in the Greenland seas, and to Kinraid, now one of the best harpooners in any whaler that sailed off the coast.

"There's three things to be afeard on," said Robson, authoritatively: "there's the ice, that's bad; there's dirty weather, that's worse; and there's whales theirselves, as is t' worst of all; leastways, they was in my day; t' darned brutes may ha' larnt better manner sin'. When I were young, they could never be got to let theirsels be harpooned wi'out floundering and making play wi' their tails and their fins, till t' sea were all in a foam, and t' boats' crews was all o'er wi' spray, which i' them latitudes is a kind o' shower-bath not needed."

"Th' whales hasn't mended their manners, as you call it," said Kinraid; "but t' ice is not to be spoken lightly on. I were once in th' ship *John*, of Hull, and we were in good green water, and were keen after whales; and ne'er thought harm of a great gray iceberg as were on our lee-bow, a mile or so off; it looked as if it had been there from the days of Adam, and were likely to see th' last man out, and it ne'er a bit bigger nor smaller in all them thousands and thousands o' years. Well, the fast-boats were out after a fish, and I were specksioneer in one; and we were so keen after capturing our whale, that none on us ever saw that we were drifting away from them right into deep shadow o' th' iceberg. But we were set upon our whale, and I harpooned it; and as soon as it were dead we lashed its fins together, and fastened its tail to our boat;

and then we took breath and looked about us, and away from us a little space were th' other boats, wi' two other fish making play, and as likely as not to break loose, for I may say as I were th' best harpooner on board the *John*, wi'out saying great things o' mysel'. So I says, 'My lads, one o' you stay i' th' boat by this fish,'—the fins o' which, as I said, I'd reeved a rope through mysel', and which was as dead as Noah's grandfather—'and th' rest on us shall go off and help th' other boats wi' their fish.' For, you see, we had another boat close by in order to sweep th' fish. (I suppose they swept fish i' your time, master?)"

"Ay, ay!" said Robson; "one boat lies still holding t' end o' th' line; t' other makes a circuit round t' fish."

"Well! luckily for us we had our second boat, for we all got into it, ne'er a man on us was left i' th' fast-boat. And says I, 'But who's to stay by t' dead fish?' And no man answered, for they were all as keen as me for to go and help our mates; and we thought as we could come back to our dead fish, as had a boat for a buoy, once we had helped our mate. So off we rowed, every man Jack on us, out o' the black shadow o' th' iceberg, as looked as steady as t' pole-star. Well! we had na' been a dozen fathoms away fra' th' boat as we had left, when crash! down wi' a roaring noise, and then a gulp of the deep waters, and then a shower o' blinding spray; and when we had wiped our eyes clear, and getten our hearts down again fra' our mouths, there were never a boat nor a glittering belly o' e'er a great whale to be seen; but t' iceberg were there, still and grim, as if a hundred ton or more had fallen off all in a mass, and crushed down boat, and fish, and all, into th' deep water, as goes half through the earth in them latitudes. Th' coalminers round about Newcastle way may come upon our good boat if they mine deep enough, else ne'er another man will see her. And I left as good a clasp-knife in her as ever I clapt eyes on."

"But what a mercy no man stayed in her," said Bell.

"Why, mistress, I reckon we a' must die some way; and I'd as soon go down into the deep waters, as be choked up wi' moulds."

"But it must be so cold," said Sylvia, shuddering and giving a little poke to the fire to warm her fancy.

"Cold!" said her father, "what do ye stay-at-homes know about cold, a should like to know. If ye'd been where a were once, north latitude 81, in such a frost as ye' ha' never known, no, not i' deep winter, and it were June i' them seas, and a whale i' sight, and a were off in a boat after her; an' t' ill-mannered brute, as soon as she were harpooned, ups wi' her big awkward tail, and struck t' boat i' her stern, and chucks me out int' t' water. That were cold, a can tell the'! First, I smarted all ower me, as if my skin were suddenly stript off me; and next, every bone i' my body had getten t' toothache, and there were a great roar i' my ears, an' a great dizziness i' my eyes; an' t' boat's crew kept throwing out their oars, an' a kept clutching at 'em, but a could na' make out where they was, my eyes dazzled so wi' t' cold, an' I thought I were bound for 'kingdom come,' an' a tried to remember t' Creed as a might die a Christian. But all a could think on was, 'What is your name, M or N?' an' just as a were giving up both words and life, they heerd me aboard. But, bless ye, they had but one oar; for they'd thrown a' t' others after me; so, yo' may reckon, it were some time afore we could reach t' ship; an', a've heerd tell, a were a precious sight to look on, for my clothes was just hard frozen to me, an' my hair a'most as big a lump o' ice as yon iceberg he was a-telling us on; they rubbed me as missus there were rubbing t' hams yesterday, and gav' me brandy; an' a ha' ne'er getten t' frost out o' my bones for a' their rubbin', and a deal o' brandy as I 'ave ta'en sin'. Talk o' cold! it's little yo' women known o' cold!"

"But there's heat, too, i' some places," said Kinraid. "I was once a voyage i' an American. They goes for th' most part south, to where you come round to t' cold again; and they'll stay there for three year at a time, if need be, going into winter harbor i' some o' th' Pacific Islands. Well, we were i' th' southern seas, a-seeking for good whaling-ground; and, close on our larboard beam, there were a great wall o' ice, as much as sixty feet high. And says our captain—as were a daredevil, if ever a man were—'There'll be an opening in yon dark gray wall, and into that opening I'll sail, if I coast along it till th' day o' judgment.' But, for all our sailing, we never seemed to come nearer to th' opening. The waters were rocking beneath us, and the sky were steady above us; and th' ice rose out o' the waters, and seemed to reach up into the sky. We sailed on, and we sailed on, for more days nor I could count. Our captain were a strange, wild man, but once he looked a little pale when he came upo' deck after his turn-in, and saw the green-gray ice going straight up on our beam. Many on us thought as the ship were bewitched for th' captain's words; and we got to speak low, and to say our prayers o' nights, and a kind o' dull silence came into th' very air; our voices did na' rightly seem our own.

And we sailed on, and we sailed on. All at once, th' man as were on watch gave a cry: he saw a break in the ice, as we'd begun to think were everlasting; and we all gathered towards the bows, and the captain called to th' man at the helm to keep her course, and cocked his head, and began to walk the quarterdeck jaunty again. And we came to a great cleft in th' long weary rock of ice: and the sides o' th' cleft were not jagged, but went straight sharp down into th' foaming waters. But we took but one look at what lay inside, for our captain, with a loud cry to God, bade the helmsman steer nor'ards away fra' th' mouth o' Hell. We all saw wi' our own eyes, inside that fearsome wall o' ice—seventy mile long, as we could swear to—inside that gray, cold ice, came leaping flames, all red and yellow wi' heat o' some unearthly kind, out o' th' very waters o' the sea; making our eyes dazzle wi' their scarlet blaze, that shot up as high, nay, higher than th' ice around, yet never so much as a shred on 't was melted. They did say that some beside our captain saw the black devils dart hither and thither, quicker than the very flames themselves; anyhow, *he* saw them. And as he knew it were his own daring as had led him to have that peep at terrors forbidden to any on us afore our time, he just dwined away, and we hadn't taken but one whale afore our captain died, and first mate took th' command. It were a prosperous voyage, but, for all that, I'll never sail those seas again, nor ever take wage aboard an American again."

"Eh, dear! but it's awful t' think o' sitting wi' a man that has seen th' doorway into hell," said Bell, aghast.

Sylvia had dropped her work, and sat gazing at Kinraid with fascinated wonder.

Daniel was just a little annoyed at the admiration which his own wife and daughter were bestowing on the specksioneer's wonderful stories, and he said——

"Ay, ay. If a'd been a talker, ye'd ha' thought a deal more on me nor ye've ever done yet. A've seen such things and done such things.

"Tell us, father!" said Sylvia, greedy and breathless.

"Some on 'em is past telling," he replied, "an' some is not to be had for t' asking, seeing as how they might bring a man into trouble. But, as a said, if a had a fancy to reveal all as is on my mind a could make t' hair on your heads lift up your caps—well, we'll say an inch, at least. Thy mother, lass, has heerd one or two on 'em. Thou mind's the story o' my ride on a whale's back, Bell?

That'll maybe be within this young fellow's comprehension o' th' danger; thou's heerd me tell it, hasn't ta?"

"Yes," said Bell; "but it's a long time ago; when we was courting."

"An' that's afore this young lass were born, as is a'most up to woman's estate. But sin' those days a ha' been o'er busy to tell stories to my wife, an' as a'll warrant, she's forgotten it; an' as Sylvia here never heerd it, if ye'll fill your glass, Kinraid, ye shall ha' t' benefit o't.

"A were a specksioneer mysel', though, after that, a rayther directed my talents int' t' smuggling branch o' my profession; but a were once a whaling aboord t' *Aimwell* of Whitby. An' we was anchored off t' coast o' Greenland one season; an' we had getten a cargo o' seven whale; but our captain he were a keen-eyed chap, an' ne'er above doing any man's work; an' once seeing a whale he throws himself int' a boat an' goes off to it, making signals to me, an' another specksioneer as were off for diversion i' another boat, for to come after him sharp. Well, afore we comes alongside, captain had harpooned t' fish; an' says he, 'Now, Robson, all ready! give into her again when she comes to t' top,' an' I stands up, right leg foremost, harpoon all ready, as soon as ever I catched a sight o' t' whale, but ne'er a fin could a see. 'Twere no wonder, for she were right below t' boat in which a were; and when she wanted to rise, what does t' great ugly brute do but come wi' her head, as is like cast iron, up bang again t' bottom o' t' boat. I were thrown up in t' air like a shuttlecock, me an' my line an' my harpoon—up we goes, an' many a good piece o' timber wi' us, an' many a good fellow too; but a had t' look after mysel' an' a were up high i' t' air, afore I could say Jack Robison, an' a thowt a were safe for another dive int' saut water; but i'stead a comes down plump on t' back o' t' whale. Ay! ye may stare, master, but there a were, an' main an' slippery it were, only a sticks my harpoon intil her an' steadies mysel', an' looks abroad o'er the vast o' waves, and gets sea-sick in a manner, an' puts up a prayer as she mayn't dive, and it were as good a prayer for wishing it might come true, as ever t' clargyman an t' clerk too put up i' Monkshaven church. Well, a reckon it were heerd, for all a were in them north latitudes, for she keeps steady, an' a does my best for t' keep steady; an' 'deed a was too steady, for a was fast wi' t' harpoon line, all knotted and tangled about me. T' captain, he sings out for me to cut it; but it's easy singin' out, and it's noane so easy fumblin' for your knife i' t' pocket o' your drawers, when ye've t' hold hard wi' t' other hand on t' back of a whale, swimming fourteen knots an hour.

At last a thinks to mysel' a can't get free o' t' line, and t' line is fast to t' harpoon, and t' harpoon is fast to t' whale; and t' whale may go down fathoms deep whenever t' maggot stirs i' her head; an' t' water's cold, an' noane good for drownin' in; a can't get free o' t' line, and a canna' get my knife out o' my breeches' pocket though t' captain should ca' it mutiny to disobey orders, and t' line's fast to t' harpoon—let's see if t' harpoon's fast to t' whale. So a tugged, and a lugged, and t' whale didn't mistake it for ticklin', but she cocks up her tail, and throws out showers o' water as were ice or ever it touched me; but a pulls on at t' shank, an' a were only afeard as she wouldn't keep at t' top wi' it sticking in her; but at last t' harpoon broke, an' just i' time, for a reckon she was near as tired o' me as a were on her, and down she went; an' a had hard work to make for t' boats as was near enough to catch me; for what wi' t' whale's being but slippery an' t' water bein' cold, an' me hampered wi' t' line an' t' piece o' harpoon, it's a chance, missus, as thou had stopped an oud maid."

"Eh dear a' me!" said Bell, "how well I mind your telling me that tale! It were twenty-four year ago come October. I thought I never could think enough on a man as had rode on a whale's back!"

"Yo' may learn t' way of winning t' women," said Daniel, winking at the specksioneer.

And Kinraid immediately looked at Sylvia. It was no premeditated action; it came as naturally as wakening in the morning when his sleep was ended; but Sylvia colored as red as any rose at his sudden glance,—colored so deeply that he looked away until he thought she had recovered her composure, and then he sat gazing at her again. But not for long, for Bell suddenly starting up did all but turn him out of the house. It was late, she said, and her master was tired, and they had a hard day before them next day; and it was keeping Ellen Corney up; and they had had enough to drink,—more than was good for them, she was sure, for they had both been taking her in with their stories, which she had been foolish enough to believe. No one saw the real motive of all this almost inhospitable haste to dismiss her guest, how the sudden fear had taken possession of her that he and Sylvia were "fancying each other." Kinraid had said early in the evening that he had come to thank her for her kindness in sending the sausages, as he was off to his own home near Newcastle in a day or two. But now he said, in reply to Daniel Robson, that he would step in another night before long and hear some more of the old man's yarns.

"But there a were, an' main an' slippery it were, only a sticks my harpoon intil her, an' steadies mysel'."

HOW CAPTAIN JOHN RIBAULT
PLANTED A COLONY IN FLORIDA

Richard Hakluyt

M Y LORD Admiral of Chastillon, a noble man more desirous of the public than of his private benefit, understanding the pleasure of the King his prince, which was to discover new and strange countries, caused vessels fit for this purpose to be made ready with all diligence, and men to be levied meet for such an enterprise: among whom he chose Captain John Ribault, a man in truth expert in sea causes: which having received his charge, set himself to sea the year 1562, the eighteenth of February, accompanied only with two of the King's ships, but so well furnished with gentlemen, (of whose number I myself was one) and with old soldiers, that he had means to achieve some notable thing and worthy of eternal memory. Having therefore sailed two months, never holding the usual course of the Spaniards, he arrived in Florida landing near a cape or promontory, which is no high land, because the coast is all flat, but only rising by reason of the high woods, which at his arrival he called Cape François in honor of our France. This cape is distant from the equator about thirty degrees.

Coasting from this place towards the north, he discovered a very fair and great river, which gave him occasion to cast anchor that he might search the same the next day very early in the morning: which being done by the break of day, accompanied with Captain Fiquinville and divers other soldiers of this ship, he was no sooner arrived on the brink of the shore, but straight he per-

from "The Principal Navigations, Voyages, and Discoveries of the English Nation" by Richard Hakluyt ceived many Indian men and women, which came of purpose to that place to receive the Frenchmen with all gentleness and amity, as they well declared by the oration which their king made, and the presents of chamois skins wherewith he honored our Captain, which the day following caused a pillar of hard stone to be planted within the said river, and not far from the mouth of the same upon a little sandy knap, in which pillar the arms of France were carved and engraved. This being done he embarked himself again, to the end always to discover the coast toward the north which was his chief desire. After he had sailed a certain time he crossed over to the other side of the river, and then in the presence of certain Indians, which of purpose did attend him, he commended his men to make their prayers, to give thanks to God for that of his grace he had conducted the French nation unto these strange places without any danger at all.

The prayers being ended, the Indians which were very attentive to hearken unto them, thinking in my judgment, that we worshiped the sun, because we always had our eyes lifted up toward heaven, rose all up and came to salute the Captain John Ribault, promising to show him their king, which rose not up as they did, but remained still sitting upon green leaves of bay and palm trees: toward whom the Captain went and sat down by him, and heard him make a long discourse, but with no great pleasure, because he could not understand his language, and much less his meaning. The king gave our Captain at his departure a plume or fan of hernshaw's feathers dyed in red, and a basket made of palm boughs after the Indian fashion, and wrought very artificially, and a great skin painted and drawn throughout with the pictures of divers wild beasts so lively drawn and portrayed, that nothing lacked but life.

Soon after we returned to our ships, we weighed our anchors and hoisted our sails to discover the coast farther forward, along the which we discovered another fair river, which the Captain himself was minded to search out, and having searched it out with the king and inhabitants thereof, he named it Seine, because it is very like unto the river Seine in France. From this river we retired toward our ships, where being arrived, we trimmed our sails to sail farther toward the north, and to descry the singularities of the coast. But we had not sailed any great way before we discovered another very fair river, which caused us to cast anchor over against it, and to trim out two boats to go to search it out. We found there an isle and a king no less affable than the rest, afterward we named the river Somme. From thence we sailed about six leagues, after we discovered another river, which after we had viewed was named by us the name of Loire. And consequently we there discovered five others: whereof the first was named Cherente, the second Garonne, the third Gironde, the fourth Belle, the fifth Grande: which being very well discovered with such things as were in them, by this time in less than the space of three-score leagues we had found out many singularities along nine rivers.

Nevertheless not fully satisfied we sailed yet farther toward the north, following the course that might bring us to the river of Jordan, one of the fairest rivers of the north, and holding our wonted course, great fogs and tempests came upon us, which constrained us to leave the coast to bear toward the main sea, which was the cause that we lost the sight of our pinnaces a whole day and a night until the next day in the morning, what time the weather waxing fair and the sea calm, we discovered a river which we called Belle a Voir. After we had sailed three or four leagues, we began to espy our pinnaces which came straight toward us, and at their arrival they reported to the Captain, that while the foul weather and fogs endured, they harbored themselves in a mighty river which in bigness and beauty exceeded the former: wherewithal the Captain was exceeding joyful, for his chief desire was to find out an haven to harbor his ships and there refresh ourselves for a while. Thus making thitherward we arrived athwart the said river, (which because of the fairness and largeness thereof we named Port Royal) we struck our sails and cast anchor at ten fathom of water: for the depth is such, namely when the sea beginneth to flow, that the greatest ships of France, yea, the argosies of Venice may enter in there. Having cast anchor, the Captain with his soldiers went on shore, and he himself went first on land: where we found the place as pleasant as was possible, for it was all covered over with mighty high oaks and infinite store of cedars, and with lentiscus growing underneath them, smelling so sweetly, that the very fragrant odor only made the place to seem exceeding pleasant. As we passed through these woods we saw nothing but turkeycocks flying in the forests, partridges gray and red, little different from ours, but chiefly in bigness. We heard also within the woods the voices of stags, of bears, of lynx, of leopards, and divers other sorts of beasts unknown to us.

A little while after, John Ribault accompanied with a good number of soldiers embarked himself, desirous to sail farther up into the arm that runneth toward the west, and to search the commodities of the place. Having sailed twelve leagues at the least, we perceived a troup of Indians, which as soon as ever they espied the pinnaces, were so afraid that they fled into the woods leaving behind them a young lynx which they were aturning upon a spit: for which cause the place was called Cape Lucerne: proceeding forth on our way, we found another arm of the river, which ran toward the east, up which the Captain determined to sail and to leave the great current. A little while after they began to espy divers other Indians both men and women half hidden within the woods: who knowing not that we were such as desired their friendship, were dismayed at the first, but soon after were emboldened, for the Captain caused great store of merchandise to be showed them openly whereby they knew that we meant nothing but well unto them: and then they made a sign that we should come on land which we would not refuse. At our coming on shore divers of them came to salute our General according to their barbarous fashion. Some of them gave him skins of chamois, others little baskets made of palm leaves, some presented him with pearls, but no great number. Afterwards they went about to make an arbor to defend us in that place from the parching heat of the sun.

Notwithstanding we returned to our ships, where after we had been but one night, the Captain in the morning commanded to put into the pinnace a pillar of hard stone fashioned like a column, wherein the arms of the King of France were graven, to plant the same in the fairest place that he could find. This done, we embarked ourselves, and sailed three leagues towards the west: where we discovered a little river, up which we sailed so long, that in the end we found it returned into the great current, and in his return to make a little island separated from the firm land, where we went on shore: and by commandment of the Captain, because it was exceeding fair and pleasant, there we planted the pillar upon a hillock open round about to the view, and environed with a lake half a fathom deep of very good and sweet water. In which island we saw two stags of exceeding bigness, in respect of those which we had seen before, which we might easily have killed with our harquebuses, if the Captain had not forbidden us, moved with the singular fairness and bigness of them. But before our departure we named the little river which environed the isle, the river of Liborne.

A few days afterward John Ribault determined to return once again toward the Indians which inhabited that arm of the river which runneth toward the west, and to carry with him good store of soldiers. For his meaning was to take two Indians of this place to bring them into France, as the Queen had commanded him. With this deliberation again we took our former course so far north, that at the last we came to the self same place where at the first we found the Indians, from thence we took two Indians by the permission of the king, which thinking that they were more favored than the rest, thought themselves very happy to stay with us. But after they had stayed a while in our ships they began to be sorry, and resolved with themselves to steal away by night, and to get a little boat which we had, and by the help of the tide to sail home toward their dwellings, and by this means to save themselves. Which thing they failed not to do. The Captain cared not greatly for their departure, considering they had not been used otherwise than well: and that therefore they would not estrange themselves from the Frenchmen.

Captain Ribault therefore knowing the singular fairness of this river desired by all means to encourage some of his men to dwell there, well foreseeing that this thing might be of great importance for the King's service, and the relief of the Commonwealth of France. Therefore proceeding on with his intent, he commanded the anchors to be weighed and to set things in order to return unto the opening of the river, to the end that if the wind came fair he might pass out to accomplish the rest of his meaning. When therefore we were come to the mouth of the river, he made them cast anchor, whereupon we stayed without discovering anything all the rest of the day. The next day he commanded that all the men of his ship should come up upon the deck, saying that he had somewhat to say unto them. They all came up, and immediately the Captain began to speak unto them in this manner.

I think there is none of you that is ignorant of how great consequence this our enterprise is, and also how acceptable it is unto our young King. Therefore my friends (as one desiring your honor and benefit) I would not fail to advertise you all of the exceeding good hap which should fall to them, which, as men of valor and worthy courage, would make trial in this our first discovery of the benefits and commodities of this new land. I pray you therefore all to advise yourselves thereof, and to declare your minds freely unto me, protesting that I will so well imprint your names in the King's ears, and the other princes, that your renown shall hereafter shine unquenchable through our realm of France.

He had scarcely ended his oration, but the greatest part of our soldiers replied: that a greater pleasure could never betide them, perceiving well the acceptable service which by this means they should do unto their Prince: besides that this thing should be for the increase of their honors: therefore they besought the Captain, before he departed out of the place, to begin to build them a fort, which they hoped afterward to finish, and to leave them munition necessary for their defense. Whereupon John Ribault being as glad as might be to see his men so well willing, determined the next day to search the most fit and convenient place to be inhabited. Wherefore he embarked himself very early in the morning and commanded them to follow him that were desirous to inhabit there, to the intent that they might like the better of the place. Having sailed up the great river on the north side, he discovered a small river, which entered into the island, which he would not fail to search out. Which done, and finding the same deep enough to harbor therein galleys and galliots in good number, proceeding farther, he found a very open place, joining upon the brink thereof, where he went on land, and seeing the place fit to build a fortress in, and commodious for them that were willing to plant there, he resolved incontinent to cause the bigness of the fortification to be measured out. And considering that there stayed but six and twenty there, he caused the fort to be made in length but sixteen fathom, and thirteen in breadth, with flanks according to the proportion thereof. The measure being taken by me and Captain Salles, we sent unto the ships for men, and to bring shovels, pickaxes and other instruments necessary to make the fortification. We travailed so diligently, that in a short space the fort was made in some sort defensible. In which meantime John Ribault caused victuals and warlike munition to be brought for the defense of the place. After he had furnished them with all such things as they had need of, he determined to take his leave of them. But before his departure he used this speech unto Captain Albert, which he left in this place.

Captain Albert, I have to request you in the presence of all these men, that you would quit yourself so wisely in your charge, and govern so modestly your small company which I leave you, which with so good cheer remaineth under your obedience, that I never have occasion but to commend you, and to recount unto the King (as I am desirous) the faithful service which before us all you undertake to do him in his new France: and you companions, (quoth he to the soldiers) I beseech you also to esteem of Captain Albert as if he were myself that stayed here with you, yielding him that obedience which a true soldier oweth unto his General and Captain, living as brethren one with another, without all dissention: and in so doing God will assist you and bless your enterprises.

Having ended his exhortation, we took our leaves of each of them, and sailed toward our ships, calling the fort by the name of Charlesfort, and the river by the name Chenonceau. The next day we determined to depart from this place being as well contented as was possible that we had so happily ended our business.

Our men after our departure never rested, but night and day did fortify themselves, being in good hope that after their fort was finished, they would begin to discover farther up within the river. It happened one day, as certain of them were in cutting of roots in the groves, that they espied on the sudden an Indian that hunted the deer, which finding himself so near upon them, was much dismayed, but our men began to draw near unto him and to use him so courteously, that he became assured and followed them to Charlesfort, where every man sought to do him pleasure. Captain Albert was very joyful of his coming, which after he had given him a shirt and some other trifles, he asked him of his dwelling: the Indian answered him that it was farther up within the river, and that he was vassal of King Audusta: he also showed him with his hand the limits of his habitation After much other talk the Indian desired leave to depart, because it drew toward night, which Captain Albert granted him very willingly.

Certain days after the Captain determined to sail toward Audusta, where being arrived, by reason of the honest entertainment which he had given to the Indian, he was so courteously received, that the king talked with him of nothing else but of the desire which he had to become his friend: giving him besides to understand that he being his friend and ally, he should have the amity of four other kings, which in might and authority were able to do much for his sake: besides all this, in his necessity they might be able to succor him with victuals. One of these kings was called Mayon, another Hoya, the third Touppo, and the fourth Stalame. He told him moreover, that they would be very glad, when they should understand the news of his coming, and there-fore he prayed him to vouchsafe to visit them. The Captain willingly consented unto him, for the desire that he had to purchase friends in that place. Therefore they departed the next morning very early, and first arrived at the house of King Touppo, and afterward went into the other kings' houses, ex-cept the house of King Stalame. He received of each of them all the amiable courtesies that might be: they showed themselves to be as affectioned friends unto him as was possible, and offered unto him a thousand small presents. After that he had remained by the space of certain days with these strange kings, he determined to take his leave: and being come back to the house of Audusta, he commanded all his men to go aboard their pinnace: for he was minded to go towards the country of King Stalame, which dwelt toward the north the distance of fifteen great leagues from Charlesfort. Therefore as they sailed up the river they entered into a great current, which they followed so far till they came at last to the house of Stalame: which brought him into his lodging, where he sought to make them the best cheer he could devise. He presented immediately unto Captain Albert his bow and arrows, which is a sign and confirmation of alliance between them. He presented him with chamois skins. The Captain seeing the best part of the day was now past, took his leave of King Stalame to return to Charlesfort, where he arrived the day following. By this time the friendship was grown so great between our men and King Audusta, that in a manner all things were common between him and them: in such sort that this good Indian king did nothing of importance, but he called our men thereunto. For when the time drew near of the celebrating their feasts of Toya, which are ceremonies most strange to recite, he sent ambassadors to our men to request them on his behalf to be there present whereunto they agreed most willingly.

When the feast was finished our men returned unto Charlesfort; where having remained but a while their victual began to wax short, which forced them to have recourse unto their neighbors, and to pray them to succor them in their necessity: which gave them part of all the victuals which they had, and kept no more unto themselves than would serve to sow their fields. They gave them also counsel to go toward the countries of King Covexis a man of might and renown in this province, which maketh his abode toward the south abounding at all seasons and replenished with such quantity of mill, corn, and beans that by his only succor they might be able to live a very long time. But before they should come into his territories, they were to repair unto a king called Ovade the brother of Covexis, which in mill, beans, and corn was no less wealthy, and withal is very liberal, and which would be very joyful if he might but once see them. Our men perceiving the good relation which the Indians made them of those two kings resolved to go thither; for they felt already the necessity which oppressed them. Therefore they made request unto King Maccou, that it would please him to give them one of his subjects to guide them the right way thither: whereupon he condescended very willingly, knowing that without his favor they should have much ado to bring their enterprise to pass. Wherefore after they had given order for all things necessary for the voyage, they put themselves to sea, and sailed so far that in the end they came into the country of Ovade, which they found to be in the river Belle. Being there arrived they advertised the king by one of the guides which they brought with them, how that (having heard of his great liberality) they had put to sea to come to beseech him to succor them with victuals in their great want and necessity: and that in so doing, he should bind them all hereafter to remain his faithful friends and loyal defenders against all his enemies. This good Indian as soon ready to do them pleasure, as they were to demand it, commanded his subjects that they should fill our pinnace with mill and beans. Afterward he caused them to bring him six pieces of his tapestry made like little coverlets, and gave them to our men with so liberal a mind, as they easily perceived the desire which he had to become their friend. In recompense of all these gifts our men gave him two cutting hooks and certain other trifles, wherewith he held himself greatly satisfied. This being done, our men took their leave of the king, which for their farewell, said nothing else but that they should return if they wanted victuals, and that they might assure themselves of him, that they should never want anything that was in his power. Wherefore they embarked themselves, and sailed towards Charlesfort, which from this place might be some five and twenty leagues distant.

But as soon as our men thought themselves at their ease, and free from the dangers whereunto they had exposed themselves night and day in gathering together of victuals here and there: lo, even as they were asleep, the fire caught in their lodgings with such fury, being increased by the wind, that the room that was built for them before our men's departure, was consumed in an instant, without being able to save anything, saving a little of their victuals. Whereupon our men being far from all succor, found themselves in such extremity, that without the aid of almighty God, they had been quite and clean out of all hope. For the next day betimes in the morning the King Audusta and King Maccou came thither, accompanied with a very good company of Indians, which knowing the misfortune, were very sorry for it. And then they uttered unto their subjects the speedy diligence which they were to use in building another house, showing unto them that the Frenchmen were their loving friends, and in less than twelve hours, they had begun and finished a house which was very near as great as the former. Which being ended, they returned home fully contented with a few cutting hooks, and hatchets, which they received of our men.

Behold therefore how our men behaved themselves very well hitherto, although they had endured many great mishaps. But misfortune or rather the just judgment of God would have it, that those which could not be overcome by fire nor water, should be undone by their own selves. This is the common fashion of men, which cannot continue in one state, and had rather to overthrow themselves, than not to attempt some new thing daily. We have infinite example in the ancient histories, especially of the Romans, unto which number this little handful of men, being far from their country and absent from their countrymen, have also added this present example. They entered therefore into partialities and dissensions, which began about a soldier named Guernache, which was a drummer of the French bands: which, as it was told me, was very cruelly hanged by his own captain, and for a small fault: which captain also using to threaten the rest of his soldiers which stayed behind under his obedience, and peradventure (as it is to be presumed) were not so obedient to him as they should have been, was the cause that they fell into a mutiny, because that many times he put his threatenings in execution: whereupon they so chased him, that at the last they put him to death. And the principal occasion that moved them thereunto was, because he degraded another soldier named La Chere (which he had banished) and because he had not performed his promise: for he had promised to send him victuals, from eight days to eight days, which thing he did not, but said on the contrary, that he would be glad to hear of his death. He said moreover, that he would chastise others also, and used so evil sounding speeches, that honesty forbiddeth me to repeat them. The soldiers seeing his madness to increase from day to day, and fearing to fall into the dangers of the other, resolved to kill him. Having executed their purpose, they went to seek the soldier that was banished, which was in a small island distant from Charlesfort about three leagues, where they found him almost half dead for hunger. When they were come home again, they assembled themselves together to choose one to be governor over them whose name was Nicolas Barre a man worthy of commendation, and one which knew so well to quit himself of his charge, that all rancor and dissension ceased among them, and they lived peaceably one with another.

During this time, they began to build a small pinnace, with hope to return into France, if no succor came unto them, as they expected from day to day. And though there were no men among them that had any skill, notwithstanding necessity, which is the mistress of all sciences, taught them the way to build it. And after it was finished, they thought of nothing else saving how to furnish it with all things necessary to undertake the voyage. But they wanted those things that of all others were most needful, as cordage and sails, without which the enterprise could not come to effect. Having no means to recover these things, they were in worse case than at the first, and almost ready to fall into despair. But that good God, which never forsaketh the afflicted, did succor them in their necessity.

As they were in these perplexities King Audusta and Maccou came to them, accompanied with two hundred Indians at the least, whom our Frenchmen went forth to meet withal, and showed the king in what need of cordage they stood: who promised them to return within two days, and to bring so much as should suffice to furnish the pinnace with tackling. Our men being pleased with these good news and promises, bestowed upon them certain cutting hooks and shirts. After their departure our men sought all means to recover rosin in the woods, wherein they cut pine trees round about, out of which they drew sufficient reasonable quantity to bray the vessel. Also they gathered a kind of moss which groweth on the trees of this country, to serve to calk the same withal. There now wanted nothing but sails, which they did make of their own shirts and of their sheets. Within few days after the Indian king returned to Charlesfort with so good store of cordage, that there was found sufficient for tackling of the small pinnace. Our men as glad as might be, used great liberality towards them, and at their leaving of the country, left them all the merchandise that remained, leaving them thereby so fully satisfied, that they departed from them with all the contentation of the world. They went forward therefore to finish the brigantine, and used so speedy diligence, that within a short time afterward they made it ready furnished with all things. In the mean season the wind became so fit for their purpose that it seemed to invite them to put to the sea: which they did without delay, after they had set all their things in order. But before they departed they embarked their artillery, their forge and other munitions of war which Captain Ribault had left them, and then as much mill as they could gather together. But being drunken with the too excessive joy, which they had conceived for

They were surprised with calms which did so much hinder them, that in three weeks they sailed not above five and twenty leagues.

their returning into France, or rather deprived of all foresight and consideration, without regarding the inconstancy of the winds, which change in a moment, they put themselves to sea, and with so slender victuals, that the end of
their enterprise became unlucky and unfortunate.

For after they had sailed the third part of their way, they were surprised
with calms which did so much hinder them, that in three weeks they sailed not
above five and twenty leagues. During this time their victuals consumed and
became so short, that every man was constrained to eat not past twelve grains
of mill by the day, which may be in value as much as twelve peas. Yea, and
this felicity lasted not long: for their victuals failed them altogether at once:
and they had nothing for their more assured refuge but their shoes and leather
jerkins which they did eat. Touching their beverage, some of them drank
the sea water: and they remained in such desperate necessity a very long space,
during the which part of them died for hunger. Beside this extreme famine,
which did so grievously oppress them, they fell every minute of an hour out
of all hope ever to see France again, insomuch that they were constrained to
cast the water continually out, that on all sides entered into their bark. And
every day they fared worse and worse: for after they had eaten up their shoes
and their leather jerkins, there arose so boisterous a wind and so contrary to
their course, that in the turning of a hand, the waves filled their vessel half
full of water and bruised it upon the one side. Being now more out of hope
than ever to escape out of this extreme peril, they cared not for casting out of
the water which now was almost ready to drown them. And as men resolved
to die, everyone fell down backward, and gave themselves over altogether
unto the will of the waves. When as one of them a little having taken heart
unto him declared unto them how little way they had to sail, assuring them,
that if the wind held, they should see land within three days. This man did
so encourage them, that after they had thrown the water out of the pinnace
they remained three days without eating or drinking, except it were of the
sea water. When the time of his promise was expired, they were more troubled than they were before, seeing they could not descry any land. Wherefore in this extreme despair certain among them made this motion that it was
better that one man should die, than that so many men should perish: they
agreed therefore that one should die to sustain the others. Which thing was
executed in the person of La Chere, of whom we have spoken heretofore,

whose flesh was divided equally among his fellows: a thing so pitiful to recite, that my pen is loth to write it.

After so long time and tedious travels, God of his goodness using his accustomed favor, changed their sorrow into joy, and showed unto them the sight of land. Whereof they were so exceeding glad, that the pleasure caused them to remain a long time as men without sense: whereby they let the pinnace float this and that way without holding any right way or course. But a small English bark boarded the vessel, in the which there was a Frenchman which had been in the first voyage into Florida, who easily knew them, and spake unto them, and afterward gave them meat and drink. Incontinently they recovered their natural courages, and declared unto him at large all their navigation. The Englishmen consulted a long while what were best to be done, and in fine they resolved to put on land those that were most feeble, and to carry the rest unto the Queen of England, which purposed at that time to send into Florida. This you see in brief that which happened to them which Captain John Ribault had left in Florida.

THE RAFT OF ODYSSEUS

~~~~~~

Homer

So soon as early Dawn shone forth, the rosy-fingered, anon Odysseus put on him a mantle and doublet, and the nymph clad her in a great shining robe, light of woof and gracious, and about her waist she cast a fair golden girdle, and a veil withal upon her head. Then she considered of the sending of Odysseus, the great-hearted. She gave him a great ax, fitted to his grasp, an ax of bronze double-edged, and with a goodly handle of olive wood fastened well. Next she gave him a polished adze, and she led the way to the border of the isle where tall trees grew, alder and poplar, and pine that reacheth unto heaven, seasoned long since and sere, that might lightly float for him. Now after she had shown him where the tall trees grew, Calypso, the fair goddess, departed homeward. And he set to cutting timber, and his work went busily. Twenty trees in all he felled, and then trimmed them with the ax of bronze, and deftly smoothed them, and over them made straight the line. Meanwhile Calypso, the fair goddess, brought him augers, so he bored each piece and jointed them together, and then made all fast with trenails and dowels. Wide as is the floor of a broad ship of burden, which some man well skilled in carpentry may trace him out, of such beam did Odysseus fashion his broad raft. And thereat he wrought, and set up the deckings, fitting them to the close-set uprights, and finished them off with long gunwales, and therein he set a mast, and a yard-arm fitted thereto, and moreover he made him a rudder to guide the craft. And he fenced it with wattled osier withies from stem to stern, to be a bulwark against the wave, and piled up wood to back them.

from "The Odyssey" by Homer. Translated by Butcher and Lang. By courtesy of The Macmillan Company.

Meanwhile Calypso, the fair goddess, brought him web of cloth to make him sails; and these too he fashioned very skilfully. And he made fast therein braces and halyards and sheets, and at last he pushed the raft with levers down to the fair salt sea.

It was the fourth day when he had accomplished all. And, lo, on the fifth, the fair Calypso sent him on his way from the island, when she had bathed him and clad him in fragrant attire. Moreover, the goddess placed on board the ship two skins, one of dark wine, and another, a great one, of water, and corn too in a wallet, and she set therein a store of dainties to his heart's desire, and sent forth a warm and gentle wind to blow. And goodly Odysseus rejoiced as he set his sails to the breeze. So he sate and cunningly guided the craft with the helm, nor did sleep fall upon his eyelids, as he viewed the Pleiads and Boötes, that setteth late, and the Bear, which they likewise call the Wain, which turneth ever in one place, and keepeth watch upon Orion, and alone hath no part in the baths of Ocean. This star, Calypso, the fair goddess, bade him to keep ever on the left as he traversed the deep. Ten days and seven he sailed traversing the deep, and on the eighteenth day appeared the shadowy hills of the land of the Phaeacians, at the point where it lay nearest to him; and it showed like a shield in the misty deep.

Now the lord, the shaker of the earth, on his way from the Ethiopians espied him afar off from the mountains of the Solymi: even thence he saw Odysseus as he sailed over the deep; and he was mightily angered in spirit, and shaking his head he communed with his own heart. "Lo now, it must be that the gods at the last have changed their purpose concerning Odysseus, while I was away among the Ethiopians. And now he is nigh to the Phaeacian land, where it is ordained that he escape the great issues of the woe which hath come upon him. But, methinks, that even yet I will drive him far enough in the path of suffering."

With that he gathered the clouds and troubled the waters of the deep, grasping his trident in his hands; and he roused all storms of all manner of winds, and shrouded in clouds the land and sea: and down sped night from heaven. The East Wind and the South Wind clashed, and the stormy West, and the North, that is born in the bright air, rolling onward a great wave. Then were the knees of Odysseus loosened and his heart melted, and heavily he spake to his own great spirit:

"Oh, wretched man that I am! what is to befal me at the last? I fear that indeed the goddess spake all things truly, who said that I should fill up the measure of sorrow on the deep, or ever I came to mine own country; and lo, all these things have an end. In such wise doth Zeus crown the wide heaven with clouds, and hath troubled the deep, and the blasts rush on of all the winds; yea, now is utter doom assured me. Thrice blessed those Danaans, yea, four times blessed, who perished on a time in wide Troy-land, doing a pleasure to the sons of Atreus! Would to God that I too had died, and met my fate on that day when the press of Trojans cast their bronze-shod spears upon me, fighting for the body of the son of Peleus! So should I have gotten my dues of burial, and the Achaeans would have spread my fame; but now it is my fate to be overtaken by a pitiful death."

Even as he spake, the great wave smote down upon him, driving on in terrible wise, that the raft reeled again. And far therefrom he fell, and lost the helm from his hand; and the fierce blast of the jostling winds came and brake his mast in the midst, and sail and yard-arm fell afar into the deep. Long time the water kept him under, nor could he speedily rise from beneath the rush of the mighty wave: for the garments hung heavy which fair Calypso gave him. But late and at length he came up, and spat forth from his mouth the bitter salt water, which ran down in streams from his head. Yet even so forgat he not his raft, for all his wretched plight, but made a spring after it in the waves, and clutched it to him, and sat in the midst thereof, avoiding the issues of death; and the great wave swept it hither and thither along the stream. And as the North Wind in the harvest tide sweeps the thistle-down along the plain, and close the tufts cling each to other, even so the winds bare the raft hither and thither along the main. Now the South would toss it to the North to carry, and now again the East would yield it to the West to chase.

But the daughter of Cadmus marked him, Ino of the fair ankles, Leucothea, who in time past was a maiden of mortal speech, but now in the depths of the salt sea she had gotten her share of worship from the gods. She took pity on Odysseus in his wandering and travail, and she rose, like a sea-gull on the wing, from the depth of the mere, and sat upon the well-bound raft and spake saying:

"Hapless one, wherefore was Poseidon, shaker of the earth, so wondrous wroth with thee, seeing that he soweth for thee the seeds of many evils? Yet shall he not make a full end of thee, for all his desire. But do even as I tell thee, and methinks thou art not witless. Cast off these garments, and leave the raft to drift before the winds, but do thou swim with thine hands and strive to win a footing on the coast of the Phaeacians, where it is decreed that thou escape. Here, take this veil imperishable and wind it about thy breast; so is there no fear that thou suffer aught or perish. But when thou hast laid hold of the mainland with thy hands, loose it from off thee and cast it into the wine-dark deep far from the land, and thyself turn away."

With that the goddess gave the veil, and for her part dived back into the heaving deep, like a sea-gull: and the dark wave closed over her. But the steadfast goodly Odysseus pondered, and heavily he spake to his own brave spirit:

"Ah, woe is me! Can it be that some one of the immortals is weaving a new snare for me, that she bids me quit my raft? Nay verily, I will not yet obey, for I had sight of the shore yet a long way off, where she told me that I might escape. I am resolved what I will do;—and methinks on this wise it is best. So long as the timbers abide in the dowels, so long will I endure steadfast in affliction, but so soon as the wave hath shattered my raft asunder, I will swim, for meanwhile no better counsel may be."

While yet he pondered these things in his heart and soul, Poseidon, shaker of the earth, stirred against him a great wave, terrible and grievous, and vaulted from the crest, and therewith smote him. And as when a great tempestuous wind tosseth a heap of parched husks, and scatters them this way and that, even so did the wave scatter the long beams of the raft. But Odysseus bestrode a single beam, as one rideth on a courser, and stript him of the garments which fair Calypso gave him. And presently he wound the veil beneath his breast, and fell prone into the sea, outstretching his hands as one eager to swim. And the lord, the shaker of the earth, saw him and shook his head, and communed with his own soul. "Even so, after all thy sufferings, go wandering over the deep, till thou shalt come among a people, the fosterlings of Zeus. Yet for all that I deem not that thou shalt think thyself too lightly afflicted." Therewith he lashed his steeds of the flowing manes, and came to Aegae, where is his lordly home.

But Athene, daughter of Zeus, turned to new thoughts. Behold, she bound up the courses of the other winds, and charged them all to cease and be still; but she roused the swift North and brake the waves before him, that so Odysseus, of the seed of Zeus, might mingle with the Phaeacians, lovers of the oar, avoiding death and the fates.

So for two nights and two days he was wandering in the swell of the sea, and much his heart boded of death. But when at last the fair-tressed Dawn brought the full light of the third day, thereafter the breeze fell, and lo, there was a breathless calm, and with a quick glance ahead, (he being upborn on a great wave), he saw the land very near.   And even as when most welcome to his children is the sight of a father's life, who lies in sickness and strong pains long wasting away, some angry god assailing him; and to their delight the gods have loosed him from his trouble; so welcome to Odysseus showed land and wood; and he swam onward being eager to set foot on the strand.   But when he was within earshot of the shore, and heard now the thunder of the sea against the reefs—for the great wave crashed against the dry land belching in terrible wise, and all was covered with foam of the sea,—for there were no harbors for ships nor shelters, but jutting headlands and reefs and cliffs; then at last the knees of Odysseus were loosened and his heart melted, and in heaviness he spake to his own brave spirit:

"Ah me! now that beyond all hope Zeus hath given me sight of land, and withal I have cloven my way through this gulf of the sea, here there is no place to land on from out of the gray water.   For without are sharp crags, and round them the wave roars surging, and sheer the smooth rock rises, and the sea is deep thereby, so that in no wise may I find firm foothold and escape my bane, for as I fain would go ashore, the great wave may haply snatch and dash me on the jagged rock—and a wretched endeavor that would be.   But if I swim yet further along the coast to find, if I may, spits that take the waves aslant and havens of the sea, I fear lest the storm-winds catch me again and bear me over the teeming deep, making heavy moan; or else some god may even send forth against me a monster from out of the shore water; and many such pastureth the renowned Amphitrite.   For I know how wroth against me hath been the great Shaker of the Earth.

Whilst yet he pondered these things in his heart and mind, a great wave bore him to the rugged shore. There would he have been stript of his skin and all his bones been broken, but that the goddess, gray-eyed Athene, put a thought into his heart.   He rushed in, and with both his hands clutched the rock, whereto he clung till the great wave went by.   So he escaped that peril, but again with backward wash it leapt on him and smote him and cast him forth into the deep.   And as when the cuttlefish is dragged forth from his chamber, the many pebbles clinging to his suckers, even so was the skin stript from his strong hand against the rocks, and the great wave closed over him.   There of a truth would luckless Odysseus have perished beyond that which was ordained, had not gray-eyed Athene given him sure counsel. He rose from the line of the breakers that belch upon the shore, and swam outside, ever looking landwards, to find, if he might, spits that take the waves aslant, and havens of the sea. But when he came in his swimming over against the mouth of a fair-flowing river, whereby the place seemed best in his eyes, smooth of rocks, and withal there was a covert from the wind, Odysseus felt the river running, and prayed to him in his heart:

"Hear me, O king, whosoever thou art; unto thee am I come, as to one to whom prayer is made, while I flee the rebukes of Poseidon from the deep. Yea, reverend even to the deathless gods is that man who comes as a wanderer, even as I now have come to thy stream and to thy knees after much travail. Nay pity me, O king; for I avow myself thy suppliant."

So spake he, and the god straightway stayed his stream and withheld his waves, and made the water smooth before him, and brought him safely to the mouths of the river. And his knees bowed and his stout hands fell, for his heart was broken by the brine. And his flesh was all swollen and a great stream of sea water gushed up through his mouth and nostrils. So he lay without breath or speech, swooning, such terrible weariness came upon him. But when now his breath returned and his spirit came to him again, he loosed from off him the veil of the goddess, and let it fall into the salt flowing river. And the great wave bare it back down the stream, and lightly Ino caught it in her hands. Then Odysseus turned from the river, and fell back in the reeds, and kissed earth, the grain-giver, and heavily he spake unto his own brave spirit:

"Ah, woe is me! what is to betide me? what shall happen unto me at the last? If I watch in the river bed all through the careful night, I fear that the bitter frost and fresh dew may overcome me, as I breathe forth my life for faintness, for the river breeze blows cold betimes in the morning. But if I climb the hill-side up to the shady wood, and there take rest in the thickets, though perchance the cold and weariness leave hold of me, and sweet sleep may come over me, I fear lest of wild beasts I become the spoil and prey."

So as he thought thereon this seemed to him the better way. He went up to the wood, and found it nigh the water in a place of wide prospect. So he crept beneath twin bushes that grew from one stem, both olive trees, one of them wild olive. Through these the force of the wet winds blew never, neither did the bright sun light on it with his rays, nor could the· rain pierce through, so close were they twined either to other; and thereunder crept Odysseus, and anon he heaped together with his hands a broad couch; for of fallen leaves there was great plenty, enough to cover two or three men in winter time, however hard the weather. And the steadfast goodly Odysseus beheld it and rejoiced, and he laid him in the midst thereof and flung over him the fallen leaves. And as when a man hath hidden away a brand in the black embers at an upland farm, one that hath no neighbors nigh, and so saveth the seed of fire, that he may not have to seek a light otherwhere, even so did Odysseus cover him with the leaves. And Athene shed sleep upon his eyes, that so it might soon release him from his weary travail, overshadowing his eyelids.

THE DEVIL-FISH

Victor Hugo

I T IS difficult for those who have not seen it to believe in the existence of the devil-fish.

Compared to this creature, the ancient hydras are insignificant.

At times we are tempted to imagine that the vague forms which float in our dreams may encounter in the realm of the Possible attractive forces, having power to fix their lineaments, and shape living beings, out of these creatures of our slumbers. The Unknown has power over these strange visions, and out of them composes monsters. Orpheus, Homer, and Hesiod imagined only the Chimera: Providence has created this terrible creature of the sea.

Creation abounds in monstrous forms of life. The wherefore of this perplexes and affrights the religious thinker.

If terror were the object of its creation, nothing could be imagined more perfect than the devil-fish.

The whale has enormous bulk, the devil-fish is comparatively small; the jararaca makes a hissing noise, the devil-fish is mute; the rhinoceros has a horn, the devil-fish has none; the scorpion has a dart, the devil-fish has no dart; the shark has sharp fins, the devil-fish has no fins; the vespertilio-bat has wings with claws, the devil-fish has no wings; the porcupine has his spines, the devil-fish has no spines; the sword-fish has his sword, the devil-fish has none; the torpedo has its electric spark, the devil-fish has none; the toad has its poison, the devil-fish has none; the viper has its venom, the devil-fish has no venom; the lion has its talons, the devil-fish has no talons; the griffon has its beak, the devil-fish has no beak; the crocodile has its jaws, the devil-fish has no teeth.

from "Toilers of the Sea" by Victor Hugo

The devil-fish has no muscular organization, no menacing cry, no breast-plate, no horn, no dart, no claw, no tail with which to hold or bruise; no cut-ting fins, or wings with nails, no prickles, no sword, no electric discharge, no poison, no talons, no beak, no teeth. Yet he is of all creatures the most formi-dably armed.

What, then, is the devil-fish? It is the sea vampire.

The swimmer who, attracted by the beauty of the spot, ventures among breakers in the open sea, where the still waters hide the splendors of the deep, or in the hollows of unfrequented rocks, in unknown caverns abounding in sea plants, testacea, and crustacea, under the deep portals of the ocean, runs the risk of meeting it. If that fate should be yours, be not curious, but fly. The intruder enters there dazzled; but quits the spot in terror.

This frightful apparition, which is always possible among the rocks in the open sea, is a grayish form which undulates in the water. It is of the thickness of a man's arm, and in length nearly five feet. Its outline is ragged. Its form resembles an umbrella closed, and without handle. This irregular mass ad-vances slowly towards you. Suddenly it opens, and eight radii issue abruptly from around a face with two eyes. These radii are alive: their undulation is like lambent flames; they resemble, when opened, the spokes of a wheel, of four or five feet in diameter. A terrible expansion! It springs upon its prey.

The devil-fish harpoons its victim.

It winds around the sufferer, covering and entangling him in its long folds. Underneath it is yellow; above, a dull, earthy hue: nothing could render that inexplicable shade dust colored. Its form is spider-like, but its tints are like those of the chameleon. When irritated it becomes violet. Its most horrible characteristic is its softness.

Its folds strangle, its contact paralyzes.

It has an aspect like gangrened or scabrous flesh. It is a monstrous embodi-ment of disease.

It adheres closely to its prey, and cannot be torn away; a fact which is due to its power of exhausting air. The eight antennæ, large at their roots, diminish gradually, and end in needle-like points. Underneath each of these feelers range two rows of pustules, decreasing in size, the largest ones near the head, the smaller at the extremities. Each row contains twenty-five of these. There are, therefore, fifty pustules to each feeler, and the creature possesses in the whole four hundred. These pustules are capable of acting like cupping-glasses.

They are cartilaginous substances, cylindrical, horny, and livid. Upon the large species they diminish gradually from the diameter of a five-franc piece to the size of a split pea. These small tubes can be thrust out and withdrawn by the animal at will. They are capable of piercing to a depth of more than an inch.

This sucking apparatus has all the regularity and delicacy of a key-board. It stands forth at one moment and disappears the next. The most perfect sensitiveness cannot equal the contractibility of these suckers; always proportioned to the internal movement of the animal, and its exterior circumstances. The monster is endowed with the qualities of the sensitive plant.

This animal is the same as those which mariners call Poulps; which science designates Cephalopteræ, and which ancient legends call Krakens. It is the English sailors who call them "Devil-fish," and sometimes Bloodsuckers. In the Channel Islands they are called *pieuvres*.

They are rare at Guernsey, very small at Jersey; but near the island of Sark are numerous as well as very large.

An engraving in Sonnini's edition of Buffon represents a Cephaloptera crushing a frigate. Denis Montfort, in fact, considers the Poulp, or Octopod, of high latitudes, strong enough to destroy a ship. Bory Saint Vincent doubts this; but he shows that in our regions they will attack men. Near Brecq-Hou, in Sark, they show a cave where a devil-fish a few years since seized and drowned a lobster-fisher. Peron and Lamarck are in error in their belief that the "poulp" having no fins cannot swim. He who writes these lines has seen with his own eyes, at Sark, in the cavern called the Boutiques, a pieuvre swimming and pursuing a bather. When captured and killed, this specimen was found to be four English feet broad, and it was possible to count its four hundred suckers. The monster thrust them out convulsively in the agony of death.

According to Denis Montfort, one of those observers whose marvelous intuition sinks or raises them to the level of magicians, the poulp is almost endowed with the passions of man: it has its hatreds. In fact, in the Absolute to be hideous is to hate.

Hideousness struggles under the natural law of elimination, which necessarily renders it hostile.

When swimming, the devil-fish rests, so to speak, in its sheath. It swims with all its parts drawn close. It may be likened to a sleeve sewn up with a closed fist within. The protuberance, which is the head, pushes the water aside and advances with a vague undulatory movement. Its two eyes, though large, are indistinct, being of the color of the water.

When in ambush, or seeking its prey, it retires into itself, grows smaller and condenses itself. It is then scarcely distinguishable in the submarine twilight.

At such times, it looks like a mere ripple in the water. It resembles anything except a living creature.

The devil-fish is crafty. When its victim is unsuspicious, it opens suddenly.

A glutinous mass, endowed with a malignant will, what can be more horrible?

It is in the most beautiful azure depths of the limpid water that this hideous, voracious polyp delights. It always conceals itself, a fact which increases its terrible associations. When they are seen, it is almost invariably after they have been captured.

At night, however, and particularly in the hot season, it becomes phosphorescent. These horrible creatures have their passions; their submarine nuptials. Then it adorns itself, burns and illumines; and from the height of some rock, it may be seen in the deep obscurity of the waves below, expanding with a pale irradiation—a spectral sun.

The devil-fish not only swims, it walks. It is partly fish, partly reptile. It crawls upon the bed of the sea. At these times, it makes use of its eight feelers, and creeps along in the fashion of a species of swift-moving caterpillar.

It has no blood, no bones, no flesh. It is soft and flabby; a skin with nothing inside. Its eight tentacles may be turned inside out like the fingers of a glove.

It has a single orifice in the center of its radii, which appears at first to be neither the vent nor the mouth. It is, in fact, both one and the other. The orifice performs a double function. The entire creature is cold.

The jelly-fish of the Mediterranean is repulsive. Contact with that animated gelatinous substance which envelopes the bather, in which the hands sink, and the nails scratch ineffectively; which can be torn without killing it, and which can be plucked off without entirely removing it—that fluid and yet tenacious creature which slips through the fingers, is disgusting; but no horror can equal the sudden apparition of the devil-fish, that Medusa with its eight serpents.

No grasp is like the sudden strain of the cephaloptera.

It is with the sucking apparatus that it attacks. The victim is oppressed by a vacuum drawing at numberless points: it is not a clawing or a biting, but an indescribable scarification. A tearing of the flesh is terrible, but less terrible than a sucking of the blood. Claws are harmless compared with the horrible action of these natural air-cups. The talons of the wild beast enter into your flesh; but with the cephaloptera it is you who enter into the creature. The muscles swell, the fibers of the body are contorted, the skin cracks under the loathsome oppression, the blood spurts out and mingles horribly with the lymph of the monster, which clings to its victim by innumerable hideous mouths. The hydra incorporates itself with the man; the man becomes one with the hydra. The specter lies upon you: the tiger can only devour you; the devil-fish, horrible, sucks your life-blood away. He draws you to him, and into himself; while bound down, glued to the ground, powerless, you feel yourself gradually emptied into this horrible pouch, which is the monster itself.

These strange animals, Science, in accordance with its habit of excessive caution even in the face of facts, at first rejects as fabulous; then she decides to observe them; then she dissects, classifies, catalogues, and labels; then procures specimens, and exhibits them in glass cases in museums. They enter then into her nomenclature; are designated mollusks, invertebrata, radiata: she determines their position in the animal world a little above the calamaries, a little below the cuttle-fish; she finds for these hydras of the sea an analogous creature in fresh water called the argyronecte: she divides them into great, medium, and small kinds; she admits more readily the existence of the small than of the large species, which is, however, the tendency of science in all countries, for she is by nature more microscopic than telescopic. She regards them from the point of view of their construction, and calls them Cephaloptera; counts their antennæ, and calls them Octopedes. This done, she leaves them. Where science drops them, philosophy takes them up.

Philosophy in her turn studies these creatures. She goes both less far and further. She does not dissect, but meditate. Where the scalpel has labored, she plunges the hypothesis. She seeks the final cause. Eternal perplexity of the thinker. These creatures disturb his ideas of the Creator. They are hideous surprises. They are the death's-head at the feast of contemplation. The philosopher determines their characteristics in dread. They are the concrete forms of evil. What attitude can he take towards this treason of creation against herself? To whom can he look for the solution of these riddles? The Possible is a terrible matrix. Monsters are mysteries in their concrete form.

Portions of shade issue from the mass, and something within detaches itself, rolls, floats, condenses, borrows elements from the ambient darkness, becomes subject to unknown polarisations, assumes a kind of life, furnishes itself with some unimagined form from the obscurity, and with some terrible spirit from the miasma, and wanders ghostlike among living things. It is as if night itself assumed the forms of animals. But for what good? with what object? Thus we come again to the eternal questioning.

These animals are indeed phantoms as much as monsters. They are proved and yet improbable. Their fate is to exist in spite of *à priori* reasonings. They are the amphibia of the shore which separates life from death. Their unreality makes their existence puzzling. They touch the frontier of man's domain and people the region of chimeras. We deny the possibility of the vampire, and the cephaloptera appears. Their swarming is a certainty which disconcerts our confidence. Optimism, which is nevertheless in the right, becomes silenced in their presence. They form the visible extremity of the dark circles. They mark the transition of our reality into another. They seem to belong to that commencement of terrible life which the dreamer sees confusedly through the loophole of the night.

That multiplication of monsters, first in the Invisible, then in the Possible, has been suspected, perhaps perceived by magi and philosophers in their austere ecstasies and profound contemplations. Hence the conjecture of a material hell. The demon is simply the invisible tiger. The wild beast which devours souls has been presented to the eyes of human beings by St. John, and by Dante in his vision of Hell.

If, in truth, the invisible circles of creation continue indefinitely, if after one there is yet another, and so forth in illimitable progression; if that chain, which for our part we are resolved to doubt, really exist, the cephaloptera at one extremity proves Satan at the other. It is certain that the wrongdoer at one end proves the existence of wrong at the other.

Every malignant creature, like every perverted intelligence, is a sphinx. A terrible sphinx propounding a terrible riddle; the riddle of the existence of Evil.

It is this perfection of evil which has sometimes sufficed to incline powerful intellects to a faith in the duality of the Deity, towards that terrible bifrons of the Manichæans.

A piece of silk stolen during the last war from the palace of the Emperor of

China represents a shark eating a crocodile, who is eating a serpent, who is devouring an eagle, who is preying on a swallow, who in his turn is eating a caterpillar.

All nature which is under our observation is thus alternately devouring and devoured. The prey prey on each other.

Learned men, however, who are also philosophers, and therefore optimists in their view of creation, find, or believe they find, an explanation. Among others, Bonnet of Geneva, that mysterious exact thinker, who was opposed to Buffon, as in later times Geoffrey St. Hilaire has been to Cuvier, was struck with the idea of the final object. His notions may be summed up thus: universal death necessitates universal sepulture; the devourers are the sextons of the system of nature. All created things enter into and form the elements of other. To decay is to nourish. Such is the terrible law from which not even man himself escapes.

In our world of twilight this fatal order of things produces monsters. You ask for what purpose. We find the solution here.

But *is* this the solution? Is this the answer to our questionings? And if so, why not some different order of things? Thus the question returns.

Let us live: be it so.

But let us endeavor that death shall be progress. Let us aspire to an existence in which these mysteries shall be made clear. Let us follow that conscience which leads us thither.

For let us never forget that the highest is only attained through the high.

Such was the creature in whose power Gilliatt had fallen for some minutes.

The monster was the inhabitant of the grotto; the terrible genii of the place. A kind of somber demon of the water.

All the splendors of the cavern existed for it alone.

On the day of the previous month when Gilliatt had first penetrated into the grotto, the dark outline, vaguely perceived by him in the ripples of the secret waters, was this monster. It was here in its home.

When entering for the second time into the cavern in pursuit of the crab, he had observed the crevice in which he supposed that the crab had taken refuge, the pieuvre was there lying in wait for prey.

Is it possible to imagine that secret ambush?

No bird would brood, no egg would burst to life, no flower would dare to open, no breast to give milk, no heart to love, no spirit to soar, under the influence of that apparition of evil watching with sinister patience in the dusk.

Gilliatt had thrust his arm deep into the opening; the monster had snapped at it. It held him fast, as the spider holds the fly.

He was in the water up to his belt; his naked feet clutching the slippery roundness of the huge stones at the bottom; his right arm bound and rendered powerless by the flat coils of the long tentacles of the creature, and his body almost hidden under the folds and cross folds of this horrible bandage.

Of the eight arms of the devilfish three adhered to the rock, while five encircled Gilliatt. In this way, clinging to the granite on the one hand, and with the other to its human prey, it enchained him to the rock. Two hundred and fifty suckers were upon him, tormenting him with agony and loathing. He was grasped by gigantic hands, the fingers of which were each nearly a yard long, and furnished inside with living blisters eating into the flesh.

As we have said, it is impossible to tear oneself from the folds of the devil-fish. The attempt ends only in a firmer grasp. The monster clings with more determined force. Its effort increases with that of its victim; every struggle produces a tightening of its ligatures.

Gilliatt had but one resource, his knife.

His left hand only was free; but the reader knows with what power he could use it. It might have been said that he had two right hands.

His open knife was in his hand.

The antenna of the devilfish cannot be cut; it is a leathery substance impossible to divide with the knife, it slips under the edge; its position in attack also is such that to cut it would be to wound the victim's own flesh.

The creature is formidable, but there is a way of resisting it. The fishermen of Sark know this, as does anyone who has seen them execute certain movements in the sea. The porpoises know it also; they have a way of biting the cuttlefish which decapitates it. Hence the frequent sight on the sea of pen-fish, poulps, and cuttlefish without heads.

The cephaloptera, in fact, is only vulnerable through the head.

Gilliatt was not ignorant of this fact.

He had never seen a devilfish of this size. His first encounter was with one of the larger species. Another would have been powerless with terror.

With the devilfish, as with a furious bull, there is a certain moment in the

He struck it with the knife clenched in his left hand.

conflict which must be seized. It is the instant when the bull lowers the neck; it is the instant when the devilfish advances its head. The movement is rapid. He who loses that moment is destroyed.

The things we have described occupied only a few moments. Gilliatt, however, felt the increasing power of its innumerable suckers.

The monster is cunning; it tries first to stupefy its prey. It seizes and then pauses awhile.

Gilliatt grasped his knife; the sucking increased.

He looked at the monster, which seemed to look at him.

Suddenly it loosened from the rock its sixth antenna, and darting it at him, seized him by the left arm.

At the same moment it advanced its head with a violent movement. In one second more its mouth would have fastened on his breast. Bleeding in the sides, and with his two arms entangled, he would have been a dead man.

But Gilliatt was watchful. He avoided the antenna, and at the moment when the monster darted forward to fasten on his breast, he struck it with the knife clenched in his left hand. There were two convulsions in opposite directions; that of the devilfish and that of its prey. The movement was rapid as a double flash of lightnings.

He had plunged the blade of his knife into the flat slimy substance, and by a rapid movement, like the flourish of a whip in the air, describing a circle round the two eyes, he wrenched the head off as a man would draw a tooth.

The struggle was ended. The folds relaxed. The monster dropped away, like the slow detaching of bands. The four hundred suckers, deprived of their sustaining power, dropped at once from the man and the rock. The mass sank to the bottom of the water.

Breathless with the struggle, Gilliatt could perceive upon the stones at his feet two shapeless, slimy heaps, the head on one side, the remainder of the monster on the other.

Fearing, nevertheless, some convulsive return of his agony, he recoiled to avoid the reach of the dreaded tentacles.

But the monster was quite dead.

Gilliatt closed his knife.

AN IMPRISONED THUNDERSTORM

Victor Hugo

THE CAPTAIN and lieutenant rushed towards the gun-deck, but could not get down. All the gunners were pouring up in dismay. Something terrible had just happened.

One of the carronades of the battery, a twenty-four pounder, had broken loose.

This is the most dangerous accident that can possibly take place on shipboard. Nothing more terrible can happen to a sloop of war in open sea and under full sail.

A cannon that breaks its moorings suddenly becomes some strange, supernatural beast. It is a machine transformed into a monster. That short mass on wheels moves like a billiard-ball, rolls with the rolling of the ship, plunges with the pitching, goes, comes, stops, seems to meditate, starts on its course again, shoots like an arrow, from one end of the vessel to the other, whirls around, slips away, dodges, rears, bangs, crashes, kills, exterminates. It is a battering ram capriciously assaulting a wall. Add to this, the fact that the ram is of metal, the wall of wood.

It is matter set free; one might say, this eternal slave was avenging itself; it seems as if the total depravity concealed in what we call inanimate things had escaped, and burst forth all of a sudden; it appears to lose patience, and to take a strange mysterious revenge; nothing more relentless than this wrath of the inanimate. This enraged lump leaps like a panther, it has the clumsiness of an elephant, the nimbleness of a mouse, the obstinacy of an ax, the uncertainty of the billows, the zigzag of the lightning, the deafness of the grave. It weighs

from "Ninety-Three" by Victor Hugo

ten thousand pounds, and it rebounds like a child's ball. It spins and then abruptly darts off at right angles.

And what is to be done? How put an end to it? A tempest ceases, a cyclone passes over, a wind dies down, a broken mast can be replaced, a leak can be stopped, a fire extinguished, but what will become of this enormous brute of bronze? How can it be captured? You can reason with a bulldog, astonish a bull, fascinate a boa, frighten a tiger, tame a lion; but you have no resource against this monster, a loose cannon. You cannot kill it, it is dead; and at the same time it lives. It lives with a sinister life which comes to it from the infinite. The deck beneath it gives it full swing. It is moved by the ship, which is moved by the sea, which is moved by the wind. This destroyer is a toy. The ship, the waves, the winds, all play with it, hence its frightful animation. What is to be done with this apparatus? How fetter this stupendous engine of destruction? How anticipate its comings and goings, its returns, its stops, its shocks? Any one of its blows on the side of the ship may stave it in. How fortell its frightful meanderings? It is dealing with a projectile, which alters its mind, which seems to have ideas, and changes its direction every instant. How check the course of what must be avoided? The horrible cannon struggles, advances, backs, strikes right, strikes left, retreats, passes by, disconcerts expectation, grinds up obstacles, crushes men like flies. All the terror of the situation is in the fluctuations of the flooring. How fight an inclined plane subject to caprices? The ship has, so to speak, in its belly, an imprisoned thunderstorm, striving to escape; something like a thunderbolt rumbling above an earthquake.

In an instant the whole crew was on foot. It was the fault of the gun captain, who had neglected to fasten the screw-nut of the mooring-chain, and had insecurely clogged the four wheels of the gun carriage; this gave play to the sole and the framework, separated the two platforms, and finally the breeching. The tackle had given way, so that the cannon was no longer firm on its carriage. The stationary breeching, which prevents recoil, was not in use at this time. A heavy sea struck the port, the carronade insecurely fastened, had recoiled and broken its chain, and began its terrible course over the deck.

To form an idea of this strange sliding, let one image a drop of water running over glass.

At the moment when the fastenings gave way, the gunners were in the battery. Some in groups, others scattered about, busied with the customary work among sailors getting ready for a signal for action. The carronade, hurled forward by the pitching of the vessel, made a gap in this crowd of men and crushed four at the first blow; then sliding back and shot out again as the ship rolled, it cut in two a fifth unfortunate, and knocked a piece of the battery against the larboard side with such force as to unship it. This caused the cry of distress just heard. All the men rushed to the companion-way. The gun deck was vacated in a twinkling.

The enormous gun was left alone. It was given up to itself. It was its own master, and master of the ship. It could do what it pleased. This whole crew, accustomed to laugh in time of battle, now trembled. To describe the terror is impossible.

Captain Boisberthelot and Lieutenant la Vieuville, although both dauntless men, stopped at the head of the companion-way and dumb, pale, and hesitating, looked down on the deck below. Someone elbowed past and went down.

It was their passenger, the peasant, the man of whom they had just been speaking a moment before.

Reaching the foot of the companion-way, he stopped.

The cannon was rushing back and forth on the deck. One might have supposed it to be the living chariot of the Apocalypse. The marine lantern swinging overhead added a dizzy shifting of light and shade to the picture. The form of the cannon disappeared in the violence of its course, and it looked now black in the light, now mysteriously white in the darkness.

It went on in its destructive work. It had already shattered four other guns and made two gaps in the side of the ship, fortunately above the water-line, but where the water would come in, in case of heavy weather. It rushed frantically against the framework; the strong timbers withstood the shock; the curved shape of the wood gave them great power of resistance; but they creaked beneath the blows of this huge club, beating on all sides at once, with a strange sort of ubiquity. The percussions of a grain of shot shaken in a bottle are not swifter or more senseless. The four wheels passed back and forth over the dead men, cutting them, carving them, slashing them, till the five corpses were a score of stumps rolling across the deck; the heads of the dead men seemed to cry out; streams of blood curled over the deck with the rolling of the vessel; the planks, damaged in several places, began to gape open. The whole ship was filled with the horrid noise and confusion.

The captain promptly recovered his presence of mind and ordered everything that could check and impede the cannon's mad course to be thrown through the hatchway down on the gun deck—mattresses, hammocks, spare sails, rolls of cordage, bags belonging to the crew, and bales of counterfeit assignats, of which the corvette carried a large quantity—a characteristic piece of English villainy regarded as legitimate warfare.

But what could these rags do? As nobody dared to go below to dispose of them properly, they were reduced to lint in a few minutes.

There was just sea enough to make the accident as bad as possible. A tempest would have been desirable, for it might have upset the cannon, and with its four wheels once in the air there would be some hope of getting it under control. Meanwhile, the havoc increased.

There were splits and fractures in the masts, which are set into the framework of the keel and rise above the decks of ships like great, round pillars. The convulsive blows of the cannon had cracked the mizzen-mast, and had cut into the main-mast.

The battery was being ruined. Ten pieces out of thirty were disabled; the breaches in the side of the vessel were increasing, and the corvette was beginning to leak.

The old passenger, having gone down to the gun deck, stood like a man of stone at the foot of the steps. He cast a stern glance over this scene of devastation. He did not move. It seemed impossible to take a step forward. Every movement of the loose carronade threatened the ship's destruction. A few moments more and shipwreck would be inevitable.

They must perish or put a speedy end to the disaster; some course must be decided on; but what? What an opponent was this carronade! Something must be done to stop this terrible madness—to capture this lightning—to overthrow this thunderbolt.

Boisberthelot said to La Vieuville,—

"Do you believe in God, chevalier?"

La Vieuville replied: "Yes—no. Sometimes."

"During a tempest."

"Yes, and in moments like this."

"God alone can save us from this," said Boisberthelot.

Everybody was silent, letting the carronade continue its horrible din.

Outside, the waves beating against the ship responded with their blows to the shocks of the cannon. It was like two hammers alternating.

Suddenly, in the midst of this inaccessible ring, where the escaped cannon was leaping, a man was seen to appear, with an iron bar in his hand. He was the author of the catastrophe, the captain of the gun, guilty of criminal carelessness, and the cause of the accident, the master of the carronade. Having done the mischief, he was anxious to repair it. He had seized the iron bar in one hand, a tiller-rope with a slip-noose in the other, and jumped down the hatchway to the gun deck.

Then began an awful sight; a Titanic scene; the contest between gun and gunner; the battle of matter and intelligence, the duel between man and the inanimate.

The man stationed himself in a corner, and with bar and rope in his two hands, he leaned against one of the riders, braced himself on his legs, which seemed two steel posts, and livid, calm, tragic, as if rooted to the deck, he waited.

He waited for the cannon to pass by him.

The gunner knew his gun, and it seemed to him as if the gun ought to know him. He had lived long with it. How many times he had thrust his hand into its mouth! It was his own familiar master. He began to speak to it as if it were his dog.

"Come!" he said. Perhaps he loved it.

He seemed to wish it to come to him.

But to come to him was to come upon him. And then he would be lost. How could he avoid being crushed? That was the question. All looked on in terror.

Not a breast breathed freely, unless perhaps that of the old man, who was alone in the battery with the two contestants, a stern witness.

He might be crushed himself by the cannon. He did not stir.

Beneath them the sea blindly directed the contest.

At the moment when the gunner, accepting this frightful hand-to-hand conflict, challenged the cannon, some chance rocking of the sea caused the carronade to remain for an instant motionless and as if stupefied. "Come, now!" said the man. It seemed to listen.

Suddenly it leaped towards him. The man dodged the blow.

The battle began. Battle unprecedented. Frailty struggling against the invulnerable. The gladiator of flesh attacking the beast of brass. On one side, brute, force; on the other, a human soul.

All this was taking place in semi-darkness. It was like the shadowy vision of a miracle.

A soul—strange to say, one would have thought the cannon also had a soul; but a soul full of hatred and rage. This sightless thing seemed to have eyes. The monster appeared to lie in wait for the man. One would have at least believed that there was craft in this mass. It also chose its time. It was a strange, gigantic insect of metal, having or seeming to have the will of a demon. For a moment this colossal locust would beat against the low ceiling overhead, then it would come down on its four wheels like a tiger on its four paws, and begin to run at the man. He, supple, nimble, expert, writhed away like an adder from all these lightning movements. He avoided a collision, but the blows which he parried fell against the vessel, and continued their work of destruction.

An end of broken chain was left hanging to the carronade. This chain had in some strange way become twisted about the screw of the cascabel. One end of the chain was fastened to the gun-carriage. The other, left loose, whirled desperately about the cannon, making all its blows more dangerous.

The screw held it in a firm grip, adding a thong to a battering-ram, making a terrible whirlwind around the cannon, an iron lash in a brazen hand. This chain complicated the contest.

However, the man went on fighting. Occasionally, it was the man who attacked the cannon; he would creep along the side of the vessel, bar and rope in hand; and the cannon, as if it understood, and as though suspecting some snare, would flee away. The man, bent on victory, pursued it.

Such things cannot long continue. The cannon seemed to say to itself, all of a sudden, "Come, now! Make an end of it!" and it stopped. One felt that the crisis was at hand. The cannon, as if in suspense, seemed to have, or really had—for to all it was a living being—a ferocious malice prepense. It made a sudden, quick dash at the gunner. The gunner sprang out of the way, let it pass by, and cried out to it with a laugh, "Try it again!" The cannon, as if enraged, smashed a carronade on the port side; then, again seized by the invisible sling which controlled it, it was hurled to the starboard side at the man, who made his escape. Three carronades gave way under the blows of the cannon; then, as if blind and not knowing what more to do, it turned its back on the man, rolled from stern to bow, injured the stern and made a breach in the planking of the prow. The man took refuge at the foot of the steps, not far from the old man who was looking on. The gunner held his iron bar in rest. The cannon seemed to notice it, and without taking the trouble to turn around, slid back on the man, swift as the blow of an ax. The man, driven against the side of the ship, was lost. The whole crew cried out with horror.

But the old passenger, till this moment motionless, darted forth more quickly than any of this wildly swift rapidity. He seized a package of counterfeit assignats, and, at the risk of being crushed, succeeded in throwing it between the wheels of the carronade. This decisive and perilous movement could not have been made with more exactness and precision by a man trained in all the exercises described in Durosel's "Manual of Gun Practice at Sea."

The package had the effect of a clog. A pebble may stop a log, the branch of a tree turn aside an avalanche. The carronade stumbled. The gunner, taking advantage of this critical opportunity, plunged his iron bar between the spokes of one of the hind wheels. The cannon stopped. It leaned forward. The man using the bar as a lever, held it in equilibrium. The heavy mass was overthrown, with the crash of a falling bell, and the man, rushing with all his might, dripping with prespiration, passed the slip-noose around the bronze neck of the subdued monster.

It was ended. The man had conquered. The ant had control over the mastodon; the pigmy had taken the thunderbolt prisoner.

The mariners and sailors clapped their hands.

The whole crew rushed forward with cables and chains, and in an instant the cannon was secured.

THE PHANTOM ISLAND

Washington Irving

"THERE ARE more things in heaven and earth than are dreamed of in our philosophy," and among these may be placed that marvel and mystery of the seas, the Island of St. Brandan. Those who have read the history of the Canaries, the fortunate islands of the ancients, may remember the wonders told of this enigmatical island. Occasionally it would be visible from their shores, stretching away in the clear bright west, to all appearance substantial like themselves, and still more beautiful. Expeditions would launch forth from the Canaries to explore this land of promise. For a time its sun-gilt peaks and long, shadowy promontories would remain distinctly visible but in proportion as the voyagers approached, peak and promontory would gradually fade away until nothing would remain but blue sky above and deep blue water below. Hence this mysterious isle was stigmatized by ancient cosmographers with the name of Aprositus or the Inaccessible. The failure of numerous expeditions sent in quest of it, both in ancient and modern days, have at length caused its very existence to be called in question, and it has been rashly pronounced a mere optical illusion, like the Fata Morgana of the Straits of Messina, or has been classed with those unsubstantial regions known to mariners as Cape Fly Away and the coast of Cloud Land.

Let us not permit, however, the doubts of worldly-wise sceptics to rob us of all the glorious realms owned by happy credulity in days of yore. Be assured, O reader of easy faith!—thou for whom it is my delight to labor—be assured that such an island actually exists, and has from time to time been revealed to the gaze and trodden by the feet of favored mortals. Historians and

from "Wolfert's Roost" by Washington Irving

philosophers may have their doubts, but its existence has been fully attested by that inspired race, the poets; who, being gifted with a kind of second sight, are enabled to discern those mysteries of nature hidden from the eyes of ordinary men. To this gifted race it has ever been a kind of wonderland. Here once bloomed, and perhaps still blooms, the famous garden of the Hesperides, with its golden fruit. Here, too, the sorceress Armida had her enchanted garden, in which she held the Christian paladin, Rinaldo, in delicious but inglorious thraldom, as set forth in the immortal lay of Tasso. It was in this island that Sycorax the witch held sway, when the good Prospero and his infant daughter Miranda were wafted to its shores. Who does not know the tale as told in the magic page of Shakespeare? The isle was then

> . . . "full of noises,
> Sounds, and sweet airs, that give delight, and hurt not."

The island, in fact, at different times, has been under the sway of different powers, genii of earth, and air, and ocean, who have made it their shadowy abode. Hither have retired many classic but broken-down deities, shorn of almost all their attributes, but who once ruled the poetic world. Here Neptune and Amphitrite hold a diminished court, sovereigns in exile. Their ocean-chariot, almost a wreck lies bottom upward in some seabeaten cavern; their pursy Tritons and haggard Nereids bask listlessly like seals about the rocks. Sometimes those deities assume, it is said, a shadow of their ancient pomp, and glide in state about a summer sea; and then, as some tall Indiaman lies becalmed with idly flapping sail, her drowsy crew may hear the mellow note of the Triton's shell swelling upon the ear as the invisible pageant sweeps by.

On the shores of this wondrous isle the kraken heaves its unwieldy bulk and wallows many a rood. Here the sea-serpent, that mighty but much-contested reptile, lies coiled up during the intervals of its revelations to the eyes of true believers. Here even the Flying Dutchman finds a port, and casts his anchor, and furls his shadowy sail, and takes a brief repose from his eternal cruisings.

In the deep bays and harbors of the island lies many a spell-bound ship, long since given up as lost by the ruined merchant. Here, too, its crew, long, long bewailed in vain, lie sleeping from age to age in mossy grottos, or wander about in pleasing oblivion of all things. Here in caverns are garnered up the priceless treasures lost in the ocean. Here sparkles in vain the diamond and flames the carbuncle. Here are piled up rich bales of Oriental silks, boxes of pearls, and piles of golden ingots.

Such are some of the marvels related of this island, which may serve to throw light upon the following legend, of unquestionable truth, which I recommend to the implicit belief of the reader.

The Adalantado of the Seven Cities

A Legend of St. Brandan

IN THE early part of the fifteenth century, when Prince Henry of Portugal, of worthy memory, was pushing the career of discovery along the western coast of Africa, and the world was resounding with reports of golden regions on the mainland, and new-found islands in the ocean, there arrived at Lisbon an old bewildered pilot of the seas, who had been driven by tempests, he knew not whither, and raved about an island far in the deep, upon which he had landed, and which he had found peopled with Christians, and adorned with noble cities.

The inhabitants, he said, having never before been visited by a ship, gathered round, and regarded him with surprise. They told him they were descendants of a band of Christians, who fled from Spain when that country was conquered by the Moslems. They were curious about the state of their fatherland, and grieved to hear that the Moslems still held possession of the kingdom of Granada. They would have taken the old navigator to church, to convince him of their orthodoxy; but, either through lack of devotion, or lack of faith in their words, he declined their invitation, and preferred to return on board of his ship. He was properly punished. A furious storm arose, drove him from his anchorage, hurried him out to sea, and he saw no more of the unknown island.

This strange story caused great marvel in Lisbon and elsewhere. Those versed in history remembered to have read, in an ancient chronicle, that, at the time of the conquest of Spain, in the eighth century, when the blessed cross was cast down and the crescent erected in its place, and when Christian churches were turned into Moslem mosques, seven bishops, at the head of seven bands of pious exiles, had fled from the peninsula, and embarked in quest of some ocean island, or distant land, where they might found seven Christian cities, and enjoy their faith unmolested.

The fate of these saints errant had hitherto remained a mystery, and their story had faded from memory; the report of the old tempest-tossed pilot, however, revived this long-forgotten theme; and it was determined by the pious and enthusiastic that the island thus accidentally discovered was the identical place of refuge whither the wandering bishops had been guided by a protecting Providence, and where they had folded their flocks.

This most excitable of worlds has always some darling object of chimerical enterprise; the "Island of the Seven Cities" now awakened as much interest and longing among zealous Christians as has the renowned city of Timbuctoo among adventurous travelers, or the Northeast passage among hardy navigators; and it was a frequent prayer of the devout, that these scattered and lost portions of the Christian family might be discovered and reunited to the great body of Christendom.

No one, however, entered into the matter with half the zeal of Don Fernando de Ulmo, a young cavalier of high standing in the Portuguese court, and of most sanguine and romantic temperament. He had recently come to his estate, and had run the round of all kinds of pleasures and excitements when this new theme of popular talk and wonder presented itself. The Island of the Seven Cities became now the constant subject of his thoughts by day, and his dreams by night; it even rivaled his passion for a beautiful girl, one of the greatest belles of Lisbon, to whom he was betrothed. At length his imagination became so inflamed on the subject, that he determined to fit out an expedition, at his own expense, and set sail in quest of this sainted island. It could not be a cruise of any great extent; for, according to the calculations of the tempest-tossed pilot, it must be somewhere in the latitude of the Canaries; which at that time, when the new world was as yet undiscovered, formed the frontier of ocean enterprise. Don Fernando applied to the crown for countenance and protection. As he was a favorite at court, the usual patronage was readily extended to him; that is to say, he received a commission from the king, Don Ioam II., constituting him Adalantado, or military governor, of any country he might discover, with the single proviso, that he should bear all the expenses of the discovery, and pay a tenth of the profits to the crown.

Don Fernando now set to work in the true spirit of a projector. He sold acre after acre of solid land, and invested the proceeds in ships, guns, ammunition, and sea-stores. Even his old family mansion in Lisbon was mortgaged without scruple, for he looked forward to a palace in one of the Seven Cities, of which he was to be Adalantado. This was the age of nautical romance, when the thoughts of all speculative dreamers were turned to the ocean. The scheme of Don Fernando, therefore, drew adventurers of every kind. The merchant promised himself new marts of opulent traffic; the soldier hoped to sack and plunder some one or other of those Seven Cities; even the fat monk shook off the sleep and sloth of the cloister, to join in a crusade which promised such increase to the possessions of the Church.

One person alone regarded the whole project with sovereign contempt and growing hostility. This was Don Ramiro Alvarez, the father of the beautiful Serafina, to whom Don Fernando was betrothed. He was one of those perverse, matter-of-fact old men, who are prone to oppose everything speculative and romantic. He had no faith in the Island of the Seven Cities; regarded the projected cruise as a crack-brained freak; looked with angry eye and internal heart-burning on the conduct of his intended son-in-law, chaffering away solid lands for lands in the moon; and scoffingly dubbed him Adalantado of Cloud Land. In fact, he had never really relished the intended match, to which his consent had been slowly extorted by the tears and entreaties of his daughter. It is true he could have no reasonable objections to the youth, for Don Fernando was the very flower of Portuguese chivalry. No one could excel him at the tilting match, or the riding at the ring; none was more bold and dexterous in the bull fight; none composed more gallant madrigals in praise of his lady's charms, or sang them with sweeter tones to the accompaniment of her guitar; nor could anyone handle the castanets and dance the bolero with more captivating grace. All these admirable qualities and endowments, however, though they had been sufficient to win the heart of Serafina, were nothing in the eyes of her unreasonable father. Oh Cupid, god of Love! why will fathers always be so unreasonable?

The engagement to Serafina had threatened at first to throw an obstacle in the way of the expedition of Don Fernando, and for a time perplexed him in the extreme. He was passionately attached to the young lady; but he was also passionately bent on this romantic enterprise. How should he reconcile the two passionate inclinations? A simple and obvious arrangement at length presented itself,—marry Serafina, enjoy a portion of the honeymoon at once, and defer the rest until his return from the discovery of the Seven Cities!

He hastened to make known this most excellent arrangement to Don Ramiro, when the long-smothered wrath of the old cavalier burst forth. He reproached him with being the dupe of wandering vagabonds and wild schemers, and with squandering all his real possessions, in pursuit of empty bubbles. Don Fernando was too sanguine a projector, and too young a man to listen tamely to such language. He acted with what is technically called "becoming spirit." A high quarrel ensued; Don Ramiro pronounced him a madman, and forbade all farther intercourse with his daughter until he should give proof of returning sanity by abandoning this madcap enterprise; while Don Fernando flung out of the house, more bent than ever on the expedition, from the idea of triumphing over the incredulity of the graybeard, when he should return successful. Don Ramiro's heart misgave him. Who knows, thought he, but this crack-brained visionary may persuade my daughter to elope with him, and share his throne in this unknown paradise of fools? If I could only keep her safe until his ships are fairly out at sea!

He repaired to her apartment, represented to her the sanguine, unsteady character of her lover and the chimerical value of his schemes, and urged the propriety of suspending all intercourse with him until he should recover from his present hallucination. She bowed her head as if in filial acquiescence, whereupon he folded her to his bosom with parental fondness and kissed away a tear that was stealing over her cheek, but as he left the chamber quietly turned the key in the lock; for though he was a fond father and had a high opinion of the submissive temper of his child, he had a still higher opinion of the conservative virtues of lock and key, and determined to trust to them until the caravels should sail. Whether the damsel had been in anywise shaken in her faith as to the schemes of her lover by her father's eloquence, tradition does not say; but certain it is, that, the moment she heard the key turn in the lock, she became a firm believer in the Island of the Seven Cities.

The door was locked; but her will was unconfined. A window of the chamber opened into one of those stone balconies, secured by iron bars, which project like huge cages from Portuguese and Spanish houses. Within this balcony the beautiful Sarafina had her birds and flowers, and here she was accustomed to sit on moonlight nights as in a bower, and touch her guitar and sing like a wakeful nightingale. From this balcony an intercourse was now maintained between the lovers, against which the lock and key of Don Ramiro were of no avail. All day would Fernando be occupied hurrying the equipments of his ships, but evening found him in sweet discourse beneath his lady's window.

At length the preparations were completed. Two gallant caravels lay at anchor in the Tagus ready to sail at sunrise. Late at night by the pale light of a waning moon the lover had his last interview. The beautiful Sarafina was sad at heart and full of dark forebodings; her lover full of hope and confidence. "A few short months," said he, "and I shall return in triumph. Thy father will then blush at his incredulity, and hasten to welcome to his house the Adalantado of the Seven Cities."

The gentle lady shook her head. It was not on this point she felt distrust. She was a thorough believer in the Island of the Seven Cities, and so sure of the success of the enterprise that she might have been tempted to join it had not the balcony been high and the grating strong. Other considerations induced that dubious shaking of the head. She had heard of the inconstancy of the seas, and the inconstancy of those who roam them. Might not Fernando meet with other loves in foreign ports? Might not some peerless beauty in one or other of those Seven Cities efface the image of Serafina from his mind? Now let the truth be spoken, the beautiful Serafina had reason for her disquiet. If Don Fernando had any fault in the world, it was that of being rather inflammable and apt to take fire from every sparkling eye. He had been somewhat of a rover among the sex on shore, what might he be on sea?

She ventured to express her doubt, but he spurned at the very idea. "What! be false to Serafina! He bow at the shrine of another beauty? Never! never!" Repeatedly did he bend his knee, and smite his breast, and call upon the silver moon to witness his sincerity and truth.

He retorted the doubt, "Might not Serafina herself forget her plighted faith? Might not some wealthier rival present himself while he was tossing on the sea; and, backed by her father's wishes, win the treasure of her hand!"

The beautiful Serafina raised her white arms between the iron bars of the balcony, and, like her lover, invoked the moon to testify her vows. Alas! how little did Fernando know her heart. The more her father should oppose, the more would she be fixed in faith. Though years should intervene, Fer-

Evening found him in sweet discourse beneath his lady's window.

nando on his return would find her true. Even should the salt sea swallow him up (and her eyes shed salt tears at the very thought), never would she be the wife of another! Never, never, never! She drew from her finger a ring gemmed with a ruby heart, and dropped it from the balcony, a parting pledge of constancy.

Thus the lovers parted with many a tender word and plighted vow. But will they keep those vows? Perish the doubt! Have they not called the constant moon to witness?

With the morning dawn the caravels dropped down the Tagus, and put to sea. They steered for the Canaries, in those days the regions of nautical discovery and romance, and the outposts of the known world, for as yet Columbus had not steered his daring barks across the ocean. Scarce had they reached those latitudes when they were separated by a violent tempest. For many days was the caravel of Don Fernando driven about at the mercy of the elements; all seamanship was baffled, destruction seemed inevitable and the crew were in despair. All at once the storm subsided; the ocean sank into a calm; the clouds which had veiled the face of heaven were suddenly withdrawn, and the tempest-tossed mariners beheld a fair and mountainous island, emerging as if by enchantment from the murky gloom. They rubbed their eyes and gazed for a time almost incredulously, yet there lay the island spread out in lovely landscapes, with the late stormy sea laving its shores with peaceful billows.

The pilot of the caravel consulted his maps and charts; no island like the one before him was laid down as existing in those parts; it is true he had lost his reckoning in the late storm, but, according to his calculations, he could not be far from the Canaries; and this was not one of that group of islands. The caravel now lay perfectly becalmed off the mouth of a river, on the banks of which, about a league from the sea, was descried a noble city, with lofty walls and towers, and a protecting castle.

After a time, a stately barge with sixteen oars was seen emerging from the river, and approaching the caravel. It was quaintly carved and gilt; the oarsmen were clad in antique garb, their oars painted of a bright crimson, and they came slowly and solemnly, keeping time as they rowed to the cadence of an old Spanish ditty. Under a silken canopy in the stern, sat a cavalier richly clad, and over his head was a banner bearing the sacred emblem of the cross.

When the barge reached the caravel, the cavalier stepped on board. He was tall and gaunt; with a long Spanish visage, moustaches that curled up to his eyes, and a forked beard. He wore gauntlets reaching to his elbows, a Toledo blade strutting out behind, with a basket hilt, in which he carried his handkerchief. His air was lofty and precise, and bespoke indisputably the hidalgo. Thrusting out a long spindle leg, he took off a huge sombrero, and swaying it until the feather swept the ground, accosted Don Fernando in the old Castilian language, and with the old Castilian courtesy, welcoming him to the Island of the Seven Cities.

Don Fernando was overwhelmed with astonishment. Could this be true? Had he really been tempest-driven to the very land of which he was in quest?

It was even so. That very day the inhabitants were holding high festival in commemoration of the escape of their ancestors from the Moors. The arrival of the caravel at such a juncture was considered a good omen, the accomplishment of an ancient prophecy through which the Island was to be restored to the great community of Christendom. The cavalier before him was grand-chamberlain, sent by the alcayde to invite him to the festivities of the capital.

Don Fernando could scarce believe that this was not all a dream. He made known his name and the object of his voyage. The grand chamberlain declared that all was in perfect accordance with the ancient prophecy, and that the moment his credentials were presented, he would be acknowledged as the Adalantado of the Seven Cities. In the meantime the day was waning; the barge was ready to convey him to the land, and would as assuredly bring him back.

Don Fernando's pilot, a veteran of the seas, drew him aside and expostulated against his venturing, on the mere word of a stranger, to land in a strange barge on an unknown shore. Who knows, Senor, what land this is, or what people inhabit it?"

Don Fernando was not to be dissuaded. Had he not believed in this island when all the world doubted? Had he not sought it in defiance of storm and tempest, and was he now to shrink from its shores when they lay before him in calm weather? In a word, was not faith the very corner-stone of his enterprise?

Having arrayed himself, therefore, in gala dress befitting the occasion, he took his seat in the barge. The grand chamberlain seated himself opposite The rowers plied their oars, and renewed the mournful old ditty, and the gorgeous but unwieldly barge moved slowly through the water.

The night closed in before they entered the river, and swept along past rock and promontory, each guarded by its tower. At every post they were challenged by the sentinel.

"Who goes there?"

"The Adalantado of the Seven Cities."

"Welcome, Senor Adalantado. Pass on."

Entering the harbor they rowed close by an armed galley of ancient form. Soldiers with crossbows patrolled the deck.

"Who goes there?"

"The Adalantado of the Seven Cities."

"Welcome, Senor Adalantado. Pass on."

They landed at a broad flight of stone steps, leading up between two massive towers, and knocked at the watergate. A sentinel, in ancient steel casque, looked from the barbican.

"Who is there?"

"The Adalantado of the Seven Cities."

"Welcome, Senor Adalantado."

The gate swung open, grating upon rusty hinges. They entered between two rows of warriors in Gothic armor, with crossbows, maces, battle-axes, and faces old-fashioned as their armor. There were processions through the streets, in commemoration of the landing of the seven Bishops and their followers, and bonfires at which effigies of losel Moors expiated their invasion of Christendom by a kind of *auto-da-fé*. The groups round the fires, uncouth in their attire, looked like the fantastic figures that roam the streets in Carnival time. Even the dames who gazed down from Gothic balconies hung with antique tapestry, resembled effigies dressed up in Christmas mummeries. Everything, in short, bore the stamp of former ages, as if the world had suddenly rolled back for several centuries. Nor was this to be wondered at. Had not the Island of the Seven Cities been cut off from the rest of the world for several hundred years; and were not these the modes and customs of Gothic Spain before it was conquered by the Moors?

Arrived at the palace of the alcayde, the grand chamberlain knocked at the portal. The porter looked through a wicket, and demanded who was there.

"The Adalantado of the Seven Cities."

The portal was thrown wide open. The grand chamberlain led the way up a vast, heavily moulded, marble staircase, and into a hall of ceremony, where was the alcayde with several of the principal dignitaries of the city, who had a marvelous resemblance, in form and feature, to the quaint figures in old illuminated manuscripts.

The grand chamberlain stepped forward and announced the name and title of the stranger guest, and the extraordinary nature of his mission. The announcement appeared to create no extraordinary emotion or surprise, but to be received as the anticipated fulfillment of a prophecy.

The reception of Don Fernando, however, was profoundly gracious, though in the same style of stately courtesy which everywhere prevailed. He would have produced his credentials, but this was courteously declined. The evening was devoted to high festivity; the following day, when he should enter the port with his caravel, would be devoted to business, when the credentials would be received in due form, and he inducted into office as Adalantado of the Seven Cities.

Don Fernando was now conducted through one of those interminable suites of apartments, the pride of Spanish palaces, all furnished in a style of obsolete magnificence. In a vast saloon, blazing with tapers, was assembled all the aristocracy and fashion of the city,—stately dames and cavaliers, the very counterpart of the figures in the tapestry which decorated the walls. Fernando gazed in silent marvel. It was a reflex of the proud aristocracy of Spain in the time of Roderick the Goth.

The festivities of the evening were all in the style of solemn and antiquated ceremonial. There was a dance, but it was as if the old tapestry were put in motion, and all the figures moving in stately measure about the floor. There was one exception, and one that told powerfully upon the susceptible Adalantado. The alcayde's daughter—such a ripe, melting beauty! Her dress, it is true, like the dresses of her neighbors, might have been worn before the flood, but she had the black Andalusian eye, a glance of which, through its long dark lashes, is irresistible. Her voice, too, her manner, her undulating movements, all smacked of Andalusia, and showed how female charms may be transmitted from age to age, and clime to clime, without ever going out of fashion. Those who know the witchery of the sex, in that most amorous part of amorous old Spain, may judge of the fascination to which Don Fernando was exposed, as he joined in the dance with one of its most captivating descendants.

He sat beside her at the banquet! such an old-world feast! such obsolete

dainties!   At the head of the table the peacock, that bird of state and ceremony, was served up in full plumage on a golden dish.   As Don Fernando cast
his eyes down the glittering board, what a vista presented itself of odd heads
and head-dresses; of formal bearded dignitaries and stately dames, with cas-
tellated locks and towering plumes!   Is it to be wondered at that he should
turn with delight from these antiquated figures to the alcayde's daughter, all
smiles and dimples, and melting looks and melting accents?   Beside, for I wish
to give him every excuse in my power, he was in a particularly excitable mood
from the novelty of the scene before him, from this realization of all his hopes
and fancies, and from frequent draughts of the wine-cup, presented to him at
every moment by officious pages during the banquet.

In a word—there is no concealing the matter—before the evening was over,
Don Fernando was making love outright to the alcayde's daughter.   They
had wandered together to a moon-lit balcony of the palace, and he was charming her ear with one of those love ditties with which, in a like balcony, he had
serenaded the beautiful Serafina.

The damsel hung her head coyly.   "Ah! Senor, these are flattering words;
but you cavaliers, who roam the seas, are unsteady as its waves.   Tomorrow
you will be throned in state, Adalantado of the Seven Cities; and will think
no more of the alcayde's daughter."

Don Fernando in the intoxication of the moment called the moon to witness
his sincerity.   As he raised his hand in adjuration, the chaste moon cast a ray
upon the ring that sparkled on his finger.   It caught the damsel's eye.   "Signor
Adalantado," said she archly, "I have no great faith in the moon, but give me
that ring upon your finger in piedge of the truth of what you profess."

The gallant Adalantado was taken by surprise; there was no parrying this
sudden appeal; before he had time to reflect, the ring of the beautiful Serafina glittered on the finger of the alcayde's daughter.

At this eventful moment the chamberlain approached with lofty demeanor,
and announced that the barge was waiting to bear him back to the caravel.   I
forbear to relate the ceremonious partings with the alcayde and his dignitaries,
and the tender farewell of the alcayde's daughter.   He took his seat in the
barge opposite the grand chamberlain.   The rowers plied their crimson oars
in the same slow and stately manner, to the cadence of the same mournful old
ditty.   His brain was in a whirl with all that he had seen, and his heart now
and then gave him a twinge as he thought of his temporary infidelity to the

beautiful Serafina. The barge sallied out into the sea, but no caravel was to be seen; doubtless she had been carried to a distance by the current of the river. The oarsmen rowed on; their monotonous chant had a lulling effect. A drowsy influence crept over Don Fernando. Objects swam before his eyes. The oarsmen assumed odd shapes as in a dream. The grand chamberlain grew larger and larger, and taller and taller. He took off his huge sombrero, and held it over the head of Don Fernando, like an extinguisher over a candle. The latter cowered beneath it; he felt himself sinking in the socket.

"Good night! Senor Adalantado of the Seven Cities!" said the grand chamberlain.

The sombrero slowly descended—Don Fernando was extinguished!

How long he remained extinct no mortal man can tell. When he returned to consciousness, he found himself in a strange cabin, surrounded by strangers. He rubbed his eyes, and looked round him wildly. Where was he?—On board a Portuguese ship, bound to Lisbon. How came he there?—He had been taken senseless from a wreck drifting about the ocean.

Don Fernando was more and more confounded and perplexed. He recalled, one by one, everything that had happened to him in the Island of the Seven Cities, until he had been extinguished by the sombrero of the grand chamberlain. But what had happened to him since? What had become of his caravel? Was it the wreck of her on which he had been found floating?

The people about him could give no information on the subject. He entreated them to take him to the Island of the Seven Cities, which could not be far off; told them all that had befallen him there; that he had but to land to be received as Adalantado; when he would reward them magnificently for their services.

They regarded his words as the ravings of delirium, and in their honest solicitude for the restoration of his reason, administered such rough remedies that he was fain to drop the subject and observe a cautious taciturnity.

At length they arrived in the Tagus, and anchored before the famous city of Lisbon. Don Fernando sprang joyfully on shore, and hastened to his ancentral mansion. A strange porter opened the door, who knew nothing of him or his family; no people of the name had inhabited the house for many a year.

He sought the mansion of Don Ramiro. He approached the balcony beneath which he had bidden farewell to Serafina. Did his eyes deceive him?

No! There was Serafina herself among the flowers in the balcony. He raised his arms toward her with an exclamation of rapture. She cast upon him a look of indignation, and, hastily retiring, closed the casement with a slam that testified her displeasure.

Could she have heard of his flirtation with the alcayde's daughter? But that was mere transient gallantry. A moment's interview would dispel every doubt of his constancy.

He rang at the door; as it was opened by the porter he rushed up-stairs; sought the well-known chamber, and threw himself at the feet of Serafina. She started back with affright, and took refuge in the arms of a youthful cavalier.

"What mean you, Senor," cried the latter, "by this intrusion?"

"What right have you to ask the question?" demanded Don Fernando fiercely.

"The right of an affianced suitor!"

Don Fernando started and turned pale. "Oh, Serafina! Serafina!" cried he, in a tone of agony; "is this thy plighted constancy?"

"Serafina? What mean you by Serafina, Senor? If this be the lady you intend, her name is Maria."

"May I not believe my senses? May I not believe my heart?" cried Don Fernando. "Is not this Serafina Alvarez, the original of yon portrait, which, less fickle than herself, still smiles on me from the wall?"

"Holy Virgin!" cried the young lady, casting her eyes upon the portrait. "He is talking of my great-grandmother!"

An explanation ensued, if that could be called an explanation which plunged the unfortunate Fernando into tenfold perplexity. If he might believe his eyes, he saw before him his beloved Serafina; if he might believe his ears, it was merely her hereditary form and features, perpetuated in the person of her great-granddaughter.

His brain began to spin. He sought the office of the Minister of Marine, and made a report of his expedition, and of the Island of the Seven Cities, which he had so fortunately discovered. Nobody knew anything that he had undertaken the enterprise under a formal contract with the crown, and had received a regular commission, constituting him Adalantado. This must be matter of record, and he insisted loudly that the books of the department should be consulted. The wordy strife at length attracted the attention of an old-gray-headed clerk, who sat perched on a high stool, at a high desk, with iron-rimmed spectacles on the top of a thin, pinched nose, copying records into an enormous folio. He had wintered and summered in the department for a great part of a century, until he had almost grown to be a piece of the desk at which he sat; his memory was a mere index of official facts and documents, and his brain was little better than red tape and parchment. After peering down for a time from his lofty perch, and ascertaining the matter in controversy, he put his pen behind his ear, and descended. He remembered to have heard something from his predecessor about an expedition of the kind in question, but then it had sailed during the reign of Don Ioam II., and he had been dead at least a hundred years. To put the matter beyond dispute, however, the archives of the Torre do Tombo, that sepulcher of old Portuguese documents, were diligently searched, and a record was found of a contract between the crown and one Fernando de Ulmo, for the discovery of the Island of the Seven Cities, and of a commission secured to him as Adalantado of the country he might discover.

"There!" cried Don Fernando, triumphantly, "there you have proof, before your own eyes, of what I have said. I am the Fernando de Ulmo specified in that record. I have discovered the Island of the Seven Cities, and am entitled to be Adalantado, according to contract."

The story of Don Fernando had certainly, what is pronounced the best of historical foundation, documentary evidence; but when a man in the bloom of youth, talked of events that had taken place above a century previously, as having happened to himself, it is no wonder that he was set down for a madman.

The old clerk looked at him from above and below his spectacles, shrugged his shoulders, stroked his chin, reascended his lofty stool, took the pen from behind his ears, and resumed his daily and eternal task, copying records into the fiftieth volume of a series of gigantic folios. The other clerks winked at each other shrewdly, and dispersed to their several places, and poor Don Fernando, thus left to himself, flung out of the office, almost driven wild by these repeated perplexities.

In the confusion of his mind, he instinctively repaired to the mansion of Alverez, but it was barred against him. To break the delusion under which the youth apparently labored, and to convince him that the Serafina about whom he raved was really dead, he was conducted to her tomb. There she lay a stately matron, cut out in alabaster; and there lay her husband beside her; a portly cavalier, in armor; and there knelt, on each side, the effigies of a numerous progeny, proving that she had been a fruitful vine. Even the very monument gave evidence of the lapse of time; the hands of her husband, folded as if in prayer, had lost their fingers, and the face of the once lovely Serafina was without a nose.

Don Fernando felt a transient glow of indignation at beholding this monumental proof of the inconstancy of his mistress; but who could expect a mistress to remain constant during a whole century of absence? And what right had he to rail about constancy, after what had passed between himself and the alcayde's daughter? The unfortunate cavalier performed one pious act of tender devotion; he had the alabaster nose of Serafina restored by a skillful statuary, and then tore himself from the tomb.

He could now no longer doubt the fact that, somehow or other, he had skipped over a whole century, during the night he had spent at the Island of the Seven Cities; and he was now as complete a stranger in his native city, as if he had never been there. A thousand times did he wish himself back to that wonderful island, with its antiquated banquet halls, where he had been so courteously received; and now that the once young and beautiful Serafina was nothing but a great-grandmother in marble, with generations of descendants, a thousand times would he recall the melting black eyes of the alcayde's daughter, who doubtless, like himself was still flourishing in fresh juvenility, and breathe a secret wish that he was seated by her side.

He would at once have set on foot another expedition at his own expense, to cruise in search of the sainted island, but his means were exhausted. He endeavored to rouse others to the enterprise, setting forth the certainty of profitable results, of which his own experience furnished such unquestionable proof. Alas! no one would give faith to his tale; but looked upon it as the feverish dream of a shipwrecked man. He persisted in his efforts; holding forth in all places and all companies, until he became an object of jest and jeer to the light-minded, who mistook his earnest enthusiasm for a proof of insanity; and the very children in the streets bantered him with the title of "The Adalantado of the Seven Cities."

Finding all efforts in vain, in his native city of Lisbon, he took shipping for the Canaries, as being nearer the latitude of his former cruise, and inhabited by people given to nautical adventure. Here he found ready listeners to his story; for the old pilots and mariners of those parts were notorious island-hunters, and devout believers in all the wonders of the seas. Indeed, one and all treated his adventure as a common occurrence, and turning to each other, with a sagacious nod of the head, observed, "He has been at the Island of St. Brandan."

They then went on to inform him of that great marvel and enigma of the ocean; of its repeated appearance to the inhabitants of their islands; and of the many but ineffectual expeditions that had been made in search of it. They took him to a promontory of the island of Palma, whence the shadowy St. Brandan had oftenest been descried, and they pointed out the very tract in the west where its mountains had been seen.

Don Fernando listened with rapt attention. He had no longer a doubt that this mysterious and fugacious island must be the same with that of the Seven Cities; and that some supernatural influence connected with it had operated upon himself, and made the events of a night occupy the space of a century.

He endeavored, but in vain, to rouse the islanders to another attempt at discovery; they had given up the phantom island as indeed inaccessible. Fernando, however, was not to be discouraged. The idea wore itself deeper and deeper in his mind, until it became the engrossing subject of his thoughts and object of his being. Every morning he would repair to the promontory of Palma, and sit there throughout the livelong day, in hopes of seeing the fairy mountains of St. Brandan peering above the horizon; every evening he returned to his home, a disappointed man, but ready to resume his post on the following morning.

His assiduity was all in vain. He grew gray in his ineffectual attempt; and was at length found dead at his post. His grave is still shown in the island of Palma, and a cross is erected on the spot where he used to sit and look out upon the sea, in hopes of the reappearance of the phantom island.

THE IRON-CLADS

Mary Johnston

SUPPER OVER, Edward went down to the house quarter to speak to the men and women there; then, in the parlor, at the piano, he played with his masterly touch "The Last Waltz," and then he came to the fire, took his grandfather's chair, and described to the women the battle at sea.

"We were encamped on the Warwick River—infantry, and a cavalry company, and a battalion from New Orleans. Around us were green flats, black mud, winding creeks, waterfowl, earthworks, and what guns they could give us. At the mouth of the river, across the channel, we had sunk twenty canal boats, to the end that Burnside should not get by. Besides the canal boats and the guns and the waterfowl there was a deal of fever—malarial—of exposure, of wet, of moldy bread, of homesickness and general desolation. Some courage existed, too, and singing at times. We had been down there a long time among the marshes—all winter, in fact. About two weeks ago——"

"Oh, Edward, were you very homesick?"

"Devilish. For the certain production of a very curious feeling, give me picket duty on a wet marsh underneath the stars! Poetic places—marshes— with a strong suggestion about them of The Last Man. . . . Where was I? Down to our camp one morning about two weeks ago came El Capitan Colorado—General Magruder, you know—gold lace, stars, and black plume! With him came Lieutenant Wood, C. S. N. We were paraded——"

"Edward, try as I may, I cannot get over the strangeness of your being in the ranks!"

Edward laughed. "There's many a better man than I in them, Aunt Lucy!

from "The Long Roll" by Mary Johnston. By permission of Houghton Mifflin Company.

They make the best of crows'-nests from which to spy on life, and that is what I always wanted to do—to spy on life!—The men were paraded, and Lieutenant Wood made us a speech. 'The old Merrimac, you know, men, that was burnt last year when the Yankees left Norfolk?—well, we've raised her, and cut her down to her berth deck, and made of her what we call an iron-clad. An iron-clad is a new man-of-war that's going to take the place of the old. The Merrimac is not a frigate any longer; she's the iron-clad Virginia, and we rather think she's going to make her name remembered. She's over there at the Gosport Navy Yard, and she's almost ready. She's covered over with iron plates, and she's got an iron beak, or ram, and she carries ten guns. On the whole, she's the ugliest beauty that you ever saw! She's almost ready to send to Davy Jones's locker a Yankee ship or two. Commodore Buchanan commands her, and you know who he is! She's got her full quota of officers, and, the speaker excepted, they're as fine a set as you'll find on the high seas! But man-of-war's men are scarcer, my friends, than hen's teeth! It's what comes of having no maritime population. Every man Jack that isn't on our few little ships is in the army—and the Virginia wants a crew of three hundred of the bravest of the brave! Now, I am talking to Virginians and Louisianians. Many of you are from New Orleans, and that means that some of you may very well have been seamen—seamen at an emergency, anyhow! Anyhow, when it comes to an emergency Virginians and Louisianians are there to meet it—on sea or on land! Just now there is an emergency—the Virginia's got to have a crew. General Magruder, for all he's got only a small force with which to hold a long line—General Magruder, like the patriot that he is, has said that I may ask this morning for volunteers. Men! any seaman among you has the chance to gather laurels from the strangest deck of the strangest ship that ever you saw! No fear for the laurels! They're fresh and green even under our belching smokestack. The Merrimac is up like the phœnix; and the last state of her is greater than the first, and her name is going down in history! Louisianians and Virginians, who volunteers?'

"About two hundred volunteered——"

"Edward, what did you know about seamanship?"

"Precious little. Chiefly, Unity, what you have read to me from novels. But the laurels sounded enticing, and I was curious about the ship. Well, Wood chose about eighty—all who had been seamen or gunners and a baker's dozen of ignoramuses beside. I came in with that portion of the elect. And off we went, in boats, across the James to the southern shore and to the Gosport Navy Yard. That was a week before the battle."

"What does it look like, Edward—the Merrimac?"

"It looks, Judith, like Hamlet's cloud. Sometimes there is an appearance of a barn with everything but the roof submerged—or of Noah's Ark, three fourths under water! Sometimes, when the flag is flying, she has the air of a piece of earthworks, mysteriously floated off into the river. Ordinarily, though, she is rather like a turtle, with a chimney sticking up from her shell. The shell is made of pitch pine and oak, and it is covered with two-inch thick plates of Tredegar iron. The beak is of cast iron, standing four feet out from the bow; that, with the rest of the old berth deck, is just awash. Both ends of the shell are rounded for pivot guns. Over the gun deck is an iron grating on which you can walk at need. There is the pilot-house covered with iron, and there is the smokestack. Below are the engines and boilers, condemned after the Merrimac's last cruise, and, since then, lying in the ooze at the bottom of the river. They are very wheezy, trembling, poor old men of the sea! It was hard work to get the coal for them to eat; it was brought at last from away out in Montgomery County, from the Price coal-fields. The guns are two 7-inch rifles, two 6-inch rifles, and six 9-inch smoothbores; ten in all.—Yes, call her a turtle, plated with iron; she looks as much like that as like anything else.

"When we eighty men from the Warwick first saw her, she was swarming with workmen. They continued to cover her over, and to make impossible any drill or exercise upon her. Hammer, hammer upon belated plates from the Tredegar! Tinger, tinker with the poor old engines! Make shift here and make shift there; work through the day and work through the night, for there was a rumor abroad that the Ericsson, that we knew was building, was coming down the coast! There was no chance to drill, to become acquainted with the turtle and her temperament. Her species had never gone to war before, and when you looked at her there was room for doubt as to how she would behave! Officers and men were strange to one another—and the gunners could not try the guns for the swarming workmen. There wasn't so much of the Montgomery coal that it could be wasted on experiments in firing up—and, indeed, it seemed wise not to experiment at all with the ancient engines! So we stood about the navy yard, and looked down the Elizabeth and across the flats to Hampton Roads, where we could see the Cumberland, the

Congress, and the Minnesota, Federal ships lying off Newport News—and the workmen riveted the last plates—and smoke began to come out of the smokestack—and suddenly Commodore Buchanan, with his lieutenants behind him, appeared between us and the Merrimac—or the Virginia. Most of us still call her the Merrimac. It was the morning of the eighth. The sun shone brightly and the water was very blue—blue and still. There were seagulls, I remember, flying overhead, screaming as they flew—and the marshes were growing emerald——"

"Yes, yes! What did Commodore Buchanan want?"

"Don't be impatient, Molly! You women don't in the least look like Griseldas! Aunt Lucy has the air of her pioneer great-grandmother who has heard an Indian calling! And as for Judith—Judith!"

"Yes, Edward."

"Come back to Greenwood. You looked a listening Jeanne d'Arc. What did you hear?"

"I heard the engines working, and the sea fowl screaming, and the wind in the rigging of the Cumberland. Go on, Edward."

"We soldiers turned seamen came to attention. 'Get on board, men,' said Commodore Buchanan. 'We are going out in the Roads and introduce a new era.' So off the workmen came and on we went—the flag officers and the lieutenants and the midshipmen and the surgeons and the volunteer aides and the men. The engineers were already below and the gunners were looking at the guns. The smoke rolled up very black, the ropes were cast off, a bugle blew, out streamed the stars and bars, all the workmen on the dock swung their hats, and down the Elizabeth moved the Merrimac. She moved slowly enough with her poor old engines, and she steered badly, and she drew twenty-two feet, and she was ugly, ugly, ugly,—poor thing!

"Now we were opposite Craney Island, at the mouth of the Elizabeth. There's a battery there, you know, part of General Colston's line, and there are forts upon the main along the James. All these were now crowded with men, hurrahing, waving their caps. . . . As we passed Craney they were singing 'Dixie.' So we came out into the James to Hampton Roads.

"Now all the southern shore from Willoughby's Spit to Ragged Island is as grey as a dove, and all the northern shore from Old Point Comfort to Newport News is blue where the enemy has settled. In between are the shining Roads. Between the Rip Raps and Old Point swung at anchor the Roanoke, the Saint Lawrence, a number of gunboats, store ships, and transports, and also a French man-of-war. Far and near over the Roads were many small craft. The Minnesota, a large ship, lay halfway between Old Point and Newport News. At the latter place there is a large Federal garrison, and almost in the shadow of its batteries rode at anchor the frigate Congress and the sloop Cumberland. The first had fifty guns, the second thirty. The Virginia, or the Merrimac, or the turtle, creeping out from the Elizabeth, crept slowly and puffing black smoke into the South Channel. The pilot, in his iron-clad pilot-house no bigger than a hickory nut, put her head to the northwest. The turtle began to swim toward Newport News.

"Until now not a few of us within her shell, and almost all of the soldiers and the forts along the shore, had thought her upon a trial trip only,—down the Elizabeth, past Craney Island, turn at Sewell's Point, and back to the dock of the Gosport Navy Yard! When she did not turn, the cheering on the shore stopped; you felt the breathlessness. When she passed the point and took to the South Channel, when her head turned upstream, when she came abreast of the Middle Ground, when they saw that the turtle was going to fight, from along the shore to Craney and from Sewell's Point there arose a yell. Every man in grey yelled. They swung hat or cap; they shouted themselves hoarse. All the flags streamed suddenly out, trumpets blared, the sky lifted, and we drank the sunshine in like wine; that is, some of us did. To others it came cold like hemlock against the lip. Fear is a horrible sensation. I was dreadfully afraid——"

"Edward!"

"Dreadfully. But you see I didn't tell anyone I was afraid, and that makes all the difference! Besides, it wore off. . . . It was a spring day and high tide, and the Federal works at Newport News and the Congress and the Cumberland and the more distant Minnesota all looked asleep in the calm, sweet weather. Washing day it was on the Congress, and clothes were drying in the rigging. That aspect as of painted ships, painted breastworks, a painted sea-piece, lasted until the turtle reached mid-channel. Then the other side woke up. Upon the shore appeared a blue swarm—men running to and fro. Bugles signaled. A commotion, too, arose upon the Congress and the Cumberland. Her head toward the latter ship, the turtle puffed forth black smoke and wallowed across the channel. An uglier poor thing you never saw, nor a bolder! Squat to the water, belching black smoke, her engines wheezing and repining, unwieldy of management, her bottom scraping every hummock of sand in all the shoaly Roads—ah, she was ugly and courageous! Our two small gunboats, the Raleigh and the Beaufort, coming from Norfolk, now overtook us,—we went on together. I was forward with the crew of the 7-inch pivot gun. I could see through the port, above the muzzle. Officers and men, we were all cooped under the turtle's shell; in order by the open ports, and the guns all ready. . . . We came to within a mile of the Cumberland, tall and graceful with her masts and spars and all the blue sky above. She looked a swan, and we, the Ugly Duckling. . . . Our ram, you know, was under water—seventy feet of the old berth deck, ending in a four-foot beak of cast iron. . . . We came nearer. At three quarters of a mile, we opened with the bow gun. The Cumberland answered, and the Congress, and their gunboats and shore batteries. Then began a frightful uproar that shook the marshes and sent the sea birds screaming. Smoke arose, and flashing fire, and an excitement—an excitement—an excitement.— Then it was, ladies, that I forgot to be afraid. The turtle swam on, toward the Cumberland, swimming as fast as Montgomery coal and the engines that had lain at the bottom of the sea could make her go. There was a frightful noise within her shell, a humming, a shaking. The Congress, the gunboats and the shore batteries kept firing broadsides. There was an enormous, thundering noise, and the air was grown sulphurous cloud. Their shot came pattering like hail, and like hail it rebounded from the iron-clad. We passed the Congress—very close to her tall side. She gave us a withering fire. We returned it, and steered on for the Cumberland. A word ran from end to end of the turtle's shell, 'We are going to ram her—stand by, men!'

"Within easy range we fired the pivot gun. I was of her crew; half naked we were, powder-blackened and streaming with sweat. The shell she sent burst above the Cumberland's stern pivot, killing or wounding most of her crew that served it. . . . We went on. . . . Through the port I could now see the Cumberland plainly, her starboard side just ahead of us, men in the shrouds and running to and fro on her deck. When we were all but on her, her starboard blazed. That broadside tore up the carriage of our pivot gun, cut another off at the trunnions, and the muzzle from a third, riddled the smokestack and steam-pipe, carried away an anchor, and killed or wounded nineteen men. The Virginia answered with three guns; a cloud of smoke came between the iron-clad and the armed sloop; it lifted—and we were on her. We struck her under the fore rigging with a dull and grinding sound. The iron beak with which we were armed was wrested off.

"The Virginia shivered, hung a moment, then backed clear of the Cumberland, in whose side there was now a ragged and a gaping hole. The pilot in the iron-clad pilot-house turned her head upstream. The water was shoal; she had to run up the James some way before she could turn and come back to attack the Congress. Her keel was in the mud; she was creeping now like a land turtle, and all the iron shore was firing at her. . . . She turned at last in freer water and came down the Roads. Through the port we could see the Cumberland that we had rammed. She had listed to port and was sinking. The water had reached her main deck; all her men were now on the spar deck, where they yet served the pivot guns. She fought to the last. A man of ours, stepping for one moment through a port to the outside of the turtle's shell, was cut in two. As the water rose and rose, the sound of her guns was like a lessening thunder. One by one they stopped. . . . To the last she flew her colors. The Cumberland went down.

"By now there had joined us the small, small James River squadron that had been anchored far up the river. The Patrick Henry had twelve guns, the Jamestown had two, and the Teaser one. Down they scurried like three valiant marsh hens to aid the turtle. With the Beaufort and the Raleigh there were five valiant pygmies, and they fired at the shore batteries, and the shore batteries answered like an angry Jove with solid shot, with shell, with grape, and with canister! A shot wrecked the boiler of the Patrick Henry, scalding to death the men who were near. . . . The turtle sank a transport steamer lying alongside the wharf at Newport News, and then she rounded the point and bore down upon the Congress.

"The frigate had showed discretion, which is the better part of valor. Noting how deeply we drew, she had slipped her cables and run aground in the shallows where she was safe from the ram of the Merrimac. We could get no nearer than two hundred feet. There we took up position, and there we began to rake her, the Beaufort, the Raleigh, and the Jamestown giving us what aid they might. She had fifty guns, and there were the heavy shore batteries, and below her the Minnesota. This ship, also aground in the Middle Channel, now came into action with a roar. A hundred guns were trained upon the Merrimac. The iron hail beat down every point, not iron-clad, that showed above our shell. The muzzles of two guns were shot away, the stanchions, the boat davits, the flagstaff. Again and again the flagstaff fell, and again and again we replaced it. At last we tied the colors to the smokestack. Beside the nineteen poor fellows that the Cumberland's guns had mowed down, we now had other killed and wounded. Commodore Buchanan was badly hurt, and the flag lieutenant, Minor. The hundred guns thundered against the Merrimac, and the Merrimac thundered against the Congress. The tall frigate and her fifty guns wished herself an iron-clad; the swan would have blithely changed with the ugly duckling. We brought down her main-mast, we disabled her guns, we strewed her decks with blood and anguish (war is a wild beast, nothing more, and I'll hail the day when it lies slain). We smashed in her sides and we set her afire. She hauled down her colors and ran up a white flag. The Merrimac ceased firing and signaled to the Beaufort. The Beaufort ran alongside, and the frigate's ranking officer gave up his colors and his sword. The Beaufort's and the Congress's own boats removed the crew and the wounded. . . . The shore batteries, the Minnesota, the picket boat Zouave, kept up a heavy firing all the while upon the Merrimac, upon the Raleigh and the Jamestown, and also upon the Beaufort. We waited until the crew was clear of the Congress, and then we gave her a round of hot shot that presently set her afire from stem to stern. This done, we turned to other work.

"The Minnesota lay aground in the North Channel. To her aid hurrying up from Old Point came the Roanoke and the Saint Lawrence. Our own batteries at Sewell's Point opened upon these two ships as they passed, and they answered with broadsides. We fed our engines, and under a billow of black smoke ran down to the Minnesota. Like the Congress, she lay upon a sand bar, beyond fear of ramming. We could only maneuver for deep water, near enough to her to be deadly. It was now late afternoon. I could see through the port of the bow pivot the slant sunlight upon the water, and how the blue of the sky was paling. The Minnesota lay just ahead; very tall she looked, another of the Congress breed; the old warships singing their death song. As we came on we fired the bow gun, then, lying nearer her, began with broadsides. But we could not get near enough; she was lifted high upon the sand, the tide was going out, and we drew twenty-three feet. We did her great harm, but we were not disabling her. An hour passed and the sun drew on to setting. The Roanoke turned and went back under the guns of Old Point, but the Saint Lawrence remained to thunder at the turtle's iron shell. The Merrimac was most unhandy, and on the ebb tide there would be shoals enough between us and a berth for the night. . . . The Minnesota could not get away, at dawn she would be yet aground, and we would then take her for our prize. 'Stay till dusk, and the blessed old iron box will ground herself where Noah's flood won't float her!' The pilot ruled, and in the gold and purple sunset we drew off. As we passed, the Minnesota blazed with all her guns; we answered her, and answered, too, the Saint Lawrence. The evening star was shining when we anchored off Sewell's Point. The wounded were taken ashore, for we had no place for wounded men under the turtle's shell. Commodore Buchanan leaving us, Lieutenant Catesby ap Roger Jones took command.

"I do not remember what we had for supper. We had not eaten since early morning, so we must have had something. But we were too tired to think or to reason or to remember. We dropped beside our guns and slept, but not for long. Three hours, perhaps, we slept, and then a whisper seemed to run through the Merrimac. It was as though the iron-clad herself had spoken, 'Come! watch the Congress die!' Most of us arose from beside the guns and mounted to the iron grating above, to the top of the turtle's shell. It was a night as soft as silk; the water smooth, in long, faint, olive swells; a half-moon in the sky. There were lights across at Old Point, lights on the battery at the Rip Raps, lights in the frightened shipping, huddled under the guns of Fortress Monroe, lights along either shore. There were lanterns in the rigging of the Minnesota where she lay upon the sand bar, and lanterns on the Saint Lawrence and the Roanoke. As we looked a small moving light, as low as possible to the water, appeared between the Saint Lawrence and the Minnesota. A man said, 'What's that? Must be a rowboat.' Another answered, 'It's going too fast for a rowboat—funny! right on the water like that!' 'A launch, I reckon,' said a third, 'with plenty of rowers. Now it's behind the Minnesota.'— 'Shut up, you talkers,' said a midshipman, 'I want to look at the Congress!'

"Four miles away, off Newport News, lay the burning Congress. In the still, clear night, she seemed almost at hand. All her masts, her spars, and her rigging showed black in the heart of a great ring of firelight. Her hull, lifted high by the sand bank which held her, had round red eyes. Her ports were windows lit from within. She made a vision of beauty and of horror. One by one, as they were reached by the flame, her guns exploded—a loud and awful sound in the night above the Roads. We stood and watched that sea picture, and we watched in silence. We are seeing giant things, and ere this war is ended we shall see more. At two o'clock in the morning the fire reached her powder magazine. She blew up. A column like the Israelite's Pillar shot to the zenith; there came an earthquake sound, sullen and deep; when all cleared there was only her hull upborne by the sand and still burning. It burned until the dawn, when it smoldered and went out."

The narrator arose, walked the length of the parlor, and came back to the four women. "Haven't you had enough for tonight? Unity looks sleepy, and Judith's knitting has lain this half-hour on the floor. Judith!"

Molly spoke. "Judith says that if there is fighting around Richmond she is going there to the hospitals, to be a nurse. The doctors here say that she does better than anyone——"

"Go on, Edward," said Judith. "What happened at dawn?"

"We got the turtle in order, and those ancient mariners, our engines, began to work, wheezing and slow. We ran up a new flagstaff, and every man stood to the guns, and the Merrimac moved from Sewell's Point, her head turned to the Minnesota, away across, grounded on a sand bank in the North Channel. The sky was as pink as the inside of a shell, and a thin white mist hung over the marshes and the shore and the great stretch of Hampton Roads. It was so thin that the masts of the ships huddled below Fortress Monroe rose clear of it into the flush of the coming sun. All their pennants were flying—the French man-of-war, and the northern ships. At that hour the sea-gulls are abroad, searching for their food. They went past the ports, screaming and moving their silver wings.

"The Minnesota grew in size. Every man of us looked eagerly—from the pilot-house, from the bow ports, and as we drew parallel with her from the ports of the side. We fired the bow gun as we came on and the shot told. There was some cheering; the morning air was so fine and the prize so sure! The turtle was in spirits—poor old turtle with her battered shell and her flag put back as fast as it was torn away! Her engines, this morning, were mortal slow and weak; they wheezed and whined, and she drew so deep that, in that shoaly water, she went aground twice between Sewell's Point and the stretch she had now reached of smooth pink water, with the sea-gulls dipping between her and the Minnesota. Despite the engines she was happy, and the gunners were all ready at the starboard ports——"

Leaning over, he took the poker and stirred the fire.

> "The best-laid schemes o' mice and men
> Gang aft agley—"

Miss Lucy's needles clicked. "Yes, the papers told us. The Ericsson."

"There came," said Edward, "there came from behind the Minnesota a cheese-box on a shingle. It had lain there hidden by her bulk since midnight. It was its single light that we had watched and thought no more of! A cheese-box on a shingle—and now it darted into the open as though a boy's arm had sent it! It was little beside the Minnesota. It was little even beside the turtle. There was a silence when we saw it, a silence of astonishment. It had come so quietly upon the scene—a *deus ex machina*, indeed, dropped from the clouds between us and our prey. In a moment we knew it for the Ericsson— the looked-for other iron-clad we knew to be a-building. The Monitor, they call it. . . . The shingle was just awash; the cheese-box turned out to be a revolving turret, mail-clad and carrying two large, modern guns—11-inch. The whole thing was armored, had the best of engines, and drew only twelve feet. . . . Well, the Merrimac had a startled breath, to be sure—there is no denying the drama of the Monitor's appearance—and then she righted and began firing. She gave to the cheese-box, or to the armored turret, one after the other, three broadsides. The turret blazed and answered, and the balls rebounded from each armored champion." He laughed. "By Heaven! it was like our old favorites, Ivanhoe and De Bois Guilbert—the ugliest squat gnomes of an Ivanhoe and of a Brian de Bois Guilbert that ever came out of a nightmare! We thundered in the lists, and then we passed each other, turned, and again encountered. Sometimes we were a long way apart, and sometimes there was not ten feet of water between those sunken decks from which arose the iron shell of the Merrimac and the iron turret of the Monitor. She fired every seven minutes; we as rapidly as we could load. Now it was the bow gun, now the after pivot, now a full broadside. Once or twice we thought her done for, but always her turret revolved, and her 11-inch guns opened again. In her lighter draught she had a great advantage; she could turn and wind where we could not. The Minnesota took a hand, and an iron battery

The shots struck above the ports of the after guns.

from the shore. We were striving to ram the Ericsson, but we could not get close to her; our iron beak, too, was sticking in the side of the sunken Cumberland—we could only ram with the blunt prow. The Minnesota, as we passed, gave us all her broadside guns—a tremendous fusillade at point-blank range, which would have sunk any ship of the swan breed. The turtle shook off shot and shell, grape and canister, and answered with her bow gun. The shell which it threw entered the side of the frigate, and, bursting amidship, exploded a store of powder and set the ship on fire. Leaving disaster aboard the Minnesota, we turned and sunk the tugboat Dragon. Then come maneuver and maneuver to gain position where we could ram the Monitor. . . .

"We got it at last. The engines made an effort like the leap of the spirit before expiring. 'Go ahead! Full speed!' We went; we bore down upon the Monitor, now in deeper water. But at the moment that we saw victory she turned. Our bow, lacking the iron beak, gave but a glancing stroke. It was heavy as it was; the Monitor shook like a man with the ague, but she did not share the fate of the Cumberland. There was no ragged hole in her side; her armor was good, and held. She backed, gathered herself together, then rushed forward, striving to ram us in her turn. But our armor, too, was good, and held. Then she came upon the Merrimac's quarter, laid her bow against the shell, and fired her 11-inch guns twice in succession. We were so close, each to the other, that it was as though two duelists were standing upon the same cloak. Frightful enough was the concussion of those guns.

"That charge drove in the Merrimac's iron side three inches or more. The shots struck above the ports of the after guns, and every man at those guns was knocked down by the impact and bled at the nose and ears. The Monitor dropped astern, and again we turned and tried to ram her. But her far lighter draught put her where we could not go; our bow, too, was now twisted and splintered. Our powder was getting low. We did not spare it, we could not; we sent shot and shell continuously against the Monitor, and she answered in kind. Monitor and Merrimac, we went now this way, now that, the Ericsson much the lighter and quicker, the Merrimac fettered by her poor old engines, and her great length, and her twenty-three feet draught. It was two o'clock in the afternoon. . . . The duelists stepped from off the cloak, tried operations at a distance, hung for a moment in the wind of indecision, then put down the match from the gunners' hands. The Monitor darted from us, her head toward the shoal water known as the Middle Ground. She reached it and rested triumphant, out of all danger from our ram, and yet where she could still protect the Minnesota. . . . A curious silence fell upon the Roads; sullen like the hush before a thunderstorm, and yet not like that, for we had had the thunderstorm. It was the stillness, perhaps, of exhaustion. It was late afternoon, the fighting had been heavy. The air was filled with smoke; in the water were floating spars and wreckage of the ships we had destroyed. The weather was sultry and still. The dogged booming of a gun from a shore battery sounded lonely and remote as a bell buoy. The tide was falling; there were sand-bars enough between us and Sewell's Point. We waited an hour. The Monitor was rightly content with the Middle Ground, and would not come back for all our charming. We fired at intervals, upon her and upon the Minnesota, but at last our powder grew so low that we ceased. The tide continued to fall, and the pilot had much to say. . . . The red sun sank in the west; the engineers fed the ancient mariners with Montgomery coal; black smoke gushed forth and pilots felt their way into the South Channel, and slowly, slowly back toward Sewell's Point. The day closed in a murky evening with a taste of smoke in the air. In the night-time the Monitor went down the Roads to Fortress Monroe, and in the morning we took the Merrimac into dry dock at Norfolk. Her armor was dented all over, though not pierced. Her bow was bent and twisted, the iron beak lost in the side of the Cumberland. Her boats were gone, and her smokestack as full of holes as any colander, and the engines at the last gasp. Several of the guns were injured, and coal and powder and ammunition all lacked. We put her there—the dear and ugly warship, the first of the iron-clads—we put her there in dry dock, and there she's apt to stay for some weeks to come. Lieutenant Wood was sent to Richmond with the report for the president and the secretary of the navy. He carried, too, the flag of the Congress, and I was one of the men detailed for its charge. . . . And now I have told you of the Merrimac and the Monitor."

Rising, he went to the piano, sat down and played "Malbrook s'en va-t-en guerre." Miss Lucy took up her knitting, and knitted very rapidly, her eyes now upon her nephew, now upon her father's portrait. Judith, rising from the old cross-stitch tabouret where she had been sitting, laid a fresh log on the fire, then went and stood beside the long window, looking out upon the rainy night.

"What," asked Edward between two chords, "what do you hear from the Valley?"

Unity answered: "General Banks has crossed the Potomac and entered Winchester—poor, poor Winchester! General Jackson hasn't quite five thousand men. He has withdrawn toward Woodstock. In spite of that dreadful Romney march, General Johnston and the soldiers seem to have confidence in him——"

Molly came in with her soft little voice. "Major Stafford has been transferred. He is with General Ewell on the Rappahannock. He writes to Judith every week. They are beautiful letters—they make you see everything that is done."

"What do you hear from Richard Cleave?"

"He never writes."

Judith came back from the window. "It is raining, raining! The petals are falling from the pyrus japonica, and all the trees are bending! Edward, war is terrible, but it lifts you up. . . ." She locked her hands behind her head. "It lifts you up, out in the storm or listening to what the ships have done, or to the stories that are told! And then you look at the unploughed land, and you wait for the bulletins, and you go to the hospital down there, . . . and you say, 'Never—oh, nevermore let us have war!'"

HOW AMYAS THREW HIS SWORD INTO THE SEA

Charles Kingsley

YES, IT is over; and the great Armada is vanquished. It is lulled for a while, the everlasting war which is in heaven, the battle of Iran and Turan, of the children of light and of darkness, of Michael and his angels against Satan and his fiends; the battle which slowly and seldom, once in the course of many centuries, culminates and ripens into a day of judgment, and becomes palpable and incarnate; no longer a mere spiritual fight, but one of flesh and blood, wherein simple men may choose their sides without mistake, and help God's cause not merely with prayer and pen, but with sharp shot and cold steel. A day of judgment has come, which has divided the light from the darkness, and the sheep from the goats, and tried each man's work by the fire; and, behold, the devil's work, like its maker, is proved to have been, as always, a lie and a sham, and a windy boast, a bladder which collapses at the merest pin-prick. Byzantine empires, Spanish Armadas, triple-crowned Papacies, Russian Despotisms, this is the way of them, and will be to the end of the world. One brave blow at the big bullying phantom, and it vanishes in sulphur stench; while the children of Israel, as of old, see the Egyptians dead on the seashore,— they scarce know how, save that God has done it,—and sing the song of Moses and of the Lamb.

And now, from England and the Netherlands, from Germany and Geneva, and those poor Vaudois shepherd-saints, whose bones for generations past

"Lie scattered on the Alpine mountains cold;"

from "Westward Ho!" by Charles Kingsley

to be, indeed, the seed of the Church, and a germ of new life, liberty, and civilization, even in these very days returning good for evil to that Piedmont which has hunted them down like the partridges on the mountains;—from all of Europe, from all of mankind, I had almost said, in which lay the seed of future virtue and greatness, of the destinies of the new-discovered world, and the triumphs of the coming age of science, arose a shout of holy joy, such as the world had not heard for many a weary and bloody century; a shout which was the prophetic birth-pæan of North America, Australia, New Zealand, the Pacific Islands, of free commerce and free colonization over the whole earth.

"There was in England, by the commandment of her Majesty," say Van Meteran, "and likewise in the United Provinces, by the direction of the States, a solemn festival day publicly appointed, wherein all persons were solemnly enjoined to resort unto yᵉ Church, and there to render thanks and praises unto God, and yᵉ preachers were commanded to exhort yᵉ people thereunto. The aforesaid solemnity was observed upon the 29th of November: which day was wholly spent in fasting, prayer, and giving of thanks.

"Likewise the Queen's Majesty herself, imitating yᵉ ancient Romans, rode into London in triumph, in regard of her own and her subjects' glorious deliverance. For being attended upon very solemnly by all yᵉ principal Estates and officers of her Realm, she was carried through her said City of London in a triumphant Chariot, and in robes of triumph, from her Palace unto yᵉ said Cathedral Church of St. Paul, out of yᵉ which yᵉ Ensigns and Colors of yᵉ vanquished Spanish hung displayed. And all yᵉ Citizens of London, in their liveries, stood on either side yᵉ street, by their several Companies, with their ensigns and banners, and the streets were hanged on both sides with blue Cloth, which, together with yᵉ aforesaid banners, yielded a very stately and gallant prospect. Her Majestie being entered into yᵉ Church together with her Clergy and nobles, gave thanks unto God, and caused a public Sermon to be preached before her at Paul's Cross; wherein none other argument was handled, but that praise, honor, and glory might be rendered unto God, and that God's Name might be extolled by thanksgiving. And with her own princely voice she most Christianly exhorted yᵉ people to do yᵉ same; whereunto yᵉ people, with a loud acclamation, wished her a most long and happy life to yᵉ confusion of her foes."

Yes, as the medals struck on the occasion said, "It came, it saw, and it fled!"

And whither?   Away and northward, like a herd of frightened deer, past the Orkneys and Shetlands, catching up a few hapless fishermen as guides, past the coast of Norway, there, too, refused water and food by the brave descendants of the Vikings; and on northward ever towards the lonely Faroes, and the everlasting dawn which heralds round the Pole the midnight sun.

Their water is failing; the cattle must go overboard; and the wild northern sea echoes to the shrieks of drowning horses.   They must homeward at least, somehow, each as best he can.   Let them meet again at Cape Finisterre, if indeed they ever meet.   Medina Sidonia, with some five-and-twenty of the soundest and best victualed ships, will lead the way, and leave the rest to their fate.   He is soon out of sight; and forty more, the only remnant of that mighty host, come wandering wearily behind, hoping to make the south-west coast of Ireland, and have help, or, at least, fresh water there, from their fellow Romanists.   Alas for them!——

> "Make Thou their way dark and slippery,
> And follow them up ever with Thy storm."

For now comes up from the Atlantic, gale on gale; and few of that hapless remnant reached the shores of Spain.

And where are Amyas and the Vengeance all this while?

At the fifty-seventh degree of latitude, the English fleet, finding themselves growing short of provision, and having been long since out of powder and ball, turn southward toward home, "thinking it best to leave the Spaniard to those uncouth and boisterous northern seas."   A few pinnaces are still sent onward to watch their course; and the English fleet, caught in the same storms which scattered the Spaniards, "with great danger and industry reached Harwich port, and there provide themselves of victuals and ammunition," in case the Spaniard should return; but there is no need for that caution.   Parma, indeed, who cannot believe that the idle at Halle, after all his compliments to it, will play him so scurvy a trick, will watch for weeks on Dunkirk dunes, hoping against hope for the Armada's return, casting anchors, and spinning rigging to repair their losses.

> "But lang lang may his ladies sit,
> With their fans intill their hand,
> Before they see Sir Patrick Spens
> Come sailing to the land."

The Armada is away on the other side of Scotland, and Amyas is following in its wake.

For when the Lord High Admiral determined to return, Amyas asked leave to follow the Spaniard; and asked, too, of Sir John Hawkins, who happened to be at hand, such ammunition and provision as could be afforded him, promising to repay the same like an honest man, out of his plunder if he lived, out of his estate if he died; lodging for that purpose bills in the hands of Sir John, who, as a man of business, took them, and put them in his pocket among the thimbles, string, and tobacco; after which Amyas, calling his men together, reminded them once more of the story of the Rose of Torridge and Don Guzman de Soto, and then asked——

"Men of Bideford, will you follow me? There will be plunder for those who love plunder; revenge for those who love revenge; and for all of us (for we all love honor) the honor of having never left the chase as long as there was a Spanish flag in English seas."

And every soul on board replied, that they would follow Sir Amyas Leigh around the world.

There is no need for me to detail every incident of that long and weary chase; how they found the *Sta. Catharina*, attacked her, and had to sheer off, she being rescued by the rest; how when Medina's squadron left the crippled ships behind, they were all but taken or sunk, by thrusting into the midst of the Spanish fleet to prevent her escaping with Medina; how they crippled her, so that she could not beat to windward out into the ocean, but was fain to run south, past the Orkneys, and down through the Minch, between Cape Wrath and Lewis; how the younger hands were ready to mutiny, because Amyas, in his stubborn haste, ran past two or three noble prizes which were all but disabled, among others one of the great galliasses, and the two great Venetians, *La Ratta* and *La Belanzara*—which were afterwards, with more than thirty other vessels, wrecked on the west coast of Ireland; how he got fresh water, in spite of certain "Hebridean Scots" of Skye, who, after reviling him in an unknown tongue, fought with him a while, and then embraced him and his men with howls of affection, and were not much more decently clad, nor more civilized, than his old friends of California; how he pacified his men by letting them pick the bones of a great Venetian which was going on shore upon Islay, (by which they got booty enough to repay them for the whole voyage,) and offended them again by refusing to land and plunder two great

Spanish wrecks on the Mull of Cantire (whose crews, by-the-bye, James tried
to smuggle off secretly into Spain in ships of his own, wishing to play, as
usual, both sides of the game at once; but the Spaniards were stopped at Yar-
mouth till the council's pleasure was known—which was, of course, to let
the poor wretches go on their way, and be hanged elsewhere); how they passed
a strange island, half black, half white, which the wild people called Raghery,
but Cary christened it "the drowned magpie;" how the *Sta. Catharina* was
near lost on the Isle of Man, and then put into Castleton (where the Manx-
men slew a whole boat's-crew with their arrows), and then put out again,
when Amyas fought with her a whole day, and shot away her mainyard; how
the Spaniard blundered down the coast of Wales, not knowing whither he
went; how they were both nearly lost on Holyhead, and again on Bardsey
Island; how they got on a lee shore in Cardigan Bay, before a heavy westerly
gale, and the *Sta. Catharina* ran aground on Sarn David, one of those strange
subaqueous pebble-dykes which are said to be the remnants of the lost land of
Gwalior, destroyed by the carelessness of Prince Seithenin the drunkard, at
whose name each loyal Welshman spits; how she got off again at the rising of
the tide, and fought with Amyas a fourth time; how the wind changed, and
she got round St. David's Head;—these, and many more moving accidents of
this eventful voyage, I must pass over without details, and go on to the end;
for it is time that the end should come.

It was now the sixteenth day of the chase. They had seen, the evening before, St. David's Head, and then the Welsh coast round Milford Haven, loom-
ing out black and sharp before the blaze of the inland thunderstorm; and it
had lightened all round them during the fore part of the night, upon a light
south-western breeze.

In vain they had strained their eyes through the darkness, to catch, by the
fitful glare of the flashes, the tall masts of the Spaniard. Of one thing at least
they were certain, that with the wind as it was, she could not have gone far to
the westward; and to attempt to pass them again, and go northward, was more
than she dare do. She was probably lying-to ahead of them, perhaps between
them and the land; and when, a little after midnight, the wind chopped up to
the west, and blew stiffly till daybreak, they felt sure that, unless she had attempted the desperate expedient of running past them, they had her safe in the
mouth of the Bristol Channel. Slowly and wearily broke the dawn, on such
a day as often follows heavy thunder; a sunless, drizzly day, roofed with low

dingy cloud, barred, and netted, and festooned with black, a sign that the storm is only taking breath a while before it bursts again; while all the narrow horizon is dim and spongy with vapor drifting before a chilly breeze. As the day went on, the breeze died down, and the sea fell to a long glassy foam-flecked roll, while overhead brooded the inky sky, and round them the leaden mist shut out alike the shore and the chase.

Amyas paced the sloppy deck fretfully and fiercely. He knew that the Spaniard could not escape; but he cursed every moment which lingered between him and that one great revenge which blackened all his soul. The men sat sulkily about the deck, and whistled for a wind; the sails flapped idly against the masts; and the ship rolled in the long troughs of the sea, till her yard-arm almost dipped right and left.

"Take care of those guns. You will have something loose next," growled Amyas.

"We will take care of the guns, if the Lord will take care of the wind," said Yeo.

"We shall have plenty before night," said Cary, "and thunder too."

"So much the better," said Amyas. "It may roar till it splits the heavens, if it does but let me get my work done."

"He's not far off, I warrant," said Cary. "One lift of the cloud, and we should see him."

"To windward of us, as likely as not," said Amyas. "The devil fights for him, I believe. To have been on his heels sixteen days, and not sent this through him yet!" And he shook his sword impatiently.

So the morning wore away, without a sign of a living thing, not even a passing gull; and the black melancholy of the heaven reflected itself in the black melancholy of Amyas. Was he to lose his prey after all? The thought made him shudder with rage and disappointment. It was intolerable. Anything but that.

"No, God!" he cried, "let me but once feel this in his accursed heart, and then—strike me dead, if Thou wilt!"

"The Lord have mercy on us," cried John Brimblecombe. "What have you said?"

"What is that to you, sir? There, they are piping to dinner. Go down. I shall not come."

And Jack went down, and talked in a half-terrified whisper of Amyas's ominous words.

All thought that they portended some bad luck, except old Yeo.

"Well, Sir John," said he, "and why not? What better can the Lord do for a man, than take him home when he has done his work? Our captain is wilful and spiteful, and must needs kill his man himself; while for me, I don't care how the Don goes, provided he does go. I owe him no grudge, nor any man. May the Lord give him repentance, and forgive him all his sins; but if I could but see him once safe ashore, as he may be ere nightfall, on the Morestone or the back of Lundy, I would say, 'Lord, now lettest Thou Thy servant depart in peace,' even if it were the lightning which was sent to fetch me."

"But, Master Yeo, a sudden death?"

"And why not a sudden death, Sir John? Even fools long for a short life and a merry one, and shall not the Lord's people pray for a short death and a merry one? Let it come as it will to old Yeo. Hark! there's the captain's voice!"

"Here she is!" thundered Amyas from the deck; and in an instant all were scrambling up the hatchway as fast as the frantic rolling of the ship would let them.

Yes. There she was. The cloud had lifted suddenly, and to the south a ragged bore of blue sky let a long stream of sunshine down on her tall masts and stately hull, as she lay rolling some four or five miles to the eastward; but as for land, none was to be seen.

"There she is; and here we are," said Cary; "but where is here? and where is there? How is the tide, master?"

"Running up Channel by this time, sir."

"What matters the tide?" said Amyas, devouring the ship with terrible and cold blue eyes. "Can't we get at her?"

"Not unless some one jumps out and shoves behind," said Cary. "I shall down again and finish that mackerel, if this roll has not chucked it to the cockroaches under the table."

"Don't jest, Will! I can't stand it," said Amyas, in a voice which quivered so much that Cary looked at him. His whole frame was trembling like an aspen. Cary took his arm, and drew him aside.

"Dear old lad," said he as they leaned over the bulwarks, "what is this? You are not yourself, and have not been these four days."

"No. I am not Amyas Leigh- I am my brother's avenger. Do not reason with me, Will: when it is over, I shall be merry old Amyas again," and he passed his hand over his brow.

"Do you believe," said he, after a moment, "that men can be possessed by devils?"

"The Bible says so."

"If my cause were not a just one, I should fancy I had a devil in me. My throat and heart are as hot as the pit. Would to God it were done, for done it must be! Now go."

Cary went away with a shudder. As he passed down the hatchway he looked back. Amyas had got the hone out of his pocket, and was whetting away again at his sword-edge, as if there was some dreadful doom on him, to whet, and whet for ever.

The weary day wore on. The strip of blue sky was curtained over again, and all was dismal as before, though it grew sultrier every moment; and now and then a distant mutter shook the air to westward. Nothing could be done to lessen the distance between the ships, for the *Vengeance* had had all her boats carried away but one, and that was much too small to tow her; and while the men went down again to finish dinner, Amyas worked on at his sword, looking up every now and then suddenly at the Spaniard, as if to satisfy himself that it was not a vision which had vanished.

About two Yeo came up to him.

"He is ours safely now, sir. The tide has been running to the eastward for this two hours."

"Safe as a fox in a trap. Satan himself cannot take him from us!"

"But God may," said Brimblecombe simply.

"Who spoke to you, sir? If I thought that He—There comes the thunder at last!"

And as he spoke, an angry growl from the westward heavens seemed to answer his wild words, and rolled and loudened nearer and nearer, till right over their heads it crashed against some cloud-cliff far above, and all was still.

Each man looked in the other's face: but Amyas was unmoved.

"The storm is coming," said he, "and the wind in it. It will be Eastward-ho now, for once, my merry men all!"

"Eastward-ho never brought us luck," said Jack in an undertone to Cary. But by this time all eyes were turned to the north-west, where a black line along the horizon began to define the boundary of sea and air, till now all dim in mist.

"There comes the breeze."

"And there the storm, too."

And with that strangely accelerating pace which some storms seem to possess, the thunder, which had been growling slow and seldom far away, now rang peal on peal along the cloudy floor above their heads.

"Here comes the breeze. Round with the yards, or we shall be taken aback."

The yards creaked round; the sea grew crisp around them; the hot air swept their cheeks, tightened every rope, filled every sail, bent her over. A cheer burst from the men as the helm went up, and they staggered away before the wind, right down upon the Spaniard, who lay still becalmed.

"There is more behind, Amyas," said Cary. "Shall we not shorten sail a little?"

"No. Hold on every stitch," said Amyas. "Give me the helm, man. Boatswain, pipe away to clear for fight."

It was done, and in ten minutes the men were all at quarters, while the thunder rolled louder and louder overhead, and the breeze freshened fast.

"The dog has it now. There he goes!" said Cary.

"Right before the wind. He has no liking to face us."

"He is running into the jaws of destruction," said Yeo. "An hour more will send him either right up the Channel, or smack on shore somewhere."

"There! he has put his helm down. I wonder if he sees land?"

"He is like a March hare beat out of his country," said Cary, "and don't know whither to run next."

Cary was right. In ten minutes more the Spaniard fell off again, and went away dead down wind, while the *Vengeance* gained on him fast. After two hours more, the four miles had diminished to one, while the lightning flashed nearer and nearer as the storm came up; and from the vast mouth of a black cloud-arch poured so fierce a breeze that Amyas yielded unwillingly to hints which were growing into open murmurs, and bade shorten sail.

On they rushed with scarcely lessened speed, the black arch following fast, curtained by one flat grey sheet of pouring rain, before which the water was boiling in a long white line; while every moment, behind the watery veil, a keen blue spark leapt down into the sea, or darted zigzag through the rain.

"We shall have it now, and with a vengeance; this will try your tackle, Master," said Cary.

The functionary answered with a shrug, and turned up the collar of his rough frock, as the first drops flew stinging round his ears. Another minute, and the squall burst full upon them in rain, which cut like hail,—hail which lashed the sea into froth, and wind which whirled off the heads of the surges, and swept the waters into one white seething waste. And above them, and behind them, and before them, the lightning leapt and ran, dazzling and blinding, while the deep roar of the thunder was changed to sharp ear-piercing cracks.

"Get the arms and ammunition under cover, and then below with you all," shouted Amyas from the helm.

"And heat the pokers in the galley fire," said Yeo, "to be ready if the rain puts our linstocks out. I hope you'll let me stay on deck, sir, in case——"

"I must have some one, and who better than you? Can you see the chase?"

No; she was wrapped in the grey whirlwind. She might be within half-a-mile of them for aught they could have seen of her.

And now Amyas and his old liegeman were alone. Neither spoke; each knew the other's thoughts, and knew that they were his own. The squall blew fiercer and fiercer, the rain poured heavier and heavier. Where was the Spaniard?

"If he has laid-to, we may overshoot him, sir!"

"If he has tried to lay-to, he will not have a sail left in the bolt-ropes, or perhaps a mast on deck. I know the stiffneckedness of those Spanish tubs. Hurrah! there he is, right on our larboard bow!"

There she was indeed, two musket-shots off, staggering away with canvas split and flying.

"He has been trying to hull, sir, and caught a buffet," said Yeo, rubbing his hands. "What shall we do now?"

"Range alongside, if it blow live imps and witches, and try our luck once more. Pah! how this lightning dazzles!"

On they swept, gaining fast on the Spaniard.

"Call the men up, and to quarters; the rain will be over in ten minutes," said Amyas.

"Shame!" cried Amyas, hurling his sword far into the sea.

Yeo ran forward to the gangway; and sprang back again, with a face white and wild——

"Land right ahead! Port your helm, sir! For the love of God, port your helm!"

Amyas, with the strength of a bull, jammed the helm down, while Yeo shouted to the men below.

She swung round. The masts bent like whips; crack went the foresail like a cannon. What matter? Within two hundred yards of them was the Spaniard; in front of her, and above her, a huge dark bank rose through the dense hail, and mingled with the clouds; and at its foot, plainer every moment, pillars and spouts of leaping foam.

"What is it, Morte? Hartland?"

It might be anything for thirty miles.

"Lundy!" said Yeo. "The south end! I see the head of the Shutter in the breakers! Hard a-port yet, and get her close-hauled as you can, and the Lord may have mercy on us still! Look at the Spaniard!"

Yes, look at the Spaniard!

On their left hand, as they broached-to, the wall of granite sloped down from the clouds toward an isolated peak of rock, some two hundred feet in height. Then a hundred yards of roaring breaker upon a sunken shelf, across which the race of the tide poured like a cataract; then, amid a column of salt smoke, the Shutter, like a huge black fang, rose waiting for its prey; and between the Shutter and the land, the great galleon loomed dimly through the storm.

He, too, had seen his danger, and tried to broach-to. But his clumsy mass refused to obey the helm; he struggled a moment, half hid in foam; fell away again, and rushed upon his doom.

"Lost! lost! lost!" cried Amyas madly, and throwing up his hands, let go the tiller. Yeo caught it just in time.

"Sir! sir! What are you at? We shall clear the rock yet."

"Yes!" shouted Amyas in his frenzy; "but he will not!"

Another minute. The galleon gave a sudden jar, and stopped. Then one long heave and bound, as, if to free herself. And then her bows lighted clean upon the Shutter.

An awful silence fell on every English soul. They heard not the roaring of wind and surge: they saw not the blinding flashes of lightning; but they heard one long ear-piercing wail to every saint in heaven rise from five hundred human throats; they saw the mighty ship heel over from the wind, and sweep headlong down the cataract of the race, plunging her yards into the foam, and showing her whole black side even to her keel, till she rolled clean over, and vanished for ever and ever.

"Shame!" cried Amyas, hurling his sword far into the sea, "to lose my right, my right! when it was in my very grasp!   Unmerciful!"

A crack which rent the sky, and made the granite ring and quiver; a bright world of flame, and then a blank of utter darkness, against which stood out, glowing red-hot, every mast, and sail, and rock, and Salvation Yeo as he stood just in front of Amyas, the tiller in his hand.   All red-hot, transfigured into fire; and behind, the black, black night.

FOG

Jack London

I SCARCELY KNOW where to begin, though I sometimes facetiously place the cause of it all to Charley Furuseth's credit. He kept a summer cottage in Mill Valley, under the shadow of Mount Tamalpais, and never occupied it except when he loafed through the winter months and read Nietzsche and Schopenhauer to rest his brain. When summer came on, he elected to sweat out a hot and dusty existence in the city and to toil incessantly. Had it not been my custom to run up to see him every Saturday afternoon and to stop over till Monday morning, this particular January Monday morning would not have found me afloat on San Francisco Bay.

Not but that I was afloat in a safe craft, for the *Martinez* was a new ferry-steamer, making her fourth or fifth trip on the run between Sausalito and San Francisco. The danger lay in the heavy fog which blanketed the bay, and of which, as a landsman, I had little apprehension. In fact, I remember the placid exaltation with which I took up my position on the forward upper deck, directly beneath the pilot-house, and allowed the mystery of the fog to lay hold of my imagination. A fresh breeze was blowing, and for a time I was alone in the moist obscurity—yet not alone, for I was dimly conscious of the presence of the pilot, and of what I took to be the captain, in the glass house above my head.

I remember thinking how comfortable it was, this division of labor which made it unnecessary for me to study fogs, winds, tides, and navigation, in order to visit my friend who lived across the arm of the sea. It was good

from "The Sea-Wolf" by Jack London. Published by the Macmillan Company. By permission of Charmian London.

that men should be specialists, I mused. The peculiar knowledge of the pilot and captain sufficed for many thousands of people who knew no more of the sea and navigation than I knew. On the other hand, instead of having to devote my energy to the learning of a multitude of things, I concentrated it upon a few particular things, such as, for instance, the analysis of Poe's place in American literature—an essay of mine, by the way, in the current *Atlantic*. Coming aboard, as I passed through the cabin, I had noticed with greedy eyes a stout gentleman reading the *Atlantic*, which was open at my very essay. And there it was again, the division of labor, the special knowledge of the pilot and captain which permitted the stout gentleman to read my special knowledge on Poe while they carried him safely from Sausalito to San Francisco.

A red-faced man, slamming the cabin door behind him and stumping out on the deck, interrupted my reflections, though I made a mental note of the topic for use in a projected essay which I had thought of calling "The Necessity for Freedom: A Plea for the Artist." The red-faced man shot a glance up at the pilot-house, gazed around at the fog, stumped across the deck and back (he evidently had artificial legs), and stood still by my side, legs wide apart, and with an expression of keen enjoyment on his face. I was not wrong when I decided that his days had been spent on the sea.

"It's nasty weather like this here that turns heads gray before their time," he said, with a nod toward the pilot-house.

"I had not thought there was any particular strain," I answered. "It seems as simple as A, B, C. They know the direction by compass, the distance, and the speed. I should not call it anything more than mathematical certainty."

"Strain!" he snorted. "Simple as A, B, C! Mathematical certainty!"

He seemed to brace himself up and lean backward against the air as he stared at me. "How about this here tide that's rushin' out through the Golden Gate?" he demanded, or bellowed, rather. "How fast is she ebbin'? What's the drift, eh? Listen to that, will you? A bell-buoy, and we're a-top of it! See 'em alterin' the course!"

From out of the fog came the mournful tolling of a bell, and I could see the pilot turning the wheel with great rapidity. The bell, which had seemed straight ahead, was now sounding from the side. Our own whistle was blowing hoarsely, and from time to time the sound of other whistles came to us from out of the fog.

"That's a ferry-boat of some sort," the newcomer said, indicating a whistle off to the right. "And there! D'ye hear that? Blown by mouth. Some scow schooner, most likely. Better watch out, Mr. Schooner-man. Ah, I thought so. Now hell's a-poppin' for somebody!"

The unseen ferry-boat was blowing blast after blast, and the mouth-blown horn was tooting in terror-stricken fashion.

"And now they're payin' their respects to each other and tryin' to get clear," the red-faced man went on, as the hurried whistling ceased.

His face was shining, his eyes flashing with excitement, as he translated into articulate language the speech of the horns and sirens. "That's a steam siren a-goin' it over there to the left. And you hear that fellow with a frog in his throat—a steam schooner as near as I can judge, crawlin' in from the Heads against the tide."

A shrill little whistle, piping as if gone mad, came from directly ahead and from very near at hand. Gongs sounded on the *Martinez*. Our paddle-wheels stopped, their pulsing beat died away, and then they started again. The shrill little whistle, like the chirping of a cricket amid the cries of great beasts, shot through the fog from more to the side and swiftly grew faint and fainter. I looked to my companion for enlightenment.

"One of them dare-devil launches," he said. "I almost wish we'd sunk him, the little rip! They're the cause of more trouble. And what good are they? Any jackass gets aboard one and runs it from hell to breakfast, blowin' his whistle to beat the band and tellin' the rest of the world to look out for him, because he's comin' and can't look out for himself! Because he's comin'! And you've got to look out, too! Right of way! Common decency! They don't know the meanin' of it!"

I felt quite amused at his unwarranted choler, and while he stumped indignantly up and down I fell to dwelling upon the romance of the fog. And romantic it certainly was—the fog, like the gray shadow of infinite mystery, brooding over the whirling speck of earth; and men, mere motes of light and sparkle, cursed with an insane relish for work, riding their steeds of wood and steel through the heart of the mystery, groping their way blindly through the Unseen, and clamoring and clanging in confident speech the while their hearts are heavy with incertitude and fear.

The voice of my companion brought me back to myself with a laugh. I too had been groping and floundering, the while I thought I rode clear-eyed through the mystery.

"Hello; somebody comin' our way," he was saying. "And d'ye hear that? He's comin' fast. Walking right along. Guess he don't hear us yet. Wind's in wrong direction."

The fresh breeze was blowing right down upon us, and I could hear the whistle plainly, off to one side and a little ahead.

"Ferry-boat?" I asked.

He nodded, then added, "Or he wouldn't be keepin' up such a clip." He gave a short chuckle. "They're gettin' anxious up there."

I glanced up. The captain had thrust his head and shoulders out of the pilot-house, and was staring intently into the fog as though by sheer force of will he could penetrate it. His face was anxious, as was the face of my companion, who had stumped over to the rail and was gazing with a like intentness in the direction of the invisible danger.

Then everything happened, and with inconceivable rapidity. The fog seemed to break away as though split by a wedge, and the bow of a steamboat emerged, trailing fog-wreaths on either side like seaweed on the snout of Leviathan. I could see the pilot-house and a white-bearded man leaning partly out of it, on his elbows. He was clad in a blue uniform, and I remembered noting how trim and quiet he was. His quietness, under the circumstances, was terrible. He accepted Destiny, marched hand in hand with it, and coolly measured the stroke. As he leaned there, he ran a calm and speculative eye over us, as though to determine the precise point of the collision, and took no notice whatever when our pilot, white with rage, shouted, "Now you've done it!"

On looking back, I realize that the remark was too obvious to make rejoinder necessary.

"Grab hold of something and hang on," the red-faced man said to me. All his bluster had gone, and he seemed to have caught the contagion of preternatural calm. "And listen to the women scream," he said grimly—almost bitterly, I thought, as though he had been through the experience before.

The vessels came together before I could follow his advice. We must have been struck squarely amidships, for I saw nothing, the strange steamboat having passed boyond my line of vision. The *Martinez* heeled over, sharply, and there was a crashing and rending of timber. I was thrown flat on the wet deck, and before I could scramble to my feet I heard the scream of the women. This it was, I am certain,—the most indescribable of blood-curdling sounds,—

that threw me into a panic. I remembered the life-preservers stored in the cabin, but was met at the door and swept backward by a wild rush of men and women. What happened in the next few minutes I do not recollect, though I have a clear remembrance of pulling down life-preservers from the overhead racks, while the red-faced man fastened them about the bodies of an hysterical group of women. This memory is as distinct and sharp as that of any picture I have seen. It is a picture, and I can see it now,—the jagged edges of the hole in the side of the cabin, through which the gray fog swirled and eddied; the empty upholstered seats, littered with all the evidences of sudden flight, such as packages, hand satchels, umbrellas, and wraps; the stout gentleman who had been reading my essay, encased in cork and canvas, the magazine still in his hand, and asking me with monotonous insistence if I thought there was any danger; the red-faced man, stumping gallantly around on his artificial legs and buckling life-preservers on all comers; and finally, the screaming bedlam of women.

This it was, the screaming of the women, that most tried my nerves. It must have tried, too, the nerves of the red-faced man, for I have another picture which will never fade from my mind. The stout gentleman is stuffing the magazine into his overcoat pocket and looking on curiously. A tangled mass of women, with drawn, white faces and open mouths, is shrieking like a chorus of lost souls; and the red-faced man, his face now purplish with wrath, and with arms extended overhead as in the act of hurling thunderbolts, is shouting, "Shut up! Oh, shut up!"

I remember the scene impelled me to sudden laughter, and in the next instant I realized I was becoming hysterical myself; for these were women of my own kind, like my mother and sisters, with the fear of death upon them and unwilling to die. And I remember that the sounds they made reminded me of the squealing of pigs under the knife of the butcher, and I was struck with horror at the vividness of the analogy. These women, capable of the most sublime emotions, of the tenderest sympathies, were open-mouthed and screaming. They wanted to live, they were helpless, like rats in a trap, and they screamed.

The horror of it drove me out on deck. I was feeling sick and squeamish, and sat down on a bench. In a hazy way I saw and heard men rushing and shouting as they strove to lower the boats. It was just as I had read descriptions of such scenes in books. The tackles jammed. Nothing worked. One boat lowered away with the plugs out, filled with women and children and then with water, and capsized. Another boat had been lowered by one end, and still hung in the tackle by the other end, where it had been abandoned. Nothing was to be seen of the strange steamboat which had caused the disaster, though I heard men saying that she would undoubtedly send boats to our assistance.

I descended to the lower deck. The *Martinez* was sinking fast, for the water was very near. Numbers of the passengers were leaping overboard. Others, in the water, were clamoring to be taken aboard again. No one heeded them. A cry arose that we were sinking. I was seized by the consequent panic, and went over the side in a surge of bodies. How I went over I do not know, though I did know, and instantly, why those in the water were so desirous of getting back on the steamer. The water was cold—so cold that it was painful. The pang, as I plunged into it, was as quick and sharp as that of fire. It bit to the marrow. It was like the grip of death. I gasped with the anguish and shock of it, filling my lungs before the life-preserver popped me to the surface. The taste of the salt was strong in my mouth, and I was strangling with the acrid stuff in my throat and lungs.

But it was the cold that was most distressing. I felt that I could survive but a few minutes. People were struggling and floundering in the water about me. I could hear them crying out to one another. And I heard, also, the sound of oars. Evidently the strange steamboat had lowered its boats. As the time went by I marveled that I was still alive. I had no sensation whatever in my lower limbs, while a chilling numbness was wrapping about my heart and creeping into it. Small waves, with spiteful foaming crests, continually broke over me and into my mouth, sending me off into more strangling paroxysms.

The noises grew indistinct, though I heard a final and despairing chorus of screams in the distance and knew that the *Martinez* had gone down. Later,— how much later I have no knowledge,—I came to myself with a start of fear. I was alone. I could hear no calls or cries—only the sound of the waves, made weirdly hollow and reverberant by the fog. A panic in a crowd, which partakes of a sort of community of interest, is not so terrible as a panic when one is by oneself; and such a panic I now suffered. Whither was I drifting? The red-faced man had said that the tide was ebbing through the Golden Gate. Was I, then, being carried out to sea? And the life-preserver in which I floated? Was it not liable to go to pieces at any moment? I had heard of such things being made of paper and hollow rushes which quickly became saturated and lost all buoyancy. And I could not swim a stroke. And I was alone, floating, apparently, in the midst of a gray primordial vastness. I confess that a madness seized me, that I shrieked aloud as the women had shrieked, and beat the water with my numb hands.

How long this lasted I have no conception, for a blankness intervened, of which I remember no more than one remembers of troubled and painful sleep. When I aroused, it was as after centuries of time; and I saw, almost above me and emerging from the fog, the bow of a vessel, and three triangular sails, each shrewdly lapping the other and filled with wind. Where the bow cut the water there was a great foaming and gurgling, and I seemed directly in its path. I tried to cry out, but was too exhausted. The bow plunged down, just missing me and sending a swash of water clear over my head. Then the long, black side of the vessel began slipping past, so near that I could have touched it with my hands. I tried to reach it, in a mad resolve to claw into the wood with my nails, but my arms were heavy and lifeless. Again I strove to call out, but made no sound.

The stern of the vessel shot by, dropping, as it did so, into a hollow between the waves; and I caught a glimpse of a man standing at the wheel, and of another man who seemed to be doing little else than smoke a cigar. I saw the smoke issuing from his lips as he slowly turned his head and glanced out over the water in my direction. It was a careless, unpremeditated glance, one of those haphazard things men do when they have no immediate call to do anything in particular, but act because they are alive and must do something.

But life and death were in that glance. I could see the vessel being swallowed up in the fog; I saw the back of the man at the wheel, and the head of the other man turning, slowly turning, as his gaze struck the water and casually lifted along it toward me. His face wore an absent expression, as of deep thought, and I became afraid that if his eyes did light upon me he would nevertheless not see me. But his eyes did light upon me, and looked squarely into mine; and he did see me, for he sprang to the wheel, thrusting the other man aside, and whirled it round and round, hand over hand, at the same time shouting orders of some sort. The vessel seemed to go off at a tangent to its former course and leapt almost instantly from view into the fog.

I felt myself slipping into unconsciousness, and tried with all the power of my will to fight above the suffocating blankness and darkness that was rising around me. A little later I heard the stroke of oars, growing nearer and nearer, and the calls of a man. When he was very near I heard him crying, in vexed fashion, "Why in hell don't you sing out?" This meant me, I thought, and then the blankness and darkness rose over me.

ICELAND FISHERMEN

Pierre Loti

AROUND ICELAND they had now that rare weather which the sailors call the *"white calm"*; nothing stirred in the air, as if all the breezes were drained and exhausted.

The sky was covered all over with a heavy whitish veil which grew darker down towards the horizon, changing first to heavy gray and lower down to the somber shades of tin. And beneath, the motionless waters shone in a pale light wearying the eye and passing a shiver all over the body.

At that moment the waters rippled, nothing but ripples playing over the sea, producing light rings like those on a mirror made by blowing. The glittering expanse seemed all covered with a net-work of indistinct design, interwoven and twisted, being quickly effaced and very fleeting.

It was impossible to tell whether this was eternal evening or endless morning; the sun no more indicates any hour, but remains always there to preside over the resplendence of mortal things, being itself only another ring, almost with no outline, growing infinitely big by a dim halo.

Yann and Sylvestre, busy fishing side by side, were singing: *Jean-François de Nantes*, that song with no end to it, amusing themselves with its very monotony, and, looking at each other with a sly wink, they laughed at the childish drollery of repeating that same refrain over and over again, and trying each time to put new fervor in it. Their cheeks were flushed in the sea atmosphere; the air they inhaled was pure and vivifying; they filled their lungs with it,—the source of all vigor and all life.

from "An Iceland Fisherman" by Pierre Loti

Yet there were appearances of non-existence around them, those of extinguished lives and those of things not created yet; the light had no warmth; objects remained motionless as if frozen under the gaze of that spectral eye,— the sun.

The *Marie* cast on the expanse a shadow long as the evening, looking greenish in the midst of the polished surface, reflecting the whiteness of the sky. In this shadow, which did not reflect, one could distinguish through the transparent surface all that was going on below it: countless fishes, thousands of myriads, all alike, gliding quietly in the same direction, as if they had the same goal in view in their eternal march. These were codfish, executing their evolutions together, all marching in parallel lines, giving an effect of gray hatchings and continually moving forward with a rapid quivering that gave a fluid appearance to this mass of silent lives. Sometimes with an abrupt movement of the tail, all turned round at one time showing the silvery scales of their bellies, and then the same movement of the tail, the same turn of the body would propagate through the whole group with slow undulations, like so many metal plates shining between two sheets of water.

The sun, already very low, was still on the decline; then surely this was evening. The nearer it descended to the lead-colored zones, its ring became clearer and more real. You could stare at it as at the moon. It still shone; but you could imagine it to be not very far out in the space; it seemed as though if one sailed on a vessel to the edge of the horizon, one would come across that big, sorry-looking balloon, floating in the air a few yards above the waters.

The fishing was going on, and looking in the calm water, it could be seen how it was done: the codfish with a gluttonous movement came to get a bite and when feeling themselves pricked they shook themselves, thus making only the matter worse. Every minute with both hands the fishermen quickly pulled their lines, throwing them in the boat to be cleaned and flattened out.

The Paimpolese flotilla was dispersed over this tranquil mirror animating the water. There could be seen little boats in the far distance hoisting their sails, though there was not a breath of breeze, looking all white and their outlines well cut against the gray background of the horizon.

On this day the occupation of the Icelander was so quiet, was so easy;— the occupation of a young girl. . . .

Jean François de Nantes
Jean-François,
Jean-François!

They were singing like two big boys. And Yann cared very little that he was so handsome and had such a noble look. He was a child only with Sylvestre, singing and playing only with him; on the contrary, he was reserved with the others and always very haughty and grave; very gentle when they needed his help, always kind and at their service when he was not vexed.

While they were singing this song two others, a few steps away, were singing something else, some other chant composed of drowsiness, of healthy vigor and vague melancholy.

Nobody was weary, and the time passed. Below in the cabin they had always fire in the iron-stove and the lid of the hatchway was kept closed to give the illusion of night to those sleeping. They needed very little air when asleep; people with less robust constitutions, brought up in the cities, would want much more; but the lungs having been inflated all day long with the clear air of these regions they also needed rest and they hardly moved. There one can crouch in any kind of a hole like animals.

After finishing their work they could sleep any time they liked. In this perpetual daylight the hours don't differ much from each other. And it was with a sound sleep that they rested, without dreams, without tossing about.

If they happened to think about women, their sleep would be disturbed. Their eyes would never close at the thought that the fishing would end in six weeks, and that they would find new loves or return to the old ones. But this hardly happened; or, they thought about it in a rather honest manner; they recalled to mind their wives and fiancées, their sisters and parents. . . . But with a habitual continence and absorbed in their work, during this long period their feelings ran through another channel. . . .

"Jean-François de Nantes;
Jean-François,
Jean-François!"

. . . Now they were looking at something hardly perceptible; far away in the gray horizon, a smoke was rising above the waters like a microscopic tail, of a different gray color, of a little darker shade than that of the sky.

It was impossible to tell whether this was eternal evening or endless morning.

With eyes accustomed to pierce the farthest corner of the sky they had soon perceived it:——

"A steamboat yonder!"

"I have an idea," said the captain looking at it carefully, "I have an idea that is a steamboat of the Government,—the cruiser coming to make its round. . . ."

This vague smoke was bringing to the fishermen news from France, and among others, a certain letter from a grandmother written by the hand of a young girl.

It approached slowly; soon they could see its black hull,—it was really the cruiser making a tour of inspection among these fiords of the west.

At the same time, a light breeze having risen blowing sharp, began to stir up here and there the dead waters; it traced over the shining mirror designs of bluish green, lengthening in paths, opening like a fan, and branching in the form of madrepores; thus it came up with a whistling as if to herald the end of the immense torpor, enveloping everything. And the sky, its veil being torn to shreds, became now clear. The mists fell once more over the horizon like accumulated heaps of gray waddings building up moldering walls around the sea. The two mirrors between which stood the fishermen—one above and the other down below—both took again their perfect transparency, as if the vapor dimming them had been wiped out. The weather was changing, but not in an agreeable manner.

And from different points of the sea, from different directions of the expanse, were fast arriving fishing vessels, all belonging to France, roaming in these latitudes, from Brittany, Normandy, Boulogne, and Dunkirk. Like birds floating together at a call they gathered around the cruiser; they came even from the empty corner of the horizon, their little grayish wings were seen everywhere. They suddenly peopled the waste.

No longer drifting they had opened their sails to the newly stirring fresh breezes, and now they were fast approaching with great speed.

Iceland, too, was seen in the distance, seeming as if it also would hurry to get nearer; it began to show gradually, more distinctly its high mountains and bare rocks, which have been lighted only on one side, or from underneath and unwillingly, as it were. Next to it there rose another Iceland, of the same color, accentuated by degrees; but this one was chimerical, and whose gigantic mountains were nothing but condensation of vapor. The sun, ever low and lagging, unable to climb higher, was seen through this illusory island in such a way as if it stood in front of it, this being incomprehensible and puzzling to the eye. It had no longer any halo, and its round disk had regained its well-defined shape, and it looked like a poor, yellow dying planet that had remained there undecided in the midst of a chaos. . . .

The cruiser, which by this time had come to a standstill, was surrounded by Icelander pleiads. Boats, like so many nutshells, lowered from the vessels, hurried to the cruiser, packed with rough, long-bearded fellows. They were asking for every sort of thing, just like children. Some wanted medicines for small cuts; others, mending materials; some provisions, and some others, letters. Some of these wild-looking fellows were brought over by their captains to be put in irons to make penance for their mutinous conduct. As they had all seen service in the Government, this seemed quite natural to them. And when the narrow spardeck was crowded with four or five of these big fellows with iron rings round their ankles, the old mates who had padlocked them would tell them:—"Lie down crosswise, boys, that people may pass," and they would obey them readily, even with a smile.

This time there were many letters for the Icelanders. Among others two for the *Marie, Captain Guermeur,* one of which was addressed to *Monsieur Gaos, Yann;* and the other for *Monsieur Moan, Sylvestre.* (This latter having arrived by the *Danemark* to Reickavick, where the cruiser had picked it up.)

The steward, taking them out of his canvas bag, distributed them, having a lot of trouble in reading the addresses written by hands not much used to that kind of work.

Thereupon the commander said:

"Hurry and make haste, the barometer is falling."

He felt somewhat troubled, seeing so many small nutshells afloat, and so many fishermen assembled in these dangerous regions.

Yann and Sylvestre always read their letters together. This time they were read by the gleam of the midnight sun which was shining above the horizon with the same look of a dead star.

Their arms around each other's shoulders they sat by themselves in a corner of the deck reading very slowly to understand the better the news from home.

In Yann's letter Sylvestre found news of Marie, his young fiancée; in that of Sylvestre, Yann read the funny stories of Grandmother Yvonne, who had not her equal in amusing those away from home. And he read also the last paragraph which concerned him specially: "My Greetings to Son Gaos."

Having finished reading the letters Sylvestre timidly showed his letter to Yann, trying to make him appreciate the handwriting.

"See what a nice hand this is, Yann, isn't it?" But Yann, who knew too well whose writing that was, shrugging his shoulders turned his head one side, which meant that he was disgusted to always hear about Gaud.

Whereupon Sylvestre carefully folded the scorned piece of paper, and putting it back in the envelope slipped it in his waistcoat pocket, next to his heart, muttering gloomily to himself:

"I am pretty sure, they never will marry . . . But what can he possibly have against her? . . ."

. . . The bell of the cruiser struck midnight, and they still sat there dreaming of home, of the absent ones and a thousand other things, as in a reverie. . . .

Then the eternal sun having just dipped its edge in the sea, commenced to climb up slowly.

And it was morning. . . .

. . . The Iceland sun had also changed its appearance, and the day opened with a sinister morning. Totally freed of its veil, it spread about long rays, which shot through the heavens like jets that announced the approach of bad weather.

The weather had been fine for the last few days; that was to end very soon. The wind blew over this group of boats, as if it wanted, by scattering them, to clear the sea. And they began to disperse, to flee like a routed army, pursued by this menace written in the air and which was not to be ignored.

It was blowing harder and harder, giving the shiver to men and vessels.

The waves, still quite small, were chasing each other to be heaped in a mass. At first they were crowned with white foam spread on their tops in folds; then with a shriveling began to exhale steam; it looked as if they were boiling; and the sharp din increased every minute.

Nobody thought about fishing now, but all gave their attention to the managing of the boats.

The lines had been long ago drawn in. They all hurried to move on. Some, in search of a shelter in the fiords trying to reach there in time. Others preferred to round the southern point of Iceland, considering it much safer to be in the open sea, having ahead of them plenty of space to run before the wind. They could still see each other. Here and there, in the trough of the sea, the sails wagged, poor little wet things, tired and flying, but were always put to rights, like a child's toy made of pith, which after being blown over resumes its erect attitude.

The great heap of clouds, which stood compact like an island on the western horizon, was now breaking up overhead and the fragments were being scattered all over the sky. This heap seemed inexhaustible: the wind extended, diffused and stretched it, bringing out to view an indefinite line of dark curtains, hanging over the clear, yellowish sky, now turned livid, cold and dreary.

The wind blew harder and harder, agitating everything.

The cruiser had made for the sheltering coves of Iceland. Only the fishing craft was left on this seething sea, which had taken a sinister look and a dreadful color. They pushed on their preparations for foul weather. Between them the distance was fast increasing, and some were lost sight of.

The waves, curling up in volutes, were supplanting each other, then mingling climbed one over the other, thus swelling higher and higher. Between them the hollows were deepened.

In a few hours, everything was plowed and upset in this watery region, where all was so calm and tranquil but yesterday; and in place of the former silence, now there reigned a deafening uproar. All this agitation of the present, what a dissolving spectacle, unconscious, useless, and all so quickly done! To what purpose all these! . . . what mystery of blind destruction! . . .

The clouds managed to enshroud the heavens, and still issuing from the west, piled in layers, hurrying on swiftly and darkening everything. Only a few yellow patches were left uncovered, through which the sun streamed down its last sheaves of rays, and the water, almost green, was gradually striped in white foam.

At noon the *Marie* was all ready to face foul weather. Her hatchways were closed; and her sails storm-reefed; she bounded along light and agile. In the midst of the disorder now commencing she seemed to gambol like a big por-

poise, whose delight is in tempests. With only a foresail, she was simply
"scudding before the wind,"—an expression used by sailors to designate this
gait.

All was steeped in darkness overhead; a close crushing vault with some coal-
black, shapeless spots spread over it, looking like a dome almost immovable;
and it was necessary to watch it sharply to ascertain that, on the contrary, it
was in a full swing of motion,—endless gray sheets hastening to pass on, and
ceaselessly replaced by others issuing forth from the depths of the horizon,—
draperies of darkness unwinding as from a never-ending roll. . . .

The *Marie* was flying before the wind, faster and faster; and the wind itself
was flying before something mysterious and terrible. The gale, the sea, the
Marie, and the clouds, all alike, possessed by the same madness, were flying
swiftly in the same direction. The wind hurried the quickest, next the surging billows rising slowly and heavily ran after it, last the *Marie* was carried
along by this general movement. Wavelets, with their pallid crests, rolling
in a perpetual tumble, were fast pursuing her; and she, always overtaken and
outrun, managed to escape by means of the deep furrows left in her wake,
upon whose eddies their fury was spent.

An illusion of lightness was the main thing to be noticed in this spectacle of
flight; without any trouble and effort she seemed to bound along. When the
Marie was lifted on the waves it was without a jerk, as it was raised by the
wind, and her descent was only a sliding with the same sensation in the stomach as when one shoots down in a "Russian car" the chutes or like imaginary
falls in dreams. She seemed to slide backwards, the flying mountain stealing
away from under her, to continue on its onward movement; then she would
suddenly plunge down in one of those hollows that were moving on also. She
touched, without getting wet or bruising herself, the frightful depths which
were, like the rest, fleeing; which were fleeing and disappearing like smoke,
like nothing. . . .

It was very dark in the depths of these watery hollows. After leaping over
each wave you could see another coming from behind; that one was still larger
and of a greenish hue in its transparency, and which hurried to approach in
furious convolution with crests ready to close, as if saying:

"Wait till I clutch you; and then I will swallow you up. . . ."

. . . But no, it has only lifted you up, just as a feather is lifted by the shrug of shoulders; it has only passed gently under you, with its seething froth, and the roar of a cataract.

And so on continuously. But always they grew bigger. Wave succeeded wave, getting more enormous, like long chains of mountains, whose valleys began to be frightful. And all this wild madness of movement was accelerating under a sky growing darker and darker, in the midst of an all-pervading uproar.

This was, surely, bad weather, and it was necessary to be watchful; but they had much open space ahead of them, much space to run in! And then this same year the *Marie* had passed the season in the westernmost parts of Iceland fisheries, so that in this furious way that they were traversing over the sea towards east, they were getting nearer home.

Yann and Sylvestre were at the helm, fastened by the waist. They still sang the song of *Jean-François de Nantes;* intoxicated by movement and swiftness, they sang at the top of their voices, laughing that they could not hear each other in this deafening uproar, amusing themselves by turning their heads to sing against the wind and so lose breath.

"Well, my boys, does it smell close up here too?" asked Guermeur, putting out his bearded face through the half-open hatchway, like the devil, ready to jump out of his box.

Oh! no, it did not smell close up there, sure enough. They were not afraid, having the exact notion of the dangers they had to grapple with, having confidence in their boat, and in the strength of their arms, and because she had danced this same wild dance for forty years of Iceland voyages, under the protection of the Virgin in faïence, always smiling between bouquets of artificial flowers. . . .

> Jean-François de Nantes;
> Jean-François,
> Jean-François!

Generally speaking, nothing was possible to see very far around them; a few hundred meters away everything took on an aspect of vague fright; pallid crests were frothing, obstructing the view. One would imagine himself to be in the midst of a narrow, but constantly changing, scene; and, moreover, objects were sunk in a sort of watery smoke, fleeting like a cloud, with great swiftness over the entire surface of the sea.

But, at intervals, a cleft was opened in the northwest, whence a sudden veering of the wind might come; then a shivering light would gleam over the horizon, a languishing reflection play on the white turbulent waves, making the vault of the heavens seem covered with duskier shadows. And these open spots in the sky were sad to behold; these distant glimpses filled the heart with dismay; for it made them see that the same chaos and the same fury were everywhere,—ever behind the wide, empty horizon, and infinitely beyond. The terror was unlimited; and one felt alone in the midst of all!

An unearthly clamor was issuing from earthly objects, like a prelude of the Apocalypse, spreading fright, as if the end of the world was at hand. Thus could be distinguished myriads of voices; they came from above, hissing and roaring, as if from a far distance,—so immense was their volume. And this was the wind, the moving power of this disorder, the invisible force directing everything. It was frightful, but there were other noises besides, nearer, more material, more menacing, that made the water boil and seethe as on live coal. . . .

All the time this was increasing.

And, in spite of their aspect of flight, the sea commenced to cover them, "to eat them up" as they said. At first sprays lashed from behind and masses of water hurled with a big force, smashing almost everything. The waves were swelling to dizzy heights; and yet, being divided into proportional parts, around which could be seen greenish fragments, formed of the falling water splashed by the wind. They fell in heavy masses on the deck with a crash, and the *Marie* shuddered all over, as if with pain. On account of the white foam spattered all around, nothing could be seen; and when the squalls were groaning madly she would rush in the whirlwind like the dust on the roads in summer time. A heavy rain was now pouring down in torrents slantingly, almost horizontally; and all in a mass hissed, slashed, and wounded like thongs.

They both stood at the helm, fastened and standing firm, dressed in oilskins, durable and glossy like the skin of the shark, which were tightened with tarred cord, close on the neck and at the wrists and ankles, to prevent the water from running in; and it all trickled down over them; and when it poured down harder, they doubled up their backs and held fast, so as not to be thrown overboard. The skin of their cheeks was burning and every minute their breath getting short. After each heavy fall of water they looked at each other, smiling at the look their beards presented, all covered with salt.

In the long run, however, this was getting very fatiguing; all this fury and madness, instead of getting appeased, always continued in their exasperating paroxysm. The rage of man and that of the beast becomes exhausted, and does not last very long;—but they have to submit for a long time to the fury of inanimate objects, that have neither cause nor purpose, and are mysterious as life itself and death.

Jean-François de Nantes;
Jean-François,
Jean-François!

Still the refrain of the old song taken up unconsciously passed from time to time through their blanched lips, but only like something voiceless. Excess of motion and uproar had intoxicated them, and in spite of their youth, their smiles were only grimaces, and their teeth, shattered by the shivering cold, their eyes, half closed, under their burning and beating eyelids, were glazed in wild helplessness. Nailed to the helm like two marble buttresses they made all the necessary movements with their shriveled and blue hands, almost without thinking, by the sheer habit of the muscles. With their hair streaming and mouths contracted, they had an outlandish look, all the primitive savagery of man reappearing.

They could no longer see each other! They were conscious only of being there side by side. In moments of greatest danger every time that a new mountain, overhanging from behind, came roaring to knock their boat with a dull crash, one of their hands would move mechanically to make the sign of the cross. They no longer had thoughts for anything, neither for Gaud, nor for woman, nor for marriage. This lasted very long. Drunk by the din, by fatigue and by cold, everything in their heads was a blank. They were but two pillars of stiffened flesh clinging to that helm; only two strong beasts cramped there by instinct, determined not to die.

MR. MIDSHIPMAN EASY
MAKES A BET

Captain Marryat

THE AURORA sailed on the second day, and with a fine breeze stood across, making as much northing as easting; the consequence was, that one fine morning they saw the Spanish coast before they saw the Toulon fleet. Mr. Pottyfar took his hands out of his pockets, because he could not examine the coast through a telescope without so doing; but this, it is said, was the first time that he had done so on the quarter-deck from the day that the ship had sailed from Port Mahon. Captain Wilson was also occupied with his telescope, so were many of the officers and midshipmen, and the men at the mast-heads used their eyes, but there was nothing but a few small fishing-boats to be seen. So they all went down to breakfast, as the ship was hove-to close in with the land.

"What will Easy bet," said one of the midshipmen, "that we don't see a prize today?"

"I will not bet that we do not see a vessel; but I'll bet you what you please that we do not take one before twelve o'clock at night."

"No, no, that won't do; just let the tea-pot travel over this way, for it's my forenoon watch."

"It's a fine morning," observed one of the mates, of the name of Martin; "but I've a notion it won't be a fine evening."

"Why not?" inquired another.

"I've now been eight years in the Mediterranean, and know something about the weather. There's a watery sky, and the wind is very steady. If we are not under double-reefed topsails tonight, say I'm no conjurer."

from "Mr. Midshipman Easy" by Captain Marryat

"That you will be, all the same, if we are under bare poles," said another.

"You're devilish free with your tongue, my youngster. Easy, pull his ears for me."

"Pull them easy, Jack, then," said the boy, laughing.

"All hands make sail!" now resounded at the hatchways.

"There they are, depend upon it," cried Gascoigne, catching up his hat and bolting out of the berth, followed by all the others except Martin, who had just been relieved, and thought that his presence in the waist might be dispensed with for the short time, at least, which it took him to swallow a cup of tea.

It was very true; a galliot and four lateen vessels had just made their appearance round the easternmost point, and, as soon as they observed the frigate, had hauled their wind. In a minute the Aurora was under a press of canvas, and the telescopes were all directed to the vessels.

"All deeply laden, sir," observed Mr. Hawkins, the chaplain; "how the topsail of the galliot is scored!"

"They have a fresh breeze just now," observed Captain Wilson to the first lieutenant.

"Yes, sir; and it's coming down fast."

"Hands by the royal halyards, there!"

The Aurora careened with the canvas to the rapidly increasing breeze.

"Topgallant-sheet and halyards!"

"Luff you may, quartermaster! luff, I tell you! A small pull of that weather main-topgallant brace; that will do!" said the master.

"Top-men, aloft there! Stand by to clew up the royals! and, Captain Wilson, shall we take them in? I'm afraid of that pole; it bends now like a coachwhip," said Mr. Pottyfar, looking up aloft, with his hands in both pockets.

"In royals—lower away!"

"They are going about, sir," said the second lieutenant, Mr. Haswell.

"Look out!" observed the chaplain; "it's coming."

Again the breeze increases, and the frigate was borne down.

"Hands reef topsails in stays, Mr. Pottyfar."

"Ay, ay, sir; 'bout ship."

The helm was put down, and the topsails lowered and reefed in stays.

"Very well, my lads, very well indeed," said Captain Wilson.

Again the topsails were hoisted and topgallant-sheets home. It was a strong

breeze, although the water was smooth and the Aurora dashed through at the
rate of eight miles an hour, with her weather leeches lifting.

"Didn't I tell you so?" said Martin to his messmates on the gangway; "but
there's more yet, my boys."

"We must take the topgallant-sails off her," said Captain Wilson, looking
aloft; for the frigate now careened to her bearings, and the wind was increasing and squally. "Try them a little longer;" but another squall came suddenly: the halyards were lowered, and the sails clewed up and furled.

In the mean time the frigate had rapidly gained upon the vessels, which still
carried on every stitch of canvas, making short tacks in shore. The Aurora
was again put about with her head toward them, and they were not two points
on her weather-bow. The sky, which had been clear in the morning, was
now overcast; the sun was obscured with opaque white clouds, and the sea
was rising fast. Another ten minutes, and then they were under double-reefed
topsails, and the squalls were accompanied with heavy rain. The frigate now
dashed through the waves, foaming in her course, and straining under the
press of sail. The horizon was so thick that the vessels ahead were no longer
to be seen.

"We shall have it, I expect," said Captain Wilson.

"Didn't I say so?" observed Martin to Gascoigne. "We take no prizes this
day, depend upon it."

"We must have another hand to the wheel, sir, if you please," said the
quartermaster, who was assisting the helmsman.

Mr. Pottyfar, with his hands concealed as usual, stood by the capstern. "I
fear, sir, we cannot carry the mainsail much longer."

"No," observed the chaplain, "I was thinking so."

"Captain Wilson, if you please, we are very close in," said the master; "don't
you think we had better go about?"

"Yes, Mr. Jones. Hands about ship—and yes, by heavens, we must! up
mainsail."

The mainsail was taken off, and the frigate appeared to be immediately relieved. She no longer jerked and plunged as before.

"We're very near the land, Captain Wilson; thick as it is, I think I can make
out the loom of it—shall we wear round, sir?" continued the master.

"Yes, hands, wear ship—put the helm up."

It was but just in time, for, as the frigate flew round, describing a circle, as she payed off before the wind, they could perceive the breakers lashing the precipitous coast, not two cables' length from them.

"I had no idea we were so near," observed the captain, compressing his lips. "Can they see anything of those vessels?"

"I have not seen them this quarter of an hour, sir," replied the signal-man, protecting his glass from the rain under his jacket.

"How's her head now, quartermaster?"

"South-southeast, sir."

The sky now assumed a different appearance—the white clouds had been exchanged for others dark and murky, the wind roared at intervals, and the rain came down in torrents. Captain Wilson went down into the cabin to examine the barometer.

"The barometer has risen," said he on his return on deck. "Is the wind steady?"

"No, sir, she's up and off three points."

"This will end in a southwester."

The wet and heavy sails now flapped from the shifting of the wind.

"Up with the helm, quartermaster."

"Up it is—she's off to south-by-west."

The wind lulled, the rain came down in a deluge—for a minute it was quite calm, and the frigate was on an even keel.

"Man the braces. We shall be taken aback directly, depend upon it."

The braces were hardly stretched along before this was the case. The wind flew round to the southwest with a loud roar, and it was fortunate that they were prepared—the yards were braced round, and the master asked the captain what course they were to steer.

"We must give it up," observed Captain Wilson, holding on by the belaying pin. "Shape our course for Cape Sicie, Mr. Jones."

And the Aurora flew before the gale, under her foresail and top-sails close reefed. The weather was now so thick that nothing could be observed twenty yards from the vessel; the thunder pealed, and the lightning darted in every direction over the dark expanse. The watch was called as soon as the sails were trimmed and all who could went below, wet, uncomfortable, and disappointed.

"What an old Jonah you are, Martin," said Gascoigne.

"Yes I am," replied he; "but we have the worst to come yet, in my opinion.

I recollect not two hundred miles from where we are now we had just such a gale in the Favorite, and we as nearly went down when——"

At this moment a tremendous noise was heard above, a shock was felt throughout the whole ship, which trembled fore and aft as if it was about to fall into pieces; loud shrieks were followed by plaintive cries; the lower deck was filled with smoke and the frigate was down on her beam ends. Without exchanging a word, the whole of the occupants of the berth flew out, and were up the hatchway, not knowing what to think, but convinced that some dreadful accident had taken place.

On their gaining the deck it was at once explained; the foremast of the frigate had been struck by lightning, had been riven into several pieces, and had fallen over the larboard bow, carrying with it the main-topmast and jib-boom. The jagged stump of the foremast was in flames and burned brightly, notwithstanding the rain fell in torrents. The ship, as soon as the foremast and main-topmast had gone overboard, broached-to furiously, throwing the men over the wheel and dashing them senseless against the carronades; the forecastle, the fore part of the main-deck, and even the lower deck, were spread with men either killed or seriously wounded, or insensible from the electric shock. The frigate was on her beam-ends and the sea broke furiously over her; all was dark as pitch, except the light from the blazing stump of the foremast, appearing like a torch, held up by the wild demons of the storm, or when occasionally the gleaming lightning cast a momentary glare, threatening every moment to repeat its attack upon the vessel, while the deafening thunder burst almost on their devoted heads. All was dismay and confusion for a minute or two; at last Captain Wilson, who had himself lost his sight for a short time, called for the carpenter and axes—they climbed up, that is, two or three of them, and he pointed to the mizzen-mast; the master was also there, and he cut loose the axes for the seamen to use; in a few minutes the mizzen-mast fell over the quarter, and the helm being put hard up, the frigate payed off and slowly righted. But the horror of the scene was not yet over. The boatswain, who had been on the forecastle, had been led below, for his vision was gone forever. The men who lay scattered about had been examined, and they were assisting them down to the care of the surgeon, when the cry of "Fire!" issued from the lower deck. The ship had taken fire at the coal-hole and carpenter's store-room, and the smoke that now ascended was intense.

"Call the drummer," said Captain Wilson, "and let him beat to quarters—all hands to their stations—let the pumps be rigged and the buckets passed along. Mr. Martin, see that the wounded men are taken down below. Where's Mr. Haswell? Mr. Pottyfar, station the men to pass the water on by hand on the lower deck. I will go there myself. Mr. Jones, take charge of the ship."

Pottyfar, who actually had taken his hands out of his pockets, hastened down to comply with the captain's orders on the main-deck as Captain Wilson descended to the deck below.

"I say, Jack, this is very different from this morning," observed Gascoigne.

"Yes," replied Jack, "so it is; but I say, Gascoigne, what's the best thing to do? When the chimney's on fire on shore, they put a wet blanket over it."

"Yes," replied Gascoigne; "but when the coal-hole's on fire on board, they will not find that sufficient."

"At all events, wet blankets must be a good thing, Ned, so let us pull out the hammocks; cut the lanyards and get some out—we can but offer them, you know, and if they do no good, at least it will show our zeal."

"Yes, Jack, and I think when they turn in again, those whose blankets you take will agree with you, that zeal makes the service very uncomfortable. However, I think you are right."

The two midshipmen collected three or four hands, and in a very short time they had more blankets than they could carry—there was no trouble in wetting them, for the main-deck was afloat—and followed by the men they had collected, Easy and Gascoigne went down with large bundles in their arms to where Captain Wilson was giving directions to the men.

"Excellent, Mr. Easy! excellent, Mr. Gascoigne!" said Captain Wilson. "Come, my lads, throw them over now, and stamp upon them well;" the men's jackets and the captain's coat had already been sacrificed to the same object.

Easy called the other midshipmen, and they went up for a further supply; but there was no occasion, the fire had been smothered; still, the danger had been so great that the fore magazine had been floated. During all this, which lasted perhaps a quarter of an hour, the frigate had rolled gunwale under, and many were the accidents which occurred. At last, all danger from fire had ceased, and the men were ordered to return to their quarters, when three officers and forty-seven men were found absent—seven of them were dead, most of them were already under the care of the surgeon, but some were still lying in the scuppers.

No one had been more active or more brave during this time of danger than Mr. Hawkins, the chaplain. He was everywhere, and when Captain Wilson went down to put out the fire, he was there encouraging the men and exerting himself most gallantly. He and Mesty came aft when all was over, one just as black as the other. The chaplain sat down and wrung his hands— "God forgive me!" said he, "God forgive me!"

"Why so, sir?" said Easy, who stood near; "I am sure you need not be ashamed of what you have done."

"No, no, not ashamed of what I've done; but, Mr. Easy—I have sworn so, sworn such oaths at the men in my haste—I, the chaplain! God forgive me! I meant nothing." It was very true that Mr. Hawkins had sworn a great deal during his exertions, but he was at that time the quarter-deck officer and not the chaplain; the example to the men and his gallantry had been most serviceable.

"Indeed, sir," said Easy, who saw that the chaplain was in great tribulation, and hoped to pacify him, "I was certainly not there all the time, but I only heard you say, 'God bless you, my men! be smart,' and so on; surely, that is not swearing."

"Was it *that* I said, Mr. Easy, are you sure? I really had an idea that I had d——d them all in heaps, as some of them deserved—no, no, not deserved. Did I really bless them—nothing but bless them?"

"Yes, sir," said Mesty, who perceived what Jack wanted; "it was nothing, I assure you, but 'God bless you, Captain Wilson! Bless your heart, my good men! Bless the king!' and so on. You do nothing but shower down blessing and wet blanket."

"I told you so," said Jack.

"Well, Mr. Easy, you've made me very happy," replied the chaplain; "I was afraid it was otherwise."

So indeed it was, for the chaplain had sworn like a boatswain; but, as Jack and Mesty had turned all his curses into blessings, the poor man gave himself absolution, and shaking hands with Jack, hoped he would come down into the gun-room, and take a glass of grog; nor did he forget Mesty, who received a good allowance at the gun-room door, to which Jack gladly consented, as the rum in the middy's berth had all been exhausted after the rainy morning—but

Jack was interrupted in his third glass, by somebody telling him the captain wanted to speak with Mr. Hawkins and with him.

Jack went up, and found the captain on the quarter-deck with the officers.

"Mr. Easy," said Captain Wilson, "I have sent for you, Mr. Hawkins, and Mr. Gascoigne, to thank you on the quarter-deck for your exertions and presence of mind on this trying occasion." Mr. Hawkins made a bow, Gascoigne said nothing, but he thought of having extra leave when they arrived at Malta. Jack felt inclined to make a speech, and began something about when there was danger that it leveled every one to an equality even on board a man-of-war.

"By no means, Mr. Easy," replied Captain Wilson, "it does the very contrary, for it proves which is the best man, and those who are the best raise themselves at once above the rest."

Jack was very much inclined to argue the point, but he took the compliment and held his tongue, which was the wisest thing he could have done; so he made his bow, and was about to go down into the midshipmen's berth when the frigate was pooped by a tremendous sea, which washed all those who did not hold on down into the waist. Jack was among the number, and naturally catching at the first object which touched him, he caught hold of the chaplain by the leg, who commenced swearing most terribly, but before he could finish the oath, the water which had burst into the cabin through the windows—for the dead-lights, in the confusion, had not yet been shipped—burst out the cross bulk-heads, sweeping like a torrent the marine, the cabin-door, and everything else in its force, and floating Jack and the chaplain with several others down the main hatchway on to the lower deck. The lower deck being also full of water, men and chests were rolling and tossing about, and Jack was sometimes in company with the chaplain, and at other times separated; at last they both recovered their legs, and gained the midshipmen's berth, which although afloat was still a haven of security. Mr. Hawkins spluttered and spit, and so did Jack, until he began to laugh.

"This is very trying, Mr. Easy," said the chaplain; "very trying indeed to the temper. I hope I have not sworn—I hope not."

"Not a word," said Jack—"I was close to you all the time—you only said, 'God preserve us!' "

"Only that? I was afraid that I said 'God d—mn it!' "

"Quite a mistake, Mr. Hawkins. Let's go into the gun-room and try to wash this salt water out of our mouths, and then I will tell you all you said, as far as I could hear it, word for word."

So Jack by this means got another glass of grog, which was very acceptable in his wet condition, and made himself very comfortable, while those on deck were putting on the dead-lights, and very busy setting the goose wings of the mainsail to prevent the frigate from being pooped a second time.

THE FLIGHT OF THE SMUGGLERS

John Masefield

B Y THIS time the other smugglers had become alarmed. The longboat gun, which worked on a slide abaft all, was cleared, and the two little cohorns, or hand-swivel guns, which pointed over the sides, were trained and loaded. A man swarmed up the mainmast to look around. 'The cutter's bearing up to close,' he called out. 'I see she's the Salcombe boat.'

'That shows they have information,' said Marah grimly, 'otherwise they'd not be looking for us here. Someone had been talking to his wife.' He hailed the masthead again. 'Have the frigates seen us yet?'

For answer, the man took a hurried glance to windward, turned visibly white to the lips, and slid down a rope to the deck. 'Bearing down fast, under stunsails,' he reported. 'The cutter's signaled them with her topsail. There's three frigates coming down,' he added.

'Right,' said Marah. 'I'll go up and see for myself.'

He went up, and came down again looking very ugly. He evidently thought that he was in a hole. 'As she goes,' he called to the helmsman, 'get all you can on the sheets, boys. Now, Jim, you're up a tree; you're within an hour of being pressed into the Navy. How'd ye like to be a ship's boy, hey, and get tickled up by a bo'sum rope-end?'

'I shouldn't like it at all,' I answered.

'You'll like it a jolly sight less than that,' said he, 'and it's what you'll probably be. We're ten miles from home. The cutter's in the road. The frigates will be on us in half-an-hour. It will be a mighty close call, my son; we shall have to fight to get clear.'

from "Jim Davis" by John Masefield

At that instant of time something went overhead with a curious whanging whine.

'That's a three-pound ball,' said Marah, pointing to a spurt upon a wave. 'The cutter wants us to stop and have breakfast with 'em.'

'Whang,' went another shot, flying far overhead. 'Fire away,' said Marah. 'You're more than a mile away; you will not hit us at that range.'

He shifted his course a little, edging more towards the shore, so as to cut transversely across the cutter's bows. We ran for twenty minutes in the course of the frigates; by that time the cutter was within half a mile and the frigates within three miles of us. All the cutter's guns were peppering at us; a shot or two went through our sail, one shot knocked a splinter from our fiferail.

'They shoot a treat, don't they?' said Marah. 'Another minute and they will be knocking away a spar.'

Just as he spoke, there came another shot from the cutter; something aloft went 'crack'; a rope unreeved from its pulley and rattled on to the deck; the mizzen came down in a heap: the halliards had been cut clean through. The men leaped to repair the damage; it took but a minute or two, but we had lost way; the next shot took us square amidships and tore off a yard of our lee side.

'We must give them one in return,' he said. 'Aft to the gun, boys.'

The men trained the long gun on the cutter. 'Oh, Marah,' I said, 'don't fire on Englishmen.'

'Who began the firing?' he answered. 'I'm going to knock away some of their sails. Stand clear of the breach,' he shouted, as he pulled the trigger-spring.

The gun roared and recoiled; a hole appeared as if by magic in the swelling square foresail of the cutter. 'Load with bar-shot and chain,' said Marah. 'Another like that and we shall rip the whole sail off. Mind your eye. There goes her gun again.'

This time the shot struck the sea beside us, sending a spout of water over our rail. Again Marah pulled his trigger-string, the gun fell over on its side, and the cutter's mast seemed to collapse into itself as though it were wrapping itself up in its own canvas. A huge loose clue of sail—the foresail's starboard leach—flew up into the air; the boom swung after it; the gaff toppled over from above; we saw the topmast dive like a lunging rapier into the sea. We had torn the foresail in two, and the shot passing on had smashed the foremast just below the cap. All her sails lay in a confused heap just forward of the mast.

'That's done her,' said one of the smugglers. 'She can't even use her gun now.'

'Hooray!' cried another. 'We're the boys for a lark.'

'Are you?' said Marah. 'We got the frigates to clear yet, my son. They'll be in range in two minutes or less. Look at them.'

Tearing after us, in chase, under all sail, came the frigates. Their bows were burrowing into white heaps of foam; we could see the red portlids and the shining gun-muzzles; we could see the scarlet coats of the marines, and the glint of brass on the poops. A flame spurted from the bows of the leader. She was firing a shot over us to bid us heave to. The smugglers looked at each other; they felt that the game was up. Bang! Another shot splashed into the sea beside us, and bounded on from wave to wave, sending up huge splashes at each bound. A third shot came from the second frigate, but this also missed. Marah was leaning over our lee rail, looking at the coast of France, still several miles away. 'White water,' he cried suddenly. 'Here's the Green Stones. We shall do them yet.'

I could see no green stones, but a quarter of a mile away, on our port-hand, the sea was all a cream of foam above reefs and sands just covered by the tide. If they were to help us, it was none too soon, for by this time the leading frigate was only a hundred yards from us. Her vast masts towered over us. I could look into her open bow ports; I could see the men at the bow guns waiting for the word to fire. I have often seen ships since then, but I never saw any ship so splendid and so terrible as that one. She was the *Laocoon*, and her figurehead was twined with serpents. The line of her ports was of a dull yellow color, and as all her ports were open, the portlids made scarlet marks all along it. Her great lower studding sail swept out from her side for all the world like a butterfly-net, raking the top of the sea for us. An officer stood on the forecastle with a speaking-trumpet in his hand.

'Stand by!' cried Marah. 'They're going to hail us.'

'Ahoy, the lugger there!' yelled the officer. 'Heave to at once or I sink you. Heave to.'

'Answer him in French,' said Marah to one of the men.

A man made some answer in French; I think he said he didn't understand. The officer told a marine to fire at us. The bullet whipped through the mizzen.

'Bang' went one of the main-deck guns just over our heads. We felt a rush and shock, and our mizzen mast and sail went over the side.

Marah stood up and raised his hand. 'We surrender, sir!' he shouted; 'we surrender! Down helm, boys.'

We swung round on our keel, and came to the wind. We saw the officer nod approval and speak a word to the sailing-master, and then the great ship lashed past us, a mighty, straining, heaving fabric of beauty, whose lower studding sails were wet half-way to their irons.

'Now for it!' said Marah. He hauled his wind, and the lugger shot off towards the broken water. 'If we get among those shoals,' he said, 'we're safe as houses. The frigate's done. She's going at such a pace they will never stop her. Not till she's gone a mile. Not without they rip the masts out of her. That officer ought to have known that trick. That will be a lesson to you, Mr. Jim. If ever you're in a little ship, and you get chased by a big ship, you keep on till she's right on top of you, and then luff hard all you know, and the chances are you'll get a mile start before they come round to go after you.'

We had, in fact, doubled like a hare, and the frigate, like a greyhound, had torn on ahead, unable to turn. We saw her lower stunsail boom carry away as they took in the sail, and we could see her seamen running to their quarters ready to brace the yards and bring the ship to her new course. The lugger soon gathered way and tore on, but it was now blowing very fresh indeed, and the sea before us was one lashing smother of breakers. Marah seemed to think nothing of that; he was watching the frigates. One, a slower sailer than the other, was sailing back to the fleet; the second had hove to about a mile away, with her long-boat lowered to pursue us. The boat was just clear of her shadow; crowding all sail in order to get to us. The third ship, the ship which we had tricked, was hauling to the wind, with her light canvas clued up for furling. In a few moments she was braced up and standing towards us, but distant about a mile.

Suddenly both frigates opened fire, and the great cannon balls ripped up the sea all round us.

'They'll sink us, sure,' said one of the smugglers with a grin.

The men all laughed, and I laughed too; we were all so very much interested in what was going to happen. The guns fired steadily one after the other in a long rolling roar. The men laughed at each shot.

'They couldn't hit the sea,' they said derisively. 'The navy gunners are no use at all.'

'No,' said Marah, 'they're not. But if they keep their course another half-minute they'll be on the sunk reef, and a lot of 'em 'll be drowned. I wonder will the old *Laocoon* take a hint.'

'Give 'em the pennant,' said Gateo.

'Ay, give it 'em,' said half-a-dozen others. 'Don't let 'em wreck.'

Marah opened the flag-locker, and took out a blue pennant (it had a white ball in the middle of it), which he hoisted to his main truck. 'Let her go off,' he cried to the helmsman.

For just a moment we lay broadside on to the frigate, a fair target for her guns, so that she could see the pennant blowing out clear.

'You see, Jim?' asked Marah. 'That pennant means "You are standing in to danger." Now we will luff again.'

'I don't think they saw it, gov'nor,' said one of the sailors as another shot flew over us. 'They'll have to send below to get their glasses, those blind navy jokers.'

'Off,' said Marah quickly; and again we lay broadside on, tumbling in the swell, shipping heavy sprays.

This time they saw it, for the *Laocoon's* helm was put down, her great sails shivered and threshed, and she stood off on the other tack. As she stood away we saw an officer leap on to the taffrail, holding on by the mizzen backstays.

'Tar my wig,' said Marah, 'if he isn't bowing to us!'

Sure enough the officer took off his hat to us and bowed gracefully.

'Polite young man,' said Marah. 'We will give them the other pennant.'

Another flag, a red pennant, was hoisted in place of the blue. 'Wishing you a pleasant voyage,' said Marah. 'Now luff, my sons. That long-boat will be on to us.'

Indeed, the long-boat had crept to within six hundred yards of us; it was time we were moving, though the guns were no longer firing on us from the ships.

'Mind your helm, boys,' said Marah as he went forward to the bows. 'I've got to con you through a lot of bad rocks. You'll have to steer small or die.'

THE GREAT WHITE WHALE

Herman Melville

First Day

THAT NIGHT, in the mid-watch, when the old man—as his wont at inter-vals—stepped forth from the scuttle in which he leaned, and went to his pivot-hole, he suddenly thrust out his face fiercely, snuffing up the sea air as a sagacious ship's dog will, in drawing nigh to some barbarous isle. He de-clared that a whale must be near. Soon that peculiar odor, sometimes to a great distance given forth by the living Sperm Whale, was palpable to all the watch; nor was any mariner surprised when, after inspecting the compass, and then the dog-vane, and then ascertaining the precise bearing of the odor as nearly as possible, Ahab rapidly ordered the ship's course to be slightly altered, and the sail to be shortened.

The acute policy dictating these movements was sufficiently vindicated at daybreak by the sight of a long sleek on the sea directly and lengthwise ahead, smooth as oil, and resembling in the pleated watery wrinkles bordering it, the polished metallic-like marks of some swift tide-rip, at the mouth of a deep, rapid stream.

"Man the mastheads! Call all hands!"

Thundering with the butts of three clubbed handspikes on the forecastle deck, Daggoo roused the sleepers with such judgment claps that they seemed to exhale from the scuttle, so instantaneously did they appear with their clothes in their hands.

"What d'ye see?" cried Ahab, flattening his face to the sky.

"Nothing, nothing, sir!" was the sound hailing down in reply.

from "Moby Dick" by Herman Melville

"T'gallant-sails! stunsails alow and aloft, and on both sides!"

All sail being set, he now cast loose the life-line, reserved for swaying him to the mainroyal masthead; and in a few moments they were hoisting him thither, when, while but two-thirds of the way aloft, and while peering ahead through the horizontal vacancy between the maintopsail and top-gallant-sail, he raised a gull-like cry in the air, "There she blows!—there she blows! A hump like a snowhill! It is Moby Dick!"

Fired by the cry which seemed simultaneously taken up by the three look-outs, the men on deck rushed to the rigging to behold the famous whale they had so long been pursuing. Ahab had now gained his final perch, some feet above the other lookouts, Tashtego standing just beneath him on the cap of the top-gallant-mast, so that the Indian's head was almost on a level with Ahab's heel. From this height the whale was now seen some mile or so ahead, at every roll of the sea revealing his high sparkling hump, and regularly jetting his silent spout into the air. To the credulous mariners it seemed the same silent spout they had so long ago beheld in the moonlit Atlantic and Indian Oceans.

"And did none of ye see it before?" cried Ahab, hailing the perched men all around him.

"I saw him almost that same instant, sir, that Captain Ahab did, and I cried out," said Tashtego.

"Not the same instant; not the same—no, the doubloon is mine, Fate reserved the doubloon for me. *I* only; none of ye could have raised the White Whale first. There she blows! there she blows!—there she blows! There again!—there again!" he cried, in long-drawn, lingering, methodic tones, attuned to the gradual prolongings of the whale's visible jets. "He's going to sound! In stunsails! Down top-gallant-sails! Stand by three boats. Mr. Starbuck, remember, stay on board, and keep the ship. Helm there! Luff, luff a point! So; steady, man, steady! There go flukes! No, no; only black water! All ready the boats there? Stand by, stand by! Lower me, Mr. Starbuck; lower, lower,—quick, quicker!" and he slid through the air to the deck.

"He is heading straight to leeward, sir," cried Stubb; "right away from us; cannot have seen the ship yet."

"Be dumb, man! Stand by the braces! Hard down the helm!—brace up! Shiver her!—shiver her! So; well that! Boats, boats!"

Soon all the boats but Starbuck's were dropped; all the boatsails set—all the paddles plying; with rippling swiftness, shooting to leeward; and Ahab heading the onset. A pale, death-glimmer lit up Fedallah's sunken eyes; a hideous motion gnawed his mouth.

Like noiseless nautilus shells, their light prows sped through the sea; but only slowly they neared the foe. As they neared him, the ocean grew still more smooth; seemed drawing a carpet over its waves; seemed a noon-meadow, so serenely it spread. At length the breathless hunter came so nigh his seemingly unsuspecting prey, that his entire dazzling hump was distinctly visible, sliding along the sea as if an isolated thing, and continually set in a revolving ring of finest, fleecy, greenish foam. He saw the vast involved wrinkles of the slightly projecting head beyond. Before it, far out on the soft Turkish-rugged waters, went the glistening white shadow from his broad, milky forehead, a musical rippling playfully accompanying the shade; and behind, the blue waters interchangeably flowed over into the moving valley of his steady wake; and on either hand bright bubbles arose and danced by his side. But these were broken again by the light toes of hundreds of gay fowl softly feathering the sea, alternate with their fitful flight; and like to some flagstaff rising from the painted hull of an argosy, the tall but shattered pole of a recent lance projected from the White Whale's back; and at intervals one of the cloud of soft-toed fowls hovering, and to and fro skimming like a canopy over the fish, silently perched and rocked on this pole, the long tail feathers streaming like pennons.

A gentle joyousness—a mighty mildness of repose in swiftness, invested the gliding whale. Not the white bull Jupiter swimming away with ravished Europa clinging to his graceful horns; his lovely, leering eyes sideways intent upon the maid; with smooth bewitching fleetness, rippling straight for the nuptial bower in Crete; not Jove did surpass the glorified White Whale as he so divinely swam.

On each soft side—coincident with the parted swell, that but once laving him, then flowed so wide away—on each bright side, the whale shed off enticings. No wonder there had been some among the hunters who namelessly transported and allured by all this serenity, had ventured to assail it; but had fatally found that quietude but the vesture of tornadoes. Yet calm, enticing calm, oh, whale! thou glidest on, to all who for the first time eye thee, no matter how many in that same way thou may'st have bejuggled and destroyed before.

*The tall but shattered pole of a recent lance projected from
the white whale's back.*

And thus, through the serene tranquilities of the tropical sea, among waves whose hand-clappings were suspended by exceeding rapture, Moby Dick moved on, still withholding from sight the full terrors of his submerged trunk, entirely hiding the wretched hideousness of his jaw. But soon the fore part of him slowly rose from the water; for an instant his whole marbleized body formed a high arch, like Virginia's Natural Bridge, and warningly waving his bannered flukes in the air, the grand god revealed himself, sounded, and went out of sight. Hoveringly halting, and dipping on the wing, the white sea-fowls longingly lingered over the agitated pool that he left.

With oars apeak, and paddles down, the sheets of their sails adrift, the three boats now stilly floated, awaiting Moby Dick's reappearance.

"An hour," said Ahab, standing rooted in his boat's stern, and he gazed beyond the whale's place, towards the dim blue spaces and wide wooing vacancies to leeward. It was only an instant; for again his eyes seemed whirling round in his head as he swept the watery circle. The breeze now freshened; the sea began to swell.

"The birds!—the birds!" cried Tashtego.

In long Indian file, as when herons take wing, the white birds were now all flying towards Ahab's boat; and when within a few yards began fluttering over the water there, wheeling round and round, with joyous, expectant cries. Their vision was keener than man's; Ahab could discover no sign in the sea. But suddenly as he peered down and down into its depths, he profoundly saw a white living spot no bigger than a white weasel, with wonderful celerity uprising, and magnifying as it rose, till it turned, and then there were plainly revealed two long crooked rows of white, glistening teeth, floating up from the undiscoverable bottom. It was Moby Dick's open mouth and scrolled jaw; his vast, shadowed bulk still half blending with the blue of the sea. The glittering mouth yawned beneath the boat like an open-doored marble tomb; and giving one sidelong sweep with his steering oar, Ahab whirled the craft aside from this tremendous apparition. Then, calling upon Fedallah to change places with him, went forward to the bows, and seizing Perth's harpoon, commanded his crew to grasp their oars and stand by to stern.

Now, by reason of this timely spinning round the boat upon its axis, its bow, by anticipation, was made to face the whale's head while yet under water. But as if perceiving this stratagem, Moby Dick, with that malicious intelligence ascribed to him, sidelingly transplanted himself, as it were, in an instant, shooting his plaited head lengthwise beneath the boat.

Through and through; through every plank and each rib, it thrilled for an instant, the whale obliquely lying on his back, in the manner of a biting shark, slowly and feelingly taking its bows full within his mouth, so that the long, narrow, scrolled lower jaw curled high up into the open air, and one of the teeth caught in a rowlock. The bluish pearl-white of the inside of the jaw was within six inches of Ahab's head, and reached higher than that. In this attitude the White Whale now shook the slight cedar as a mildly cruel cat her mouse. With unastonished eyes Fedallah gazed, and crossed his arms; but the tiger-yellow crew were tumbling over each other's heads to gain the uttermost stern.

And now, while both elastic gunwales were springing in and out, as the whale dallied with the doomed craft in this devilish way; and from his body being submerged beneath the boat, he could not be darted at from the bows, for the bows were almost inside of him, as it were; and while the other boats involuntarily paused, as before a quick crisis impossible to withstand, then it was that monomaniac Ahab, furious with this tantalizing vicinity of his foe, which placed him all alive and helpless in the very jaws he hated; frenzied with all this, he seized the long bone with his naked hands, and wildly strove to wrench it from its gripe. As now he thus vainly strove, the jaw slipped from him; the frail gunwales bent in, collapsed, and snapped, as both jaws, like an enormous shears, sliding further aft, bit the craft completely in twain, and locked themselves fast again in the sea, midway between the two floating wrecks. These floated aside, the broken ends drooping, the crew at the stern-wreck clinging to the gunwales, and striving to hold fast to the oars to lash them across.

At that preluding moment, ere the boat was yet snapped, Ahab, the first to perceive the whale's intent, by the crafty upraising of his head, a movement that loosed his hold for the time; at that moment his hand had made one final effort to push the boat out of the bite. But only slipping further into the whale's mouth, and tilting over sideways as it slipped, the boat had shaken off his hold on the jaw; spilled him out of it, as he leaned to the push; and so he fell flat-faced upon the sea.

Ripplingly withdrawing from his prey, Moby Dick now lay at a little distance, vertically thrusting his oblong white head up and down in the billows; and at the same time slowly revolving his whole spindled body; so that when his vast wrinkled forehead rose—some twenty or more feet out of the water— the now rising swells, with all their confluent waves, dazzling broke against it; vindictively tossing their shivered spray still higher into the air.[1]   So, in a gale, the but half baffled Channel billows only recoil from the base of the Eddystone, triumphantly to overleap its summit with their scud.

But soon resuming his horizontal attitude, Moby Dick swam swiftly round and round the wrecked crew; sideways churning the water in his vengeful wake, as if lashing himself up to still another and more deadly assault.   The sight of the splintered boat seemed to madden him, as the blood of grapes and mulberries cast before Antiochus's elephants in the book of Maccabees.   Meanwhile Ahab half smothered in the foam of the whale's insolent tail, and too much of a cripple to swim,—though he could still keep afloat, even in the heart of such a whirlpool as that; helpless Ahab's head was seen, like a tossed bubble which the least chance shock might burst.   From the boat's fragmentary stern, Fedallah incuriously and mildly eyed him; the clinging crew, at the other drifting end, could not succor him; more than enough was it for them to look to themselves.   For so revolvingly appalling was the White Whale's aspect, and so planetarily swift the ever-contracting circles he made, that he seemed horizontally swooping upon them.   And though the other boats, unharmed, still hovered hard by, still they dared not pull into the eddy to strike, lest that should be the signal for the instant destruction of the jeopardized castaways, Ahab and all; nor in that case could they themselves hope to escape.   With straining eyes then, they remained on the outer edge of the direful zone, whose center had now become the old man's head.

Meantime, from the beginning all this had been descried from the ship's mastheads; and squaring her yards, she had borne down upon the scene; and was now so nigh, that Ahab in the water hailed her;—"Sail on the"—but that moment a breaking sea dashed on him from Moby Dick, and whelmed him for the time.   But struggling out of it again, and chancing to rise on a towering crest, he shouted,—"Sail on the whale!—Drive him off!"

The *Pequod*'s prows were pointed; and breaking up the charmed circle, she effectually parted the White Whale from his victim.   As he sullenly swam off, the boats flew to the rescue.

Dragged into Stubb's boat with bloodshot, blinded eyes, the white brine caking in his wrinkles; the long tension of Ahab's bodily strength did crack, and helplessly he yielded to his body's doom: for a time, lying all crushed in the bottom of Stubb's boat, like one trodden under foot of herds of elephants. Far inland, nameless wails came from him, as desolate sounds from out ravines.

But this intensity of his physical prostration did but so much the more abbreviate it. In an instant's compass, great hearts sometimes condense to one deep pang, the sum-total of those shallow pains kindly diffused through feebler men's whole lives. And so, such hearts, though summary in each one suffering; still, if the gods decree it, in their lifetime aggregate a whole age of woe, wholly made up of instantaneous intensities; for even in their pointless centers, those noble natures contain the entire circumferences of inferior souls.

"The harpoon," said Ahab, half-way rising, and draggingly leaning on one bended arm—"is it safe?"

"Aye, sir, for it was not darted; this is it," said Stubb, showing it.

"Lay it before me;—any missing men?"

"One, two, three, four, five;—there were five oars, sir, and here are five men."

"That's good.—Help me, man; I wish to stand. So, so, I see him! there! there! going to leeward still; what a leaping spout!—Hands off from me! The eternal sap runs up in Ahab's bones again! Set the sail; out oars; the helm!"

It is often the case that when a boat is stove, its crew, being picked up by another boat, help to work that second boat; and the chase is thus continued with what is called double-banked oars. It was thus now. But the added power of the boat did not equal the added power of the whale, for he seemed to have treble-banked his every fin; swimming with a velocity which plainly showed, that if now, under these circumstances, pushed on, the chase would prove an indefinitely prolonged, if not a hopeless one; nor could any crew endure for so long a period, such an unintermitted, intense straining at the oar; a thing barely tolerable only in some one brief vicissitude. The ship itself, then, as it sometimes happens, offered the most promising intermediate means of overtaking the chase. Accordingly, the boats now made for her, and were soon swayed up to their cranes—the two parts of the wrecked boat having been previously secured by her—and then hoisting everything to her side, and stacking her canvas high up, and sideways outstretching it with stunsails, like the double-jointed wings of an albatross; the *Pequod* bore down in the leeward wake of Moby Dick. At the well-known, methodic intervals, the whale's glittering spout was regularly announced from the manned mastheads; and when he would be reported as just gone down, Ahab would take the time, and then pacing the deck, binnacle-watch in hand, so soon as the last second of the allotted hour expired, his voice was heard.—"Whose is the doubloon now? D'ye see him?" and if the reply was, "No, sir!" straightway he commanded them to lift him to his perch. In this way the day wore on; Ahab, now aloft and motionless; anon, unrestingly pacing the planks.

As he was thus walking, uttering no sound, except to hail the men aloft, or to bid them hoist a sail still higher, or to spread one to a still greater breadth— thus to and fro pacing, beneath his slouched hat, at every turn he passed his own wrecked boat, which had been dropped upon the quarter-deck, and lay there reversed; broken bow to shattered stern. At last he paused before it; and as in an already over-clouded sky fresh troops of clouds will sometimes sail across, so over the old man's face there now stole some such added gloom as this.

Stubb saw him pause; and perhaps intending, not vainly, though, to evince his own unabated fortitude, and thus keep up a valiant place in his captain's mind, he advanced, and eyeing the wreck exclaimed—"The thistle the ass refused; it pricked his mouth too keenly, sir; ha! ha!"

"What soulless thing is this that laughs before a wreck? Man, man! did I not know thee brave as fearless fire (and as mechanical) I could swear thou wert poltroon. Groan nor laugh should be heard before a wreck."

"Aye, sir," said Starbuck, drawing near, " 'tis a solemn sight; an omen, and an ill one."

"Omen? omen?—the dictionary! If the gods think to speak outright to man, they will honorably speak outright; not shake their heads, and give an old wife's darkling hint.—Begone! Ye two are the opposite poles of one thing; Starbuck is Stubb reversed, and Stubb is Starbuck; and ye two are all mankind; and Ahab stands alone among the millions of the peopled earth, nor gods nor men his neighbors! Cold, cold—I shiver!—How now? Aloft there! D'ye see him? Sing out for every spout, though he spout ten times a second!"

The day was nearly done; only the hem of his golden robe was rustling. Soon, it was almost dark, but the look-out men still remained unset.

"Can't see the spout now, sir;—too dark"—cried a voice from the air.

"How heading when last seen?"

"As before, sir,—straight to leeward."

"Good! he will travel slower now 'tis night. Down royals and top-gallant stunsails, Mr. Starbuck. We must not run over him before morning; he's making a passage now, and may heave-to a while. Helm there! keep her full before the wind!—Aloft! come down!—Mr. Stubb, send a fresh hand to the foremast head, and see it manned till morning."—Then advancing towards the doubloon in the mainmast—"Men, this gold is mine, for I earned it; but I shall let it abide here till the White Whale is dead; and then, whosoever of ye first raises him, upon the day he shall be killed, this gold is that man's; and if on that day I shall again raise him, then, ten times its sum shall be divided among all of ye! Away now!—the deck is thine, sir."

And so saying, he placed himself half-way within the scuttle, and slouching his hat, stood there till dawn, except when at intervals rousing himself to see how the night wore on.

Second Day

At daybreak, the three mastheads were punctually manned afresh.

"D'ye see him?" cried Ahab after allowing a little space for the light to spread.

"See nothing, sir."

"Turn up all hands and make sail! he travels faster than I thought for;—the top-gallant-sails!—aye, they should have been kept on her all night. But no matter—'tis but resting for the rush."

Here be it said, that this pertinacious pursuit of one particular whale, continued through day into night, and through night into day, is a thing by no means unprecedented in the South Sea fishery. For such is the wonderful skill, prescience of experience, and invincible confidence acquired by some great natural geniuses among the Nantucket commanders, that from the simple observation of a whale when last described, they will, under certain given circumstances, pretty accurately foretell both the direction in which he will continue to swim for a time, while out of sight, as well as his probable rate of progression during that period. And, in these cases, somewhat as a pilot, when about losing sight of a coast, whose general trending he well knows, and which he desires shortly to return to again, but at some further point; like as this pilot stands by his compass, and takes the precise bearing of the cape at present visible, in order the more certainly to hit aright the remote, unseen headland, eventually to be visited: so does the fisherman, at his compass, with the whale; for after being chased, and diligently marked, through several hours of daylight, then, when night obscures the fish, the creature's future wake through the darkness is almost as established to the sagacious mind of the hunter, as the pilot's coast is to him. So that to this hunter's wondrous skill, the proverbial evanescence of a thing writ in water, a wake, is to all desired purposes wellnigh as reliable as the steadfast land. And as the mighty iron Leviathan of the modern railway is so familiarly known in its every pace, that, with watches in their hands, men time his rate as doctors that of a baby's pulse; and lightly say of it, "the up train or the down train will reach such or such a spot, at such or such an hour," even so, almost, there are occasions when these Nantucketers time that other Leviathan of the deep, according to the observed humor of his speed; and say to themselves, "So many hours hence this whale will have gone two hundred miles, will have about reached this or that degree of latitude or longitude." But to render this acuteness at all successful in the end, the wind and the sea must be the whaleman's allies; for of what present avail to the becalmed or windbound mariner is the skill that assures him he is exactly ninety-three leagues and a quarter from his port? Inferable from these statements are many collateral subtle matters touching the chase of whales.

The ship tore on; leaving such a furrow in the sea as when a cannon-ball, missent, becomes a ploughshare and turns up the level field.

"By salt and hemp!" cried Stubb, "but this swift motion of the deck creeps up one's legs and tingles at the heart. This ship and I are two brave fellows!—Ha! ha! Some one take me up, and launch me, spine-wise, on the sea,—for by live-oaks! my spine's a keel. Ha, ha! we go the gait that leaves no dust behind!"

"There she blows—she blows!—she blows!—right ahead!" was now the masthead cry.

"Aye, aye!" cried Stubb; "I knew it—ye can't escape—blow on and split your spout, O whale! the mad fiend himself is after ye! blow your trump—blister your lungs!—Ahab will dam off your blood, as a miller shuts his water-gate upon the stream!"

And Stubb did but speak out for well-nigh all that crew. The frenzies of the chase had by this time worked them bubblingly up, like old wine worked anew. Whatever pale fears and forebodings some of them might have felt before; these were not only now kept out of sight through the growing awe of Ahab, but they were broken up, and on all sides routed, as timid prairie hares that scatter before the bounding bison.   The hand of Fate had snatched all their souls; and by the stirring perils of the previous day; the rack of the past night's suspense; the fixed, unfearing, blind, reckless way in which their wild craft went plunging towards its flying mark; by all these things, their hearts were bowled along.   The wind that made great bellies of their sails, and rushed the vessel on by arms invisible as irresistible; this seemed the symbol of that unseen agency which so enslaved them to the race.

They were one man, not thirty.   For as the one ship that held them all; though it was put together of all contrasting things—oak, and maple, and pine wood; iron, and pitch, and hemp—yet all these ran into each other in the one concrete hull, which shot on its way, both balanced and directed by the long central keel; even so, all the individualities of the crew.   This man's valor, that man's fear; guilt and guiltiness, all varieties were welded into oneness, and were all directed to that fatal goal which Ahab their one lord and keel did point to.

The rigging lived.   The mastheads, like the tops of tall palms, were outspreadingly tufted with arms and legs.   Clinging to a spar with one hand, some reached forth the other with impatient wavings; others, shading their eyes from the vivid sunlight, sat far out on the rocking yards; all the spars in full bearing of mortals, ready and ripe for their fate.   Ah! how they still strove through that infinite blueness to seek out the thing that might destroy them!

"Why sing ye not out for him, if ye see him?" cried Ahab, when, after the lapse of some minutes since the first cry, no more had been heard.   "Sway me up, men; ye have been deceived; not Moby Dick casts one odd jet that way, and then disappears."

It was even so; in their headlong eagerness, the men had mistaken some other thing for the whale-spout, as the event itself soon proved; for hardly had Ahab reached his perch; hardly was the rope belayed to its pin on deck, when he struck the key-note to an orchestra, that made the air vibrate as with the combined discharges of rifles.   The triumphant halloo of thirty buckskin lungs was heard, as—much nearer to the ship than the place of the imaginary jet, less than a mile ahead—Moby Dick bodily burst into view!   For not by any calm and indolent spoutings; not by the peaceable gush of that mystic fountain in his head, did the White Whale now reveal his vicinity; but by the far more wondrous phenomenon of breaching.   Rising with his utmost velocity from the furthest depths, the Sperm Whale thus booms his entire bulk into the pure element of air, and piling up a mountain of dazzling foam, shows his place to the distance of seven miles and more. In those moments, the torn, enraged waves he shakes off seem his mane; in some cases this breaching is his act of defiance.

"There she breaches! there she breaches!" was the cry, as in his immeasurable bravadoes the White Whale tossed himself salmon-like to Heaven. So suddenly seen in the blue plain of the sea, and relieved against the still bluer margin of the sky, the spray that he raised, for the moment, intolerably glittered and glared like a glacier; and stood there gradually fading and fading away from its first sparkling intensity, to the dim mistiness of an advancing shower in a vale.

"Aye, breach your last to the sun, Moby Dick!" cried Ahab, "thy hour and thy harpoon are at hand!—Down! down all of ye, but one man at the fore. The boats!—stand by!"

Unmindful of the tedious rope-ladders of the shrouds, the men, like shooting stars, slid to the deck, by the isolated backstays and halyards; while Ahab, less dartingly, but still rapidly, was dropped from his perch.

"Lower away," he cried, so soon as he had reached his boat—a spare one, rigged the afternoon previous. "Mr. Starbuck, the ship is thine—keep away from the boats but keep near them. Lower, all!"

As if to strike a quick terror into them, by this time being the first assailant himself, Moby Dick had turned, and was now coming for the three crews. Ahab's boat was central; and cheering his men, he told them he would take the whale head-and-head,—that is, pull straight up to his forehead,—a not uncommon thing; for when within a certain limit, such a course excludes the coming onset from the whale's sidelong vision. But ere that close limit was gained, and while yet all three boats were plain as the ship's three masts to his eye; the White Whale churning himself into furious speed, almost in an instant as it were, rushing among the boats with open jaws, and a lashing tail, offered appalling battle on every side; and heedless of the irons darted at him from every boat, seemed only intent on annihilating each separate plank of which those boats were made. But skilfully maneuvered, incessantly wheeling like trained chargers in the field; the boats for a while eluded him; though, at times, but by a plank's breadth; while all the time, Ahab's unearthly slogan tore every other cry but his to shreds.

But at last in his untraceable evolutions, the White Whale so crossed and re-crossed, and in a thousand ways entangled the slack of the three lines now fast to him, that they foreshortened, and, of themselves, warped the devoted boats towards the planted irons in him; though now for a moment the whale drew aside a little, as if to rally for a more tremendous charge. Seizing that opportunity, Ahab first paid out more line: and then was rapidly hauling and jerking in upon it again—hoping that way to disencumber it of some snarls—when lo! —a sight more savage than the embattled teeth of sharks!

Caught and twisted—corkscrewed in the mazes of the line—loose harpoons and lances, with all their bristling barbs and points, came flashing and dripping up to the chocks in the bows of Ahab's boat. Only one thing could be done. Seizing the boat-knife, he critically reached within—through—and then, without—the rays of steel; dragged in the line beyond, passed it, inboard, to the bowsman, and then, twice sundering the rope near the chocks— dropped the intercepted fagot of steel into the sea; and was all fast again. That instant, the White Whale made a sudden rush among the remaining tangles of the other lines; by so doing, irresistibly dragged the more involved boats of Stubb and Flask towards his flukes; dashed them together like two rolling husks on a surf-beaten beach, and then, diving down into the sea, disappeared in a boiling maelstrom, in which, for a space, the odorous cedar chips of the wrecks danced round and round, like the grated nutmeg in a swiftly stirred bowl of punch.

While the two crews were yet circling in the waters, reaching out after the revolving line-tubs, oars, and other floating furniture, while aslope little Flask bobbed up and down like an empty vial, twitching his legs upwards to escape the dreaded jaws of sharks; and Stubb was lustily singing out for someone to ladle him up; and while the old man's line—now parting—admitted of his pulling into the creamy pool to rescue whom he could;—in that wild simultaneousness of a thousand concreted perils,—Ahab's yet unstricken boat seemed drawn up towards Heaven by invisible wires,—as arrow-like, shooting perpendicularly from the sea, the White Whale dashed his broad forehead against its bottom, and sent it, turning over and over, into the air; till it fell again—gunwale downwards—and Ahab and his men struggled out from under it, like seals from a seaside cave.

The first uprising momentum of the whale—modifying its direction as he struck the surface—involuntarily launched him along it, to a little distance from the center of the destruction he had made; and with his back to it, he now lay for a moment slowly feeling with his flukes from side to side; and whenever a stray oar, bit of plank, the least chip or crumb of the boats touched his skin, his tail swiftly drew back, and came sideways, smiting the sea. But soon, as if satisfied that his work for that time was done, he pushed his plaited forehead through the ocean, and trailing after him the intertangled lines, continued his leeward way at a traveler's methodic pace.

As before, the attentive ship having described the whole fight, again came bearing down to the rescue, and dropping a boat, picked up the floating mariners, tubs, oars, and whatever else could be caught at, and safely landed them on her decks. Some sprained shoulders, wrists, and ankles; livid contusions; wrenched harpoons and lances: inextricable intricacies of rope; shattered oars and planks; all these were there; but no fatal or even serious ill seemed to have befallen anyone. As with Fedallah the day before, so Ahab was now found grimly clinging to his boat's broken half, which afforded a comparatively easy float; nor did it so exhaust him as the previous day's mishap.

But when he was helped to the deck, all eyes were fastened upon him; as instead of standing by himself he still half-hung upon the shoulder of Starbuck, who had thus far been the foremost to assist him. His ivory leg had been snapped off, leaving but one short sharp splinter.

"Aye, aye, Starbuck, 'tis sweet to lean sometimes, be the leaner who he will; and would old Ahab had leaned oftener than he has."

"The ferrule has not stood, sir," said the carpenter, now coming up; "I put good work into that leg."

"But no bones broken, sir, I hope," said Stubb with true concern.

"Aye! and all splintered to pieces, Stubb!—d'ye see it.—But even with a broken bone, old Ahab is untouched; and I account no living bone of mine one jot more me, than this dead one that's lost. Nor White Whale, nor man, nor fiend, can so much as graze old Ahab in his own proper and inaccessible being. Can any lead touch yonder floor, any mast scrape yonder roof?— Aloft there! which way?"

"Dead to leeward, sir."

"Up helm, then; pile on the sail again, shipkeepers! down the rest of the spare boats and rig them—Mr. Starbuck, away, and muster the boat's crews."

"Let me first help thee towards the bulwarks, sir."

"Oh, oh, oh! how this splinter gores me now! Accursed fate! that the unconquerable captain in the soul should have such a craven mate!"

"Sir?"

"My body, man, not thee. Give me something for a cane—there, that shivered lance will do. Muster the men. Surely I have not seen him yet. By heaven, it cannot be!—missing?—quick! call them all."

The old man's hinted thought was true. Upon mustering the company, the Parsee was not there.

"The Parsee!" cried Stubb—"he must have been caught in——"

"The black vomit wrench thee!—run all of ye above, alow, cabin, forecastle—find him—not gone—not gone!"

But quickly they returned to him with the tidings that the Parsee was nowhere to be found.

"Aye, sir," said Stubb—"caught among the tangles of your line—I thought I saw him dragging under."

"*My* line? *my* line? Gone?—gone? What means that little word?—What death-knell rings in it, that old Ahab shakes as if he were the belfry. The harpoon, too!—toss over the litter there,—d'ye see it?—the forged iron, men, the White Whale's—no, no, no,—blistered fool! this hand did dart it!—'tis in the fish!—Aloft there! Keep him nailed—Quick!—all hands to the rigging of the boats—collect the oars—harpooneers! the irons, the irons!—hoist the royals higher—a pull on the sheets!—helm there! steady, steady for your life! I'll ten times girdle the unmeasured globe; yea and dive straight through it, but I'll slay him yet!"

"Great God! but for one single instant show thyself," cried Starbuck; "never never wilt thou capture him, old man.—In Jesus' name no more of this, that's worse than devil's madness. Two days chased; twice stove to splinters; thy very leg once more snatched from under thee; thy evil shadow gone—all good angels mobbing thee with warnings:—what more wouldst thou have?— Shall we keep chasing this murderous fish till he swamps the last man? Shall we be dragged by him to the bottom of the sea? Shall we be towed by him to the infernal world? Oh, oh!—Impiety and blasphemy to hunt him more!"

"Starbuck, of late I've felt strangely moved to thee; ever since that hour we both saw—thou know'st what, in one another's eyes. But in this matter of the whale, be the front of thy face to me as the palm of this hand—a lipless, unfeatured blank. Ahab is for ever Ahab, man. This whole act's immutably decreed. 'Twas rehearsed by thee and me a billion years before this ocean rolled. Fool! I am the Fates' lieutenant; I act under orders. Look thou, underling! that thou obeyest mine.—Stand round me, men. Ye see an old man cut down to the stump; leaning on a shivered lance; propped up on a lonely foot. 'Tis Ahab—his body's part; but Ahab's soul's a centipede, that moves upon a hundred legs. I feel strained, half stranded, as ropes that tow dismasted frigates in a gale; and I may look so. But ere I break, ye'll hear me crack; and till ye hear *that*, know that Ahab's hawser tows his purpose yet. Believe ye, men, in the things called omens? Then laugh aloud, and cry encore! For ere they drown, drowning things will twice rise to the surface; then rise again, to sink for evermore. So with Moby Dick—two days he's floated—tomorrow will be the third. Aye, men, he'll rise once more—but only to spout his last! D'ye feel brave men, brave?"

"As fearless fire," cried Stubb.

"And as mechanical," muttered Ahab. Then as the men went forward, he muttered on:—"The things called omens! And yesterday I talked the same to Starbuck there, concerning my broken boat. Oh! how valiantly I seek to drive out of others' hearts what's clinched so fast in mine!—The Parsee— the Parsee!—gone, gone? and he was to go before:—but still was to be seen again ere I could perish—How's that?—There's a riddle now might baffle all the lawyers backed by the ghosts of the whole line of judges:—like a hawk's beak it pecks my brain. *I'll, I'll* solve it, though!"

When dusk descended, the whale was still in sight to leeward.

So once more the sail was shortened, and everything passed nearly as on the previous night; only, the sound of hammers, and the hum of the grindstone was heard till nearly daylight, as the men toiled by lanterns in the complete and careful rigging of the spare boats and sharpening their fresh weapons for the morrow. Meantime, of the broken keel of Ahab's wrecked craft the carpenter made him another leg; while still as on the night before, slouched Ahab stood fixed within his scuttle; his hid heliotrope glance anticipatingly gone backward on its dial; set due eastward for the earliest sun.

Third Day

The morning of the third day dawned fair and fresh, and once more the solitary night-man at the fore-masthead was relieved by crowds of the daylight lookouts, who dotted every mast and almost every spar.

"D'ye see him?" cried Ahab; but the whale was not yet in sight.

"In his infallible wake, though; but follow that wake, that's all. Helm there; steady, as thou goest, and hast been going. What a lovely day again! were it a new-made world, and made for a summer-house to the angels, and this morning the first of its throwing open to them, a fairer day could not dawn upon that world. Here's food for thought, had Ahab time to think, but Ahab never thinks; he only feels, feels, feels, *that's* tingling enough for mortal man! to think's audacity. God only has that right and privilege. Thinking is, or ought to be a coolness and a calmness; and our poor hearts throb, and our poor brains beat too much for that. And yet, I've sometimes thought my brain was very calm—frozen calm, this old skull cracks so, like a glass in which the contents turn to ice, and shiver it. And still this hair is growing now; this moment growing, and heat must breed it; but no, it's like that sort of common grass that will grow anywhere, between the earthly clefts of Greenland ice or in Vesuvius lava. How the wild winds blow it; they whip it about me as the torn shreds of split sails lash the tossed ship they cling to. A vile wind that has no doubt blown ere this through prison corridors and cells, and wards of hospitals, and ventilated them, and now comes blowing hither as innocent as fleeces. Out upon it!—it's tainted. Were I the wind, I'd blow no more on such a wicked, miserable world. I'd crawl somewhere to a cave, and slink there. And yet, 'tis a noble and heroic thing, the wind! who ever conquered it? In every fight it has the last and bitterest blow. Run tilting at it, and you but run through it. Ha! a coward wind that strikes stark naked men, but will not stand to receive a single blow. Even Ahab is a braver thing—a nobler thing than *that*. Would now the wind but had a body; but all the things that most exasperate and outrage mortal man, all these things are bodiless, but only bodiless as objects, not as agents. There's a most special, a most cunning, oh, a most malicious difference! And yet, I say again, and swear it now, that there's something all glorious and gracious in the wind. These warm Trade Winds, at least, that in the clear heavens blow straight on, in strong and steadfast, vigorous mildness; and veer not from their mark, however the baser currents of the sea may turn and tack, and the mightiest Mississippis of the land shift and swerve about, uncertain where to go at last. And by the eternal Poles; these same Trades that so directly blow my good ship on; these Trades, or something like them—something so unchangeable, and full as strong, blow my keeled soul along! To it! Aloft there! What d'ye see?"

"Nothing, sir."

"Nothing! and noon at hand! The doubloon goes a-begging! See the sun!

Aye, aye, it must be so. I've oversailed him. How, got the start? Aye, he's chasing *me* now; not I, *him*—that's bad; I might have known it, too. Fool! the lines—the harpoons he's towing. Aye, aye, I have run him by last night. About! about! Come down, all of ye, but the regular lookouts! Man the braces!"

Steering as she had done, the wind had been somewhat on the *Pequod's* quarter, so that now being pointed in the reverse direction, the braced ship sailed hard upon the breeze as she rechurned the cream in her own white wake.

"Against the wind he now steers for the open jaw," murmured Starbuck to himself, as he coiled the new-hauled main-brace upon the rail. "God keep us, but already my bones feel damp within me, and from the inside wet my flesh. I misdoubt me that I disobey my God in obeying him!"

"Stand by to sway me up!" cried Ahab, advancing to the hempen basket. "We should meet him soon."

"Aye, aye, sir," and straightway Starbuck did Ahab's bidding, and once more Ahab swung on high.

A whole hour now passed; gold-beaten out to ages. Time itself now held long breaths with keen suspense. But at last, some three points off the weatherbow, Ahab descried the spout again, and instantly from the three mastheads three shrieks went up as if the tongues of fire had voiced it.

"Forehead to forehead I meet thee, this third time, Moby Dick! On deck there!—brace sharper up; crowd her into the wind's eye. He's too far off to lower yet, Mr. Starbuck. The sails shake! Stand over the helmsman with a topmaul! So, so; he travels fast, and I must down. But let me have one more good round look aloft here at the sea; there's time for that. An old, old sight, and yet somehow so young; aye, and not changed a wink since I first saw it, a boy, from the sandhills of Nantucket! The same!—the same!—the same to Noah as to me. There's a soft shower to leeward. Such lovely leewardings! They must lead somewhere—to something else than common land, more palmy than the palms. Leeward! the White Whale goes that way; look to windward, then; the better if the bitter quarter. But good-bye, good-bye, old masthead! What's this?—green? aye, tiny mosses in these warped cracks. No such green weather stains on Ahab's head! There's the difference now between man's old age and matter's. But aye, old mast, we both grow old together; sound in our hulls, though, are we not, my ship? Aye, minus a leg, that's all. By heaven! this dead wood has the better of my live flesh every way. I can't compare with it; and I've known some ships made of dead trees outlast the lives of men made of the most vital stuff of vital fathers. What's that he said? he should still go before me, my pilot; and yet to be seen again? But where? Shall I have eyes at the bottom of the sea, supposing I descend those endless stairs? and all night I've been sailing from him, wherever he did sink to. Aye, aye, like many more thou told'st direful truth as touching thyself, O Parsee; but, Ahab, there thy shot fell short. Good-bye, masthead—keep a good eye upon the whale, the while I'm gone. We'll talk tomorrow, nay, tonight, when the White Whale lies down there, tied by head and tail."

He gave the word; and still gazing round him, was steadily lowered through the cloven blue air to the deck.

In due time the boats were lowered; but as standing in his shallop's stern, Ahab just hovered upon the point of the descent, he waved to the mate,—who held one of the tackle-ropes on deck—and bade him pause.

"Starbuck!"

"Sir?"

"For the third time my soul's ship starts upon this voyage, Starbuck."

"Aye, sir, thou wilt have it so."

"Some ships sail from their ports, and ever afterwards are missing, Starbuck!"

"Truth, sir: saddest truth."

"Some men die at ebb tide; some at low water; some at the full of the flood;—and I feel now like a billow that's all one crested comb, Starbuck. I am old;—shake hands with me, man."

Their hands met; their eyes fastened; Starbuck's tears the glue.

"Oh, my captain, my captain!—noble heart—go not—go not!—see, its a brave man that weeps; how great the agony of the persuasion then!"

"Lower away!"—cried Ahab, tossing the mate's arm from him. "Stand by the crew!"

In an instant the boat was pulling round close under the stern.

"The sharks! the sharks!" cried a voice from the low cabin-window there; "O master, my master, come back!"

But Ahab heard nothing; for his own voice was high-lifted then; and the boat leaped on.

Yet the voice spake true; for scarce had he pushed from the ship, when numbers of sharks, seemingly rising from out dark waters beneath the hull, maliciously snapped at the blades of the oars, every time they dipped in the water; and in this way accompanied the boat with their bites. It is a thing not uncommonly happening to the whale-boats in those swarming seas; the sharks at times apparently following them in the same prescient way that vultures hover over the banners of marching regiments in the east. But these were the first sharks that had been observed by the *Pequod* since the White Whale had been first described; and whether it was that Ahab's crew were all such tiger-yellow barbarians, and therefore their flesh more musky to the senses of the sharks—a matter sometimes well known to affect them,—however it was, they seemed to follow that one boat without molesting the others.

"Heart of wrought steel!" murmured Starbuck, gazing over the side, and following with his eyes the receding boat—"canst thou yet ring boldly to that sight?—lowering thy keel among ravening sharks, and followed by them, open-mouthed, to the chase; and this the critical third day?—For when three days flow together in one continuous intense pursuit; be sure the first is the morning, the second the noon, and the third the evening and the end of that thing—be that end what it may. Oh! my God! what is this that shoots through me, and leaves me so deadly calm, yet expectant,—fixed at the top of a shudder! Future things swim before me, as in empty outlines and skeletons; all the past is somehow grown dim. Mary, girl! thou fadest in pale glories behind me; boy! I seem to see but thy eyes grown wondrous blue. Strangest problems of life seem clearing; but clouds sweep between—Is my journey's end coming? My legs feel faint; like his who has footed it all day. Feel thy heart,—beats it yet?—Stir thyself, Starbuck!—stave it off—move, move! speak aloud!—Masthead there! See ye my boy's hand on the hill?—Crazed; —aloft there!—keep thy keenest eye upon the boats:—mark well the whale! —Ho! again!—drive off that hawk! see! he pecks—he tears the vane"— pointing to the red flag flying at the main-truck—"Ha! he soars away with it!—Where's the old man now? sees't thou that sight, oh Ahab!—shudder, shudder!"

The boats had not gone very far, when by a signal from the mastheads—a downward pointed arm, Ahab knew that the whale had sounded; but intend-ing to be near him at the next rising, he held on his way a little sideways from the vessel; the becharmed crew maintaining the profoundest silence, as the head-beat waves hammered and hammered against the opposing bow.

"Drive, drive in your nails, oh ye waves! to their uttermost heads drive them in! ye but strike a thing without a lid; and no coffin and no hearse can be mine:—and hemp only can kill me! Ha! ha!"

Suddenly the waters around them slowly swelled in broad circles; then quickly upheaved, as if sideways sliding from a submerged berg of ice, swiftly rising to the surface. A low rumbling sound was heard; a subterraneous hum; and then all held their breaths; as bedraggled with trailing ropes, and harpoons, and lances, a vast form shot lengthwise, but obliquely from the sea. Shrouded in a thin drooping veil of mist, it hovered for a moment in the rainbowed air; and then fell swamping back into the deep. Crushed thirty feet upwards, the waters flashed for an instant like heaps of fountains, then brokenly sank in a shower of flakes, leaving the circling surface creamed like new milk round the marble trunk of the whale.

"Give way!" cried Ahab to the oarsmen and the boats darted forward to the attack; but maddened by yesterday's fresh irons that corroded in him, Moby Dick seemed combinedly possessed by all the angels that fell from heaven. The wide tiers of welded tendons overspreading his broad white forehead, beneath the transparent skin, looked knitted together; as head on, he came churning his tail among the boats; and once more flailed them apart; spilling out the irons and lances from the two mates' boats, and dashing in one side of the upper part of their bows, but leaving Ahab's almost without a scar.

While Daggoo and Queequeg were stopping the strained planks; and as the whale swimming out from them, turned, and showed one entire flank as he shot by them again; at that moment a quick cry went up. Lashed round and round to the fish's back; pinioned in the turns upon turns in which, during the past night, the whale had reeled the involutions of the lines around him, the half torn body of the Parsee was seen; his sable raiment frayed to shreds; his distended eyes turned full upon old Ahab.

The harpoon dropped from his hand.

"Befooled, befooled!"—drawing in a long lean breath—"Aye, Parsee! I see thee again.—Aye, and thou goest before; and this, *this* then is the hearse that thou didst promise. But I hold thee to the last letter of thy word. Where is the second hearse? Away, mates, to the ship! those boats are useless now; repair them if ye can in time, and return to me; if not, Ahab is enough to die—

Down, men! the first thing that but offers to jump from this boat I stand in, that thing I harpoon.   Ye are not other men, but my arms and my legs; and so obey me.—Where's the whale? gone down again?"

But he looked too nigh the boat; for as if bent upon escaping with the corpse he bore and as if the particular place of the last encounter had been but a stage in his leeward voyage, Moby Dick was now again steadily swimming forward; and had almost passed the ship,—which thus far had been sailing in the contrary direction to him, though for the present her headway had been stopped.   He seemed swimming with his utmost velocity, and now only intent upon pursuing his own straight path in the sea.

"Oh! Ahab," cried Starbuck, "not too late is it, even now, the third day, to desist.   See! Moby Dick seeks thee not.   It is thou, thou, that madly seekest him!"

Setting sail to the rising wind, the lonely boat was swiftly impelled to leeward, by both oars and canvas.   And at last when Ahab was sliding by the vessel, so near as plainly to distinguish Starbuck's face as he leaned over the rail, he hailed him to turn the vessel about, and follow him, not too swiftly, at a judicious interval.   Glancing upwards, he saw Tashtego, Queequeg, and Daggoo, eagerly mounting to the three mastheads; while the oarsmen were rocking in the two staved boats which had just been hoisted to the side, and were busily at work in repairing them.   One after the other, through the port-holes, as he sped, he also caught flying glimpses of Stubb and Flask, busying themselves on deck among bundles of new irons and lances.   As he saw all this; as he heard the hammers in the broken boats; far other hammers seemed driving a nail into his heart.   But he rallied.   And now marking that the vane or flag was gone from the main masthead, he shouted to Tashtego, who had just gained that perch, to descend again for another flag, and a hammer and nails, and so nail it to the mast.

Whether fagged by the three days' running chase, and the resistance to his swimming in the knotted hamper he bore; or whether it was some latent deceitfulness and malice in him: whichever was true, the White Whale's way now began to abate, as it seemed, from the boat so rapidly nearing him once more; though indeed the whale's last start had not been so long a one as before. And still as Ahab glided over the waves the unpitying sharks accompanied him; and so pertinaciously stuck to the boat; and so continually bit at the plying oars, that the blades became jagged and crunched, and left small splinters in the sea, at almost every dip.

"Heed them not! those teeth but give new rowlocks to your oars. Pull on! 'tis the better rest, the shark's jaw than the yielding water."

"But at every bite, sir, the thin blades grow smaller and smaller."

"They will last long enough! pull on!—But who can tell"—he muttered—"whether these sharks swim to feast on a whale or on Ahab?—But pull on! Aye, all alive, now—we near him. The helm! take the helm; let me pass,"—and so saying, two of the oarsmen helped him forward to the bows of the still flying boat.

At length as the craft was cast to one side, and ran ranging along with the White Whale's flank, he seemed strangely oblivious of its advance—as the whale sometimes will—and Ahab was fairly within the smoky mountain mist, which, thrown off from the whale's spout, curled round his great, Monadnock hump. He was even thus close to him; when, with body arched back, and both arms lengthwise highlifted to the poise, he darted his fierce iron, and his far fiercer curse into the hated whale. As both steel and curse sank to the socket, as if sucked into a morass, Moby Dick sideways writhed; spasmodically rolled his nigh flank against the bow, and, without staving a hole in it, so suddenly canted the boat over, that had it not been for the elevated part of the gunwale to which he then clung, Ahab would once more have been tossed into the sea. As it was, three of the oarsmen—who foreknew not the precise instant of the dart, and were therefore unprepared for its effects—these were flung out; but so fell, that, in an instant two of them clutched the gunwale again, and rising to its level on a combing wave, hurled themselves bodily inboard again; the third man helplessly drooping astern, but still afloat and swimming.

Almost simultaneously, with a mighty volition or ungraduated, instantaneous swiftness, the White Whale darted through the weltering sea. But when Ahab cried out to the steersman to take new turns with the line, and hold it so; and commanded the crew to turn round on their seats, and tow the boat up to the mark; the moment the treacherous line felt that double strain and tug, it snapped in the empty air!

"What breaks in me? Some sinew cracks!—'tis whole again; oars! oars! Burst in upon him!"

Hearing the tremendous rush of the sea-crashing boat, the whale wheeled round to present his blank forehead at bay; but in that evolution, catching sight of the nearing black hull of the ship; seemingly seeing in it the source of all his persecutions; bethinking it—it may be—a larger and nobler foe; of a sudden, he bore down upon its advancing prow, smiting his jaws amid fiery showers of foam.

Ahab staggered; his hand smote his forehead. "I grow blind; hands! stretch out before me that I may yet grope my way. Is't nigh?"

"The whale! The ship!" cried the cringing oarsmen.

"Oars! oars! Slope downwards to thy depths, O sea, that ere it be for ever too late, Ahab may slide this last, last time upon his mark! I see: the ship! the ship! Dash on, my men! Will ye not save my ship?"

But as the oarsmen violently forced their boat through the sledge-hammering seas, the before whale-smitten bow-ends of two planks burst through, and in an instant almost, the temporarily disabled boat lay nearly level with the waves; its half-wading, splashing crew, trying hard to stop the gap and bale out the pouring water.

Meantime, for that one beholding instant, Tashtego's masthead hammer remained suspended in his hand; and the red flag, half-wrapping him as with a plaid, then streamed itself straight out from him, as his own forward-flowing heart; while Starbuck and Stubb, standing upon the bowsprit beneath, caught sight of the down-coming monster just as soon as he.

"The whale, the whale! Up helm, up helm! Oh, all ye sweet powers of air, now hug me close! Let not Starbuck die, if die he must, in a woman's fainting fit. Up helm, I say—ye fools, the jaw! the jaw! Is this the end of all my bursting prayers? all my life-long fidelities? Oh, Ahab, Ahab, lo, thy work. Steady! helmsman, steady. Nay, nay! Up helm again! He turns to meet us! Oh, his unappeasable brow drives on towards one, whose duty tells him he cannot depart. My God, stand by me now!"

"Stand not by me, but stand under me, whoever you are that will now help Stubb; for Stubb, too, sticks here. I grin at thee, thou grinning whale! Whoever helped Stubb, or kept Stubb awake, but Stubb's own unwinking eye? And now poor Stubb goes to bed upon a mattress that is all too soft; would it were stuffed with brushwood! I grin at thee, thou grinning whale! Look ye, sun, moon and stars! I call ye assassins of as good a fellow as ever spouted up his ghost. For all that, I would yet ring glasses with ye, would ye but hand the cup! Oh, oh, oh, oh! thou grinning whale, but there'll be plenty of gulping soon! Why fly ye not, O, Ahab? For me, off shoes and jacket to it, let Stubb die in his drawers! A most moldy and oversalted death, though;—cherries! cherries! cherries! Oh, Flask, for one red cherry ere we die!"

"Cherries? I only wish that we were where they grow. Oh, Stubb, I hope my poor mother's drawn my part-pay ere this; if not, few coppers will come to her now, for the voyage is up."

From the ship's bows, nearly all the seamen now hung inactive; hammers, bits of plank, lances, and harpoons, mechanically retained in their hands, just as they had darted from their various employments; all their enchanted eyes intent upon the whale, which from side to side strangely vibrating his predestinating head, sent a broad band of overspreading semicircular foam before him as he rushed. Retribution, swift vengeance, eternal malice were in his whole aspect, and spite of all that mortal man could do, the solid white buttress of his forehead smote the ship's starboard bow, till men and timbers reeled. Some fell flat upon their faces. Like dislodged trucks, the heads of the harpooneers aloft shook on their bull-like necks. Through the breach, they heard the waters pour, as mountain torrents down a flume.

"The ship! The hearse!—the second hearse!" cried Ahab from the boat; "its wood could only be American!"

Diving beneath the settling ship, the whale ran quivering along its keel; but turning under water, swiftly shot to the surface again, far off the other bow, but within a few yards of Ahab's boat, where, for a time, he lay quiescent.

"I turn my body from the sun. What ho, Tashtego! let me hear thy hammer. Oh! ye three unsurrendered spires of mine; thou uncracked keel; and only god-bullied hull; thou firm deck, and haughty helm, and Pole-pointed prow,—death-glorious ship! must ye then perish, and without me? Am I cut off from the last fond pride of meanest shipwrecked captains? Oh, lonely death on lonely life! Oh, now I feel my topmost greatness lies in my topmost grief. Ho, ho! from all your furthest bounds, pour ye now in, ye bold billows of my whole foregone life, and top this one piled comber of my death! Towards thee I roll, thou all-destroying but unconquering whale; to the last I grapple with thee; from hell's heart I stab at thee; for hate's sake I spit my last breath at thee. Sink all coffins and all hearses to one common pool! and since neither can be mine let me then tow to pieces, while still chasing thee, though tied to thee, thou damned whale! *Thus*, I give up the spear!"

The harpoon was darted; the stricken whale flew forward; with igniting velocity the line ran through the groove; ran foul. Ahab stopped to clear it; he did clear it; but the flying turn caught him round the neck, and voicelessly as Turkish mutes bowstring their victim, he was shot out of the boat, ere the crew knew he was gone. Next instant, the heavy eyesplice in the rope's final end flew out of the stark-empty tub, knocked down an oarsman, and smiting the sea, disappeared in its depths.

For an instant, the tranced boat's crew stood still; then turned. "The ship? Great God, where is the ship? Soon they through dim, bewildering mediums saw her sidelong fading phantom, as in the gaseous Fata Morgana; only the uppermost masts out of water; while fixed by infatuation, or fidelity, or fate, to their once lofty perches, the pagan harpooneers still maintained their sinking lookouts on the sea. And now, concentric circles seized the lone boat itself, and all its crew, and each floating oar, and every lance-pole, and spinning, animate and inanimate, all round and round in one vortex, carried the smallest chip of the *Pequod* out of sight.

But as the last whelmings intermixingly poured themselves over the sunken head of the Indian at the mainmast, leaving a few inches of the erect spar yet visible, together with long streaming yards of the flag, which calmly undulated, with ironical coincidings, over the destroying billows they almost touched;—at that instant, a red arm and a hammer hovered backwardly uplifted in the open air, in the act of nailing the flag faster and yet faster to the subsiding spar. A sky-hawk that tauntingly had followed the main-truck downwards from its natural home among the stars, pecking at the flag, and incommoding Tashtego there; this bird now chanced to intercept its broad fluttering wing between the hammer and the wood; and simultaneously feeling that ethereal thrill, the submerged savage beneath, in his death-gasp, kept his hammer frozen there; and so the bird of heaven, with unearthly shrieks, and his imperial beak thrust upwards, and his whole captive form folded in the flag of Ahab, went down with his ship, which, like Satan, would not sink to hell till she had dragged a living part of heaven along with her, and helmeted herself with it.

Now small fowls flew screaming over the yet yawning gulf; a sullen white surf beat against its steep sides; then all collapsed, and the great shroud of the sea rolled on as it rolled five thousand years ago.

ROUNDING CAPE HORN

Herman Melville

AND NOW, through drizzling fogs and vapors, and under damp, double-reefed top-sails, our wet-decked frigate drew nearer and nearer to the squally Cape.

Who has not heard of it? Cape Horn, Cape Horn—a *horn* indeed, that has tossed many a good ship. Was the descent of Orpheus, Ulysses, or Dante into Hell, one whit more hardy and sublime than the first navigator's weathering of that terrible Cape?

Turned on her heel by a fierce West Wind, many an outward-bound ship has been driven across the Southern Ocean to the Cape of Good Hope—*that* way to seek a passage to the Pacific. And that stormy Cape, I doubt not, has sent many a fine craft to the bottom, and told no tales. At those ends of the earth are no chronicles. What signify the broken spars and shrouds that, day after day, are driven before the prows of more fortunate vessels? or the tall masts, imbedded in icebergs, that are found floating by? They but hint the old story—of ships that have sailed from their ports, and never more have been heard of.

Impracticable Cape! You may approach it from this direction or that—in any way you please—from the East or from the West; with the wind astern, or abeam, or on the quarter; and still Cape Horn is Cape Horn. Cape Horn it is that takes the conceit out of fresh-water sailors, and steeps in a still salter brine the saltest. Woe betide the tyro; the fool-hardy, Heaven preserve!

Your Mediterranean captain, who with a cargo of oranges has hitherto made merry runs across the Atlantic, without so much as furling a t'-gallant-

from "White Jacket" by Herman Melville

sail, oftentimes, off Cape Horn, receives a lesson which he carries to the grave; though the grave—as is too often the case—follows so hard on the lesson that no benefit comes from the experience.

Other strangers who draw nigh to this Patagonia termination of our Continent, with their souls full of its shipwrecks and disasters—top-sails cautiously reefed, and everything guardedly snug—these strangers at first unexpectedly encountering a tolerably smooth sea, rashly conclude that the Cape, after all, is but a bugbear; they have been imposed upon by fables, and founderings and sinkings hereabouts are all cock-and-bull stories.

"Out reefs, my hearties; fore and aft set t'-gallant-sails! stand by to give her the fore-top-mast stun'-sail!"

But, Captain Rash, those sails of yours were much safer in the sail-maker's loft. For now, while the heedless craft is bounding over the billows, a black cloud rises out of the sea; the sun drops down from the sky; a horrible mist far and wide spreads over the water.

"Hands by the halyards! Let go! Clew up!"

Too late.

For ere the ropes' ends can be cast off from the pins, the tornado is blowing down to the bottom of their throats. The masts are willows, the sails ribbons, the cordage wool; the whole ship is brewed into the yeast of the gale.

And now, if, when the first green sea breaks over him, Captain Rash is not swept overboard, he has his hands full be sure. In all probability his three masts have gone by the board, and, raveled into list, his sails are floating in the air. Or, perhaps, the ship *broaches to,* or is *brought by the lee.* In either case, Heaven help the sailors, their wives and their little ones; and Heaven help the underwriters.

Familiarity with danger makes a brave man braver, but less daring. Thus with seamen: he who goes the oftenest round Cape Horn goes the most circumspectly. A veteran mariner is never deceived by the treacherous breezes which sometimes waft him pleasantly toward the latitude of the Cape. No sooner does he come within a certain distance of it—previously fixed in his own mind—than all hands are turned to setting the ship in storm-trim; and never mind how light the breeze, down come his t'-gallant-yards. He "bends" his strongest storm-sails, and lashes everything on deck securely. The ship is then ready for the worst; and if, in reeling round the headland, she receives a broadside, it generally goes well with her. If ill, all hands go to the bottom with quiet consciences.

Among sea-captains, there are some who seem to regard the genius of the Cape as a wilful, capricious jade, that must be courted and coaxed into complaisance. First, they come along under easy sails; do not steer boldly for the headland, but tack this way and that—sidling up to it. Now they woo the Jezebel with a t'-gallant-studding-sail; anon, they deprecate her wrath with double-reefed-top-sails. When, at length, her unappeasable fury is fairly aroused, and all round the dismantled ship the storm howls and howls for days together, they still persevere in their efforts. First, they try unconditional submission; furling every rag and *heaving to;* laying like a log, for the tempest to toss wheresoever it pleases.

This failing, they set a *spencer* or *try-sail*, and shift on the other tack. Equally vain! The gale sings as hoarsely as before. At last, the wind comes round fair; they drop the fore-sail; square the yards, and scud before it; their implacable foe chasing them with tornadoes, as if to show her insensibility to the last.

Other ships, without encountering these terrible gales, spend week after week endeavoring to turn this boisterous world-corner against a continual head-wind. Tacking hither and thither, in the language of sailors they *polish* the Cape by beating about its edges so long.

Le Mair and Schouten, two Dutchmen, were the first navigators who weathered Cape Horn. Previous to this, passages had been made to the Pacific by the Straits of Magellan; nor, indeed, at that period, was it known to a certainty that there was any other route, or that the land now called Terra del Fuego was an island. A few leagues southward from Terra del Fuego is a cluster of small islands, the Diegoes; between which and the former island are the Straits of Le Mair, so called in honor of their discoverer, who first sailed through them into the Pacific. Le Mair and Schouten, in their small, clumsy vessels, encountered a series of tremendous gales, the prelude to the long train of similar hardships which most of their followers have experienced. It is a significant fact, that Schouten's vessel, the *Horne*, which gave its name to the Cape, was almost lost in weathering it.

The next navigator round the Cape was Sir Francis Drake, who, on Raleigh's Expedition, beholding for the first time, from the Isthmus of Darien, the "goodlie South Sea," like a true-born Englishman, vowed, please God, to sail an English ship thereon; which the gallant sailor did, to the sore discomfiture of the Spaniards on the coasts of Chili and Peru.

But perhaps the greatest hardships on record, in making this celebrated passage, were those experienced by Lord Anson's squadron in 1736. Three remarkable and most interesting narratives record their disasters and sufferings. The first, jointly written by the carpenter and gunner of the Wager; the second by young Byron, a midshipman in the same ship; the third, by the chaplain of the Centurion. White-Jacket has them all; and they are fine reading of a boisterous March night, with the casement rattling in your ear, and the chimney-stacks blowing down upon the pavement, bubbling with raindrops.

But if you want the best idea of Cape Horn, get my friend Dana's unmatchable "Two Years Before the Mast." But you can read, and so you must have read it. His chapters describing Cape Horn must have been written with an icicle.

At the present day the horrors of the Cape have somewhat abated. This is owing to a growing familiarity with it; but, more than all, to the improved condition of ships in all respects, and the means now generally in use of preserving the health of the crews in times of severe and prolonged exposure.

Colder and colder; we are drawing nigh to the Cape. Now gregoes, pea jackets, monkey jackets, reefing jackets, storm jackets, oil jackets, paint jackets, round jackets, short jackets, long jackets, and all manner of jackets, are the order of the day, not excepting the immortal white jacket, which begins to be sturdily buttoned up to the throat, and pulled down vigorously at the skirts, to bring them well over the loins.

But, alas! those skirts were lamentably scanty; and though, with its quiltings, the jacket was stuffed out about the breasts like a Christmas turkey, and of a dry cold day kept the wearer warm enough in that vicinity, yet about the loins it was shorter than a ballet-dancer's skirts; so that while my chest was in the temperate zone close adjoining the torrid, my hapless thighs were in Nova Zembla, hardly an icicle's toss from the Pole.

Then, again, the repeated soakings and dryings it had undergone, had by this time made it shrink woefully all over, especially in the arms, so that the wristbands had gradually crawled up near to the elbows; and it required an energetic thrust to push the arm through, in drawing the jacket on.

I endeavored to amend these misfortunes by sewing a sort of canvas ruffle round the skirts, by way of a continuation or supplement to the original work, and by doing the same with the wristbands.

This is the time for oil-skin suits, dread-naughts, tarred trousers and over-alls, sea-boots, comforters, mittens, woolen socks, Guernsey frocks, Havre shirts, buffalo-robe shirts, and moose-skin drawers. Every man's jacket is his wigwam, and every man's hat his caboose.

Perfect license is now permitted to the men respecting their clothing. Whatever they can rake and scrape together they put on—swaddling themselves in old sails, and drawing old socks over their heads for night-caps. This is the time for smiting your chest with your hand, and talking loud to keep up the circulation.

Colder, and colder, and colder, till at last we spoke a fleet of icebergs bound North. After that, it was one incessant "*cold snap*," that almost snapped off our fingers and toes. Cold! It was cold as *Blue Flujin*, where sailors say fire freezes.

And now coming up with the latitude of the Cape, we stood southward to give it a wide berth, and while so doing were becalmed; ay, becalmed off Cape Horn, which is worse, far worse, than being becalmed on the Line.

Here we lay forty-eight hours, during which the cold was intense. I wondered at the liquid sea, which refused to freeze in such a temperature. The clear, cold sky overhead looked like a steel-blue cymbal, that might ring, could you smite it. Our breath came and went like puffs of smoke from pipe-bowls. At first there was a long gauky swell, that obliged us to furl most of the sails, and even send down t'-gallant-yards, for fear of pitching them overboard.

Out of sight of land, at this extremity of both the inhabitable and uninhabitable world, our peopled frigate, echoing with the voices of men, the bleating of lambs, the cackling of fowls, the gruntings of pigs, seemed like Noah's old ark itself, becalmed at the climax of the Deluge.

There was nothing to be done but patiently to await the pleasure of the elements, and "whistle for a wind," the usual practice of seamen in a calm. No fire was allowed, except for the indispensable purpose of cooking, and heating bottles of water to toast Selvagee's feet. He who possessed the largest stock of vitality, stood the best chance to escape freezing. It was horrifying.

In such weather any man could have undergone amputation with great ease, and helped take up the arteries himself.

Indeed, this state of affairs had not lasted quite twenty-four hours, when the extreme frigidity of the air, united to our increased tendency to inactivity, would very soon have rendered some of us subjects for the surgeon and his mates, had not a humane proceeding of the Captain suddenly impelled us to vigorous exercise.

And here be it said, that the appearance of the Boatswain, with his silver whistle to his mouth, at the main hatchway of the gun-deck, is always regarded by the crew with the utmost curiosity, for this betokens that some general order is about to be promulgated through the ship. What now? is the question that runs on from man to man. A short preliminary whistle is then given by "Old Yarn," as they call him, which whistle serves to collect round him, from their various stations, his four mates. Then Yarn, or Pipes, as leader of the orchestra, begins a peculiar call, in which his assistants join. This over, the order, whatever it may be, is loudly sung out and prolonged, till the remotest corner echoes again. The Boatswain and his mates are the town-criers of a man-of-war.

The calm had commenced in the afternoon: and the following morning the ship's company were electrified by a general order, thus set forth and declared: "*D'ye hear there, fore and aft! all hands skylark!*"

This mandate, nowadays never used except upon very rare occasions, produced the same effect upon the men that Exhilarating Gas would have done, or an extra allowance of "grog." For a time, the wonted discipline of the ship was broken through, and perfect license allowed. It was a Babel here, a Bedlam there, and a Pandemonium everywhere. The Theatricals were nothing compared with it. Then the faint-hearted and timorous crawled to their hiding-places, and the lusty and bold shouted forth their glee. Gangs of men, in all sorts of outlandish habiliments, wild as those worn at some crazy carnival, rushed to and fro, seizing upon whomsoever they pleased—warrant-officers and dangerous pugilists excepted—pulling and hauling the luckless tars about, till fairly baited into a genial warmth. Some were made fast to and hoisted aloft with a will: others, mounted upon oars, were ridden fore and aft on a rail, to the boisterous mirth of the spectators, any one of whom might be the next victim. Swings were rigged from the tops, or the masts; and the most reluctant wights being purposely selected, spite of all struggles, were swung from East to West, in vast arcs of circles, till almost breathless. Horn-pipes, fandangoes, Donnybrook-jigs, reels, and quadrilles, were danced under the very nose of the most mighty captain, and upon the very quarter-deck and poop. Sparring and wrestling, too, were all the vogue; *Kentucky bites* were given, and the *Indian hug* exchanged. The din frightened the sea-fowl, that flew by with accelerated wing.

It is worth mentioning that several casualties occurred, of which, however, I will relate but one. While the "skylarking" was at its height, one of the fore-top-men—an ugly-tempered devil of a Portuguese, looking on—swore that he would be the death of any man who laid violent hands upon his inviolable person. This threat being overheard, a band of desperadoes, coming up from behind, tripped him up in an instant, and in the twinkling of an eye the Portuguese was straddling an oar, borne aloft by an uproarious multitude, who rushed him along the deck at a railroad gallop. The living mass of arms all round and beneath him was so dense, that every time he inclined one side he was instantly pushed upright, but only to fall over again, to receive another push from the contrary direction. Presently, disengaging his hands from those who held them, the enraged seaman drew from his bosom an iron belaying-pin, and recklessly laid about him to right and left. Most of his persecutors fled; but some eight or ten still stood their ground, and, while bearing him aloft, endeavored to wrest the weapon from his hands. In this attempt, one man was struck on the head, and dropped insensible. He was taken up for dead, and carried below to Cuticle, the surgeon, while the Portuguese was put under guard. But the wound did not prove very serious; and in a few days the man was walking about the deck, with his head well bandaged.

This occurrence put an end to the "skylarking," further head-breaking being strictly prohibited. In due time the Portuguese paid the penalty of his rashness at the gangway; while once again the officers *shipped their quarter-deck faces.*

Ere the calm had yet left us, a sail had been discerned from the fore-top-mast-head, at a great distance, probably three leagues or more. At first it was a mere speck, altogether out of sight from the deck. By the force of attraction, or something else equally inscrutable, two ships in a calm, and equally affected by the currents, will always approximate, more or less. Though there was not a breath of wind, it was not a great while before the strange sail was described from our bulwarks; gradually, it drew still nearer.

What was she, and whence? There is no object which so excites interest and conjecture, and, at the same time, baffles both, as a sail, seen as a mere speck on these remote seas off Cape Horn.

A breeze! a breeze! for lo! the stranger is now perceptibly nearing the frigate; the officer's spy-glass pronounces her a full-rigged ship, with all sail set, and coming right down to us, though in our own vicinity the calm still reigns.

She is bringing the wind with her. Hurrah! Ay, there it is! Behold how mincingly it creeps over the sea, just ruffling and crisping it.

Our top-men were at once sent aloft to loose the sails, and presently they faintly began to distend. As yet we hardly had steerage-way. Toward sunset the stranger bore down before the wind, a complete pyramid of canvas. Never before, I venture to say, was Cape Horn so audaciously insulted. Stun'-sails alow and aloft; royals, moon-sails, and everything else. She glided under our stern, within hailing distance, and the signal-quarter-master ran up our ensign to the gaff.

"Ship ahoy!" cried the Lieutenant of the Watch, through his trumpet.

"Halloa!" bawled an old fellow in a green jacket, clapping one hand to his mouth, while he held on with the other to the mizzen-shrouds.

"What ship's that?"

"The Sultan, Indiaman, from New York, and bound to Callao and Canton, sixty days out, all well. What frigate's that?"

"The United States ship Neversink, homeward bound."

"Hurrah! hurrah! hurrah!" yelled our enthusiastic countryman, transported with patriotism.

By this time the Sultan had swept past, but the Lieutenant of the Watch could not withhold a parting admonition.

"D'ye hear? You'd better take in some of your flying-kites there. Look out for Cape Horn!"

But the friendly advice was lost in the now increasing wind. With a suddenness by no means unusual in these latitudes, the light breeze soon became a succession of sharp squalls, and our sail-proud braggadacio of an Indiaman was observed to let everything go by the run, his t'-gallant stun'-sails and flying-jib taking quick leave of the spars; the flying-jib was swept into the air, rolled together for a few minutes, and tossed about in the squalls like a

Stun'-sail aglow and aloft; royals, moon-sails, and everything else. She glided under our stern within hailing distance.

foot-ball. But the wind played no such pranks with the more prudently managed canvas of the Neversink, though before many hours it was stirring times with us.

About midnight, when the starboard watch, to which, I belonged, was below, the boatswain's whistle was heard, followed by the shrill cry of "*All hands take in sail!* jump, men, and save ship!*"

Springing from our hammocks, we found the frigate leaning over to it so steeply, that it was with difficulty we could climb the ladders leading to the upper deck.

Here the scene was awful. The vessel seemed to be sailing on her side. The main-deck guns had several days previous been run in and housed, and the port-holes closed, but the lee carronades on the quarter-deck and forecastle were plunging through the sea, which undulated over them in milk-like billows of foam. With every lurch to leeward the yard-arm-ends seemed to dip in the sea, while forward the spray dashed over the bows in cataracts, and drenched the men who were on the fore-yard. By this time the deck was alive with the whole strength of the ship's company, five hundred men, officers and all, mostly clinging to the weather bulwarks. The occasional phosphorescence of the yeasting sea cast a glare upon their uplifted faces, as a night fire in a populous city lights up the panic-stricken crowd.

In a sudden gale, or when a large quantity of sail is suddenly to be furled, it is the custom for the First Lieutenant to take the trumpet from whoever happens then to be officer of the deck. But Mad Jack had the trumpet that watch; nor did the First Lieutenant now seek to wrest it from his hands. Every eye was upon him, as if we had chosen him from among us all, to decide this battle with the elements, by single combat with the spirit of the Cape; for Mad Jack was the saving genius of the ship, and so proved himself that night. I owe this right hand, that is this moment flying over my sheet, and all my present being to Mad Jack. The ship's bows were now butting, battering, ramming, and thundering over and upon the head seas, and with a horrible wallowing sound our whole hull was rolling in the trough of the foam. The gale came athwart the deck, and every sail seemed bursting with its wild breath.

All the quarter-masters, and several of the forecastle-men, were swarming round the double-wheel on the quarter-deck. Some jumping up and down, with their hands upon the spokes; for the whole helm and galvanized keel were fiercely feverish, with the life imparted to them by the wild tempest.

"Hard *up* the helm!" shouted Captain Claret, bursting from his cabin like a ghost in his night-dress.

"Damn you!" raged Mad Jack to the quarter-masters; "hard *down*—hard *down*, I say, and be damned to you!"

Contrary orders! but Mad Jack's were obeyed. His object was to throw the ship into the wind, so as the better to admit of close-reefing the top-sails. But though the halyards were let go, it was impossible to clew down the yards, owing to the enormous horizontal strain on the canvas. It now blew a hurricane. The spray flew over the ship in floods. The gigantic masts seemed about to snap under the world-wide strain of the three entire top-sails.

"Clew down! clew down!" shouted Mad Jack, husky with excitement, and in a frenzy, beating his trumpet against one of the shrouds. But, owing to the slant of the ship, the thing could not be done. It was obvious that before many minutes something must go—either sails, rigging, or sticks; perhaps the hull itself, and all hands.

Presently a voice from the top exclaimed that there was a rent in the main-top-sail. And instantly we heard a report like two or three muskets discharged together; the vast sail was rent up and down like the Vail of the Temple. This saved the main-mast; for the yard was now clewed down with comparative ease, and the top-men laid out to stow the shattered canvas. Soon, the two remaining top-sails were also clewed down and close reefed.

Above all the roar of the tempest and the shouts of the crew, was heard the dismal tolling of the ship's bell—almost as large as that of a village church—which the violent rolling of the ship was occasioning. Imagination cannot conceive the horror of such a sound in a night-tempest at sea.

"Stop that ghost!" roared Mad Jack; "away, one of you, and wrench off the clapper!"

But no sooner was this ghost gagged, than a still more appalling sound was heard, the rolling to and fro of the heavy shot, which, on the gun-deck, had broken loose from the gun-racks, and converted that part of the ship into an immense bowling-alley. Some hands were sent down to secure them; but it was as much as their lives were worth. Several were maimed; and the midshipmen who were ordered to see the duty performed reported it impossible, until the storm abated.

The most terrific job of all was to furl the main-sail, which, at the commencement of the squalls, had been clewed up, coaxed and quieted as much as possible with the bunt-lines and slab-lines. Mad Jack waited some time for a lull, ere he gave an order so perilous to be executed. For to furl this enormous sail, in such a gale, required at least fifty men on the yard; whose weight, superadded to that of the ponderous stick itself, still further jeopardized their lives. But there was no prospect of a cessation of the gale, and the order was at last given.

At this time a hurricane of slanting sleet and hail was descending upon us; the rigging was coated with a thin glare of ice, formed within the hour.

"Aloft, main-yard-men! and all you main-top-men! and furl the main-sail!" cried Mad Jack.

I dashed down my hat, slipped out of my quilted jacket in an instant, kicked the shoes from my feet, and, with a crowd of others, sprang for the rigging. Above the bulwarks (which in a frigate are so high as to afford much protection to those on deck) the gale was horrible. The sheer force of the wind flattened us to the rigging as we ascended, and every hand seemed congealing to the icy shrouds by which we held.

"Up—up, my brave hearties!" shouted Mad Jack; and up we got, some way or other, all of us, and groped our way out on the yard-arms.

"Hold on, every mother's son!" cried an old quarter-gunner at my side. He was bawling at the top of his compass; but in the gale, he seemed to be whispering; and I only heard him from his being right to windward of me.

But his hint was unnecessary; I dug my nails into the *Jack-stays*, and swore that nothing but death should part me and them until I was able to turn round and look to windward. As yet, this was impossible; I could scarcely hear the man to leeward at my elbow; the wind seemed to snatch the words from his mouth and fly away with them to the South Pole.

All this while the sail itself was flying about, sometimes catching over our heads, and threatening to tear us from the yard in spite of all our hugging. For about three quarters of an hour we thus hung suspended right over the rampant billows, which curled their very crests under the feet of some four or five of us clinging to the lee-yard-arm, as if to float us from our place.

Presently, the word passed along the yard from windward, that we were ordered to come down and leave the sail to blow, since it could not be furled. A midshipman, it seemed, had been sent up by the officer of the deck to give the order, as no trumpet could be heard where we were.

Those on the weather yard-arm managed to crawl upon the spar and scramble down the rigging; but with us, upon the extreme leeward side, this feat was out of the question; it was, literary, like climbing a precipice to get to windward in order to reach the shrouds: besides, the entire yard was now encased in ice, and our hands and feet were so numb that we dared not trust our lives to them. Nevertheless, by assisting each other, we contrived to throw ourselves prostrate along the yard, and embrace it with our arms and legs. In this position, the stun'-sail-booms greatly assisted in securing our hold. Strange as it may appear, I do not suppose that, at this moment, the slightest sensation of fear was felt by one man on that yard. We clung to it with might and main; but this was instinct. The truth is, that, in circumstances like these, the sense of fear is annihilated in the unutterable sights that fill all the eye, and the sounds that fill all the ear. You become identified with the tempest; your insignificance is lost in the riot of the stormy universe around.

Below us, our noble frigate seemed thrice its real length—a vast black wedge, opposing its widest end to the combined fury of the sea and wind.

At length the first fury of the gale began to abate, and we at once fell to pounding our hands, as a preliminary operation to going to work; for a gang of men had now ascended to help secure what was left of the sail; we somehow packed it away, at last, and came down.

About noon the next day, the gale so moderated that we shook two reefs out of the top-sails, set new courses, and stood due east, with the wind astern.

Thus, all the fine weather we encountered after first weighing anchor on the pleasant Spanish coast, was but the prelude to this one terrific night; more especially, that treacherous calm immediately preceding it. But how could we reach our long-promised homes without encountering Cape Horn? by what possibility avoid it? And though some ships have weathered it without these perils, yet by far the greater part must encounter them. Lucky it is that it comes about midway in the homeward-bound passage, so that the sailors have time to prepare for it, and time to recover from it after it is astern.

But, sailor or landsman, there is some sort of a Cape Horn for all. Boys! beware of it; prepare for it in time. Gray-beards! thank God it is passed. And ye lucky livers, to whom, by some rare fatality, your Cape Horns are placid as Lake Lemans, flatter not yourselves that good luck is judgment and discretion; for all the yolk in your eggs, you might have foundered and gone down, had the Spirit of the Cape said the word.

THE MUTINY OF THE BOUNTY

Guy Murchie, Jr.

Dawn of the morning of April 28, 1789, found the southern Pacific ocean calm. The moon had set, leaving the sky empty but for a few stars of the first magnitude. The air was cool close to the surface of the sea, which stretched unbroken in transparent greenness from horizon to horizon.

A tiny speck in this immensity was his majesty George III.'s armed vessel the Bounty, ninety feet long in an ocean that stretched ten thousand miles. Aboard the vessel as she winged her way gently westward under full canvas lay 34-year-old William Bligh in his narrow bunk, breathing thickly. Most of the other officers also were asleep—but there was one who was wider awake than he had ever been in his life.

That man, Fletcher Christian, the young master's mate, was making his way aft to the captain's cabin, a cutlass in his hand and three armed companions at his heel. A look of ruthless determination flamed from his black eyes. He was about to take the leading role in the most famous mutiny that ever occurred in the British navy.

Let Captain Bligh tell what happened:

"Tuesday the 28th.—Just before sun-rising, while I was yet asleep, Mr. Christian, with the master-at-arms, gunner's mate, and Thomas Burkitt, seaman, came into my cabin and, seizing me, tied my hands with a cord behind my back, threatening me with instant death if I spoke or made the least noise; I, however, called as loud as I could, in hopes of assistance; but they had already secured the officers who were not of their party by placing sentinels at their doors.

from "The Mutiny of the Bounty and other Sea Stories" by Guy Murchie, Jr. By courtesy of Consolidated Book Publishers, Inc.

"There were three men at my cabin door besides the four within; Christian had only a cutlass in his hand, the others had muskets and bayonets. I was hauled out of bed and forced on deck in my shirt, suffering great pain from the tightness with which they had tied my hands. I demanded the reason of such violence, but received no other answer than abuse for not holding my tongue. The master, the gunner, the surgeon, Mr. Elphinstone (master's mate) and Nelson were kept confined below; and the fore-hatchway was guarded by sentinels.

"The boatswain and carpenter, and also the clerk, Mr. Samuel, were allowed to come upon deck, where they saw me standing abaft the mizenmast with my hands tied behind my back, under a guard, with Christian at their head. The boatswain was ordered to hoist the launch out, with a threat if he did not do it instantly *to take care of himself.*

"When the boat was out Mr. Hayward and Mr. Hallet, two of the midshipmen, and Mr. Samuel were ordered into it. I demanded what their intention was in giving this order and endeavored to persuade the people near me not to persist in such acts of violence; but it was to no effect; 'Hold your tongue, sir, or you are dead this instant,' was constantly repeated to me. . . .

"I continued my endeavors to turn the tide of affairs, when Christian changed the cutlass which he had in his hand for a bayonet that was brought to him, and, holding me with a strong gripe by the cord that tied my hands, he with many oaths threatened to kill me immediately if I would not be quiet; the villains round me had their pieces cocked and bayonets fixed. Particular people were called on to go into the boat and were hurried over the side; whence I concluded that with these people I was to be set adrift; I therefore made another effort to bring about a change, but with no other effect than to be threatened with having my brains blown out."

But by some accounts Captain Bligh was not quite so uncompromising as his own account would make him. According to Boatswain's Mate Morrison:

"When Mr. Bligh found he must get into the boat, he begged of Mr. Christian to desist, saying, 'I'll pawn my honor, I'll give my bond, Mr. Christian, never to think of this if you'll desist,' and urged him to think of his wife and family; to which Mr. Christian replied, 'No, Captain Bligh, if you had any honor things had not come to this; and if you had any regard for your wife and family you should have thought on them before and not behaved so much like a villain.'

"Lieutenant Bligh again attempted to speak, but was ordered to be silent. The boatswain also tried to pacify Mr. Christian, to whom he replied, 'It is too late; I have been in hell for this fortnight past and am determined to bear it no longer; and you know, Mr. Cole, that I have been used like a dog all the voyage.'"

Captain Bligh's journal continues:

"The boatswain and seamen who were to go in the boat were allowed to collect twine, canvas, lines, sails, cordage, an eight-and-twenty gallon cask of water, and Mr. Samuel got 150 lbs. of bread, with a small quantity of rum and wine, also a quadrant and compass; but he was forbidden on pain of death to touch either map, ephemeris, book of astronomical observations, sextant, time-keeper, or any of my surveys or drawings.

"The mutineers having forced those of the seamen whom they meant to get rid of into the boat, Christian directed a dram to be served to each of his own crew. I then unhappily saw that nothing could be done to effect the recovery of the ship; there was no one to assist me, and every endeavor on my part was answered with threats of death.

"The officers were next called on deck and forced over the side into the boat, while I was kept apart from every one, abaft the mizenmast; Christian, armed with a bayonet, holding me by the bandage that secured my hands. The guard round me had their pieces cocked; but on my daring the ungrateful wretches to fire they uncocked them.

"Isaac Martin, one of the guard over me, I saw, had an inclination to assist me, and as he fed me with shaddock (my lips being quite parched) we explained our wishes to each other by our looks; but, this being observed, Martin was removed from me. He then attempted to leave the ship, for which purpose he got into the boat; but with many threats they obliged him to return.

"The armorer, Joseph Coleman, and two of the carpenters, M'Intosh and Norman, were also kept contrary to their inclination; and they begged of me, after I was astern in the boat, to remember that they declared they had no hand in the transaction. Michael Byrne, I am told, likewise wanted to leave the ship.

"It is of no moment for me to recount my endeavors to bring back the offenders to a sense of their duty; all I could do was by speaking to them in general; but it was to no purpose, for I was kept securely bound and no one except the guard suffered to come near me.

"To Mr. Samuel I am indebted for securing my journals (without which this book would be based on memory only), and commission, with some material ship papers. Without these I had nothing to certify what I had done, and my honor and character might have been suspected, without my possessing a proper document to have defended them. All this he did with great resolution, though guarded and strictly watched. He attempted to save the time-keeper, and a box with my surveys, drawings, and remarks for fifteen years past, which were numerous; when he was hurried away with 'Damn your eyes, you are well off to get what you have.'

"It appeared to me that Christian was some time in doubt whether he should keep the carpenter or his mates; at length he determined on the latter and the carpenter was ordered into the boat. He was permitted, but not without some opposition, to take his tool chest.

"Much altercation took place among the mutinous crew during the whole business; some swore, 'I'll be damned if he does not find his way home if he gets anything with him' (meaning me); and, when the carpenter's chest was carrying away, 'Damn my eyes, he will have a vessel built in a month.' While others laughed at the helpless situation of the boat, being very deep, and so little room for those who were in her. As for Christian, he seemed as if meditating destruction on himself and everyone else.

"I asked for arms, but they laughed at me and said I was well acquainted with the people among whom I was going and therefore did not want them; four cutlasses, however, were thrown into the boat after we were veered astern.

"The officers and men being in the boat, they only waited for me, of which the master-at-arms informed Christian, who then said, 'Come, Captain Bligh, your officers and men are now in the boat, and you must go with them; if you attempt to make the least resistance you will instantly be put to death'; and without further ceremony, with a tribe of armed ruffians about me, I was forced over the side, where they untied my hands.

"Being in the boat, we were veered astern by a rope. A few pieces of pork were thrown to us, and some clothes, also the cutlasses I have already mentioned; and it was then that the armorer and carpenters called out to me to remember that they had no hand in the transaction. After having undergone a great deal of ridicule and been kept some time to make sport for these unfeeling wretches, we were at length cast adrift in the open ocean."

Nineteen men they were as they sat in the open boat in the middle of the half-legendary Pacific ocean and watched their ship sail away to the north. Their plight was not hopeless, but it was little better than that. The boat was built to hold twelve men. With nineteen, and all the gear and belongings they had been able to collect, it was so overloaded that waves slopped over the side even in this relatively calm sea.

It appeared out of the question to attempt anything but to reach the nearest land as quickly as possible, which was the island of Tofoa, lying about thirty miles to the northeast. This island did not seem too inviting, however, for it was of the same group as Annamooka, where the watering party sent ashore from the Bounty a few days back had met with a hostile reception by the natives. Without firearms, nineteen men in an overloaded open boat would be helpless at the hands of hundreds of natives in their swift canoes and armed with stones and spears and perhaps bows and arrows.

But where else could they go? Tahiti was the nearest island where they could be sure of a friendly reception, and that was some 1,500 miles away, with a trade wind blowing dead against them. The nearest friendly settlement they could think of in the other direction was a Dutch colony on the island of Timor in the East Indies, more than 3,500 miles away, and Captain Bligh was not quite positive of this. There was nothing to do but make for Tofoa.

As there was practically no wind at the time, Captain Bligh's first order—after the men had packed away their belongings and made the boat as shipshape as possible—was to take to the oars and steer for Tofoa. The men, somewhat cheered by their leader's resolute appearance, grasped the oars with a will and, changing places every hour, steadily drew nearer to the land which stood in hazy purple on the horizon.

"While the Bounty remained in sight," Bligh recorded, "she steered to the W.N.W., but I considered this only as a feint, for when we were sent away, 'Huzza for Otaheite!' was frequently heard among the mutineers."

By noon the Bounty had disappeared over the horizon. Captain Bligh put all further thoughts of her out of his mind and considered seriously what was best to be done.

"My first determination was to seek a supply of breadfruit and water at Tofoa and afterwards to sail for Tongataboo and there risk a solicitation to

Poulaho, the king, to equip my boat and grant a supply of water and provisions so as to enable us to reach the East Indies.

"The quantity of provisions I found in the boat was 150 lbs. of bread, 16 pieces of pork (each piece weighing 2 lbs.), 6 quarts of rum, 6 bottles of wine, with 28 gallons of water and 4 empty barrecoes.

"Happily the afternoon kept calm until about 4 o'clock, when we were so far to windward that, with a moderate easterly breeze which sprung up, we were able to sail. It was nevertheless dark when we got to Tofoa, where I expected to land; but the shore proved to be so steep and rocky that I was obliged to give up all thoughts of it and keep the boat under the lee of the island with two oars, for there was no anchorage. Having fixed on this mode of proceeding for the night, I served to every person half a pint of grog and each took to his rest as well as our unhappy situation would allow.

"In the morning at dawn of day," wrote Bligh, "we set off along shore in search of landing, and about 10 o'clock we discovered a stony cove at the N.W. part of the island, where I dropt the grapnel within twenty yards of the rocks. A great deal of surf ran on the shore, but, as I was unwilling to diminish our stock of provisions, I landed Mr. Samuel and some others, who climbed the cliffs and got into the country to search for supplies. . . . Towards noon Mr. Samuel returned with a few quarts of water, which he had found in holes; but he had met with no spring or any prospect of a sufficient supply in that particular."

Neither had Mr. Samuel seen any inhabitants, though he had found the remains of a fire and some deserted huts. Captain Bligh was anxious to solve this mystery, because he wanted to obtain as much water, cocoanuts, or other provisions as he could to supplement the meager supply allowed him by the mutineers and which would normally have supported nineteen men only three or four days. If there were only a few natives he meant to make friends and trade with them. If there were many, and they appeared hostile, he meant to leave the island. In either case there was no time to be lost, for the men had to eat and there was no apparent means for replenishing their supplies.

On May 1, their third day at the island, Bligh, still having no answer to the problem, sent out a last party in desperate hopes of finding natives or some source of food before quitting the island. The party at first could find not even water, "but," recorded Bligh, "they met with two men, a woman, and a child; the men came with them to the cove and brought two cocoanut shells of water. I immediately made friends with these people and sent them away for breadfruit, plantains, and water. Soon after other natives came to us, and by noon I had thirty of them about me, trading with the articles we were in want of; but I could only afford one ounce of pork and a quarter of a bread-fruit to each man for dinner, with half a pint of water, for I was fixed in not using any of the bread or water in the boat."

Buttons and beads and old shirts were the articles handed out to the natives in trade for breadfruit, cocoanuts, and other fruit. "Towards evening," wrote Bligh, "I had the satisfaction to find our stock of provisions somewhat in-creased; but the natives did not appear to have much to spare. What they brought was in such small quantities that I had no reason to hope we should be able to procure from them sufficient to stock us for our voyage."

Stormy weather, however, kept the captain from putting to sea, and the following day a new and very formidable danger was added to his troubles. Natives by the score came to the little crescent of beach where the white men were camped, some climbing down the vines that lined the cliffs, some in large canoes, and Bligh wrote, "I observed symptoms of a design against us."

Momentarily the captain regained some hope when two of the chiefs asked after Captain Cook, and one of the friendlier natives was recognized as a man the landing party had seen on Annamooka. But very shortly the water's edge was lined with some 200 natives, thus separating Bligh and most of his men, who were near the cliff's edge, from the boat a few feet off shore.

"As we had no means of improving our situation," wrote Bligh, "I told our people I would wait until sunset, by which time, perhaps, something might happen in our favor; that if we attempted to go at present we must fight our way through, which we could do more advantageously at night; and that in the meantime we would endeavor to get off to the boat what we had bought. The beach was now lined with the natives, and we heard nothing but the knocking of stones together, which they had in each hand. I knew very well this was the sign of an attack. . . .

"I carefully watched the motions of the natives, who still increased in num-ber, and found that, instead of their intention being to leave us, fires were made and places fixed on for their stay during the night. Consultations were also held among them, and everything assured me we should be attacked. . . .

"The sun was near setting when I gave the word, on which every person who was on shore with me boldly took up his proportion of things and carried them to the boat. . . . We walked down the beach, every one in a silent kind of horror." For protection Bligh kept hold of the hand of one of the natives who had been a kind of ambassador and made him walk with the white men as a human shield. The natives were just working themselves up to the necessary pitch of excitement as the whites calmly marched through their ranks, trying to look as if nothing was amiss, and made for the boat.

"I ordered the carpenter not to quit me until the other people were in the boat," wrote Bligh. "Nageete [the native whose hand Bligh had been holding], finding I would not stay, loosed himself from my hold and went off, and we all got into the boat except one man, who while I was getting on board quitted it and ran up the beach to cast the stern fast off, notwithstanding the master and others called to him to return, while they were hauling me out of the water.

"I was no sooner in the boat than the attack began by about 200 men; the unfortunate poor man who had run up the beach was knocked down, and the stones flew like a shower of shot. Many Indians got hold of the stern rope and were near hauling us on shore, and would certainly have done it if I had not had a knife in my pocket, with which I cut the rope. We then hauled off to the grapnel, everyone being more or less hurt. At this time I saw five of the natives about the poor man they had killed, and two of them were beating him about the head with stones in their hands.

"We had no time to reflect before, to my surprise, they filled their canoes with stones and twelve men came off after us to renew the attack, which they did so effectually as nearly to disable all of us. Our grapnel was foul, but Providence here assisted us; the fluke broke, and we got to our oars and pulled to sea. They, however, could paddle round us, so that we were obliged to sustain the attack without being able to return it except with such stones as lodged in the boat, and in this I found we were very inferior to them. We could not close, because our boat was lumbered and heavy, and that they knew very well; I therefore adopted the expedient of throwing overboard some cloaths, which they lost time in picking up; and as it was now almost dark, they gave over the attack and returned towards the shore, leaving us to reflect on our unhappy situation."

After this sample of the dispositions of the natives of the Friendly Islands (so named more hopefully than accurately by Captain Cook), Bligh and his men were discouraged in their intention to land at other of these islands.

"My mind was employed in considering what was best to be done," wrote Bligh, "when I was solicited by all hands to take them towards home; and when I told them no hopes of relief for them remained but what I might find at New Holland until I came to Timor, a distance of full 1,200 leagues [3,600 miles], where was a Dutch settlement, but in what part of the island I knew not, they all agreed to live on one ounce of bread and a quarter of a pint of water per day.

"Therefore, after examining our stock of provisions and recommending this as a sacred promise forever to their memory, we bore away across a sea where the navigation is but little known, in a small boat twenty-three feet long from stem to stern, deep laden with eighteen men; without a chart, and nothing but my own recollection and general knowledge of the situation of places, assisted by a book of latitudes and longitudes, to guide us. I was happy, however, to see everyone better satisfied with our situation in this particular than myself.

"Our stock of provisions consisted of about 150 lbs. of bread, 28 gallons of water, 20 lbs. of pork, 3 bottles of wine, and 5 quarts of rum. The difference between this and the quantity we had on leaving the ship was principally owing to loss in the bustle and confusion of the attack. A few cocoanuts were in the boat, and some breadfruit, but the latter was trampled to pieces."

All night they sailed, bearing away from Tofoa to the west under a reefed lug foresail. The captain divided his companions into watches and made the boat as shipshape as possible, also offering thanks to God "for our miraculous preservation."

"At daybreak on May 3d," Bligh's journal continues, "the gale increased; the sun rose very fiery and red, a sure indication of a severe gale of wind"— which was the very worst thing for a heavily loaded open boat. "At eight it blew a violent storm, and the sea ran very high, so that between the seas the sail was becalmed, and when on the top of the sea it was too much to have set; but I was obliged to carry to it, for we were now in very imminent danger and distress, the sea curling over the stern of the boat, which obliged us to bail with all our might. A situation more distressing has perhaps seldom been experienced.

"Our bread was in bags and in danger of being spoiled by the wet. To be starved to death was inevitable if this could not be prevented. I therefore began to examine what cloaths there were in the boat and what other things could be spared; and, having determined that only two suits should be kept for each person, the rest was thrown overboard, with some rope and spare sails, which lightened the boat considerably, and we had more room to bail the water out. Fortunately the carpenter had a good chest in the boat, into which I put the bread the first favorable moment."

With their most important food supply, the bread, thus made secure against the wet, the men gave their full strength to bailing, which strenuous exercise had to be kept up continuously while the storm lasted. However, the fact that they were sailing directly before the wind was of inestimable value. "We could do nothing more than keep before the sea," wrote Bligh, "in the course of which the boat performed so wonderfully well that I no longer dreaded any danger in that respect. But among the hardships we were to undergo, that of being constantly wet was not the least; the nights were very cold, and at daylight our limbs were so benumbed that we could scarce find the use of them. At this time I served a teaspoonful of rum to each person, which we all found great benefit from."

On May 4 the Fiji Islands appeared. Though they skirted the Islands, they dared not land for fear of the natives.

Directly through the middle of this archipelago Bligh sailed, the islands remaining in sight for some four days. Seeing two swift sailing canoes approaching from one island, the commander decided not to risk a meeting with these natives, who, he figured, must be much like the nearby Friendly islanders. Instead he ordered the men to let down the sails, it being nearly calm, and to row their hardest.

But the fifty-foot canoes glided nearer with apparent ease until one was only two miles away and gaining steadily. The white men needed no urging as they plied their oars, and at last, at sundown, the pursuers gave up the chase and turned back toward their island home.

Then came the rain. "Heavy rain came on at 4 o'clock," wrote Bligh, "when every person did their utmost to catch some water, and we increased our stock to 34 gallons, besides quenching our thirst for the first time since we had been at sea; but an attendant consequence made us pass the night very miserably; . . . we experienced cold and shiverings scarce to be conceived."

May 8, happily, was a fine day with sunshine. "This afternoon we cleaned out the boat, and it employed us till sun-set to get everything dry and in order. Hitherto I had issued the allowance by guess, but I now got a pair of scales, made with two cocoanut shells; and, having accidentally some pistol balls in the boat, 25 of which weighed one pound, or 16 ounces, I adopted one as the proportion of weight that each person should receive of bread at the times I served it. I also amused all hands with describing the situation of New Guinea and New Holland and gave them every information in my power, that in case any accident happened to me, those who survived might have some idea of what they were about and be able to find their way to Timor, which at present they knew nothing of more than the name, and some not that."

Ever alert to improve their lot and provide against every possible contingency, the able commander, 34 years old, cool and cheerful under this supreme test, busied himself with the problems of making the masts secure and of providing a way to keep from foundering when the next heavy storm came up.

"I got fitted a pair of shrouds for each mast," he wrote, "and contrived a canvas weather cloth round the boat and raised the quarters about nine inches by nailing on the seats of the stern sheets, which proved of great benefit to us."

Notwithstanding these improvements there were many times in succeeding stormy days when the little vessel was in great danger from the floods of water that poured over her stern as the mountainous waves, some two hundred feet apart, overtook her from behind. Again and again she would be lifted to the top of a foaming peak, where her canvas suddenly caught the full force of the gale, filling with a loud bang before she would coast stern foremost down the retreating slope of the giant wave to the trough, where her sails would again flap in the eddying air.

Bligh held the tiller much of the time himself, taking care to keep her exactly before the sea. Any slipping off this course might easily have tipped and swamped her, costing eighteen lives for a moment of carelessness.

Daily Bligh checked his latitude with the sextant left him by the mutineers, observing the sun's elevation every noon; and his longitude he estimated by calculating the difference between dawn where he was and dawn at the longitude of Tahiti as given by Mr. Nelson's watch. Both of these observations he compared with his location as indicated by a log he had devised for dead reckoning. Thus he kept fair track of his progress as he passed north of the New Hebrides Islands and bore due west to pick up the great barrier reef of New Holland (Australia).

During all this grewsome nightmare of anxiety and agony Captain Bligh maintained a hopefulness that amazed and cheered his companions. Forbidding them to take the small amount of pork all at one meal, as many desired, he explained that they could live much longer taking it bit by bit. Even the constant rains and the necessity for bailing had a bright side for him.

"For my own part," he wrote, "I consider the general run of cloudy and wet weather to be a blessing of Providence. Hot weather would have caused us to have died of thirst, and perhaps being so constantly covered with rain or sea protected us from that dreadful calamity. . . .

"Being constantly obliged to bale," he added, "was perhaps not to be reckoned an evil, as it gave us exercise." But perhaps the most valuable of Bligh's ideas for relieving the sufferings of his men was his suggestion of stripping, then dipping their clothes in the warm sea water, wringing them out, and putting them on again. This procedure, repeated often during the cold nights, must have kept many from pneumonia.

Four days before the little boat got to New Holland the company probably passed the climax of their agony and despair, for despite their exhaustion they knew they had still nearly 2,000 miles to go before they could expect much relief. "The misery we suffered this day exceeded the preceding," wrote the captain. "The night was dreadful. The sea flew over us with great force and kept us baling with horror and anxiety. At dawn of day I found everyone in a most distressed condition, and I now began to fear that another such a night would put an end to the lives of several who seemed no longer able to support such sufferings."

And then on May 28 came the coast of New Holland. "At 1 in the morning the person at the helm heard the sound of breakers, and I no sooner lifted up my head than I saw them close under our lee, not more than a quarter of a mile distant from us."

All the forenoon they sailed along the reefs that guard this northeastern tip of the continent, looking for a channel through to the smooth water inside. At last, after some anxiety because of the danger of being blown helplessly against the reef, they passed through an opening and approached the coast, which "showed itself very distinctly, with a variety of high and low land, some parts of which were covered with wood."

Seeing no natives about, some of the men slept on shore that night, and in the morning Captain Bligh made a fire with the help of his magnifying glass and cooked a stew of bread, pork, and oysters, of which there were plenty to be found along the shore. Fresh water was plentiful, too. The men soon took a new lease on life, and while some repaired the boat's damaged rudder, others explored the island where they were. It was a rocky isle less than a mile long, and covered with stunted trees, yet they found fireplaces and "two miserable wigwams, having only one side loosely covered." Also, wrote Bligh, "the track of some animal was very discernable, and Mr. Nelson agreed with me that it was the kangaroo."

On the third day, everyone feeling much refreshed (though by no means free of aches and weakness), the captain "directed every person to attend prayers, and by 4 o'clock we were preparing to embark, when twenty natives appeared, running and holloaing to us, on the opposite shore. They were armed with a spear or lance and a short weapon which they carried in their left hand; they made signs for us to come to them. On the top of the hills we saw the heads of many more; whether these were their wives and children, or others who waited for our landing, until which they meant not to show themselves, lest we might be intimidated, I cannot say; but, as I found we were discovered to be on the coast, I thought it prudent to make the best of my way, for fear of canoes. . . ."

Continuing northward all night, the castaways again landed at a little island, and here, for the first time since leaving the Bounty, developed some symptoms of mutiny. After describing how, being weary to despair, they grumbled at his orders, Bligh wrote in his diary (but deleted most of it before publication) that:

"The carpenter [Purcell] began to be insolent to a high degree, and at last told me with a mutinous aspect he was as good a man as I was. I did not see just now where this was to end; I therefore determined to strike a final blow at it, and either to preserve my command or die in the attempt; and, taking hold of a cutlass, I ordered the rascal to take hold of another and defend himself, when he called out that I was going to kill him and began to make concessions.

"I was now only assisted by Mr. Nelson, and the master [Fryer] very deliberately called out to the boatswain to put me under an arrest, and was stirring up a greater disturbance when I declared, if he interfered when I was in the execution of my duty to preserve order and regularity, and that in consequence any tumult arose, I would certainly put him to death the first person.

"This had a proper effect on this man, and he now assured me that, on the contrary, I might rely on him to support my orders and directions for the future. This is the outline of a tumult that lasted about a quarter of an hour."

On up the coast they went, with scarcely a stop. Occasionally they were able to get oysters and clams, but not in large enough quantities to store up a supply. However, they were able to catch birds, called noddies and boobies, quite often. The latter, appropriately named, would sometimes sit where they were while a man walked up and grabbed them.

By June 10 the boat was nearly to Timor, and though the men were hopeful, their condition was rapidly getting worse, with few exceptions.

"In the morning," wrote Bligh, "after a very bad night, I could see an alteration for the worse in more than half my people. . . . I had great apprehension that some could not hold out. An extreme weakness, swelled legs, hollow and ghastly countenances, great propensity to sleep, with an apparent debility of understanding, seemed to me melancholy presages of their approaching dissolution.

"At 3 in the morning," recorded the commander on June 12, "with an excess of joy, we discovered Timor." None of them knew, however, at what part of Timor the Dutch settlement was located, so they had to sail on along the shore, eagerly inspecting the wooded plains and meadows for the slightest sign of civilization.

At last they found a native living on a peninsula, who gave them some turtle meat and Indian corn and piloted them to the settlement of Coupang, where the Dutch governor received them all into his own house.

Their incredible voyage was over and stands to this day probably the most remarkable voyage in a small open boat ever completed. Considering the overloaded condition of the launch and the starvation rations for the eighteen men, that they could have reached the coast of Timor in forty-one days after leaving Tofoa, having run 3,618 miles (according to their log), is little short of a miracle.

A DESCENT INTO THE MAELSTROM

Edgar Allan Poe

WE HAD now reached the summit of the loftiest crag. For some minutes the old man seemed too much exhausted to speak.

"Not long ago," said he at length, "and I could have guided you on this route as well as the youngest of my sons; but, about three years past, there happened to me an event such as never happened before to mortal man—or, at least, such as no man ever survived to tell of—and the six hours of deadly terror which I then endured have broken me up body and soul. You suppose me a *very* old man—but I am not. It took less than a single day to change these hairs from a jetty black to white, to weaken my limbs, and to unstring my nerves, so that I tremble at the least exertion, and am frightened at a shadow. Do you know I can scarcely look over this little cliff without getting giddy?"

The "little cliff," upon whose edge he had so carelessly thrown himself down to rest that the weightier portion of his body hung over it, while he was only kept from falling by the tenure of his elbow on its extreme and slippery edge—this "little cliff" arose, a sheer unobstructed precipice of black shining rock, some fifteen or sixteen hundred feet from the world of crags beneath us. Nothing would have tempted me to within half a dozen yards of its brink. In truth so deeply was I excited by the perilous position of my companion, that I fell at full length upon the ground, clung to the shrubs around me, and dared not even glance upward at the sky—while I struggled in vain to divest myself of the idea that the very foundations of the mountain

from "Tales of Mystery and Imagination" by Edgar Allan Poe

were in danger from the fury of the wind. It was long before I could reason myself into sufficient courage to sit up and look out into the distance.

"You must get over these fancies," said the guide, "for I have brought you here that you might have the best possible view of the scene of that event I mentioned—and to tell you the whole story with the spot just under your eye."

"We are now," he continued, in that particularizing manner which distinguished him—"we are now close upon the Norwegian coast—in the sixty-eighth degree of latitude—in the great province of Nordland—and in the dreary district of Lofoden. The mountain upon whose top we sit is Helseggen, the Cloudy. Now raise yourself up a little higher—hold onto the grass if you feel giddy—so—and look out, beyond the belt of vapor beneath us, into the sea."

I looked dizzily, and beheld a wide expanse of ocean, whose waters wore so inky a hue as to bring at once to my mind the Nubian geographer's account of the *Mare Tenebrarum*. A panorama more deplorably desolate no human imagination can conceive. To the right and left, as far as the eye could reach, there lay outstretched, like ramparts of the world, lines of horridly black and beetling cliff, whose character of gloom was but the more forcibly illustrated by the surf which reared high up against it its white and ghastly crest, howling and shrieking forever. Just opposite the promontory upon whose apex we were placed, and at a distance of some five or six miles out at sea, there was visible a small, bleak-looking island; or, more properly, its position was discernable through the wilderness of surge in which it was enveloped. About two miles nearer the land, arose another of smaller size, hideously craggy and barren, and encompassed at various intervals by a cluster of dark rocks.

The appearance of the ocean, in the space between the more distant island and the shore, had something very unusual about it. Although, at the time, so strong a gale was blowing landward that a brig in the remote offing lay to under a double-reefed trysail, and constantly plunged her whole hull out of sight, still there was here nothing like a regular swell, but only a short, quick, angry cross dashing of water in every direction—as well in the teeth of the wind as otherwise. Of foam there was little except in the immediate vicinity of the rocks.

"The island in the distance," resumed the old man, "is called by the

Norwegians Vurrgh. The one midway is Moskoe. That a mile to the northward is Ambaaren. Yonder are Islesen, Hotholm, Keildhelm, Suarven, and Buckholm. Farther off—between Moskoe and Vurrgh—are Otterholm, Flimen, Sandflesen, and Stockholm. These are the true names of the places— but why it has been thought necessary to name them at all, is more than either you or I can understand. Do you hear anything? Do you see any·change in the water?"

We had now been about ten minutes upon the top of Helseggen, to which we had ascended from the interior of Lofoden, so that we had caught no glimpse of the sea until it had burst upon us from the summit. As the old man spoke, I became aware of a loud and gradually increasing sound, like the moaning of a vast herd of buffaloes upon an American prairie; and at the same moment I perceived that what seamen term the *chopping* character of the ocean beneath us, was rapidly changing into a current which set to the eastward. Even while I gazed, this current acquired a monstrous velocity. Each moment added to its speed—to its headlong impetuosity. In five minutes the whole sea as far as Vurrgh, was lashed into ungovernable fury; but it was between Moskoe and the coast that the main uproar held its sway. Here the vast bed of the waters, seamed and scarred into a thousand conflicting channels, burst suddenly into frenzied convulsion—heaving, boiling, hissing— gyrating in gigantic and innumerable vortices, and all whirling and plunging on to the eastward with a rapidity which water never elsewhere assumes, except in precipitous descents.

In a few minutes more, there came over the scene another radical alteration. The general surface grew somewhat more smooth, and the whirlpools, one by one disappeared, while prodigious streaks of foam became apparent where none had been seen before. These streaks, at length, spreading out to a great distance, and entering into combination, took unto themselves the gyratory motion of the subsided vortices, and seemed to form the germ of another more vast. Suddenly—very suddenly—this assumed a distinct and definite exist- ence, in a circle of more than half a mile in diameter. The edge of the whirl was represented by a broad belt of gleaming spray; but no particle of this slipped into the mouth of the terrific funnel, whose interior, as far as the eye could fathom it, was a smooth, shining, and jet-black wall of water, inclined to the horizon at an angle of some forty-five degrees, speeding dizzily round and round with a swaying and sweltering motion, and sending forth to the winds

A smooth, shining and jet-black wall of water sped dizzily round and round.

an appalling voice, half shriek, half roar, such as not even the mighty cataract of Niagara ever lifts up in its agony to Heaven.

The mountain trembled to its very base, and the rock rocked. I threw myself upon my face, and clung to the scant herbage in an excess of nervous agitation.

"This," said I at length, to the old man—"this *can* be nothing else than the great whirlpool of the Maelstrom."

"So it is sometimes termed," said he. "We Norwegians call it the Moskoe-strom, from the island of Moskoe in the midway."

The ordinary accounts of this vortex had by no means prepared me for what I saw. That of Jonas Ramus, which is perhaps the most circumstantial of any, cannot impart the faintest conception either of the magnificence, or of the horror of the scene—or of the wild bewildering sense of *the novel* which confounds the beholder. I am not sure from what point of view the writer in question surveyed it, nor at what time; but it could neither have been from the summit of Helseggen, nor during a storm. There are some passages of his description, nevertheless, which may be quoted for their details, although their effect is exceedingly feeble in conveying an impression of the spectacle.

"Between Lofoden and Moskoe," he says, "the depth of the water is between thirty-six and forty fathoms; but on the other side, toward Ver (Vur-rgh) this depth decreases so as not to afford a convenient passage for a vessel, without the risk of splitting on the rocks, which happens even in the calmest weather. When it is flood, the stream runs up the country between Lofoden and Moskoe with a boisterous rapidity; but the roar of its impetuous ebb to the sea is scarce equaled by the loudest and most dreadful cataracts; the noise being heard several leagues off, and the vortices or pits are of such an extent and depth, that if a ship comes within its attraction, it is inevitably absorbed and carried down to the bottom, and there beat to pieces against the rocks; and when the water relaxes, the fragments thereof are thrown up again. But these intervals of tranquillity are only at the turn of the ebb and flood, and in calm weather, and last but a quarter of an hour, its violence gradually returning. When the stream is most boisterous, and its fury heightened by a storm, it is dangerous to come within a Norway mile of it. Boats, yachts, and ships have been carried away by not guarding against it before they were carried within its reach. It likewise happens frequently, that whales come too near the stream, and are overpowered by its violence; and then it is impossible to describe their howlings and bellowings in their fruitless struggles to disengage themselves. A bear once, attempting to swim from Lofoden to Moskoe, was caught by the stream and borne down, while he roared terribly, so as to be heard on shore. Large stocks of firs and pine-trees, after being absorbed by the current, rise again broken and torn to such a degree as if bristles grew upon them. This plainly shows the bottom to consist of craggy rocks, among which they are whirled to and fro. This stream is regulated by the flux and reflux of the sea—it being constantly high and low water every six hours. In the year 1645, early in the morning of Sexagesima Sunday, it raged with such noise and impetuosity that the very stones of the houses on the coast fell to the ground."

In regard to the depth of the water, I could not see how this could have been ascertained at all in the immediate vicinity of the vortex. The "forty fathoms" most have reference only to portions of the channel close upon the shore either of Moskoe or Lofoden. The depth in the center of the Moskoe-strom must be unmeasurably greater; and no better proof of this fact is necessary than can be obtained from even the sidelong glance into the abyss of the whirl which may be had from the highest crag of Helseggen. Looking down from this pinnacle upon the howling Phlegethon below, I could not help smiling at the simplicity with which the honest Jonas Ramus records, as a matter difficult of belief, the anecdotes of the whales and the bears, for it appeared to me, in fact, a self-evident thing, that the largest ships of the line in existence, coming within the influence of that deadly attraction, could resist it as little as a feather the hurricane, and must disappear bodily and at once.

The attempts to account for the phenomenon—some of which, I remember, seemed to me sufficiently plausible in perusal—now wore a very different and unsatisfactory aspect. The idea generally received is that this, as well as three smaller vortices among the Ferroe Islands, "have no other cause than the collision of waves rising and falling, at flux and reflux, against a ridge of rocks and shelves, which confines the water so that it precipitates itself like a cataract; and thus the higher the flood rises, the deeper must the fall be, and the natural result of all is a whirlpool or vortez, the prodigious suction of which is sufficiently known by lesser experiments."—These are the words of the *Encyclopædia Britannica*. Kircher and others imagine that in the center of the channel of the Maelstrom is an abyss penetrating the globe, and issuing in some very remote part—the Gulf of Bothnia being somewhat decidedly named in one instance. This opinion, idle in itself, was the one to which, as I gazed, by imagination most readily assented; and, mentioning it to the guide, I was rather surprised to hear him say that, although it was the view almost universally entertained of the subject by the Norwegians, it nevertheless was not his own. As to the former notion he confessed his inability to comprehend it; and here I agreed with him—for, however conclusive on paper, it becomes altogether unintelligible, and even absurd, amid the thunder of the abyss.

"You have had a good look at the whirl now," said the old man, "and if you will creep round this crag, so as to get in its lee, and deaden the roar of the water, I will tell you a story that will convince you I ought to know something of the Moskoe-strom."

I placed myself as desired, and he proceeded.

"Myself and my two brothers once owned a schooner-rigged smack of about seventy tons burthen, with which we were in the habit of fishing among the islands beyond Moskoe, nearly to Vurrgh. In all violent eddies at sea there is good fishing, at proper opportunities, if one has only the courage to attempt it; but among the whole of the Lofoden coastmen, we three were the only ones who made a regular business of going out to the islands, as I tell you. The usual grounds are a great way lower down to the southward. There fish can be got at all hours, without much risk, and therefore these places are preferred. The choice spots over here among the rocks, however, not only yield the finest variety, but in far greater abundance; so that we often got in a single day, what the more timid of the craft could not scrape together in a week. In fact, we made it a matter of desperate speculation—the risk of life standing instead of labor, and courage answering for capital.

"We kept the smack in a cove about five miles higher up the coast than this; and it was our practice, in fine weather, to take advantage of the fifteen minutes' slack to push across the main channel of the Moskoe-strom, far above the pool, and then drop down upon anchorage, somewhere near Otterholm, or Sandflesen where the eddies are not so violent as elsewhere. Here we used to remain until nearly time for slack-water again, when we weighed and made for home. We never set out upon this expedition without a steady side wind for going and coming—one that we felt sure would not fail us before our return—and we seldom made a miscalculation upon this point. Twice, during six years, we were forced to stay all night at anchor on account of a dead calm, which is a rare thing indeed just about here; and once we had to remain on the grounds nearly a week, starving to death, owing to a gale which blew up shortly after our arrival, and made the channel too boisterous to be thought of. Upon this occasion we should have been driven out to sea in spite of everything (for the whirlpools threw us round and round so violently, that, at length, we fouled our anchor and dragged it) if it had not been that we drifted into one of the innumerable cross currents—here today and gone tomorrow—which drove us under the lee of Flimen, where, by good luck, we brought up.

"I could not tell you the twentieth part of the difficulties we encountered 'on the ground'—it is a bad spot to be in, even in good weather—but we made shift always to run the gauntlet of the Moskoe-strom itself without accident: although at times my heart has been in my mouth when we happened to be a minute or so behind or before the slack. The wind sometimes was not as strong as we thought it at starting, and then we made rather less way than we could wish, while the current rendered the smack unmanageable. My eldest brother had a son eighteen years old, and I had two stout boys of my own. These would have been of great assistance at such times, in using the sweeps as well as afterward in fishing—but somehow, although we ran the risk ourselves, we had not the heart to let the young ones get into the danger—for, after all said and done, it *was* a horrible danger, and that is the truth.

"It is now within a few days of three years since what I am going to tell you occurred. It was on July 10, 18—, a day which the people of this part of the world will never forget—for it was one in which blew the most terrible hurricane that ever came out of the heavens. And yet all the morning, and indeed until late in the afternoon, there was a gentle and steady breeze from the south-west, while the sun shone brightly, so that the oldest seaman among us could not have foreseen what was to follow.

"The three of us—my two brothers and myself—had crossed over to the islands about two o'clock P.M., and soon nearly loaded the smack with fine fish, which, we all remarked, were more plenty that day than we had ever known them. It was just seven, *by my watch*, when we weighed and started for home, so as to make the worst of the Strom at slack-water, which we knew would be at eight.

"We set out with a fresh wind on our starboard quarter, and for some time spanked along at a great rate, never dreaming of danger, for indeed we saw not the slightest reason to apprehend it. All at once we were taken aback by a breeze from over Helseggen. This was most unusual—something that had never happened to us before—and I began to feel a little uneasy, without exactly knowing why. We put the boat on the wind, but could make no headway at all for the eddies, and I was upon the point of proposing to return to the anchorage, when, looking astern, we saw the whole horizon covered with a singular copper-colored cloud that rose with the most amazing velocity.

"In the meantime the breeze that had headed us off fell away and we were dead becalmed, drifting about in every direction. This state of things, however, did not last long enough to give us time to think about it. In less than a minute the storm was upon us—in less than two the sky was entirely overcast—and what with this and the driving spray, it became suddenly so dark that we could not see each other in the smack.

"Such a hurricane as then blew it is folly to attempt describing. The oldest seaman in Norway never experienced anything like it. We had let our sails go by the run before it cleverly took us; but, at the first puff, both our masts went by the board as if they had been sawed off—the mainmast taking with it my youngest brother, who had lashed himself to it for safety.

"Our boat was the lightest feather of a thing that ever sat upon water. It had a complete flush deck, with only a small hatch near the bow, and this hatch it had always been our custom to batten down when about to cross the Strom, by way of precaution against the chopping seas. But for this circumstance we should have foundered at once—for we lay entirely buried for some moments. How my elder brother escaped destruction I cannot say, for I never had an opportunity of ascertaining. For my part, as soon as I had let the foresail run, I threw myself flat on deck, with my feet against the narrow gunwale of the bow, and with my hands grasping a ring-bolt near the foot of the foremast. It was mere instinct that prompted me to do this—which was undoubtedly the very best thing I could have done—for I was too much flurried to think.

"For some moments we were completely deluged, as I say, and all this time I held my breath, and clung to the bolt. When I could stand it no longer I raised myself upon my knees, still keeping hold with my hands, and thus got my head clear. Presently our little boat gave herself a shake, just as a dog does in coming out of the water, and thus rid herself, in some measure, of the seas. I was now trying to get the better of the stupor that had come over me, and to collect my senses so as to see what was to be done, when I felt some-body grasp my arm. It was my elder brother, and my heart leaped for joy, for I had made sure that he was overboard—but the next moment all this joy was turned into horror—for he put his mouth close to my ear, and screamed out the word '*Moskoe-strom!*'

"No one ever will know what my feelings were at that moment. I shook from head to foot as if I had had the most violent fit of the ague. I knew what he meant by that one word well enough—I knew what he wished to make me understand. With the wind that now drove us on, we were bound for the whirl of the Strom, and nothing could save us!

"You perceive that in crossing the Strom *channel*, we always went a long way up above the whirl, even in the calmest weather, and then had to wait and watch carefully for the slack—but now we were driving right upon the pool itself, and in such a hurricane as this! 'To be sure,' I thought, 'we shall get there just about the slack—there is some little hope in that'—but in the next moment I cursed myself for being so great a fool as to dream of hope at all. I knew very well that we were doomed, had we been ten times a ninety-ton ship.

"By this time the first fury of the tempest had spent itself, or perhaps we did not feel it so much, as we scudded before it, but at all events the sea which at first had been kept down by the wind, and lay flat and frothing, now got up into absolute mountains. A singular change, too, had come over the heavens. Around in every direction it was still as black as pitch, but nearly overhead there burst out, all at once, a circular rift of clear sky—as clear as I ever saw—and of a deep bright blue—and through it there blazed forth the full moon with a luster that I never before knew her to wear. She lit up everything about us with the greatest distinctness—but, oh God, what a scene it was to light up!

"I now made one or two attempts to speak to my brother—but in some manner which I could not understand, the din had so increased that I could not make him hear a single word, although I screamed at the top of my voice in his ear. Presently he shook his head, looking as pale as death, and held up one of his fingers, as if to say '*listen!*'

"At first I could not make out what he meant—but soon a hideous thought flashed upon me, I dragged my watch from its fob. It was not going. I glanced at its face by the moonlight, and then burst into tears as I flung it far away into the ocean. *It had run down at seven o'clock! We were behind the time of the slack, and the whirl of the Strom was in full fury!*

"When a boat is well built, properly trimmed, and not deep laden, the waves in a strong gale, when she is going large, seem always to slip from beneath her—which appears strange to a landsman—and this is what is called *riding*, in sea phrase.

"Well, so far we had ridden the swells very cleverly; but presently a gigantic sea happened to take us right under the counter, and bore us with it as it rose —up—up—as if into the sky. I would not have believed that any wave could rise so high. And then down we came with a sweep, a slide, and a plunge that made me feel sick and dizzy, as if I was falling from some lofty mountain-top in a dream. But while we were up I had thrown a quick glance around— and that one glance was all-sufficient. I saw our exact position in an instant. The Moskoe-strom whirlpool was about a quarter of a mile dead ahead—but no more like the everyday Moskoe-strom than the whirl, as you now see it, is like a mill-race. If I had not known where we were, and what we had to expect, I should not have recognized the place at all. As it was, I involun-tarily closed my eyes in horror. The lids clenched themselves together as if in a spasm.

"It could not have been more than two minutes afterward until we suddenly felt the waves subside, and were enveloped in foam. The boat made a sharp half-turn to larboard, and then shot off in its new direction like a thunderbolt. At the same moment the roaring noise of the water was completely drowned in a kind of shrill shriek—such a sound as you might imagine given out by the water-pipes of many thousand steamvessels letting off their steam all together. We were now in the belt of surf that always surrounds the whirl; and I thought, of course, that another moment would plunge us into the abyss, down which we could only see indistinctly on account of the amazing ve-locity with which we were borne along. The boat did not seem to sink into the water at all, but to skim like an air-bubble upon the surface of the surge. Her starboard side was next the whirl, and on the larboard arose the world of ocean we had left. It stood like a huge writhing wall between us and the horizon.

"It may appear strange, but now, when we were in the very jaws of the gulf, I felt more composed than when we were only approaching it. Having made up my mind to hope no more, I got rid of a great deal of that terror which unmanned me at first. I supposed it was despair that strung my nerves.

"It may look like boasting—but what I tell you is truth—I began to reflect how magnificent a thing it was to die in such a manner, and how foolish it was in me to think of so paltry a consideration as my own individual life, in view of so wonderful a manifestation of God's power. I do believe that I blushed with shame when this idea crossed my mind. After a little while I became possessed with the keenest curiosity about the whirl itself. I positively felt a *wish* to explore its depths, even at the sacrifice I was going to make; and my principal grief was that I should never be able to tell my old companions on shore about the mysteries I should see. These, no doubt, were singular fancies to occupy a man's mind in such extremity—and I have often thought since, that the revolutions of the boat around the pool might have rendered me a little light-headed.

"There was another circumstance which tended to restore my self-possession; and this was the cessation of the wind, which could not reach us in our present situation—for, as you saw for yourself, the belt of surf is considerably lower than the general bed of the ocean, and this latter now towered above us, a high, black, mountainous ridge. If you have never been at sea in a heavy gale, you can form no idea of the confusion of mind occasioned by the wind and spray together. They blind, deafen, and strangle you, and take away all power of action or reflection. But we were now, in a great measure, rid of these annoyances—just as death-condemned felons in prison are allowed petty indulgences, forbidden them while their doom is yet uncertain.

"How often we made the circuit of the belt it is impossible to say. We careened round and round for perhaps an hour, flying rather than floating, getting gradually more and more into the middle of the surge, and then nearer and nearer to its horrible inner edge. All this time I had never let go of the ring-bolt. My brother was at the stern, holding on to a large empty water-cask which had been securely lashed under the coop of the counter, and was the only thing on deck that had not been swept overboard when the gale first took us. As we approached the brink of the pit he let go his hold upon this, and made for the ring, from which, in the agony of his terror, he endeavored to force my hands, as it was not large enough to afford us both a secure grasp. I never felt deeper grief than when I saw him attempt this act—although I knew he was a madman when he did it—a raving maniac through sheer fright.

I did not care, however, to contest the point with him. I knew it could make no difference whether either of us held on at all; so I let him have the bolt, and went astern to the cask. This there was no great difficult in doing; for the smack flew round steadily enough, and upon an even keel—only swaying to and fro with the immense sweeps and swelters of the whirl. Scarcely had I secured myself in my new position, when we gave a wild lurch to starboard, and rushed headlong into the abyss. I muttered a hurried prayer to God and thought that all was over.

"As I felt the sickening sweep of the descent, I had instinctively tightened my hold upon the barrel, and closed my eyes. For some seconds I dared not open them—while I expected instant destruction, and wondered that I was not already in my death-struggles with the water. But moment after moment elapsed. I still lived. The sense of falling had ceased; and the motion of the vessel seemed much as it had been before, while in the belt of foam, with the exception that she now lay more along. I took courage and looked once again upon the scene.

"Never shall I forget the sensations of awe, horror, and admiration with which I gazed about me. The boat appeared to be hanging, as if by magic, midway down, upon the interior surface of a funnel vast in circumference, prodigious in depth, and whose perfectly smooth sides might have been mistaken for ebony, but for the bewildering rapidity with which they spun around, and for the gleaming and ghastly radiance they shot forth, as the rays of the full moon, from that circular rift amid the clouds which I have already described, streamed in a flood of golden glory along the black walls, and far away down into the inmost recesses of the abyss.

"At first I was too much confused to observe anything accurately. The general burst of terrific grandeur was all that I beheld. When I recovered myself a little, however, my gaze fell instinctively downward. In this direction I was able to obtain an unobstructed view, from the manner in which the smack hung on the inclined surface of the pool. She was quite upon an even keel—that is to say, her deck lay in a plane parallel with that of the water—but this latter sloped at an angle of forty-five degrees, so that we seemed to be lying upon our beam ends. I could not help observing, nevertheless, that I had scarcely more difficulty in maintaining my hold and footing in this situation, than if we had been upon a dead level; and this, I suppose, was owing to the speed at which we revolved.

"The rays of the moon seemed to search the very bottom of the profound gulf: but still I could make out nothing distinctly on account of a thick mist in which everything there was enveloped, and over which there hung a magnificent rainbow, like that narrow and tottering bridge which Mussulmans say is the only pathway between Time and Eternity. This mist, or spray, was no doubt occasioned by the clashing of the great walls of the funnel, as they all met together at the bottom—but the yell that went up to the heavens from out of that mist I dare not attempt to describe.

"Our first slide into the abyss itself, from the belt of foam above, had carried us to a great distance down the slope; but our further descent was by no means proportionate. Round and round we swept—not with any uniform movement—but in dizzying swings and jerks, that sent us sometimes only a few hundred yards—sometimes nearly the complete circuit of the whirl. Our progress downward, at each revolution, was slow, but very perceptible.

"Looking about me upon the wide waste of liquid ebony on which we were thus borne, I perceived that our boat was not the only object in the embrace of the whirl. Both above and below us were visible fragments of vessels, large masses of building-timber and trunks of trees, with many smaller articles, such as pieces of house furniture, broken boxes, barrels and staves. I have already described the unnatural curiosity which had taken the place of my original terrors. It appeared to grow upon me as I drew nearer and nearer to my dreadful doom. I now began to watch, with a strange interest, the numerous things that floated in our company. I *must* have been delirious, for I even sought *amusement* in speculating upon the relative velocities of their several descents toward the foam below. 'This fir-tree,' I found myself at one time saying, 'will certainly be the next thing that takes the awful plunge and disappears,' and then I was disappointed to find that the wreck of a Dutch merchant ship overtook it and went down before. At length, after making several guesses of this nature, and being deceived in all—this fact—the fact of my invariable miscalculation, set me upon a train of reflection that made my limbs again tremble, and my heart beat heavily once more.

"It was not a new terror that thus affected me, but the dawn of a more exciting *hope*. This hope arose partly from memory, and partly from present observation. I called to mind the great variety of buoyant matter that strewed the coast of Lofoden, having been absorbed and then thrown forth by the Moskoe-strom. By far the greater number of the articles were shattered in the most extraordinary way—so chafed and roughened as to have the appearance of being stuck full of splinters—but then I distinctly recollected that there were *some* of them which were not disfigured at all.   Now I could not account for this difference except by supposing that the roughened fragments were the only ones which had been *completely absorbed*—that the others had entered the whirl at so late a period of the tide, or, for some reason, had descended so slowly after entering, that they did not reach the bottom before the turn of the flood came, or of the ebb, as the case might be.   I conceived it possible, in either instance, that they might thus be whirled up again to the level of the ocean, without undergoing the fate of those which had been drawn in more early or absorbed more rapidly.   I made, also, three important observations.   The first was, that as a general rule, the larger the bodies were, the more rapid their descent—the second, that, between two masses of equal extent, the one spherical, and the other *of any other shape,* the superiority in speed of descent was with the sphere—the third, that, between two masses of equal size, the one cylindrical, and the other of any other shape, the cylinder was absorbed the more slowly.

"Since my escape, I have had several conversations on this subject with an old schoolmaster of the district; and it was from him that I learned the use of the words 'cylinder' and 'sphere.'   He explained to me—although I have forgotten the explanation—how what I observed was, in fact, the natural consequence of the forms of the floating fragments—and showed me how it happened that a cylinder, swimming in a vortex, offered more resistance to its suction, and was drawn in with greater difficulty than an equally bulky body, of any form whatever.

"There was one startling circumstance which went a great way in enforcing these observations, and rendering me anxious to turn them to account, and this was that, at every revolution, we passed something like a barrel, or else the yard or the mast of a vessel, whilst many of these things, which had been on our level when I first opened my eyes upon the wonders of the whirlpool, were now high up above us, and seemed to have moved but little from their original station.

"I no longer hesitated what to do.   I resolved to lash myself securely to the water-cask upon which I now held, to cut it loose from the counter, and to throw myself with it into the water.   I attracted my brother's attention by signs, pointed to the floating barrels that came near us, and did everything in my power to make him understand what I was about to do. I thought at length that he comprehended my design—but, whether this was the case or not, he shook his head despairingly, and refused to move from his station by the ring-bolt. It was impossible to reach him; the emergency admitted of no delay; and so, with a bitter struggle, I resigned him to his fate, fastened myself to the cask by means of the lashings which secured it to the counter, and precipitated myself with it into the sea, without another moment's hesitation.

"The result was precisely what I had hoped it might be. As it is myself who now tell you this tale—as you see that I *did* escape—and as you are already in possession of the mode in which this escape was effected, and must therefore anticipate all that I have further to say—I will bring my story quickly to conclusion. It might have been an hour, or thereabout after my quitting the smack, when, having descended to a vast distance beneath me, it made three or four wild gyrations in rapid succession and, bearing my loved brother with it, plunged headlong, at once and for ever, into the chaos of foam below. The barrel to which I was attached sunk very little farther than half the distance between the bottom of the gulf and the spot at which I leaped overboard, before a great change took place in the character of the whirlpool. The slope of the sides of the vast funnel became momently less and less steep. The gyrations of the whirl grew, gradually, less and less violent. By degrees, the froth and the rain-bow disappeared, and the bottom of the gulf seemed slowly to uprise. The sky was clear, the winds had gone down, and the full moon was setting radiantly in the west, when I found myself on the surface of the ocean, in full view of the shores of Lofoden, and above the spot where the pool of the Moskoe-strom *had been*. It was the hour of the slack—but the sea still heaved in mountainous waves from the effects of the hurricane. I was borne violently into the channel of the Strom, and in a few minutes, was hurried down the coast into the 'grounds' of the fishermen. A boat picked me up—exhausted from fatigue—and (now that the danger was removed) speechless from the memory of its horror. Those who drew me on board were my old mates and daily companions—but they knew me no more than they would have known a traveler from the spirit-land. My hair, which had been raven black the day before, was as white as you see it now. They say too that the whole expression of my countenance had changed. I told them my story—they did not believe it. I now tell it to *you*—and I can scarcely expect you to put more faith in it than did the merry fishermen of Lofoden."

SIR RICHARD GRENVILLE
AND THE SPANISH ARMADA

Sir Walter Raleigh

THE *L. Thomas Howard*, with six of her Majesty's ships, six victualers of London, the bark *Ralegh*, and two or three pinnaces riding at anchor near unto Flores, one of the westerly islands of the Azores, the last of August in the afternoon, had intelligence by one Captain Midleton, of the approach of the Spanish Armada. Which Midleton being in a very good sailer, had kept them company three days before, of good purpose, both to discover their forces the more, as also to give advice to my *L. Thomas* of their approach. He had no sooner delivered the news but the fleet was in sight: many of our ships' companies were on shore in the island: some providing ballast for their ships; others filling of water and refreshing themselves from the land with such things as they could either for money, or by force recover. By reason whereof our ships being all pestered and romaging everything out of order, very light for want of ballast. And that which was most to our disadvantage, the one half part of the men of every ship sick, and utterly unserviceable. For in the *Revenge* there were ninety diseased: in the *Bonaventure*, not so many in health as could handle her main sail. For had not twenty men been taken out of a bark of Sir George Caryes, his being commanded to be sunk, and those appointed to her, she had had hardly ever recovered England. The rest for the most part, were in little better state. The names of her Majesty's ships were these as followeth: the *Defiance*, which was Admiral, the *Revenge* Vice-Admiral, the *Bonaventure* commanded by Captain Crosse, the *Lion* by George Fenner, the *Forefight* by M. Thomas Vauisour, and the *Crane* by Dus-

from "The Last Fight of the Revenge *at Sea" by Sir Walter Raleigh*

seild.   The *Forefight* and the *Crane* being but small ships; only the other were of the middle size; the rest, besides the bark *Ralegh*, commanded by Captain Thin, were victualers, and of small force or none.   The Spanish fleet having shrouded their approach by reason of the island; were now so soon at hand, as our ships had scare time to weigh their anchors, but some of them were driven to let slip their cables, and set sail.   Sir Richard Grenville was the last weighed, to recover the men that were upon the island, which otherwise had been lost.   The *L. Thomas* with the rest very hardly recovered the wind, which Sir Richard Grenville not being able to do, was persuaded by the Master and others to cut his main sail, and cast about, and to trust to the sailing of his ship: for the squadron of Seville were on his weather bow.   But Sir Richard utterly refused to turn from the enemy, alleging that he would rather chose to die, than to dishonor himself, his country, and her Majesty's ship, persuading his company that he would pass through the two squadrons, in despite of them: and enforce those of Seville to give him way.   Which he performed upon divers of the foremost, who as the mariners term it, sprang their luff, and fell under the lee of the *Revenge*.   But the other course had been the better, and might right well have been answered in so great an impossibility of prevailing.   Notwithstanding out of the greatness of his mind, he could not be persuaded.   In the meanwhile as he attended those which were nearest him the great *San Philip* being in the wind of him, and coming towards him, becalmed his sails in such sort, as the ship could neither way nor feel the helm; so huge and high carged was the Spanish ship, being of a thousand and five hundred tons.   Who afterlaid the *Revenge* aboard.   When he was thus bereft of his sails, the ships that were under his lee luffing up, also laid him aboard: of which the next was the Admiral of the Biscaines, a very mighty and puissant ship commanded by Brittan Dona.   The said *Philip* carried three tier of ordinance on a side, and eleven pieces in every tier.   She shot eight forth right out of her chase, besides those of the stern ports.

After the *Revenge* was entangled with this *Philip*, four other boarded her; two on her larboard, and two on her starboard.   The fight thus beginning at three of the clock in the afternoon, continued very terrible all that evening. But the great *San Philip* having received the lower tier of the *Revenge*, discharged with crossbarshot, shifted herself with all diligence from her sides, utterly misliking her first entertainment.   Some say that the ship foundered, but we cannot report it for truth, unless we were assured.   The Spanish ships were filled with companies of soldiers, in some two hundred besides the mariners; in some five, in others eight hundred. In ours there were none at all beside the mariners, but the servants of the commanders and some few voluntary gentlemen only. After many interchanged volleys of great ordinance and small shot, the Spaniards deliberated to enter the *Revenge*, and made divers attempts, hoping to force her by the multitudes of their armed soldiers and musketiers, but were still repulsed again and again, and at all times beaten back, into their own ships, or into the seas. In the beginning of the fight, the *George Noble* of London, having received some shot through her by the Armados, fell under the lee of the *Revenge*, and asked Sir Richard what he would command him, being but one of the victualers and of small force: Sir Richard bid him save himself, and leave him to his fortune. After the fight had thus without intermission, continued while the day lasted and some hours of the night, many of our men were slain and hurt, and one of the great galleons of the Armada, and the Admiral of the Hulks both sunk, and in many other of the Spanish ships great slaughter was made. Some write that Sir Richard was very dangerously hurt almost in the beginning of the fight, and lay speechless for a time ere he recovered. But two of the *Revenge's* own company, brought home in a ship of line from the islands, examined by some of the lords, and others: affirmed that he was never so wounded as that he forsook the upper deck, till an hour before midnight; and then being shot into the body with a musket as he was dressing, was again shot into the head, and withall his chirurgeon wounded to death. This agreeth also with an examination taken by Sir Frances Godolphine, of four other mariners of the same ship being returned, with examination, the said Sir Frances sent unto master William Killigrue, of her Majesty's privy chamber.

But to return to the fight, the Spanish ships which attempted to board the *Revenge*, as they were wounded and beaten off, so always others came in their places, she having never less than two mighty galleons by her sides, and aboard her. So that ere the morning from three of the clock the day before, there had fifteen several Armados assailed her; and all so ill approved their entertainment, as they were by the break of day, far more willing to harken to a composition, than hastily to make any more assaults or entries. But as the day increased, so our men decreased: and as the light grew more and more, by so much more grew our discomforts. For none appeared in fight but enemies, saving one small ship called the *Pilgrim*, commanded by Jacob Whiddon, who hovered all night to see the success: but in the morning bearing with the *Revenge* was hunted like a hare amongst many ravenous hounds, but escaped.

All the powder of the *Revenge* to the last barrel was now spent, all her pikes broken, forty of her best men slain, and the most part of the rest hurt. In the beginning of the fight she had but one hundred free from sickness, and fourscore and ten sick, laid in hold upon the ballast. A small troup to man such a ship, and a weak garrison to resist so mighty an army. By those hundred all was sustained, the volleys, boarding, and enterings of fifteen ships of war, besides those which beat her at large. On the contrary, the Spanish were always supplied with soldiers brought from every squadron: all manner of arms and powder at will. Unto ours there remained no comfort at all, no hope, no supply either of ships, men, or weapons; the masts all beaten overboard, all her tackle cut asunder, her upper work altogether rased, and in effect evened she was with the water, but the very foundation or bottom of a ship, nothing being left overhead either for flight or defense. Sir Richard finding himself in this distress, and unable any longer to make resistance, having endured in this fifteen hours fight, the assault of fifteen several Armados, all by turns aboard him, and by estimation eight hundred shot of great artillery, besides many assaults and entries. And that himself and the ship must needs be possessed by the enemy, who were now all cast in a ring about him; the *Revenge* not able to move one way or other, but as she was moved with the waves and billow of the sea: commanded the Master Gunner, whom he knew to be a most resolute man, to split and sink the ship; that thereby nothing might remain of glory or victory to the Spaniards: seeing in so many hours fight, and with so great a navy they were not able to take her, having had fifteen hours time, fifteen thousand men, and fifty and three sail of men of war to perform it withall. And persuaded the company, or as many as he could induce, to yield themselves unto God, and to the mercy of none else; but as they had like valiant resolute men, repulsed so many enemies, they should not now shorten the honor of their nation, by prolonging their own lives for a few hours, or a few days. The master gunner readily condescended and divers others; but the Captain and the Master were of an other opinion, and besought Sir Richard to have care of them: alleging that the Spaniard would be as ready to entertain a composition, as they were willing to offer the same: and that there being divers sufficient and valiant men yet living, and whose wounds were not mortal, they might do their country and prince acceptable service hereafter. And (that where Sir Richard had alleged that the Spaniards should never glory to have taken one ship of her Majesty's, seeing that they had so long and so notably defended themselves) they answered, that the ship had six foot water in hold, three shot under water which were so weakly stopped, as with the first working of the sea must needs sink, and was besides so crushed and bruised, as she could never be removed out of the place.

And as the matter was thus in dispute, and Sir Richard refusing to hearken to any of those reasons: the Master of the *Revenge* (while the Captain won unto him the greater party) was convoyed aboard the General *Don Alfonso Bassan*. Who finding none over hasty to enter the *Revenge* again, doubting lest Sir Richard would have blown them up and himself, and perceiving by the report of the Master of the *Revenge* his dangerous disposition: yielded that all their lives should be saved, the company sent for England, and the better sort to pay such reasonable ransom as their estate would bear, and in the mean season to be free from galley or imprisonment. To this he so much the rather condescended as well as I have said, for fear of further loss and mischief to themselves, as also for the desire he had to recover Sir Richard Grenville; whom for his notable valor he seemed greatly to honor and admire.

When this answer was returned, and that safety of life was promised, the common sort being now at the end of their peril, the most drew back from Sir Richard and the Master Gunner, being no hard matter to dissuade men from death to life. The Master Gunner finding himself and Sir Richard thus prevented and mastered by the greater number, would have slain himself with a sword, had he not been by force withheld and locked into his cabin. Then the General sent many boats aboard the *Revenge*, and divers of our men fearing Sir Richard's disposition, stole away aboard the General and other ships. Sir Richard thus overmatched, was sent unto by Alfonso Bassan to remove out of the *Revenge*, the ship being marvelous unsavory, filled with blood and bodies of dead, and wounded men like a slaughter house. Sir Richard answered that he might do with his body what he list, for he esteemed it not, and as he was carried out of the ship he swooned, and reviving again desired the company to pray for him. The General used Sir Richard with all humanity, and left nothing unattempted that tended to his recovery, highly commending his valor and worthiness, and greatly bewailed the danger wherein he was being unto them a rare spectacle, and a resolution seldom approved, to see one ship turn toward so many enemies, to endure the charge and boarding of so many huge Armados, and to resist and repell the assaults and entries of so many soldiers.   All which and more, is confirmed by a Spanish captain of the same Armada, and a present actor in the fight, who being severed from the rest in a storm, was by the *Lion* of London a small ship taken, and is now prisoner in London.

The General Commander of the Armada, was Don Alfonso Bassan, brother to the Marquesse of Santa Cruce.   The Admiral of the Biscaine Squadron, was Brittan Dona.   Of the Squadron of Seville, Marques of Arumburch.   The hulks and flyboats were commanded by Luis Cutino.   There were slain and drowned in this fight, well near two thousand of the enemies and two especial commanders Don Luis de Saint John, and Don George de Prunaria de Mallaga, as the Spanish captain confesseth, besides divers others of special account, whereof as yet report is not made.

The Admiral of the Hulks and the Ascention of Seville, were both sunk by the side of the *Revenge;* one other recovered the rode of Saint Michels, and sunk also there; a fourth ran herself with the shore to save her men.   Sir Richard died as it is said, the second or third day aboard the General, and was by them greatly bewailed.   What became of his body, whether it were buried in the sea or on the land we know not: the comfort that remaineth to his friends is, that he hath ended his life honorably in respect of the reputation won to his nation and country, and of the same to his posterity, and that being dead, he hath not outlived his own honor.

ATTACKED BY PIRATES

Charles Reade

W IND DOWN at noon next day, and a dead calm.
  At two P.M. the weather cleared; the sun came out high in heaven's
center; and a balmy breeze from the west.

At six twenty-five, the grand orb set calm and red, and the sea was gorgeous
with miles and miles of great ruby dimples: it was the first glowing smile of
southern latitude. The night stole on so soft, so clear, so balmy, all were loth
to close their eyes on it: the passengers lingered long on deck, watching the
Great Bear dip, and the Southern Cross rise, and overhead a whole heaven of
glorious stars most of us have never seen, and never shall see in this world.
No belching smoke obscured, no plunging paddles deafened; all was musical;
the soft air sighing among the sails; the phosphorescent water bubbling from
the ship's bows; the murmurs from little knots of men on deck subdued by the
great calm: home seemed near, all danger far; Peace ruled the sea, the sky, the
heart: the ship, making a track of white fire on the deep, glided gently yet
swiftly homeward, urged by snowy sails piled up like alabaster towers against
a violet sky, out of which looked a thousand eyes of holy tranquil fire. So
melted the sweet night away.

Now carmine streaks tinged the eastern sky at the water's edge; and that
water blushed; now the streaks turned orange, and the waves below them
sparkled. Thence splashes of living gold flew and settled on the ship's white
sails, the deck, and the faces; and with no more prologue, being so near the

from "Hard Cash" by Charles Reade

line, up came majestically a huge, fiery, golden sun, and set the sea flaming liquid topaz.

Instantly the look-out at the foretop-gallant-mast-head hailed the deck below.

"STRANGE SAIL! RIGHT AHEAD!"

The strange sail was reported to Captain Dodd, then dressing in his cabin. He came soon after on deck and hailed the look-out: "Which way is she standing?"

"Can't say, sir. Can't see her move any."

Dodd ordered the boatswain to pipe to breakfast; and taking his deck glass went lightly up to the fore-top-gallant-mast crosstrees. Thence, through the light haze of a glorious morning, he espied a long low schooner, lateen-rigged, lying close under Point Leat, a small island about nine miles distant on the weather bow, and nearly in the *Agra's* course, then approaching the Straits of Gaspar, 4 latitude S.

"She is hove-to," said Dodd very gravely.

At eight o'clock, the stranger lay about two miles to windward, and still hove-to.

By this time all eyes were turned upon her, and half a dozen glasses. Everybody, except the captain, delivered an opinion. She was a Greek lying-to for water: she was a Malay coming north with canes, and short of hands: she was a pirate watching the Straits.

The captain leaned silent and somber with his arms on the bulwarks, and watched the suspected craft.

Mr. Fullalove joined the group, and leveled a powerful glass, of his own construction. His inspection was long and minute, and, while the glass was at his eye, Sharpe asked him half in a whisper, could he make out anything?

"Wal," said he, "the varmint looks considerable snaky." Then, without removing his glass, he let drop a word at a time, as if the facts were trickling into his telescope at the lens, and out at the sight. "One—two—four—seven, false ports."

There was a momentary murmur among the officers all round. But British

sailors are undemonstrative: Colonel Kenealy, strolling the deck with his cigar, saw they were watching another ship with maritime curiosity, and making comments; but he discerned no particular emotion nor anxiety in what
they said, nor in the grave low tones they said it in. Perhaps a brother seaman
would though.

The next observation that trickled out of Fullalove's tube was this: "I judge
there are too few hands on deck, and too many—white—eyeballs—glittering
at the portholes."

"Confound it," muttered Bayliss, uneasily; "how can you see that?"

Fullalove replied only by quietly handing his glass to Dodd. The captain
thus appealed to, glued his eye to the tube.

"Well, sir; see the false ports, and the white eyebrows?" asked Sharpe ironi-
cally.

"I see this is the best glass I ever looked through," said Dodd doggedly,
without interrupting his inspection.

"I think he is a Malay pirate," said Mr. Grey.

Sharpe took him up very quickly, and indeed angrily: "Nonsense. And if
he is, he won't venture on a craft of this size."

"Says the whale to the swordfish," suggested Fullalove, with a little guttural
laugh.

The captain, with the American glass at his eye, turned half round to the
man at the wheel: "Starboard!"

"Starboard it is."

"Steer south-south-east."

"Ay, ay, sir." And the ship's course was thus altered two points.

This order lowered Dodd fifty per cent in Mr. Sharpe's estimation. He
held his tongue as long as he could: but at last his surprise and dissatisfaction
burst out of him, "Won't that bring him out on us!"

"Very likely, sir," replied Dodd.

"Begging your pardon, captain, would it not be wiser to keep our course,
and show the blackguard we don't fear him?"

"When we *do!* Sharpe, he has made up his mind an hour ago whether to
lie still or bite; my changing my course two points won't change his mind, but
it may make him declare it; and *I* must know what he does intend before I run
the ship into the narrows ahead."

"Oh, I see," said Sharpe, half convinced.

The alteration in the *Agra's* course produced no movement on the part of the mysterious schooner. She lay-to under the land still, and with only a few hands on deck, while the *Agra* edged away from her and entered the Straits between Long Island and Point Leat, leaving the schooner about two miles and a half distant to the N.W.

Ah! The stranger's deck swarms black with men.

His sham ports fell as if by magic, his guns grinned through the gaps like black teeth; his huge foresail rose and filled, and out he came in chase.

The breeze was a kiss from Heaven, the sky a vaulted sapphire, the sea a million dimples of liquid, lucid gold.

The way the pirate dropped the mask, showed his black teeth, and bore up in chase, was terrible: so dilates and bounds the sudden tiger on his unwary prey. There were stout hearts among the officers of the peaceable *Agra;* but danger in a new form shakes the brave, and this was their first pirate: their dismay broke out in ejaculations not loud but deep. "Hush," said Dodd doggedly; "the lady!"

Mrs. Beresford had just come on deck to enjoy the balmy morning.

"Sharpe," said Dodd, in a tone that conveyed no suspicion to the new-comer, "set the royals and flying jib.—Port!"

"Port it is," cried the man at the helm.

"Steer due south!" And, with these words in his mouth, Dodd dived to the gun-deck.

By this time elastic Sharpe had recovered the first shock, and the order to crowd sail on the ship galled his pride and his manhood. He muttered indignantly, "The white feather!" This eased his mind, and he obeyed orders briskly as ever. While he and his hands were setting every rag the ship could carry on that tack, the other officers having unluckily no orders to execute, stood gloomy and helpless, with their eyes glued, by a sort of somber fascination, on that coming fate; and they literally jumped and jarred when Mrs. Beresford, her heart opened by the lovely day, broke in on their nerves with her light treble.

"What a sweet morning, gentlemen! After all, a voyage is a delightful

thing. Oh, what a splendid sea! and the very breeze is warm. Ah! and
there's a little ship sailing along: here, Freddy, Freddy darling, leave off
beating the sailor's legs, and come here and see this pretty ship. What a pity
it is so far off. Ah! ah! what is that dreadful noise?"

For her horrible small talk, that grated on those anxious souls like the
mockery of some infantine fiend, was cut short by ponderous blows and tremendous smashing below. It was the captain staving in water-casks: the water poured out at the scuppers.

"Clearing the lee guns," said a middy, off his guard.

Colonel Kenealy pricked up his ears, drew his cigar from his mouth, and
smelt powder. "What, for action?" said he brisky. "Where's the enemy?"

Fullalove made him a signal, and they went below.

Mrs. Beresford had not heard or not appreciated the remark: she prattled
on till she made the mates and midshipmen shudder.

Realize the situation, and the strange incongruity between the senses and
the mind in these poor fellows! The day had ripened its beauty; beneath a
purple heaven shone, sparkled, and laughed a blue sea, in whose waves the
tropical sun seemed to have fused his beams; and beneath that fair, sinless,
peaceful sky, wafted by a balmy breeze over those smiling, transparent, golden
waves, a bloodthirsty Pirate bore down on them with a crew of human tigers;
and a lady babble babble babble babble babble babble babbled in their quivering ears.

But now the captain came bustling on deck, eyed the loftier sails, saw they
were drawing well, appointed four midshipmen a staff to convey his orders:
gave Bayliss charge of the carronades, Grey of the cutlasses, and directed
Mr. Tickell to break the bad news gently to Mrs. Beresford, and to take her
below to the orlop deck; ordered the purser to serve out beef, biscuit, and
grog to all hands, saying, "Men can't work on an empty stomach: and fighting is hard work;" then beckoned the officers to come round him. "Gentlemen," said he, confidentially, "in crowding sail on this ship I had no hope of
escaping that fellow on this tack, but I was, and am, most anxious to gain the
open sea, where I can square my yards and run for it, if I see a chance. At
present I shall carry on till he comes within range: and then, to keep the Company's canvas from being shot to rags, I shall shorten sail; and to save ship
and cargo and all our lives, I shall fight while a plank of her swims. Better
be killed in hot blood than walk the plank in cold."

The officers cheered faintly; the captain's dogged resolution stirred up theirs.

The pirate had gained another quarter of a mile and more. The ship's crew were hard at their beef and grog, and agreed among themselves it was a comfortable ship. They guessed what was coming, and woe to the ship in that hour if the captain had not won their respect. Strange to say, there were two gentlemen in the *Agra* to whom the pirate's approach was not altogether unwelcome. Colonel Kenealy and Mr. Fullalove were rival sportsmen and rival theorists. Kenealy stood out for a smooth bore and a four-ounce ball; Fullalove for a rifle of his own construction. Many a doughty argument they had, and many a bragging match; neither could convert the other. At last Fullalove hinted that by going ashore at the Cape, and getting each behind a tree at one hundred yards, and popping at one another, one or other would be convinced.

"Well, but," said Kenealy, "if he is dead, he will be no wiser. Besides, to a fellow like me, who has had the luxury of popping at his enemies, popping at a friend is poor insipid work."

"That is true," said the other regretfully. "But I reckon we shall never settle it by argument."

Theorists are amazing; and it was plain, by the alacrity with which these good creatures loaded the rival instruments, that to them the pirate came not so much as a pirate as a solution. Indeed, Kenealy, in the act of charging his piece, was heard to mutter, "Now, this is lucky." However, these theorists were no sooner loaded than something occurred to make them more serious. They were sent for in haste to Dodd's cabin; they found him giving Sharpe a new order.

"Shorten sail to the taupsles and jib, get the colors ready on the halyards, and then send the men aft."

Sharpe ran out full of zeal, and tumbled over Ramgolam, who was stooping remarkably near the keyhole. Dodd hastily bolted the cabin-door, and looked with trembling lip and piteous earnestness in Kenealy's face and Fullalove's. They were mute with surprise at a gaze so eloquent and yet mysterious.

He manned himself, and opened his mind to them with deep emotion, yet not without a certain simple dignity.

"Colonel," said he, "you are an old friend; *you*, sir, are a new one; but I esteem you highly, and what my young gentlemen chaff you about, you calling all men brothers, and making that poor negro love you instead of fear you, that shows me you have a great heart. My dear friends, I have been unlucky enough to bring my children's fortune on board this ship: here it is under my shirt. Fourteen thousand pounds! This weighs me down. Oh, if they should lose it after all! Do pray give me a hand apiece and pledge your sacred words to take it home safe to my wife at Barkington, if you, or either of you, should see this bright sun set today, and I should not."

"Why, Dodd, old fellow," said Kenealy cheerfully, "this is not the way to go into action."

"Colonel," replied Dodd, "to save this ship and cargo, I must be wherever the bullets are, and I will too."

Fullalove, more sagacious than the worthy colonel, said earnestly——

"Captain Dodd, may I never see Broadway again, and never see Heaven at the end of my time, if I fail you. There's my hand."

"And mine," said Kenealy warmly.

They all three joined hands, and Dodd seemed to cling to them.

"God bless you both! God bless you! Oh, what a weight your true hands have pulled off my heart. Good-by, for a few minutes. The time is short. I'll just offer a prayer to the Almighty for wisdom, and then I'll come up and say a word to the men and fight the ship, according to my lights."

Sail was no sooner shortened and the crew ranged, than the captain came briskly on deck, saluted, jumped on a carronade, and stood erect. He was not the man to show the crew his forebodings.

(Pipe.) "Silence fore and aft."

"My men, the schooner coming up on our weather quarter is a Portuguese pirate. His character is known; he scuttles all the ships he boards, dishonors the women, and murders the crew. We cracked on to get out of the narrows, and now we have shortened sail to fight this blackguard, and teach him to molest a British ship. I promise, in the Company's name, twenty pounds prize-money to every man before the mast if we beat him off or out-maneuver him; thirty if we sink him; and forty if we tow him astern into a friendly port. Eight guns are clear below, three on the weather side, five on the lee; for, if he knows his business, he will come up on the lee quarter: if he doesn't, that is no fault of yours nor mine. The muskets are all loaded, the cutlasses ground like razors——"

"Hurrah!"

"We have got women to defend——"

"Hurrah!"

"A good ship under our feet, the God of justice overhead, British hearts in our bosoms, and British colors flying—run 'em up!—over our heads." (The ship's colors flew up to the fore, and the Union Jack to the mizzen peak.) "Now, lads, I mean to fight this ship while a plank of her (stamping on the deck) swims beneath my foot, and—what do you say?"

The reply was a fierce "hurrah!" from a hundred throats, so loud, so deep, so full of volume, it made the ship vibrate, and rang in the creeping-on pirate's ears. Fierce, but cunning, he saw mischief in those shortened sails, and that Union Jack, the terror of his tribe, rising to a British cheer; he lowered his mainsail, and crawled up on the weather quarter. Arrived within a cable's length, he double-reefed his foresail to reduce his rate of sailing nearly to that of the ship; and the next moment a tongue of flame, and then a gush of smoke, issued from his lee bow, and the ball flew screaming like a seagull over the *Agra's* mizen top. He then put his helm up, and fired his other bow-chaser, and sent the shot hissing and skipping on the water past the ship. This prologue made the novices wince. Bayliss wanted to reply with a carronade; but Dodd forbade him sternly, saying, "If we keep him aloof we are done for."

The pirate drew nearer, and fired both guns in succession, hulled the *Agra* amidships, and sent an eighteen-pound ball through her foresail. Most of the faces were pale on the quarter-deck; it was very trying to be shot at, and hit, and make no return. The next double discharge sent one shot smash through the stern cabin window, and splintered the bulwark with another, wounding a seaman slightly.

"LIE DOWN FORWARD!" shouted Dodd. "Bayliss, give him a shot."

The carronade was fired with a tremendous report, but no visible effect. The pirate crept nearer, steering in and out like a snake to avoid the carronades, and firing those two heavy guns alternately into the devoted ship. He hulled the *Agra* now nearly every shot.

The two available carronades replied noisily, and jumped as usual; they sent one thirty-two pound shot clean through the schooner's deck and side; but that was literally all they did worth speaking of.

"Curse them!" cried Dodd; "load them with grape! they are not to be trusted with ball. And all my eighteen-pounders dumb! The coward won't come alongside and give them a chance."

At the next discharge the pirate chipped the mizen mast, and knocked a sailor into dead pieces on the forecastle. Dodd put his helm down ere the smoke cleared, and got three carronades to bear, heavily laden with grape. Several pirates fell, dead or wounded, on the crowded deck, and some holes appeared in the foresail; this one interchange was quite in favor of the ship.

But the lesson made the enemy more cautious; he crept nearer, but steered so adroitly, now right astern, now on the quarter, that the ship could seldom bring more than one carronade to bear, while he raked her fore and aft with grape and ball.

In this alarming situation, Dodd kept as many of the men below as possible; but, for all he could do, four were killed and seven wounded.

Fullalove's word came too true: it was the swordfish and the whale: it was a fight of hammer and anvil; one hit, the other made a noise. Cautious and cruel, the pirate hung on the poor hulking creature's quarters and raked her at point-blank distance. He made her pass a bitter time. And her captain! To see the splintering hull, the parting shrouds, the shivered gear, and hear the shrieks and groans of his wounded; and he unable to reply in kind! The sweat of agony poured down his face. Oh, if he could but reach the open sea, and square his yards, and make a long chase of it; perhaps fall in with aid. Wincing under each heavy blow, he crept doggedly, patiently on towards that one visible hope.

At last, when the ship was cloved with shot, and peppered with grape, the channel opened; in five minutes more he could put her dead before the wind.

No! The pirate, on whose side luck had been from the first, got half a broadside to bear at long musket-shot, killed a midshipman by Dodd's side, cut away two of the *Agra's* mizen shrouds, wounded the gaff, and cut the jib-stay. Down fell that powerful sail into the water, and dragged across the ship's forefoot, stopping her way to the open sea she panted for. The mates groaned; the crew cheered stoutly, as British tars do in any great disaster: the pirates yelled with ferocious triumph, like the devils they looked.

But most human events, even calamities, have two sides. The *Agra* being brought almost to a standstill, the pirate forged ahead against his will, and the combat took a new and terrible form. The elephant gun popped and the rifle cracked in the *Agra's* mizen top, and the man at the pirate's helm jumped into the air and fell dead: both Theorists claimed him. Then the three carronades peppered him hotly; and he hurled an iron shower back with fatal effect. Then at last the long eighteen-pounders on the gun-deck got a word in. The old Niler was not the man to miss a vessel alongside in a quiet sea: he sent two round shot clean through him; the third splintered his bulwark and swept across his deck.

"His masts—fire at his masts!" roared Dodd to Monk, through his trumpet. He then got the jib clear, and made what sail he could without taking all the hands from the guns.

This kept the vessels nearly alongside a few minutes, and the fight was hot as fire. The pirate now for the first time hoisted his flag. It was black as ink. His crew yelled as it rose: the Britons, instead of quailing, cheered with fierce derision; the pirate's wild crew of yellow Malays, black chinless Papuans, and bronzed Portuguese, served their side guns, twelve-pounders, well, and with ferocious cries. The white Britons, drunk with battle now, naked to the waist, grimed with powder, and spotted like leopards with blood, their own and their mates', replied with loud undaunted cheers and a deadly hail of grape from the quarter-deck; while the master-gunner and his mates, loading with a rapidity the mixed races opposed could not rival, hulled the schooner well between wind and water, and then fired chain-shot at her masts, as ordered, and began to play the mischief with her shrouds and rigging. Meantime, Fullalove and Kenealy, aided by Vespasian, who loaded, were quietly butchering the pirate crew two a minute, and hoped to settle the question they were fighting for: smooth bore *v.* rifle; but unluckily neither fired once without killing; so "there was nothing proven."

The pirate, bold as he was, got sick of fair fighting first. He hoisted his mainsail and drew rapidly ahead, with a slight bearing to windward, and dismounted a carronade and stove in the ship's quarter-boat, by way of a parting kick.

The men hurled a contemptuous cheer after him; they thought they had beaten him off. But Dodd knew better. He was but retiring a little way to make a more deadly attack than ever: he would soon wear, and cross the *Agra's* defenseless bows, to rake her fore and aft at pistol-shot distance; or grapple, and board the enfeebled ship, two hundred strong.

Dodd flew to the helm, and with his own hands put it hard a-weather, to give the deck-guns one more chance, the last, of sinking or disabling the Destroyer. As the ship obeyed, and a deck-gun bellowed below him, he saw a vessel running out from Long Island, and coming swiftly up on his lee quarter.

It was a schooner. Was she coming to his aid?

Horror! A black flag floated from her foremast head.

While Dodd's eyes were staring almost out of his head at this deathblow to hope, Monk fired again; and just then a pale face came close to Dodd's, and a solemn voice whispered in his ear: "Our ammunition is nearly done!"

Dodd seized Sharpe's hand convulsively, and pointed to the pirate's consort coming up to finish them; and said, with the calm of a brave man's despair, "Cutlasses! and die hard!"

At that moment the master-gunner fired his last gun. It sent a chain-shot on board the retiring pirate, took off a Portuguese head and spun it clean into the sea ever so far to windward, and cut the schooner's foremast so nearly through that it trembled and nodded, and presently snapped with a loud crack, and came down like a broken tree, with the yard and sail; the latter overlapping the deck and burying itself, black flag and all, in the sea; and there, in one moment, lay the Destroyer buffeting and wriggling—like a heron on the water with his long wings broken—an utter cripple.

The victorious crew raised a stunning cheer.

"Silence!" roared Dodd, with his trumpet. "All hands make sail!"

He set his courses, bent a new jib, and stood out to windward close hauled, in hopes to make a good offing, and then put his ship dead before the wind, which was now rising to a stiff breeze. In doing this he crossed the crippled pirate's bows, within eighty yards; and sore was the temptation to rake him; but his ammunition being short, and his danger being imminent from the other pirate, he had the self-command to resist the great temptation.

He hailed the mizen top: "Can you two hinder them from firing that gun?"

"I rather think we can," said Fullalove; "eh, Colonel?" and he tapped his long rifle.

The ship no sooner crossed the schooner's bows than a Malay ran forward with a linstock. Pop went the colonel's ready carbine, and the Malay fell over dead, and the linstock flew out of his hand. A tall Portuguese, with a movement of rage, snatched it up and darted to the gun: the Yankee rifle cracked, but a moment too late. Bang! went the pirate's bow-chaser, and crashed into the *Agra's* side, and passed nearly through her.

"Ye missed him! Ye missed him!" cried the rival theorist, joyfully. He was mistaken: the smoke cleared, and there was the pirate captain leaning wounded against the mainmast with a Yankee bullet in his shoulder, and his crew uttering yells of dismay and vengeance. They jumped, and raged, and brandished their knives, and made horrid gesticulations of revenge; and the white eyeballs of the Malays and Papuans glittered fiendishly; and the wounded captain raised his sound arm and had a signal hoisted to his consort, and she bore up in chase, and jamming her fore lateen flat as a board, lay far nearer the wind than the *Agra* could, and sailed three feet to her two besides. On this superiority being made clear, the situation of the merchant vessel, though not so utterly desperate as before Monk fired his lucky shot, became pitiable enough. If she ran before the wind, the fresh pirate would cut her off: if she lay to windward, she might postpone the inevitable and fatal collision with a foe as strong as that she had only escaped by a rare piece of luck; but this would give the crippled pirate time to refit and unite to destroy her. Add to this the failing ammunition and the thinned crew!

Dodd cast his eyes all round the horizon for help.

The sea was blank.

The bright sun was hidden now; drops of rain fell, and the wind was beginning to sing, and the sea to rise a little.

"Gentlemen," said he, "let us kneel down and pray for wisdom, in this sore strait."

He and his officers kneeled on the quarter-deck. When they rose, Dodd stood rapt about a minute: his great thoughtful eye saw no more the enemy, the sea, nor anything external; it was turned inward. His officers looked at him in silence.

"Sharpe," said he at last, "there *must* be a way out of them both with such a breeze as this is now; if we could but see it."

"Ay, *if*," groaned Sharpe.

Dodd mused again.

"About ship!" said he softly, like an absent man.

"Ay, ay, sir!"

"Steer due north!" said he, still like one whose mind was elsewhere.

While the ship was coming about, he gave minute orders to the mates and the gunner, to ensure co-operation in the delicate and dangerous maneuvers that were sure to be at hand.

The wind was W.N.W: he was standing north; one pirate lay on his lee beam stopping a leak between wind and water, and hacking the deck clear of his broken mast and yards. The other, fresh, and thirsting for the easy prey, came up to weather on him and hang on his quarter, pirate fashion.

When they were distant about a cable's length, the fresh pirate, to meet the ship's change of tactics, changed his own, luffed up, and gave the ship a broadside, well aimed but not destructive, the guns being loaded with ball.

Dodd, instead of replying immediately, put his helm hard up and ran under the pirate's stern, while he was jammed up in the wind, and with his five eighteen pounders raked him fore and aft, then paying off, gave him three carronades crammed with grape and canister. The rapid discharge of eight guns made the ship tremble, and enveloped her in thick smoke; loud shrieks and groans were heard from the schooner: the smoke cleared; the pirate's mainsail hung on deck, his jib-boom was cut off like a carrot and the sail struggling; his foresail looked lace, lanes of dead and wounded lay still or writhing on his deck, and his lee scuppers ran blood into the sea. Dodd squared his yards and bore away.

The ship rushed down the wind, leaving the schooner staggered and all abroad. But not for long; the pirate wore and fired his bow chasers at the now flying *Agra*, split one of the carronades in two, and killed a Lascar, and made a hole in the foresail. This done, he hoisted his mainsail again in a trice, sent his wounded below, flung his dead overboard, to the horror of their foes, and came after the flying ship, yawing and firing his bow chasers. The ship was silent. She had no shot to throw away. Not only did she take these blows like a coward, but all signs of life disappeared on her, except two men at the wheel and the captain on the main gangway.

Dodd had ordered the crew out of the rigging, armed them with cutlasses, and laid them flat on the forecastle. He also compelled Kenealy and Fullalove to come down out of harm's way, no wiser on the smooth bore question than they went up.

The great patient ship ran environed by her foes; one destroyer right in her course, another in her wake, following her with yells of vengeance, and pounding away at her—but no reply.

Suddenly the yells of the pirates on both sides ceased, and there was a moment of dead silence on the sea.

Yet nothing fresh had happened.

Yes, this had happened: the pirates to windward and the pirates to leeward of the *Agra* had found out, at one and the same moment, that the merchant captain they had lashed, and bullied, and tortured was a patient but tremendous man. It was not only to rake the fresh schooner he had put his ship before the wind, but also by a double, daring, masterstroke to hurl his monster ship bodily on the other. Without a foresail she could never get out of her way. The pirate crew had stopped the leak, and cut away and unshipped the broken foremast, and were stepping a new one, when they saw the huge ship bearing down in full sail. Nothing easier than to slip out of her way could they get the foresail to draw; but the time was short, the deadly intention manifest, the coming destruction swift.

After that solemn silence came a storm of cries and curses, as their seamen went to work to fit the yard and raise the sail; while their fighting men seized their matchlocks and trained the guns. They were well commanded by an heroic able villain. Astern the consort thundered; but the *Agra's* response was a dead silence more awful that broadsides.

For then was seen with what majesty the enduring Anglo-Saxon fights.

One of that indomitable race on the gangway, one at the foremast, two at the wheel, conned and steered the great ship down on a hundred matchlocks and a grinning broadside, just as they would have conned and steered her into a British harbor.

"Starboard!" said Dodd, in a deep calm voice, with a motion of his hand.

"Starboard it is."

The pirate wriggled ahead a little. The man forward made a silent signal to Dodd.

"Port!" said Dodd quietly.

"Port it is."

But at this critical moment the pirate astern sent a mischievous shot and knocked one of the men to atoms at the helm.

Dodd waved his hand without a word, and another man rose from the deck, and took his place in silence, and laid his unshaking hand on the wheel stained with that man's warm blood whose place he took.

The high ship was now scarce sixty yards distant; *she seemed to know:* she reared her lofty figure-head with great awful shoots into the air.

But now the panting pirates got their new foresail hoisted with a joyful shout: it drew, the schooner gathered way, and their furious consort close on the *Agra's* heels just then scourged her deck with grape.

"Port!" said Dodd calmly.

"Port it is."

The giant prow darted at the escaping pirate. That acre of coming canvas took the wind out of the swift schooner's foresail; it flapped: oh, then she was doomed! That awful moment parted the races on board her: the Papuans and Sooloos, their black faces livid and blue with horror, leaped yelling into the sea, or crouched and whimpered; the yellow Malays and brown Portuguese, though blanched to one color now, turned on death like dying panthers, fired two cannon slap into the ship's bows, and snapped their muskets and matchlocks at their solitary executioner on the ship's gangway, and out flew their knives like crushed wasp's stings. CRASH! the Indiaman's cutwater in thick smoke beat in the schooner's broadside: down went her masts to leeward like fishing-rods whipping the water; there was a horrible shrieking yell; wild forms leaped off on the *Agra,* and were hacked to pieces almost ere they reached the deck—a surge, a chasm in the sea, filled with an instant rush of engulphing waves, a long, awful, grating, grinding noise, never to be forgotten in this world, all along under the ship's keel—and the fearful majestic monster passed on over the blank she had made, with a pale crew standing silent and awestruck on her deck; a cluster of wild heads and staring eyeballs bobbing like corks in her foaming wake, sole relic of the blotted-out Destroyer; and a wounded man staggering on the gangway, with hands uplifted and staring eyes.

Shot in two places, the head and the breast!

With a loud cry of pity and dismay, Sharpe, Fullalove, Kenealy, and others rushed to catch him; but, ere they got near, the captain of the triumphant ship fell down on his hands and knees, his head sunk over the gangway, and his blood ran fast and pattered in the midst of them on the deck he had defended so bravely.

THE DERELICT NEPTUNE

Morgan Robertson

A CROSS the Atlantic Ocean from the Gulf of Guinea to Cape St. Roque moves a great body of water—the Main Equatorial Current—which can be considered the motive power, or mainspring, of the whole Atlantic current system, as it obtains its motion directly from the ever-acting push of the tradewinds. At Cape St. Roque this broad current splits into two parts, one turning north, the other south. The northern part contracts, increases its speed, and, passing up the northern coast of South America as the Guiana Current, enters through the Caribbean Sea into the Gulf of Mexico, where it circles around to the northward; then, colored a deep blue from the fine river silt of the Mississippi, and heated from its long surface exposure under a tropical sun to an average temperature of eighty degrees, it emerges into the Florida Channel as the Gulf Stream.

From here it travels northeast, following the trend of the coast line, until, off Cape Hatteras, it splits into three divisions, one of which, the westernmost, keeps on to lose its warmth and life in Baffin's Bay. Another impinges on the Hebrides, and is no more recognizable as a current; and the third, the eastern and largest part of the divided stream, makes a wide sweep to the east and south, enclosing the Azores and the deadwater called the Sargasso Sea, then, as the African Current, runs down the coast until, just below the Canary Isles, it merges into the Lesser Equatorial Current, which, parallel to the parent stream, and separated from it by a narrow band of backwater, travels west and filters through the West Indies, making puzzling combinations with the tides, and finally bearing so heavily on the young Gulf Stream

from "Spun Yarn," by Morgan Robertson. By courtesy of Harper & Brothers.

as to give to it the sharp turn to the northward through the Florida Channel.

In the South Atlantic, the portion of the Main Equatorial Current split off by Cape St. Roque and directed south leaves the coast at Cape Frio, and at the latitude of the River Plate assumes a due easterly direction, crossing the ocean as the Southern Connecting Current. At the Cape of Good Hope it meets the cold, northeasterly Cape Horn Current, and with it passes up the coast of Africa to join the Equatorial Current at the starting-point in the Gulf of Guinea, the whole constituting a circulatory system of ocean rivers, of speed value varying from eighteen to ninety miles a day.

On a bright morning in November, 1894, a curious-looking craft floated into the branch current which, skirting Cuba, flows westward through the Bahama Channel. A man standing on the highest of two points enclosing a small bay near Cape Maisi, after a critical examination through a telescope, disappeared from the rocks, and in a few moments a light boat, of the model used by whalers, emerged from the mouth of the bay, containing this man and another. In the boat also was a coil of rope.

The one who had inspected the craft from the rocks was a tall young fellow, dressed in flannel shirt and trousers, the latter held in place by a cartridge-belt, such as is used by the American cowboy. To this was hung a heavy revolver. On his head was a broad-brimmed cork helmet, much soiled, and resembling in shape the Mexican sombrero. Beneath this head-gear was a mass of brown hair, which showed a non-acquaintance with barbers for, perhaps, months, and under this hair a suntanned face, lighted by serious gray eyes. The most noticeable feature of this face was the extreme arching of the eyebrows—a never-failing index of the highest form of courage. It was a face that would please. The face of the other was equally pleasing in its way. It was red, round, and jolly, with twinkling eyes, the whole borrowing a certain dignity from closely cut white hair and mustaches. The man was about fifty, dressed and armed like the other.

"What do you want of pistols, Boston?" he said to the younger man. "One might think this an old-fashioned, piratical cutting out."

"Oh, I don't know, Doc. It's best to have them. That hulk may be full of Spaniards, and the whole thing nothing but a trick to draw us out. But she looks like a derelict. I don't see how she got into this channel, unless she drifted up past Cape Maisi from the southward, having come in with the Guiana Current. It's all rocks and shoals to the eastward."

The boat, under the impulse of their oars, soon passed the fringing reef and came in sight of the strange craft, which lay about a mile east and half a mile off shore. "You see," resumed the younger man, called Boston, "there's a back-water inside Point Mulas, and if she gets into it she may come ashore right here."

"Where we can loot her. Nice business for a respectable practitioner like me to be engaged in! Doctor Bryce, of Havana, consorting with Fenians from Canada, exiled German socialists, Cuban horse-thieves who would be hung in a week if they went to Texas, and a long-legged sailor man who calls himself a retired naval officer, but who looks like a pirate; and all shouting for *Cuba Libre! Cuba Libre!* It's plunder you want."

"But none of us ever manufactured dynamite," answered Boston, with a grin. "How long did they have you in Moro Castle, Doc?"

"Eight months," snapped the doctor, his face clouding. "Eight months in that rathole, with the loss of my property and practice—all for devotion to science. I was on the brink of the most important and beneficent discovery in explosives the world ever dreamed of. Yes, sir, 'twound have made me famous and stopped all warfare."

"The captain told me this morning that he'd heard from Marti," said Boston, after an interval. "Good news, he said, but that's all I learned. Maybe it's from Gomez. If he'll only take hold again we can chase the Spanish off the island now. Then we'll put some of your stuff under Moro and lift it off the earth."

In a short time, details of the craft ahead, hitherto hidden by distance, began to show. There was no sign of life aboard; her spars were gone, with the exception of the foremast, broken at the hounds, and she seemed to be of about a thousand tons burden, colored a mixed brown and dingy gray, which, as they drew near, was shown as the action of iron rust on black and lead-colored paint. Here and there were outlines of painted ports. Under the stump of a shattered bowsprit projected from between bluff bows a weather-worn figurehead, representing the god of the sea. Above on the bows were wooden-stocked anchors stowed inboard, and aft on the quarters were iron davits with blocks intact—but no falls. In a few of the dead-eyes in the channels could be seen frayed rope-yarns, rotten with age, and, with the stump of the foremast, the wooden stocks of the anchors, and the teak-wood rail, of a bleached gray color. On the round stern, as they pulled under it, they spelled, in raised letters, flecked here and there with discolored gilt, the name "Neptune, of London." Unkempt and forsaken, she had come in from the mysterious sea to tell her story.

They climbed the channels, fastened the painter, and peered over the rail. There was no one in sight, and they sprang down, finding themselves on a deck that was soft and spongy with time and weather.

"She's an old tub," said Boston, scanning the gray fabric fore and aft; "one of the first iron ships built, I should think. They housed the crew under the t'gallant forecastle. See the doors forward, there? And she has a full-decked cabin—that's old style. Hatchers are all battened down, but I doubt if this tarpaulin holds water." He stepped on the main hatch, brought his weight on the ball of one foot, and turned around. The canvas crumbled to threads, showing the wood beneath. "Let's go below. If there were any Spaniards here they'd have shown themselves before this." The cabin doors were latched but not locked, and they opened them.

"Hold on," said the doctor, "this cabin may have been closed for years, and generated poisonous gases. Open that upper door, Boston."

Boston ran up the shaky poop ladder and opened the companion-way above, which let a stream of the fresh morning air and sunshine into the cabin, then, after a moment or two, descended and joined the other, who had entered from the main-deck. They were in an ordinary ship's cabin, surrounded by staterooms, and with the usual swinging lamp and tray; but the table, chairs, and floor were covered with fine dust.

"Where the deuce do you get so much dust at sea?" coughed the doctor.

"Nobody knows, Doc. Let's hunt for the manifest and the articles. This must have been the skipper's room." They entered the largest stateroom, and Boston opened an old-fashioned desk. Among the discolored documents it contained, he found one and handed it to the doctor. "Articles," he said; "look at it." Soon he took out another. "I've got it. Now we'll find what she has in her hold, and if it's worth bothering about."

"Great Scott!" exclaimed the doctor; "this paper is dated 1844, fifty years ago." Boston looked over his shoulder.

"That's so; she signed her crew at Boston, too. Where has she been all this time? Let's see this one."

The manifest was short, and stated that her cargo was 3000 barrels of lime, 8000 kids of tallow, and 2500 carboys of acid, 1700 of which were sulphuric,

Unkempt and forsaken, she had come in from the mysterious sea to tell her story.

the rest of nitric acid. "That cargo won't be much good to us, Doc. I'd hope to find something we could use. Let's find the log-book, and see what happened to her." Boston rummaged what seemed to be the first-mate's room. "Plenty of duds here," he said; "but they're ready to fall to pieces. Here's the log."

He returned with the book, and, seated at the dusty table, they turned the yellow leaves. "First departure, Highland Light, March 10, 1844," read Boston. "We'll look in the remarks column."

Nothing but the ordinary incidents of a voyage were found until they reached the date June 1st, where entry was made of the ship being "caught aback" and dismasted off the Cape of Good Hope in a sudden gale. Then followed daily "remarks" of the southeasterly drift of the ship, the extreme cold (which, with the continuance of the bad weather, prevented saving the wreck for jury-masts), and the fact that no sails were sighted.

June 6th told of her being locked in soft, slushy ice, and still being pressed southward by the never-ending gale; June 10th said that the ice was hard, and at June 15th was the terrible entry: "Fire in the hold!"

On June 16th was entered this: "Kept hatches battened down and stopped all air-holes, but the deck is too hot to stand on, and getting hotter. Crew insist on lowering the boats and pulling them northward over the ice to open water in hopes of being picked up. Good-bye." In the position columns of this date the latitude was given as 62 degrees 44 minutes S. and the longitude as 30 degrees 50 minutes E. There were no more entries.

"What tragedy does this tell of?" said the doctor. "They left this ship in the ice fifty years ago. Who can tell if they were saved?"

"Who indeed?" said Boston. "The mate hadn't much hope. He said 'Good-bye.' But one thing is certain; we are the first to board her since. I take it she stayed down there in the ice until she drifted around the Pole, and thawed out where she could catch the Cape Horn current, which took her up to the Hope. Then she came up with the South African Current till she got into the Equatorial drift, then west, and up with the Guiana Current into the Caribbean Sea to the southward of us, and this morning the flood-tide brought her through. It isn't a question of winds; they're too variable. It's currents, though it may have taken her years to get here. But the surprising part of it is that she hasn't been boarded. Let's look in the hold and see what the fire has done."

When they boarded the hulk, the sky, with the exception of a filmy haze overhanging the eastern end of the island, was clear. Now, as they emerged from the cabin, this haze had solidified and was coming—one of the black and vicious squalls of the West India seas.

"No man can tell what wind there is in them," remarked Boston, as he viewed it. "But it's pretty close to the water, and dropping rain. Hold on, there, Doc. Stay aboard. We couldn't pull ashore in the teeth of it." The doctor had made a spasmodic leap to the rail. "If the chains were shackled on, we might drop one of the hooks and hold her; but it's two hours work for a full crew."

"But we're likely to be blown away, aren't we?" asked the doctor.

"Not far. I don't think it'll last long. We'll make the boat fast astern and get out of the wet." They did so, and entered the cabin. Soon the squall, coming with a shock like that of a solid blow, struck the hulk broadside to and careened her. From the cabin door they watched the nearly horizontal rain as it swished across the deck, and listened to the·screaming of the wind, which prevented all conversation. Silently they waited—one hour—two hours—then Boston said: "This is getting serious. It's no squall. If it wasn't so late in the season I'd call it a hurricane. I'm going on deck."

He climbed the companionway stairs to the poop, and shut the scuttle behind him—for the rain was flooding the cabin—then looked around. The shore and horizon were hidden by a dense wall of gray, which seemed not a hundred feet distant. From to windward this wall was detaching great waves or sheets of almost solid water, which bombarded the ship in successive blows, to be then lost in the gray whirl to leeward. Overhead was the same dismal hue, marked by hurrying masses of darker cloud, and below was a sea of froth, white and flat; for no waves could rise their heads in that wind. Drenched to the skin, he tried the wheel and found it free in its movements. In front of it was a substantial binnacle, and within a compass, which, though sluggish, as from a well-worn pivot, was practically in good condition. "Blowing us about nor'west by west," he muttered, as he looked at it— "straight up the coast. It's better than the beach in this weather, but may land us in Havana." He examined the boat. It was full of water, and tailing to windward, held by its painter. Making sure that this was fast, he went down.

"Doc," he said, as he squeezed the water from his limp cork helmet and flattened it on the table, "have you any objections to being rescued by some craft going into Havana?"

"I have—decided objections."

"So have I; but this wind is blowing us there—sideways. Now, such a blow as this, at this time of year, will last three days at least, and I've an idea that it'll haul gradually to the south, and west towards the end of it. Where'll we be then? Either piled up on one of the Bahama keys or interviewed by the Spaniards. Now I've been thinking of a scheme on deck. We can't get back to camp for a while—that's settled. This iron hull is worth something, and if we can take it into an American port we can claim salvage. Key West is the nearest, but Fernandina is the surest. We've got a stump of a foremast and a rudder and a compass. If we can get some kind of sail up forward and bring her 'fore the wind, we can steer any course within thirty degrees of the wind line."

"But I can't steer. And how long will this voyage take? What will we eat?"

"Yes, you can steer—good enough. And, of course, it depends on food, and water, too. We'd better catch some of this that's going to waste."

In what had been the steward's storeroom they found a harness-cask with bones and dry rust in the bottom. "It's salt meat, I suppose," said the doctor, "reduced to its elements." With the handles of their pistols they carefully hammered down the rusty hoops over the shrunken staves, which were well preserved by the brine they had once held, and taking the cask on deck, cleaned it thoroughly under the scuppers—or drain-holes—of the poop, and let it stand under the stream of water to swell and sweeten itself.

"If we find more casks we'll catch some more," said Boston; "but that will last us two weeks. Now we'll hunt for her stores. I've eaten salt-horse twenty years old, but I can't vouch for what we may find here." They examined all the rooms adjacent to the cabin, but found nothing.

"Where's the lazarette in this kind of a ship?" asked Boston. "The cabin runs right aft to the stern. It must be below us." He found that the carpet was not tacked to the floor, and, raising the after end, discovered a hatch, or trap-door, which he lifted. Below, when their eyes were accustomed to the darkness, they saw boxes and barrels—all covered with the same fine dust which filled the cabin.

"Don't go down there, yet, Boston," said the doctor. "It may be full of carbonic acid gas. She's been afire, you know. Wait." He tore a strip from some bedding in one of the rooms, and, lighting one end by means of a flint and steel which he carried, lowered the smouldering rag until it rested on the pile below. It did not go out.

"Safe enough, Boston," he remarked. "But you go down; you're younger."

Boston smiled and sprang down on the pile, from which he passed up a box. "Looks like tinned stuff, Doc. Open it, and I'll look over here."

The doctor smashed the box with his foot, and found, as the other had thought, that it contained cylindrical cans; but the labels were faded with age. Opening one with his jack-knife, he tasted the contents. It was a mixture of meat and a fluid, called by sailors "soup-and-bully," and as fresh and sweet as though canned the day before.

"We're all right, Boston," he called down the hatch. "Here's as good a dish as I've tasted for months. Ready cooked, too."

Boston soon appeared. "There are some beef or pork barrels over in the wing," he said, "and plenty of this canned stuff. I don't know what good the salt meat is. The barrels seem tight, but we won't need to broach one for a while. There's a bag of coffee—gone to dust, and some hard bread that isn't fit to eat; but this'll do." He picked up the open can.

"Boston," said the doctor, "if those barrels contain meat, we'll find it cooked—boiled in its own brine, like this."

"Isn't it strange," said Boston, as he tasted the contents of the can, "that this stuff should keep so long?"

"Not at all. It was cooked thoroughly by the heat, and then frozen. If your barrels haven't burst from the expansion of the brine under the heat or cold, you'll find the meat just as good."

"But rather salty, if I'm a judge of salt-horse. Now, where's the sail-locker? We want a sail on that foremast. It must be forward."

In the forecastle they found sailor's chests and clothing in all stages of ruin, but none of the spare sails that ships carry. In the boatswain's locker, in one corner of the forecastle, however, they found some iron-strapped blocks in fairly good condition, which Boston noted. Then they opened the main-hatch, and discovered a mixed pile of boxes, some showing protruding necks of large bottles, or carboys, others nothing but the circular opening. Here and there in the tangled heap were sections of canvas sails—rolled and unrolled, but all yellow and worthless. They closed the hatch and returned to the cabin, where they could converse.

"They stowed their spare canvas in the 'tween-deck on top of the cargo," said Boston; "and the carboys——"

"And the carboys burst from the heat and ruined the sails," broke in the doctor. "But another question is, what became of that acid?"

"If it's not in the 'tween-deck yet, it must be in the hold—leaked through the hatches."

"I hope it hasn't reached the iron in the hull, Boston, my boy. It takes a long time for cold acids to act on iron after the first oxidation, but in fifty years mixed nitric and sulphuric will do lots of work."

"No fear, Doc; it had done its work when you were in your cradle. What'll we do for canvas? We must get this craft before the wind. How'll the carpet do?" Boston lifted the edge, and tried the fabric in his fingers. "It'll go," he said; "we'll double it. I'll hunt for a palm-and-needle and some twine." These articles he found in the mate's room. "The twine's no better than yarn," said he, "but we'll use four parts."

Together they doubled the carpet diagonally, and with long stitches joined the edges. Then Boston sewed into each corner a thimble—an iron ring— and they had a triangular sail of about twelve feet hoist. "It hasn't been exposed to the action of the air like the ropes in the locker forward," said Boston, as he arose and took off the palm; "and perhaps it'll last till she pays off. Then we can steer. You get the big pulley-blocks from the locker, Doc, and I'll get the rope from the boat. It's lucky I thought to bring it; I expected to lift things out of the hold with it."

At the risk of his life Boston obtained the coil from the boat, while the doctor brought the blocks. Then, together, they rove off a tackle. With the handles of their pistols they knocked bunk-boards to pieces and saved the nails; then Boston climbed the foremast, as a painter climbs a steeple—by nailing successive billets of wood above his head for steps. Next he hauled up and secured the tackle to the forward side of the mast, with which they pulled up the upper corner of their sail, after lashing the lower corners to the windlass and fiferail.

It stood the pressure, and the hulk paid slowly off and gathered headway. Boston took the wheel and steadied her at northwest by west—dead before the wind—while the doctor, at his request, brought the open can of soup and lubricated the wheel-screw with the only substitute for oil at their command; for the screw worked hard with the rust of fifty years.

Their improvised sail, pressed steadily on but one side, had held together, but now, with the first flap as the gale caught it from another direction, appeared a rent; with the next flap the rag went to pieces.

"Let her go!" sang out Boston gleefully; "we can steer now. Come here, Doc, and learn to steer."

The doctor came; and when he left that wheel, three days later, he had learned. For the wind had blown a continuous gale the whole of this time, which, with the ugly sea raised as the ship left the lee of the land, necessitated the presence of both men at the helm. Only occasionally was there a lull during which one of them could rush below and return with a can of soup. During one of these lulls Boston had examined the boat, towing half out of water, and concluded that a short painter was best with a water-logged boat, had reinforced it with a few turns of his rope from forward. In the three days they had sighted no craft except such as their own—helpless—hove-to or scudding.

Boston had judged rightly in regard to the wind. It had hauled slowly to the southward, allowing him to make the course he wished—through the Bahama and up the Florida Channel with the wind over the stern. During the day he could guide himself by landmarks, but at night, with a darkened binnacle, he could only steer blindly on with the wind at his back. The storm center, at first to the south of Cuba, had made a wide circle, concentric with the curving course of the ship, and when the latter had reached the upper end of the Florida channel, had spurted ahead and whirled out to sea across her bows. It was then that the undiminished gale, blowing nearly west, had caused Boston, in despair, to throw the wheel down and bring the ship into the trough of the sea—to drift. Then the two wet, exhausted, hollow-eyed men slept the sleep that none but sailors and soldiers know; and when they awakened, twelve hours later, stiff and sore, it was to look out on a calm, starlit evening, with an eastern moon silvering the surface of the long, northbound rollers, and showing in sharp relief a dark horizon, on which there was no sign of land or sail.

They satisfied their hunger; then Boston, with a rusty iron pot from the galley, to which he fastened the end of his rope, dipped up some of the water from over the side. It was warm to the touch, and, aware that they were in the Gulf Stream, they crawled under the musty bedding in the cabin berths and slept through the night. In the morning there was no promise of the easterly wind that Boston hoped would come to blow them to port, and they secured their boat—reeving off davit-tackles, and with the plug out, pulling it up, one end at a time, while the water drained out through the hole in the bottom.

"Now, Boston," said the doctor, "here we are, as you say, on the outer edge of the Gulf Stream, drifting out into the broad Atlantic at the rate of four miles an hour. We've got to make the best of it until something comes along; so you hunt through that store-room and see what else there is to eat, and I'll examine the cargo. I want to know where that acid went."

They opened all the hatches, and while Boston descended to the lazarette, the doctor, with his trousers rolled up, climbed down the notched steps in a stanchion. In a short time he came up wth a yellow substance in his hand, which he washed thoroughly with fresh water in Boston's improvised draw-bucket, and placed in the sun to dry. Then he returned to the 'tween-deck. After a while, Boston, rummaging the lazarette, heard him calling through the bulkhead, and joined him.

"Look here, Boston," said the doctor; "I've cleared away the muck over this hatch. It's 'corked,' as you sailormen call it. Help me get it up."

They dug the compacted oakum from the seams with their knives, and by iron rings in each corner, now eaten with rust to almost the thinness of wire, they lifted the hatch. Below was a filthy-looking layer of whitish substance, protruding from which were charred, half-burned staves. First they repeated the experiment with the smoldering rag, and finding that it burned, as before, they descended. The whitish substance was hard enough to bear their weight, and they looked around. Overhead, hung to the under side of the deck and extending the length of the hold, were wooden tanks, charred, and in some places burned through.

"She must have been built for a passenger or troop ship," said Boston. "Those tanks would water a regiment."

"Boston," answered the doctor, irrelevantly, "will you climb up and bring down an oar from the boat? Carry it down—don't throw it, my boy." Boston obliged him, and the doctor, picking his way forward, then aft, struck each tank with the oar. "Empty—all of them," he said.

He dug out with his knife a piece of the whitish substance under foot, and examined it closely in the light from the hatch.

"Boston," he said, impressively, "this ship was loaded with lime, tallow, and acids—acids above, lime and tallow down here. This stuff is neither; it is lime-soap. And, moreover, it had not been touched by acids." The doctor's ruddy face was ashen.

"Well?" asked Boston.

"Lime soap is formed by the cauticizing action of lime on tallow in the presence of water and heat. It is easy to understand this fire. One of those tanks leaked and dribbled down on the cargo, attacking the lime—which was stowed underneath, as all these staves we see on top are from tallow-kids. The heat generated by the slaking lime set fire to the barrels in contact, which in turn set fire to others, and they burned until the air was exhausted, and then went out. See, they are but partly consumed. There was intense heat in this hold, and expansion of the water in all the tanks. Are tanks at sea filled to the top?"

"Chock full, and a cap screwed down on the upper end of the pipes."

"As I thought. The expending water burst every tank in the hold, and the cargo was deluged with water, which attacked every lime barrel in the bottom layer, at least. Result—the bursting of those barrels from the ebullition of slaking lime, the melting of the tallow—which could not burn long in the closed-up space—and the mixing of it in the interstices of the lime barrels with water and lime—a boiling hot mess. What happens under such conditions?"

"Give it up," said Boston, laconically.

"Lime soap is formed, which rises, and the water beneath is in time all taken up by the lime."

"But what of it?" interrupted the other.

"Wait. I see that this hold and the 'tween-deck are lined with wood. Is that customary in iron ships?"

"Not now. It used to be a notion that an iron skin damaged the cargo; so the first iron ships were ceiled with wood."

"Are there any drains in the 'tween-deck to let water out, in case it gets into that deck from above—a sea, for instance?"

"Yes, always; three or four scupper-holes each side amidships. They lead the water into the bilges, where the pumps can reach it."

"I found up there," continued the doctor, "a large piece of wood, badly charred by acid for half its length, charred to a lesser degree for the rest. It was oval in cross section, and the largest end was charred most."

"Scupper plug. I suppose they plugged the 'tween-deck scuppers to keep any water they might ship out of the bilges and away from the lime."

"Yes, and those plugs remained in place for days, if not weeks or months, after the carboys burst, as indicated by the greater charring of the larger end of the plug. I burrowed under the debris, and found the hole which that plug fitted. It was worked loose, or knocked out of the hole by some internal movement of the broken carboys, perhaps. At any rate, it came out, after remaining in place long enough for the acids to become thoroughly mixed and for the hull to cool down. She was in the ice, remember. Boston, the mixed acid went down that hole, or others like it. Where is it now?"

"I suppose," said Boston, thoughtfully, "that it soaked up into the hold, through the skin."

"Exactly. The skin is calked with oakum, is it not?" Boston nodded.

"That oakum would contract with the charring action, as did the oakum in the hatch, and every drop of that acid—ten thousand gallons, as I have figured—has filtered up into the hold, with the exception of what remained between the frames under the skin. Have you ever studied organic chemistry?"

"Slightly."

"Then you can follow me. When tallow is saponified there is formed, from the palmitin, stearin, and olein contained, with the cauticizing agent—in this case, lime—a soap. But there are two ends to every equation, and at the bottom of this immense soap vat, held in solution by the water, which would afterwards be taken up by the surplus lime, was the other end of this equation; and as the yield from tallow of this other product is about thirty per cent., and as we start with eight thousand fifty-pound kids—four hundred thousand pounds—all of which has disappeared, we know that, sticking to the skin and sides of the barrels down here, is—or was once—one hundred and twenty thousand pounds, or sixty tons, of the other end of the equation —glycerine!"

"Do you mean, Doc," asked Boston, with a startled look, "that——"

"I mean," said the doctor, emphatically, "that the first thing the acids— mixed in the 'tween-deck to just about the right proportions, mind you—

would attack, on oozing through the skin, would be this glycerine; and the certain product of this union under intense cold—this hull was frozen in the ice, remember—would be nitro-glycerine; and, as the yield of the explosive is two hundred and twenty per cent. of the glycerine, we can be morally sure that in the bottom of this hold, each minute globule of it held firmly in a hard matrix of sulphate or nitrate of calcium—which would be formed next when the acids met the hydrates and carbonates of lime—is over one hundred and thirty tons of nitro-glycerine, all the more explosive from not being washed of free acids. Come up on deck. I'll show you something else."

Limp and nerveless, Boston followed the doctor. This question was beyond his seamanship.

The doctor brought the yellow substance—now well dried. "I found plenty of this in the 'tween-deck," he said; "and I should judge they used it to pack between the carboy boxes. It was once cotton-batting. It is now, since I have washed it, a very good sample of gun-cotton. Get me a hammer —crowbar—something hard."

Boston brought a marline-spike from the locker, and the doctor, tearing off a small piece of the substance and placing it on the iron barrel of a gipsy-winch, gave it a hard blow with the marline spike, which was nearly torn from his hand by the explosion that followed.

"We have in the 'tween-deck," said the doctor, as he turned, "about twice as many pounds of this stuff as they used to pack the carboys with; and, like the nitro-glycerine, is the more easily exploded from the impurities and free acids. I washed this for safe handling. Boston, we are adrift on a floating bomb that would pulverize the rock of Gibraltar!"

"But, doctor," asked Boston, as he leaned against the rail for support, "wouldn't there be evolution of heat from the action of the acids on the lime—enough to explode the nitro-glycerine just formed?"

"The best proof that it did not explode is the fact that this hull still floats. The action was too slow, and it was very cold down there. But I can't yet account for the acids left in the bilges. What have they been doing all these fifty years?"

Boston found a sounding-rod in the locker, which he scraped bright with his knife, then, unlaying a strand of the rope for a line, sounded the pump-well. The rod came up dry, but with a slight discoloration on the lower end, which Boston showed to the doctor.

"The acids have expended themselves on the iron frames and plates. How thick are they?"

"Plates, about five-eighths of an inch; frames, like railroad iron."

"This hull is a shell! We won't get much salvage. Get up some kind of distress signal, Boston." Somehow the doctor was now the master-spirit.

A flag was nailed to the mast, union down, to be blown to pieces with the first breeze; then another, and another, until the flag locker was exhausted. Next they hung out, piece after piece, all they could spare of the rotten bedding, until that too was exhausted. Then they found, in a locker of their boat, a flag of Free Cuba, which they decided not to waste, but to hang out only when a sail appeared.

But no sail appeared, and the craft, buffeted by gales and seas, drifted eastward, while the days became weeks, and the weeks became months. Twice she entered the Sargasso Sea—the graveyard of derelicts—to be blown out by friendly gales and resume her travels. Occasional rains replenished the stock of fresh water, but the food they found at first, with the exception of some cans of fruit, was all that came to light; for the salt meat was leathery, and crumbled to a salty dust on exposure to the air. After a while their stomachs revolted at the diet of cold soup, and they ate only when hunger compelled them.

At first they had stood watch-and-watch, but the lonely horror of the long night vigils in the constant apprehension of instant death had affected them alike, and they gave it up, sleeping and watching together. They had taken care of their boat and provisioned it, ready to lower and pull into the track of any craft that might approach. But it was four months from the beginning of this strange voyage when the two men, gaunt and hungry—with ruined digestions and shattered nerves—saw, with joy which may be imagined, the first land and the first sail that gladdened their eyes after the storm in the Florida Channel.

A fierce gale from the southwest had been driving them, broadside on, in the trough of the sea, for the whole of the preceding day and night; and the land they now saw appeared to them a dark, ragged line of blue, early in the morning. Boston could only surmise that it was the coast of Portugal or Spain. The sail—which lay between them and the land, about three miles to leeward—proved to be the try-sail of a black craft, hove-to, with bows nearly towards them.

Boston climbed the foremast with their only flag and secured it; then, from the high poop-deck, they watched the other craft, plunging and wallowing in the immense Atlantic combers, often raising her forefoot into plain view, again descending with a dive that hid the whole forward half in a white cloud of spume.

"If she was a steamer I'd call her a cruiser," said Boston; "one of England's black ones, with a storm sail on her military mainmast. She has a ram bow, and—yes, sponsors and guns. That's what she is, with her funnels and bridge carried away."

"Isn't she right in our track, Boston?" asked the doctor, excitedly. "Hadn't she better get out of our way?"

"She's got steam up—a full head; see the escape-jet? She isn't helpless. If she don't launch a boat, we'll take to ours and board her."

The distance lessened rapidly—the cruiser plunging up and down in the same spot, the derelict heaving to leeward in great, swinging leaps, as the successive seas caught her, each one leaving her half a length farther on. Soon they could make out the figures of men.

"Take us off," screamed the doctor, waving his arms, "and get out of our way!"

"We'll clear her," said Boston; "see, she's started her engine."

As they drifted down on the weather-side of the cruiser they shouted repeatedly words of supplication and warning. They were answered by a solid shot from a secondary gun, which flew over their heads. At the same time, the ensign of Spain was run up on the flagstaff.

"They're Spanish, Boston. They're firing on us. Into that boat with you! If a shot hits our cargo, we won't know what struck us."

They sprang into the boat, which luckily hung on the lee side, and cleared the falls—fastened and coiled in the bow and stern. Often during their long voyage they had rehearsed the launching of the boat in a seaway—an operation requiring quick and concerted action.

"Ready, Doc?" sang out Boston. "One, two, three—let go!" The falls overhauled with a whir, and the falling boat, striking an uprising sea with a smack, sank with it. When it raised they unhooked the tackle blocks, and pushed off with the oars just as a second shot hummed over their heads.

"Pull, Boston; pull hard—straight to windward!" cried the doctor.

The tight whaleboat shipped no water, and though they were pulling in the teeth of a furious gale, the hulk was drifting away from them, so, in a short time, they were separated from their late home by a full quarter-mile of angry sea. The cruiser had forged ahead in plain view, and, as they looked, took in the try-sail.

"She's going to wear," said Boston. "See, she's paying off."

"I don't know what 'wearing' means, Boston," panted the doctor, "but I know the Spanish nature. She's going to ram that hundred and thirty tons of nitro. Don't stop. Pull away. Hold on, there; hold on, you fools!" he shouted. "That's a torpedo; keep away from her!"

Forgetting his own injunction to "pull away," the doctor stood up, waving his oar frantically, and Boston assisted. But if their shouts and gestures were understood aboard the cruiser, they were ignored. She slowly turned in a wide curve and headed straight for the *Neptune* which had drifted to leeward of her.

What was in the minds of the officers on that cruiser's deck will never be known. Cruisers of all nations hold roving commissions in regard to derelicts, and it is fitting and proper for one of them to gently prod a "vagrant of the sea" with the steel prow and send her below to trouble no more. But it may be that the sight of the Cuban flag, floating defiantly in the gale, had something to do with the full speed at which the Spanish ship approached. When but half a length separated the two craft, a heavy sea lifted the bow of the cruiser high in air; then it sank, and the sharp steel ram came down like a butcher's cleaver on the side of the derelict.

A great semicircular wall of red shut out the gray of the sea and sky to leeward, and for an instant the horrified men in the boat saw—as people see by a lightning flash—dark lines radiating from the center of this red wall, and near this center poised on end in mid-air, with deck and sponsons still intact, a bowless, bottomless remnant of the cruiser. Then, and before the remnant sank into the vortex beneath, the spectacle went out in the darkness of unconsciousness; for a report, as of concentrated thunder, struck them down. A great wave had left the crater-like depression in the sea, which threw the boat on end, and with the inward rush of surrounding water rose a mighty gray cone, which then subsided to a hollow, while another wave followed the first. Again and again this gray pillar rose and fell, each subsidence marked by the sending forth of a wave. And long before these concentric waves had lost themselves in the battle with the storm-driven combers from the ocean, the half-filled boat, with her unconscious passengers, had drifted over the spot where lay the shattered remnant, which, with the splintered fragments of wood and iron strewn on the surface and bottom of the sea for a mile around, and the lessening cloud of dust in the air, was all that was left of the derelict *Neptune* and one of the finest cruisers in the Spanish navy.

A few days later, two exhausted, half-starved men pulled a whaleboat up to the steps of the wharf at Cadiz, where they told some lies and sold their boat. Six months after, these two men, sitting at a camp-fire of the Cuban army, read from a discolored newspaper, brought ashore with the last supplies, the following:

"By cable to the 'Herald.'"

"CADIZ, March 13, 1895.—Anxiety for the safety of the *Reina Regente* has grown rapidly to-day, and this evening it is feared, generally, that she went down with her four hundred and twenty souls in the storm which swept the southern coast on Sunday night and Monday morning. Despatches from Gibraltar say that pieces of a boat and several semaphore flags belonging to the cruiser came ashore at Ceuta and Tarifa this afternoon."

THE CRUISE OF THE TORCH

Michael Scott

A WEEK AFTER our arrival at Nassau we again sailed for Bermuda, having taken on board ten American skippers, and several other Yankees, as prisoners of war.

For the first three days after we cleared the Passages, we had fine weather. Wind at east-south-east; after that it came on to blow from the north-west, and so continued without intermission during the whole of the passage to Bermuda. On the fourth morning after we left Nassau, we descried a sail in the south-east quarter, and immediately made sail in chase. We overhauled her about noon; she hove-to, after being fired at repeatedly; and, on boarding her, we found she was a Swede from Charleston, bound to Havre-de-Grace. All the letters we could find on board were very unceremoniously broken open, and nothing having transpired that could identify the cargo as enemy's property, we were bundling over the side, when a nautical-looking subject, who had attracted my attention from the first, put in his oar.

"Lieutenant," said he, "will you allow me to put this barrel of New York apples into the boat as a present to Captain Deadeye, from Captain —— of the United States navy?"

Mr. Treenail bowed, and said he would; and we shoved off and got on board again, and now there was the devil to pay, from the perplexity old Dead-eye was thrown into, as to whether, here in the heat of the American war, he was bound to take this American captain prisoner or not. I was no party to the councils of my superiors, of course, but the foreign ship was finally allowed to continue her course.

from "Tom Cringle's Log" by Michael Scott

The next day I had the forenoon watch; the weather had lulled unexpectedly, nor was there much sea, and the deck was all alive, to take the advantage
of the fine *blink*, when the man at the mast-head sung out—"Breakers right
ahead, sir."

"Breakers!" said Mr. Splinter, in great astonishment. "Breakers!—why the
man must be mad—I say, Jenkins——"

"Breakers close under the bows," sung out the boatswain from forward.

"The devil," quoth Splinter, and he ran along the gangway, and ascended
the forecastle, while I kept close to his heels. We looked out ahead, and there
we certainly did see a splashing, and boiling, and white foaming of the ocean,
that unquestionably looked very like breakers. Gradually, this splashing and
foaming appearance took a circular whisking shape, as if the clear green sea,
for a space of a hundred yards in diameter, had been stirred about by a gigantic invisible *spurtle*, until everything hissed again; and the curious part of
it was, that the agitation of the water seemed to keep ahead of us, as if the
breeze which impelled us had also floated it onwards. At length the whirling
circle of white foam ascended higher and higher, and then gradually contracted itself into a spinning black tube, which wavered about, for all the
world, like a gigantic *lochleech*, held by the tail between the finger and
thumb, while it was poking its vast snout about in the clouds in search of a
spot to fasten on.

"Is the boat gun on the forecastle loaded?" said Captain Deadeye.

"It is, sir."

"Then luff a bit—that will do—fire."

The gun was discharged, and down rushed the black wavering pillar in a
watery *avalanche*, and in a minute after the dark heaving billows rolled over
the spot whereout it arose, as if no such thing had ever been.

This said troubling of the waters was neither more nor less than a waterspout, which again is neither more nor less than a whirlwind at sea, which
gradually whisks the water round and round, and up and up, as you see straws
so raised, until it reaches a certain height, when it invariably breaks. Before
this I had thought that a waterspout was created by some next to supernatural
exertion of the power of the Deity, in order to suck up water into the clouds,
that they, like the wine-skins in Spain, may be filled with rain.

The morning after the weather was clear and beautiful, although the wind
blew half a gale. Nothing particular happened until about seven o'clock in

the evening. I had been invited to dine with the gunroom officers this day, and everything was going on smooth and comfortable, when Mr. Splinter spoke.—"I say, master, don't you smell gunpowder?"

"Yes I do," said the little master, "or something deuced like it."

To explain the particular comfort of our position, it may be right to mention that the magazine of a brig sloop is exactly under the gunroom. Three of the American skippers had been quartered on the gunroom mess, and they were all at table. Snuff, snuff, smelled one, and another sniffled,—"Gunpowder, I guess, and in a state of ignition."

"Will you not send for the gunner, sir?" said the third.

Splinter did not like it, I saw, and this quailed me.

The captain's bell rang. "What smell of brimstone is that, steward?"

"I really can't tell," said the man, trembling from head to foot; "Mr. Splinter has sent for the gunner, sir."

"The devil!" said Deadeye, as he hurried on deck. We all followed. A search was made.

"Some matches have caught in the magazine," said one.

"We shall be up and away like sky-rockets," said another.

Several of the American masters ran out on the jibboom, coveting the temporary security of beings so far removed from the seat of the expected explosion, and all was alarm and confusion, until it was ascertained that two of the boys, little skylarking vagabonds, had stolen some pistol cartridges, and had been making lightning, as it is called, by holding a lighted candle between the fingers and putting some loose powder into the palm of the hand, and then chucking it up into the flame. They got a sound flogging, on a very unpoetical part of their corpuses, and once more the ship subsided into her usual orderly discipline. The northwester still continued, with a clear blue sky, without a cloud overhead by day, and a bright cold moon by night. It blew so hard for the three succeeding days, that we could not carry more than close-reefed topsails to it, and a reefed foresail. Indeed, towards six bells in the forenoon watch, it came thundering down with such violence, and the sea increased so much, that we had to hand the fore-topsail.

This was by no means an easy job. "Ease her a bit," said the first lieutenant,—"there—shake the wind out of her sails for a moment, until the men get the canvas"—whirl, a poor fellow pitched off the lee foreyardarm into the sea. "Up with the helm—heave him the bight of a rope." We kept away,

The gun was discharged, and down rushed the black wavering pillar in a watery avalanche.

but all was confusion, until an American midshipman, one of the prisoners on board, hove the bight of a rope at him. The man got it under his arms, and after hauling him along for a hundred yards at the least—and one may judge of the velocity with which he was dragged through the water, by the fact that it took the united strain of ten powerful men to get him in—he was brought safely on board, pale and blue, when we found that the running of the rope had crushed in his broad chest below his arms, as if it had been a girl's waist, cutting into the very muscles of it and of his back half an inch deep. He had to be bled before he could breathe, and it was an hour before the circulation could be restored, by the joint exertions of the surgeon and gunroom steward, chafing him with spirits and camphor, after he had been stripped and stowed away between the blankets in his hammock.

The same afternoon we fell in with a small prize to the squadron in the *Chesapeake*, a dismasted schooner, manned by a prize crew of a midshipman and six men. She had a signal of distress, an American ensign, with the union down, hoisted on the jury-mast, across which there was a rigged solitary lug-sail. It was blowing so hard that we had some difficulty in boarding her, when we found she was a Baltimore pilot-boat-built schooner of about 70 tons burden, laden with flour, and bound for Bermuda. But three days before, in a sudden squall, they had carried away both masts short by the board, and the only spar which they had been able to rig, was a spare topmast, which they had jammed into one of the pumps—fortunately she was as tight as a bottle—and stayed it the best way they could. The captain offered to take the little fellow who had charge of her, and his crew and cargo, on board, and then scuttle her; but no—all he wanted was a cask of water and some biscuit; and having had a glass of grog, he trundled over the side again, and returned to his desolate command. However, he afterwards brought his prize safe into Bermuda.

The weather still continued very rough, but we saw nothing until the second evening after this. The forenoon had been even more boisterous than any of the preceding, and we were all fagged enough with "make sail," and "shorten sail," and "all hands," the whole day through; and as the night fell, I found myself, for the fourth time, in the maintop. The men had just lain in from the main-topsail yard, when we heard the watch called on deck,—"Starboard watch, ahoy,"—which was a cheery sound to us of the larboard, who were thus released from duty on deck and allowed to go below.

The men were scrambling down the weather shrouds, and I was preparing to follow them, when I jammed my left foot in the grating of the top, and capsized on my nose. I had been up nearly the whole of the previous night, and on deck the whole of the day, and actively employed too, as during the greatest part of it blew a gale. I stooped down in some pain, to see what had bolted me to the grating, but I had no sooner extricated my foot, than, over-worked and over-fatigued as I was, I fell over in the soundest sleep that ever I have enjoyed before or since, the back of my neck resting on a coil of rope, so that my head hung down within it.

The rain all this time was beating on me, and I was drenched to the skin. I must have slept for four hours or so, when I was awakened by a rough thump on the side from the stumbling foot of the captain of the top, the word having been passed to shake a reef out of the topsails, the wind having rather suddenly gone down. It was done; and now broad awake, I determined not to be caught napping again, so I descended, and swung myself in on deck out of the main rigging, just as Mr. Treenail was mustering the crew at eight bells. When I landed on the quarterdeck, there he stood abaft the binnacle, with the light shining on his face, his glazed hat glancing, and the rain-drop sparkling at the brim of it. He had noticed me the moment I descended and spoke up immediately.

"Heyday, Master Cringle, you are surely out of your watch. Why, what are you doing here, eh?"

I stepped up to him, and told him the truth, that, being over-fatigued, I had fallen asleep in the top.

"Well, well, boy," said he, "never mind, go below, and turn in; if you don't take your rest, you will never be a sailor."

"But what do you see aloft?" glancing his eye upwards, and all the crew on deck as I passed them looked anxiously up also amongst the rigging, as if wondering what I saw there, for I had been so chilled in my snooze, that my neck, from resting in the cold on the coil of rope, had become stiffened and rigid to an intolerable degree; and although, when I first came on deck, I had by a strong exertion brought my *caput* to its proper bearings, yet the moment I was dismissed by my superior officer, I for my own comfort was glad to conform to the contraction of the muscle, whereby I once more staved along the deck, *glowering* up into the heavens, as if I had seen some wonderful sight there.

"What do you see aloft?" repeated Mr. Treenail, while the crew, greatly puzzled, continued to follow my eye, as they thought, and to stare up into the rigging.

"Why, sir, I have thereby got a stiff neck—that's all, sir."

"Go and turn in at once, my good boy—make haste, now—tell our steward to give you a glass of hot grog, and mind your hand that you don't get sick."

I did as I was desired, swallowed the grog, and turned in; but I could not have been in bed above an hour, when the drum beat to quarters, and I had once more to bundle out on the cold wet deck, where I found all excitement. At the time I speak of, we had been beaten by the Americans in several actions of single ships, and our discipline had improved in proportion as we came to learn by sad experience that the enemy was not to be under-valued. I found that there was a ship in sight, right ahead of us—apparently carrying all sail. A group of officers were on the forecastle with night-glasses, the whole crew being stationed in dark clusters round the guns at quarters. Several of the American skippers were forward amongst us, and they were of opinion that the chase was a man-of-war, although our own people seemed to doubt this. One of the skippers insisted that she was the *Hornet*, from the unusual short-ness of her lower masts, and the immense squareness of her yards. But the puzzle was, if it were the *Hornet*, why she did not shorten sail. Still this might be accounted for, by her either wishing to make out what we were be-fore she engaged us, or she might be clearing for action. At this moment a whole cloud of studdingsails were blown from the yards as if the booms had been carrots; and to prove that the chase was keeping a bright look-out, she immediately kept away, and finally bore up dead before the wind, under the impression, no doubt, that she would draw ahead of us, from the gear being entire, before we could rig out our light sails again.

And so she did for a time, but at length we got within gun-shot. The American masters were now ordered below, the hatches were clapped on, and the word passed to see all clear. Our shot was by this time flying over and over her, and it was evident she was not a man-of-war. We peppered away—she could not even be a privateer; we were close under her lee-quarter, and yet she had never fired a shot; and her large swaggering Yankee ensign was now run up to the peak, only to be hauled down the next moment. Hurrah! a large cotton ship, from Charlestown to Bourdeaux, prize to H.M.S. *Torch*.

She was taken possession of, and proved to be the *Natches*, of four hundred tons burden, fully loaded with cotton.

By the time we got the crew on board, and the second lieutenant, with a prize crew of fifteen men, had taken charge, the weather began to lour again, nevertheless we took the prize in tow, and continued on our voyage for the next three days, without anything particular happening. It was the middle watch, and I was sound asleep, when I was startled by a violent jerking of my hammock, and a cry "that the brig was amongst the breakers." I ran on deck in my shirt, where I found all hands, and a scene of confusion such as I never had witnessed before. The gale had increased, yet the prize had not been cast off, and the consequence was, that by some mismanagement or carelessness, the swag of the large ship had suddenly hove the brig in the wind, and taken the sails aback. We accordingly fetched stern away, and ran foul of the prize, and there we were, in a heavy sea, with our stern grinding against the cotton ship's high quarter.

The mainboom, by the first rasp that took place after I came on deck, was broken short off, and nearly twelve feet of it hove right in over the taffril; the vessels then closed, and the next rub ground off the ship's mizen channel as clean as if it had been sawed away. Officers shouting, men swearing, rigging, cracking, the vessels crashing and thumping together, I thought we were gone, when the first lieutenant seized his trumpet—"Silence, men,—hold your tongues, you cowards, and mind the word of command!"

The effect was magical.—"Brace round the foreyard! round with it—set the jib—that's it—fore-topmast—staysail—haul—never mind if the gale takes it out of the bolt rope"—a thundering flap, and away it flew in truth down to leeward, like a puff of white smoke.—"Never mind, men, the jib stands. Belay all that—down with the helm, now—don't you see she has sternway yet? Zounds! we shall be smashed to atoms if you don't mind your hands, you lubbers—main-topsail sheets let fly—there she pays off, and has headway once more, that's it—right your helm now—never mind his spanker-boom, the forestay will stand it—there—up with the helm, sir—we have cleared him—hurrah!"—And a near thing it was too, but we soon had everything snug; and although the gale continued without any intermission for ten days, at length we ran in and anchored with our prize in Five Fathom Hole, off the entrance to St. George's Harbor.

It was lucky for us that we got to anchor at the time we did, for that same afternoon, one of the most tremendous gales of wind from the westward came on that I ever saw. Fortunately it was steady, and did not veer about, and having good ground-tackle down, we rode it out well enough. The effect was very uncommon; the wind was howling over our mast-heads, and amongst the cedar bushes on the cliffs above, while on deck it was nearly calm, and there was very little swell, being a weather shore; but half a mile out at sea all was white foam, and the tumbling waves seemed to meet from north and south, leaving a space of smooth water under the lee of the island, shaped like the tail of a comet, tapering away, and gradually roughening and becoming more stormy, until the roaring billows once more owned allegiance to the genius of the storm.

There we rode, with three anchors ahead, in safety through the night; and next day, availing of a temporary lull, we ran up, and anchored off the Tanks. Three days after this, the American frigate *President* was brought in by the *Endymion*, and the rest of the squadron.

I went on board, in common with every officer in the fleet, and certainly I never saw a more superb vessel; her scantling was that of a seventy-four, and she appeared to have been fitted with great care. I got a week's leave at this time, and, as I had letters to several families, I contrived to spend my time pleasantly enough.

Bermuda, as all the world knows, is a cluster of islands in the middle of the Atlantic. There are Lord knows how many of them, but the beauty of the little straits and creeks which divide them, no man can describe who has not seen them. The town of Saint George's, for instance, looks as if the houses were cut out of chalk; and one evening the family where I was on a visit proceeded to the main island, Hamilton, to attend a ball there. We had to cross three ferries, although the distance was not above nine miles, if so far. The 'Mudian women are unquestionably beautiful—so thought Thomas Moore, a tolerable judge, before me. By the by, touching this 'Mudian ball, it was a very gay affair—the women pleasant and beautiful; but all the men, when they speak, or are spoken to, shut one eye and spit;—a lucid and succinct description of a community.

The second day of my sojourn was fine—the first fine day since our arrival —and with several young ladies of the family, I was prowling through the cedar wood above St. George's, when a dark good-looking man passed us; he was dressed in tight worsted net pantaloons and Hessian boots, and wore a blue frock-coat and two large epaulets, with rich French bullion, and a round hat. On passing he touched his hat, with much grace, and in the evening I met him in society. It was Commodore Decatur. He was very much a Frenchman in manner, or, I should rather say, in look, for although very well bred, he, for one ingredient, by no means possessed a Frenchman's volubility; still, he was an exceedingly agreeable and very handsome man.

The following day we spent in a pleasure cruise amongst the three hundred and sixty-five islands, many of them not above an acre in extent—fancy an island of an acre in extent!—with a solitary house, a small garden, a red-skinned family, a piggery, and all around clear deep pellucid water. None of the islands, or islets, rise to any great height, but they all shoot precipitously out of the water, as if the whole group had originally been one huge platform of rock, with numberless grooves subsequently chiseled out in it by art.

We had to wind our way amongst these manifold small channels for two hours, before we reached the gentleman's house where we had been invited to dine; at length, on turning a corner, with both lateen sails drawing beautifully, we ran bump on a shoal; there was no danger, and knowing that the 'Mudians were capital sailors, I sat still. Not so Captain K——, a round plump little *homo*,—"Shove her off, my boys, shove her off." She would not move, and thereupon he in a fever of gallantry jumped overboard up to the waist in full fig; and one of the men following his example, we were soon afloat. The ladies applauded, and the captain sat in his wet *breeks* for the rest of the voyage, in all the consciousness of being considered a hero. Ducks and onions are the grand staple of Bermuda, but there was a fearful dearth of both at the time I speak of; a knot of young West India merchants, who, with heavy purses and large credits on England, had at this time domiciled themselves in St. George's, to batten on the spoils of poor Jonathan, having monopolized all the good things of the place. I happened to be acquainted with one of them, and thereby had less reason to complain, but many a poor fellow, sent ashore on duty, had to put up with Lenten fare at the taverns. At length, having re-fitted, we sailed, in company with the *Rayo* frigate, with a convoy of three transports freighted with a regiment for New Orleans, and several merchantmen, bound for the West Indies.

"The still vexed Bermoothes"—I arrived at them in a gale of wind, and I sailed from them in a gale of wind. What the climate may be in the summer I don't know; but during the time I was there, it was one storm after another.

We sailed in the evening with the moon at full, and the wind at west-north-west. So soon as we got from under the lee of the land, the breeze struck us, and it came on to blow like thunder, so that we were all soon reduced to our storm staysails; and there we were, transports, merchantmen, and men-of-war, rising on the mountainous billows one moment, and the next losing sight of everything but the water and sky in the deep trough of the sea, while the seething foam was blown over us in showers from the curling manes of the roaring waves. But overhead, all this while, it was as clear as a lovely winter moon could make it, and the stars shone brightly in the deep blue sky; there was not even a thin fleecy shred of cloud racking across the moon's disk. Oh, the glories of a northwester!

But the devil seize such glory! Glory, indeed! with a fleet of transports, and a regiment of soldiers on board! Glory! why, I daresay five hundred rank and file, at the fewest, were all cascading at one and the same moment,— a thousand poor fellows turned outside in, like so many pairs of old stockings. Any glory in that? But to proceed.

Next morning the gale still continued, and when the day broke, there was the frigate standing across our bows, rolling and pitching as she tore her way through the boiling sea, under a close-reefed main-topsail and reefed foresail, with topgallant yards and royal masts, and everything that could be struck with safety in war time, down on deck. There she lay with her clear black bends, and bright white streak, and long tier of cannon on the maindeck, and the carronades on the quarterdeck and forecastle grinning through the ports in the black bulwarks, while the white hammocks, carefully covered by the hammock cloths, crowned the defenses of the gallant frigate fore and aft, as she delved through the green surge,—one minute rolling and rising on the curling white crest of a mountainous sea, amidst a hissing snow-storm of spray, with her bright copper glancing from stem to stern, and her scanty white canvas swelling aloft, and twenty feet of her keel forward occasionally hove into the air clean out of the water, as if she had been a sea-bird rushing to take wing,—and the next, sinking entirely out of sight, hull, masts and rigging, behind an intervening sea, that rose in hoarse thunder between us, threatening to overwhelm both us and her. As for the transports, the largest of the three had lost her fore-topmast, and had bore up under her foresail; another was also scudding under a close-reefed fore-topsail; but the third or headquarter ship was still lying to to windward, under her storm staysails. None of the merchant vessels were to be seen, having been compelled to bear up in the night, and to run before it under bare poles.

At length, as the sun rose, we got before the wind, and it soon moderated so far that we could carry reefed topsails and foresails; and away we all bowled, with a clear, deep, cold, blue sky, and a bright sun overhead, and a stormy leaden-colored ocean, with whitish green-crested billows, below. The sea continued to go down, and the wind to slacken, until the afternoon, when the Commodore made the signal for the *Torch* to send a boat's crew, the instant it could be done with safety, on board the dismasted ship, to assist in repairing damages, and in getting up a jury-fore-topmast.

The damaged ship was at this time on our weather-quarter; we accordingly handed the fore-topsail, and presently she was alongside. We hailed her, that we intended to send a boat on board, and desired her to heave-to, as we did, and presently she rounded to under our lee. One of the quarter-boats was manned with three of the carpenter's crew, and six good men over and above her complement; but it was no easy matter to get on board of her, let me tell you, after she had been lowered, carefully watching the rolls, with four hands in. The moment she touched the water, the tackles were cleverly unhooked, and the rest of us tumbled on board, shin leather growing scarce, when we shoved off. With great difficulty, and not without wet jackets, we, the supernumeraries, got on board, and the boat returned to the *Torch*. The evening when we landed in the lobster-box, as Jack loves to designate a transport, was too far advanced for us to do anything towards refitting that night; and the confusion, and uproar, and numberless abominations of the crowded craft, were irksome to a greater degree than I expected even, after having been accustomed to the strict and orderly discipline of a man-of-war. The following forenoon the *Torch* was ordered by signal to chase in the south-east quarter, and hauling out from the fleet, she was soon out of sight.

"There goes my house and home," said I, and a feeling of desolateness came over me, that I would have been ashamed at the time to have acknowledged.

TRAFALGAR

Robert Southey

SOON AFTER daylight Nelson came upon deck. The 21st of October was a festival in his family; because on that day his uncle, Captain Suckling, in the *Dreadnought*, with two other line of battle ships, had beaten off a French squadron of four sail of the line and three frigates. Nelson, with that sort of superstition from which few persons are entirely exempt, had more than once expressed his persuasion that this was to be the day of his battle also; and he was well pleased at seeing his prediction about to be verified. The wind was now from the west,—light breezes, with a long heavy swell. Signal was made to bear down upon the enemy in two lines; and the fleet set all sail. Collingwood, in the *Royal Sovereign*, led the lee-line of thirteen ships; the *Victory* led the weather-line of fourteen.

Blackwood went on board the *Victory* about six. He found him in good spirits, but very calm; not in that exhilaration which he had felt upon entering into battle at Aboukir and Copenhagen; he knew that his own life would be particularly aimed at, and seems to have looked for death with almost as sure an expectation as for victory. His whole attention was fixed upon the enemy. They tacked to the northward, and formed their line on the larboard tack; thus bringing the shoals of Trafalgar and St. Pedro under the lee of the British, and keeping the port of Cadiz open for themselves. This was judiciously done: and Nelson, aware of all the advantages which it gave them, made signal to prepare to anchor.

Villeneuve was a skillful seaman; worthy of serving a better master and a better cause. His plan of defense was as well conceived, and as original, as the

from "The Life of Horatio Lord Nelson" by Robert Southey

plan of attack. He formed the fleet in a double line, every alternate ship being about a cable's length to windward of her second ahead and astern. Nelson, certain of a triumphant issue to the day, asked Blackwood what he should consider as a victory. That officer answered, that, considering the handsome way in which battle was offered by the enemy, their apparent determination for a fair trial of strength, and the situation of the land, he thought it would be a glorious result if fourteen were captured. He replied: "I shall not be satisfied with less than twenty." Soon afterwards he asked him if he did not think there was a signal wanting. Captain Blackwood made answer that he thought the whole fleet seemed very clearly to understand what they were about. These words were scarcely spoken before that signal was made, which will be remembered as long as the language, or even the memory, of England shall endure—Nelson's last signal:—"England expects every man to do his duty!" It was received throughout the fleet, with a shout of answering acclamation, made sublime by the spirit which it breathed and the feeling which it expressed. "Now," said Lord Nelson, "I can do no more. We must trust to the Great Disposer of all events, and the justice of our cause. I thank God for this great opportunity of doing my duty."

He wore that day, as usual, his admiral's frock coat, bearing on the left breast four stars of the different orders with which he was invested. Ornaments which rendered him so conspicuous a mark for the enemy, were beheld with ominous apprehensions by his officers. It was known that there were riflemen on board the French ships, and it could not be doubted but that his life would be particularly aimed at. They communicated their fears to each other; and the surgeon, Mr. Beatty, spoke to the chaplain, Dr. Scott, and to Mr. Scott, the public secretary, desiring that some person would entreat him to change his dress, or cover the stars: but they knew that such a request would highly displease him. "In honor I gained them," he had said when such a thing had been hinted to him formerly, "and in honor I will die with them." Mr. Beatty, however, would not have been deterred by any fear of exciting his displeasure, from speaking to him himself upon a subject in which the weal of England as well as the life of Nelson was concerned, but he was ordered from the deck before he could find an opportunity. This was a point upon which Nelson's officers knew that it was hopeless to remonstrate or reason with him; but both Blackwood, and his own captain, Hardy, represented to him how advantageous to the fleet it would be for him to keep out of action as long as possible; and he consented at last to let the *Leviathan* and the *Temeraire*, which were sailing abreast of the *Victory*, be ordered to pass ahead. Yet even here the last infirmity of this noble mind was indulged; for these ships could not pass ahead if the *Victory* continued to carry all her sail; and so far was Nelson from shortening sail, that it was evident he took pleasure in pressing on, and rendering it impossible for them to obey his own orders. A long swell was setting into the Bay of Cadiz: our ships, crowding all sail, moved majestically before it, with light winds from the south-west. The sun shone on the sails of the enemy; and their well-formed line, with their numerous three-deckers, made an appearance which any other assailants would have thought formidable; but the British sailors only admired the beauty and the splendor of the spectacle; and, in full confidence of winning what they saw, remarked to each other, what a fine sight yonder ships would make at Spithead!

The French admiral, from the *Bucentaure*, beheld the new manner in which his enemy was advancing, Nelson and Collingwood each leading his line; and, pointing them out to his officers, he is said to have exclaimed, that such conduct could not fail to be successful. Yet Villeneuve had made his own dispositions with the utmost skill, and the fleets under his command waited for the attack with perfect coolness. Ten minutes before twelve they opened their fire. Eight or nine of the ships immediately ahead of the *Victory*, and across her bows, fired single guns at her, to ascertain whether she was yet within their range. As soon as Nelson perceived that their shot passed over him, he desired Blackwood and Captain Prowse, of the *Sirius*, to repair to their respective frigates; and, on their way, to tell all the captains of the line of battle ships that he depended on their exertions; and that, if by the prescribed mode of attack they found it impracticable to get into action immediately, they might adopt whatever they thought best, provided it led them quickly and closely alongside an enemy. As they were standing on the front of the poop, Blackwood took him by the hand, saying, he hoped soon to return and find him in possession of twenty prizes. He replied: "God bless you, Blackwood! I shall never see you again."

Nelson's column was steered about two points more to the north than Collingwood's, in order to cut off the enemy's escape into Cadiz: the lee-line, therefore, was first engaged. "See," cried Nelson, pointing to the *Royal Sovereign*, as she steered right for the center of the enemy's line, cut through it astern of the *Santa Anna*, three-decker, and engaged her at the muzzle of her guns on the starboard side: "see how that noble fellow, Collingwood, carries his ship into action!" Collingwood, delighted at being first in the heat of the fire, and knowing the feelings of his commander and old friend, turned to his captain, and exclaimed, "Rotherham, what would Nelson give to be here!" Both these brave officers, perhaps, at this moment thought of Nelson with gratitude, for a circumstance which had occurred on the preceding day. Admiral Collingwood, with some of the captains, having gone on board the *Victory* to receive instructions, Nelson inquired of him where his captain was? and was told, in reply, that they were not upon good terms with each other. "Terms!" said Nelson;—"good terms with each other!" Immediately he sent a boat for Captain Rotherham; led him, as soon as he arrived, to Collingwood, and saying, "Look, yonder are the enemy!" bade them "shake hands like Englishmen."

The enemy continued to fire a gun at a time at the *Victory*, till they saw that a shot had passed through her main-topgallant-sail; then they opened their broadsides, aiming chiefly at her rigging, in the hope of disabling her before she could close with them. Nelson, as usual, had hoisted several flags, lest one should be shot away. The enemy showed no colors till late in the action, when they began to feel the necessity of having them to strike. For this reason, the *Santissima Trinidad*, Nelson's old acquaintance, as he used to call her, was distinguishable only by her four decks; and to the bow of this opponent he ordered the *Victory* to be steered. Meantime an incessant raking fire was kept up upon the *Victory*. The admiral's secretary was one of the first who fell: he was killed by a cannon-shot, while conversing with Hardy. Captain Adair, of the marines, with the help of a sailor, endeavored to remove the body from Nelson's sight, who had a great regard for Mr. Scott; but he anxiously asked, "Is that poor Scott that's gone?" and being informed that it was indeed so, exclaimed, "Poor fellow!" Presently a double-headed shot struck a party of marines, who were drawn up on the poop, and killed eight of them: upon which Nelson immediately desired Captain Adair to disperse his men round the ship, that they might not suffer so much from being together. A few minutes afterwards a shot struck the fore brace bits on the quarter-deck, and passed between Nelson and Hardy, a splinter from the bit tearing off Hardy's buckle and bruising his foot. Both stopped, and looked anxiously at each other, each supposing the other to be wounded. Nelson then smiled, and said, "This is too warm work, Hardy, to last long."

The *Victory* had not yet returned a single gun: fifty of her men had been by this time killed or wounded, and her main-topmast, with all her studding sails and their booms, shot away. Nelson declared that, in all his battles, he had seen nothing which surpassed the cool courage of his crew on this occasion. At four minutes after twelve she opened her fire from both sides of her deck. It was not possible to break the enemy's line without running on board one of their ships: Hardy informed him of this, and asked which he would prefer. Nelson replied: "Take your choice, Hardy, it does not signify much." The master was then ordered to put the helm to port, and the *Victory* ran on board the *Redoutable*, just as her tiller ropes were shot away. The French ship received her with a broadside; then instantly let down her lower-deck ports, for fear of being boarded through them, and never afterwards fired a great gun during the action. Her tops, like those of all the enemy's ships, were filled with riflemen. Nelson never placed musketry in his tops; he had a strong dislike to the practice, not merely because it endangers setting fire to the sails, but also because it is a murderous sort of warfare, by which individuals may suffer, and a commander, now and then, be picked off, but which never can decide the fate of a general engagement.

Captain Harvey, in the *Temeraire*, fell on board the *Redoutable* on the other side. Another enemy was in like manner on board the *Temeraire:* so that these four ships formed as compact a tier as if they had been moored together, their heads lying all the same way. The lieutenants of the *Victory*, seeing this, depressed their guns of the middle and lower decks, and fired with a diminished charge, lest the shot should pass through, and injure the *Temeraire*. And because there was danger that the *Redoutable* might take fire from the lower-deck guns, the muzzles of which touched her side when they were run out, the fireman of each gun stood ready with a bucket of water, which, as soon as the gun was discharged, he dashed into the hole made by the shot. An incessant fire was kept up from the *Victory* from both sides; her larboard guns playing upon the *Bucentaure* and the huge *Santissima Trinidad*.

It had been part of Nelson's prayer that the British fleet might be distinguished by humanity in the victory which he expected. Setting an example himself, he twice gave orders to cease firing upon the *Redoutable*, supposing that she had struck, because her great guns were silent; for, as she carried no flag, there was no means of instantly ascertaining the fact. From this ship, which he had thus twice spared, he received his death. A ball fired from her mizzen-top, which, in the then situation of the two vessels, was not more than fifteen yards from that part of the deck where he was standing, struck the epaulette on his left shoulder,—about a quarter after one, just in the heat of the action. He fell upon his face, on the spot which was covered with his poor secretary's blood. Hardy, who was a few steps from him, turning round, saw three men raising him up. "They have done for me at last, Hardy," said he. "I hope not!" cried Hardy. "Yes," he replied; "my back bone is shot through." Yet even now, not for a moment losing his presence of mind, he observed, as they were carrying him down the ladder, that the tiller ropes, which had been shot away, were not yet replaced, and ordered that new ones should be rove immediately:—then, that he might not be seen by the crew, he took out his handkerchief, and covered his face and his stars.—Had he but concealed these badges of honor from the enemy, England, perhaps, would not have had cause to receive with sorrow the news of the battle of Trafalgar.

The cockpit was crowded with wounded and dying men, over whose bodies he was with some difficulty conveyed, and laid upon a pallet in the midshipmen's berth. It was soon perceived, upon examination, that the wound was mortal. This, however, was concealed from all, except Captain Hardy, the chaplain, and the medical attendants. He himself being certain, from the sensation in his back, and the gush of blood which he felt momently within his breast, that no human care could avail him, insisted that the surgeon should leave him, and attend to those to whom he might be useful: "For," said he, "you can do nothing for me." All that could be done was to fan him with paper, and frequently to give him lemonade, to alleviate his intense thirst. He was in great pain, and expressed much anxiety for the event of the action, which now began to declare itself. As often as a ship struck the crew of the *Victory* hurraed; and at every hurra a visible expression of joy gleamed in the eyes, and marked the countenance, of the dying hero. But he became impatient to see Captain Hardy; and as that officer, though often sent for, could not leave the deck, Nelson feared that some fatal cause prevented him, and repeatedly cried: "Will no one bring Hardy to me? He must be killed! He is surely dead!"—An hour and ten minutes elapsed, from the time when Nelson received his wound, before Hardy could come to him. They shook hands in silence; Hardy in vain struggling to suppress the feelings of that most painful and yet sublimest moment. "Well, Hardy," said Nelson, "how goes the day

with us?"—"Very well," replied Hardy; "ten ships have struck, but five of
their van have tacked, and show an intention of bearing down upon the *Victory*. I have called two or three of our fresh ships round, and have no doubt
of giving them a drubbing."—"I hope," said Nelson, "none of our ships have
struck?" Hardy answered, "There was no fear of that." Then, and not till
then, Nelson spoke of himself. "I am a dead man, Hardy," said he; "I am
going fast:—it will be all over with me soon. Come nearer to me. Let my
dear Lady Hamilton have my hair, and all other things belonging to me."
Hardy observed, that he hoped Mr. Beatty could yet hold out some prospect
of life. "Oh no!" he replied; "it is impossible. My back is shot through.
Beatty will tell you so." Captain Hardy then, once more, shook hands with
him; and, with a heart almost bursting, hastened upon deck.

By this time all feeling below the breast was gone, and Nelson, having made
the surgeon ascertain this, said to him: "You know I am gone. I know it. I
feel something rising in my breast"—putting his hand on his left side—"which
tells me so." And upon Beatty's inquiring whether his pain was very great,
he replied, "So great, that he wished he was dead. Yet," said he, in a lower
voice, "one would like to live a little longer too!" And after a few minutes,
in the same under-tone, he added: "What would become of poor Lady Hamilton if she knew my situation!" Next to his country she occupied his thoughts.
Captain Hardy, some fifty minutes after he had left the cockpit, returned;
and, again taking the hand of his dying friend and commander, congratulated
him on having gained a complete victory. How many of the enemy were
taken he did not know, as it was impossible to perceive them distinctly—but
fourteen or fifteen at least. "That's well," cried Nelson; "but I bargained for
twenty." And then, in a stronger voice, he said, "Anchor, Hardy; anchor."
Hardy, upon this, hinted that Admiral Collingwood would take upon himself
the direction of affairs. "Not while I live, Hardy!" said the dying Nelson,
ineffectually endeavoring to raise himself from the bed: "do you anchor."
His previous order for preparing to anchor had shown how clearly he foresaw
the necessity of this. Presently, calling Hardy back, he said to him, in a low
voice, "Don't throw me overboard"; and he desired that he might be buried
by his parents, unless it should please the king to order otherwise. Then, re-
verting to private feelings: "Take care of my dear Lady Hamilton, Hardy;
take care of poor Lady Hamilton.—Kiss me, Hardy," said he. Hardy knelt
down, and kissed his cheek: and Nelson said, "Now I am satisfied. Thank

God, I have done my duty." Hardy stood over him in silence for a moment or two, then knelt again, and kissed his forehead. "Who is that?" said Nelson; and being informed, he replied, "God bless you, Hardy." And Hardy then left him—for ever.

Nelson now desired to be turned upon his right side, and said: "I wish I had not left the deck; for I shall soon be gone." Death was, indeed, rapidly approaching. He said to the chaplain: "Doctor, I have *not* been a *great* sinner"; and, after a short pause, "Remember that I leave Lady Hamilton, and my daughter Horatia, as a legacy to my country." His articulation now became difficult; but he was distinctly heard to say, "Thank God, I have done my duty!" These words he had repeatedly pronounced; and they were the last words he uttered. He expired at thirty minutes after four,—three hours and a quarter after he had received his wound.

THE MAN
WITH THE BELT OF GOLD

Robert Louis Stevenson

MORE THAN a week went by, in which the ill-luck that had hitherto pursued the *Covenant* upon this voyage grew yet more strongly marked.
Some days she made a little way; others, she was driven actually back. At
last we were beaten so far to the south that we tossed and tacked to and fro
the whole of the ninth day, within sight of Cape Wrath and the wild rocky
coast on either hand of it. There followed on that a council of the officers,
and some decision which I did not rightly understand, seeing only the result:
that we had made a fair wind of a foul one and were running south.

The tenth afternoon there was a falling swell and a thick, wet, white fog
that hid one end of the brig from the other. All afternoon, when I went on
deck, I saw men and officers listening hard over the bulwarks—"for breakers,"
they said; and though I did not so much as understand the word, I felt danger
in the air, and was excited.

Maybe about ten at night, I was serving Mr. Riach and the captain at their
supper, when the ship struck something with a great sound, and we heard
voices singing out. My two masters leaped to their feet.

"She's struck!" said Mr. Riach.

"No, sir," said the captain. "We've only run a boat down."

And they hurried out.

The captain was in the right of it. We had run down a boat in the fog,
and she had parted in the midst and gone to the bottom with all her crew but

from "Kidnapped" by Robert Louis Stevenson

one. This man (as I heard afterwards) had been sitting in the stern as a passenger, while the rest were on the benches rowing. At the moment of the blow, the stern had been thrown into the air, and the man (having his hands free, and for all he was encumbered with a frieze overcoat that came below his knees) had leaped up and caught hold of the brig's bowsprit. It showed he had luck and much agility and unusual strength, that he should have thus saved himself from such a pass. And yet, when the captain brought him into the round-house, and I set eyes on him for the first time, he looked as cool as I did.

He was smallish in stature, but well set and as nimble as a goat; his face was of a good open expression, but sunburnt very dark, and heavily freckled and pitted with the smallpox; his eyes were unusually light and had a kind of dancing madness in them, that was both engaging and alarming; and when he took off his great-coat, he laid a pair of fine silver-mounted pistols on the table, and I saw that he was belted with a great sword. His manners, besides, were elegant, and he pledged the captain handsomely. Altogether I thought of him, at the first sight, that here was a man I would rather call my friend than my enemy.

The captain, too, was taking his observations, but rather of the man's clothes than his person. And to be sure, as soon as he had taken off the great-coat, he showed forth mighty fine for the round-house of a merchant brig: having a hat with feathers, a red waistcoat, breeches of black plush, and a blue coat with silver buttons and handsome silver lace; costly clothes, though somewhat spoiled with the fog and being slept in.

"I'm vexed, sir, about the boat," says the captain.

"There are some pretty men gone to the bottom," said the stranger, "that I would rather see on the dry land again than half a score of boats."

"Friends of yours?" said Hoseason.

"You have none such friends in your country," was the reply. "They would have died for me like dogs."

"Well, sir," said the captain, still watching him, "there are more men in the world than boats to put them in."

"And that's true, too," cried the other with spirit, "and ye seem to be a gentleman of great penetration."

"I have been in France, sir," says the captain, so that it was plain he meant more by the words than showed upon the face of them.

"Well, sir," says the other, "and so has many a pretty man, for the matter of that."

"No doubt, sir," says the captain, "and fine coats."

"Oho!" says the stranger, "is that how the wind sets?" And he laid his hand quickly on his pistols.

"Don't be hasty," said the captain. "Don't do a mischief before you see the need of it. Ye've a French soldier's coat upon your back and a Scotch tongue in your head, to be sure; but so has many an honest fellow in these days, and I dare say none the worse of it."

"So?" said the gentleman in the fine coat: "are ye of the honest party?" (meaning, Was he a Jacobite? for each side, in these sort of civil broils, takes the name of honesty for its own).

"Why, sir," replied the captain, "I am a true-blue Protestant, and I thank God for it." (It was the first word of any religion I had ever heard from him, but I learnt afterwards he was a great churchgoer while on shore.) "But for all that," says he, "I can be sorry to see another man with his back to the wall."

"Can ye so, indeed?" asked the Jacobite. "Well, sir, to be quite plain with ye, I am one of those honest gentlemen that were in trouble about the years forty-five and six; and (to be still quite plain with ye) if I got into the hands of any of the red-coated gentry, it's like it would go hard with me. Now, sir, I was for France; and there was a French ship cruising here to pick me up; but she gave us the go-by in the fog—as I wish from the heart that ye had done yoursel'! And the best that I can say is this: If ye can set me ashore where I was going, I have that upon me will reward you highly for your trouble."

"In France!" says the captain. "No, sir; that I cannot do. But where ye come from—we might talk of that."

And then, unhappily, he observed me standing in my corner, and packed me off to the galley to get supper for the gentleman. I lost no time, I promise you; and when I came back into the round-house, I found the gentleman had taken a money-belt from about his waist, and poured out a guinea or two upon the table. The captain was looking at the guineas, and then at the belt, and then at the gentleman's face; and I thought he seemed excited.

"Half of it," he cried, "and I'm your man!"

The other swept back the guineas into the belt, and put it on again under his waistcoat. "I have told ye, sir," said he, "that not one doit of it belongs to me. It belongs to my chieftain," and here he touched his hat—"and while I would be but a silly messenger to grudge some of it that the rest might come safe, I should show myself a hound indeed if I bought my own carcase any too dear. Thirty guineas on the seaside, or sixty if ye set me on the Linnhe loch. Take it, if ye will; if not, ye can do your worst."

"Ay," said Hoseason. "And if I gave ye over to the soldiers?"

"Ye would make a fool's bargain," said the other. "My chief, let me tell you, sir, is forfeited, like every honest man in Scotland. His estate is in the hands of the man they call King George; and it is his officers that collect the rents, or try to collect them. But for the honor of Scotland, the poor tenant bodies take a thought upon their chief lying in exile; and this money is a part of that very rent for which King George is looking. Now, sir, ye seem to me to be a man that understands things: bring this money within the reach of Government, and how much of it'll come to you?"

"Little enough, to be sure," said Hoseason; and then, "If they knew," he added, drily. "But I think, if I was to try, that I could hold my tongue about it."

"Ah, but I'll befool ye there!" cried the gentleman. "Play me false, and I'll play you cunning. If a hand's laid upon me, they shall ken what money it is."

"Well," returned the captain, "what must be must. Sixty guineas, and done. Here's my hand upon it."

"And here's mine," said the other.

And thereupon the captain went out (rather hurriedly, I thought), and left me alone in the round-house with the stranger.

At that period (so soon after the forty-five) there were many exiled gentlemen coming back at the peril of their lives, either to see their friends or to collect a little money; and as for the Highland chiefs that had been forfeited, it was a common matter of talk how their tenants would stint themselves to send them money, and their clansmen outface the soldiery to get it in, and run the gauntlet of our great navy to carry it across. All this I had, of course, heard tell of; and now I had a man under my eyes whose life was forfeit on all these counts and upon one more, for he was not only a rebel and a smuggler of rents, but had taken service with King Louis of France. And as if all this were not enough, he had a belt full of golden guineas round his loins. Whatever my opinions, I could not look on such a man without a lively interest.

"And so you're a Jacobite?" said I, as I set meat before him.

"Ay," said he, beginning to eat. "And you, by your long face, should be a Whig?"

"Betwixt and between," said I, not to annoy him; for indeed I was as good a Whig as Mr. Campbell could make me.

"And that's naething," said he. "But I'm saying, Mr. Betwixt-and-Between," he added, "this bottle of yours is dry; and it's hard if I'm to pay sixty guineas and be grudged a dram upon the back of it."

"I'll go and ask for the key," said I, and stepped on deck.

The fog was close as ever, but the swell almost down. They had laid the brig to, not knowing precisely where they were, and the wind (what little there was of it) not serving well for their true course. Some of the hands were still hearkening for breakers; but the captain and the two officers were in the waist with their heads together. It struck me (I don't know why) that they were after no good; and the first word I heard, as I drew softly near, more than confirmed me.

It was Mr. Riach, crying out as if upon a sudden thought:

"Couldn't we wile him out of the round-house?"

"He's better where he is," returned Hoseason; "he hasn't room to use his sword."

"Well, that's true," said Riach; "but he's hard to come at."

"Hut!" said Hoseason. "We can get the man in talk, one upon each side, and pin him by the two arms; or if that'll not hold, sir, we can make a run by both the doors and get him under hand before he has time to draw."

At this hearing, I was seized with both fear and anger at these treacherous, greedy, bloody men that I sailed with. My first mind was to run away; my second was bolder.

"Captain," said I, "the gentleman is seeking a dram, and the bottle's out. Will you give me the key?"

They all started and turned about.

"Why, here's our chance to get the firearms!" Riach cried; and then to me: "Hark ye, David," he said, "do ye ken where the pistols are?"

"Ay, ay," put in Hoseason. "David kens; David's a good lad. Ye see, David my man, yon wild Hielandman is a danger to the ship, besides being a rank foe to King George, God bless him!"

I had never been so be-Davided since I came on board; but I said Yes, as if all I heard were quite natural.

"The trouble is," resumed the captain, "that all our firelocks, great and little, are in the round-house under this man's nose; likewise the powder. Now, if I, or one of the officers, was to go in and take them, he would fall to thinking. But a lad like you, David, might snap up a horn and a pistol or two without remark. And if ye can do it cleverly, I'll bear it in mind when it'll be good for you to have friends; and that's when we come to Carolina."

Here Mr. Riach whispered him a little.

"Very right, sir," said the captain; and then to myself: "And see here, David, yon man has a beltful of gold, and I give you my word that you shall have your fingers in it."

I told him I would do as he wished, though indeed I had scarce breath to speak with; and upon that he gave me the key of the spirit locker, and I began to go slowly back to the round-house. What was I to do? They were dogs and thieves; they had stolen me from my country; they had killed poor Ransome; and was I to hold the candle to another murder? But then, upon the other hand, there was the fear of death very plain before me; for what could a boy and a man, if they were as brave as lions, against a whole ship's company?

I was still arguing it back and forth, and getting no great clearness, when I came into the round-house and saw the Jacobite eating his supper under the lamp; and at that my mind was made up all in a moment. I have no credit by it; it was by no choice of mine, but as if by compulsion, that I walked right up to the table and put my hand on his shoulder.

"Do ye want to be killed?" said I.

He sprang to his feet, and looked a question at me as clear as if he had spoken.

"Oh!" cried I, "they're all murderers here; it's a ship full of them! They've murdered a boy already. Now it's you."

"Ay, ay," said he; "but they haven't got me yet." And then looking at me curiously, "Will ye stand with me?"

"That will I!" said I. "I am no thief, nor yet murderer. I'll stand by you."

"Why, then," said he, "what's your name?"

"David Balfour," said I; and then thinking that a man with so fine a coat must like fine people, I added for the first time, "of Shaws."

It never occurred to him to doubt me, for a Highlander is used to see great gentlefolks in great poverty; but as he had no estate of his own, my words nettled a very childish vanity he had.

"My name is Stewart," he said, drawing himself up. "Alan Breck, they call me. A king's name is good enough for me, though I bear it plain and have the name of no farm-midden to clap to the hind-end of it."

And having administered this rebuke, as though it were something of a chief importance, he turned to examine our defenses.

The round-house was built very strong, to support the breaching of the seas. Of its five apertures, only the skylight and the two doors were large enough for the passage of a man. The doors, besides, could be drawn close: they were of stout oak, and ran in grooves, and were fitted with hooks to keep them either shut or open, as the need arose. The one that was already shut I secured in this fashion; but when I was proceeding to slide to the other, Alan stopped me.

"David," said he—"for I cannae bring to mind the name of your landed estate, and so will make so bold as to call you David—that door, being open, is the best part of my defenses."

"It would be yet better shut," says I.

"Not so, David," says he. "Ye see, I have but one face; but so long as that door is open and my face to it, the best part of my enemies will be in front of me, where I would aye wish to find them."

Then he gave me from the rack a cutlass (of which there were a few besides the firearms), choosing it with great care, shaking his head and saying he had never in all his life seen poorer weapons; and next he set me down to the table with a powder-horn, a bag of bullets and all the pistols, which he bade me charge.

"And that will be better work, let me tell you," said he, "for a gentleman of decent birth, than scraping plates and reaching drams to a wheen tarry sailors."

Thereupon he stood up in the midst with his face to the door, and drawing his great sword, made trial of the room he had to wield it in.

"I must stick to the point," he said, shaking his head; "and that's a pity, too. It doesn't set my genius, which is all for the upper guard. And now," said he, "do you keep on charging the pistols, and give heed to me."

I told him I would listen closely. My chest was tight, my mouth dry, the light dark to my eyes; the thought of the numbers that were soon to leap in upon us kept my heart in a flutter; and the sea which I heard washing round the brig, and where I thought my dead body would be cast ere morning, ran in my mind strangely.

"First of all," said he, "how many are against us?"

I reckoned them up; and such was the hurry of my mind, I had to cast the numbers twice. "Fifteen," said I.

Alan whistled. "Well," said he, "that can't be cured. And now follow me. It is my part to keep this door, where I look for the main battle. In that, ye have no hand. And mind and dinnae fire to this side unless they get me down; for I would rather have ten foes in front of me than one friend like you cracking pistols at my back."

I told him, indeed I was no great shot.

"And that's very bravely said," he cried in a great admiration of my candor. "There's many a pretty gentleman that wouldnae dare to say it."

"But then, sir," said I, "there is the door behind you, which they may perhaps break in."

"Ay," says he, "and that is a part of your work. No sooner the pistols charged, than ye must climb up into yon bed where ye're handy at the window; and if they lift hand against the door, ye're to shoot. But that's not all. Let's make a bit of a soldier of ye, David. What else have ye to guard?"

"There's the skylight," said I. "But indeed, Mr. Stewart, I would need to have eyes upon both sides to keep the two of them; for when my face is at the one, my back is to the other."

"And that's very true," said Alan. "But have ye no ears to your head?"

"To be sure!" cried I. "I must hear the bursting of the glass!"

"Ye have some rudiments of sense," said Alan, grimly.

But now our time of truce was come to an end. Those on deck had waited for my coming till they grew impatient; and scarce had Alan spoken, when the captain showed face in the open door.

"Stand!" cried Alan, and pointed his sword at him.

The captain stood, indeed; but he neither winced nor drew back a foot.

"A naked sword?" says he. "This is a strange return for hospitality."

"Do ye see me?" said Alan. "I am come of kings; I bear a king's name.

My badge is the oak. Do ye see my sword? It has slashed the heads off mair Whigamores than you have toes upon your feet. Call up your vermin to your back, sir, and fall on! The sooner the clash begins the sooner ye'll taste this steel throughout your vitals."

The captain said nothing to Alan, but he looked over at me with an ugly look. "David," said he, "I'll mind this"; and the sound of his voice went through me with a jar.

Next moment he was gone.

"And now," said Alan, "let your hand keep your head, for the grip is coming."

Alan drew a dirk, which he held in his left hand in case they should run in under his sword. I, on my part, clambered up into the berth with an armful of pistols and something of a heavy heart, and set open the window where I was to watch. It was a small part of the deck that I could overlook, but enough for our purpose. The sea had gone down, and the wind was steady and kept the sails quiet; so that there was a great stillness in the ship, in which I made sure I heard the sound of muttering voices. A little after, and there came a clash of steel upon the deck, by which I knew they were dealing out the cutlasses and one had been let fall: and after that, silence again.

I do not know if I was what you call afraid; but my heart beat like a bird's, both quick and little; and there was a dimness came before my eyes which I continually rubbed away, and which continually returned. As for hope, I had none; but only a darkness of despair and a sort of anger against all the world that made me long to sell my life as dear as I was able. I tried to pray, I remember, but that same hurry of my mind, like a man running, would not suffer me to think upon the words; and my chief wish was to have the thing begin and be done with it.

It came all of a sudden when it did, with a rush of feet and a roar, and then a shout from Alan, and a sound of blows and some one crying out as if hurt. I looked back over my shoulder, and saw Mr. Shuan in the doorway, crossing blades with Alan.

"That's him that killed the boy!" I cried.

"Look to your window!" said Alan; and as I turned back to my place, I saw him pass his sword through the mate's body.

It was none too soon for me to look to my own part; for my head was scarce back at the window, before five men, carrying a spare yard for a battering-ram, ran past me and took post to drive the door in. I had never fired with a pistol in my life, and not often with a gun; far less against a fellow-creature. But it was now or never; and just as they swang the yard, I cried out, "Take that!" and shot into their midst.

I must have hit one of them, for he sang out and gave back a step, and the rest stopped as if a little disconcerted. Before they had time to recover, I sent another ball over their heads; and at my third shot (which went as wide as the second) the whole party threw down the yard and ran for it.

Then I looked round again into the deck-house. The whole place was full of the smoke of my own firing, just as my ears seemed to be burst with the noise of the shots. But there was Alan, standing as before; only now his sword was running blood to the hilt, and himself so swelled with triumph and fallen into so fine an attitude, that he looked to be invincible. Right before him on the floor was Mr. Shuan, on his hands and knees; the blood was pouring from his mouth, and he was sinking slowly lower, with a terrible, white face; and just as I looked, some of those from behind caught hold of him by the heels and dragged him bodily out of the round-house. I believed he died as they were doing it.

"There's one of your Whigs for ye!" cried Alan; and then turning to me, he asked if I had done much execution.

I told him I had winged one, and thought it was the captain.

"And I've settled two," says he. "No, there's not enough blood let; they'll be back again. To your watch, David. This is but a dram before meat."

I settled back to my place, re-charging the three pistols I had fired, and keeping watch with both eye and ear.

Our enemies were disputing not far off upon the deck, and that so loudly that I could hear a word or two above the washing of the seas.

"It was Shuan bungled it," I heard one say.

And another answered him with a "Wheesht, man! He's paid the piper."

After that the voices fell again into the same muttering as before. Only now, one person spoke most of the time, as though laying down a plan, and first one and then another answered him briefly, like men taking orders. By this, I made sure they were coming on again, and told Alan.

"It's what we have to pray for," said he. "Unless we can give them a good distaste of us, and done with it, there'll be nae sleep for either you or me. But this time, mind, they'll be in earnest."

By this, my pistols were ready, and there was nothing to do but listen and wait. While the brush lasted, I had not the time to think if I was frighted; but now, when all was still again, my mind ran upon nothing else. The thought of the sharp swords and the cold steel was strong in me; and presently, when I began to hear stealthy steps and a brushing of men's clothes against the round-house wall, and knew they were taking their places in the dark, I could have found it in my mind to cry out aloud.

All this was upon Alan's side; and I had begun to think my share of the fight was at an end, when I heard some one drop softly on the roof above me.

Then there came a single call on the sea-pipe, and that was the signal. A knot of them made one rush of it, cutlass in hand, against the door; and at the same moment, the glass of the skylight was dashed in a thousand pieces, and a man leaped through and landed on the floor. Before he got his feet, I had clapped a pistol to his back, and might have shot him, too; only at the touch of him (and him alive) my whole flesh misgave me, and I could no more pull the trigger than I could have flown.

He had dropped his cutlass as he jumped, and when he felt the pistol, whipped straight round and laid hold of me, roaring out an oath; and at that either my courage came again, or I grew so much afraid as came to the same thing; for I gave a shriek and shot him in the midst of the body. He gave the most horrible, ugly groan, and fell to the floor. The foot of a second fellow, whose legs were dangling through the skylight, struck me at the same time upon the head; and at that I snatched another pistol and shot this one through the thigh, so that he slipped through and tumbled in a lump on his companion's body. There was no talk of missing, any more than there was time to aim; I clapped the muzzle to the very place and fired.

I might have stood and stared at them for long, but I heard Alan shout as if for help, and that brought me to my senses.

He had kept the door so long; but one of the seamen, while he was engaged with others, had run in under his guard and caught him about the body. Alan was dirking him with his left hand, but the fellow clung like a leech. Another had broken in and had his cutlass raised. The door was thronged with their faces. I thought we were lost, and catching up my cutlass, fell on them in flank.

But I had not time to be of help. The wrestler dropped at last; and Alan, leaping back to get his distance, ran upon the others like a bull, roaring as he went. They broke before him like water, turning, and running, and falling one against another in their haste. The sword in his hands flashed like quicksilver into the huddle of our fleeing enemies; and at every flash there came the scream of a man hurt. I was still thinking we were lost, when lo! they were all gone, and Alan was driving them along the deck as a sheep-dog chases sheep.

Yet he was no sooner out than he was back again, being as cautious as he was brave; and meanwhile the seamen continued running and crying out as if he was still behind them; and we heard them tumble one upon another into the forecastle, and clap-to the hatch upon the top.

The round-house was like a shambles; three were dead inside, another lay in his death agony across the threshold; and there were Alan and I victorious and unhurt.

He came up to me with open arms. "Come to my arms!" he cried, and embraced and kissed me hard upon both cheeks. "David," said he, "I love you like a brother. And oh, man," he cried in a kind of ecstasy, "am I no a bonny fighter?"

Thereupon he turned to the four enemies, passed his sword clean through each of them, and tumbled them out of doors one after the other. As he did so, he kept humming and singing and whistling to himself, like a man trying to recall an air; only what *he* was trying was to make one. All the while, the flush was in his face, and his eyes were as bright as a five-year-old child's with a new toy. And presently he sat down upon the table, sword in hand; the air that he was making all the time began to run a little clearer, and then clearer still; and then out he burst with a great voice into a Gaelic song.

I have translated it here, not in verse (of which I have no skill) but at least in the king's English. He sang it often afterwards, and the thing became popular; so that I have heard it, and had it explained to me, many's the time.

> This is the song of the sword of Alan:
> The smith made it,
> The fire set it;
> Now it shines in the hand of Alan Breck.
>
> Their eyes were many and bright,
> Swift were they to behold,
> Many the hands they guided:
> The sword was alone.

The dun deer troop over the hill,
They are many, the hill is one:
The dun deer vanish,
The hill remains.

Come to me from the hills of heather,
Come from the isles of the sea.
O far-beholding eagles,
Here is your meat.

Now this song which he made (both words and music) in the hour of our victory, is something less than just to me, who stood beside him in the tussle. Mr. Shuan and five more were either killed outright or thoroughly disabled; but of these, two fell by my hand, the two that came by the skylight. Four more were hurt, and of that number, one (and he not the least important) got his hurt from me. So that, altogether, I did my fair share both of the killing and the wounding, and might have claimed a place in Alan's verses. But poets have to think upon their rhymes; and in good prose talk, Alan always did me more than justice.

In the meanwhile, I was innocent of any wrong being done me. For not only I knew no word of the Gaelic; but what with the long suspense of the waiting, and the scurry and strain of our two spirits of fighting, and more than all, the horror I had of some of my own share in it, the thing was no sooner over than I was glad to stagger to a seat. There was that tightness on my chest that I could hardly breathe; the thought of the two men I had shot sat upon me like a nightmare; and all upon a sudden, and before I had a guess of what was coming, I began to sob and cry like any child.

Alan clapped my shoulder, and said I was a brave lad and wanted nothing but sleep.

"I'll take the first watch," said he. "You've done well by me, David, first and last; and I wouldn't lose you for all Appin—no, nor for Breadalbane."

So I made up my bed on the floor; and he took the first spell, pistol in hand and sword on knee, three hours by the captain's watch upon the wall. Then he roused me up, and I took my turn of three hours; before the end of which it was broad day, and a very quiet morning, with a smooth, rolling sea that tossed the ship and made the blood run to and fro on the round-house floor, and a heavy rain that drummed upon the roof. All my watch there was nothing stirring; and by the banging of the helm, I knew they had even no one at the tiller. Indeed (as I learned afterwards) there were so many of them hurt or dead, and the rest in so ill a temper, that Mr. Riach and the captain had to take turn and turn like Alan and me, or the brig might have gone ashore and nobody the wiser. It was a mercy the night had fallen so still, for the wind had gone down as soon as the rain began. Even as it was, I judged by the wailing of a great number of gulls that went crying and fishing round the ship, that she must have drifted pretty near the coast of one of the islands of the Hebrides; and at last, looking out of the door of the round-house, I saw the great stone hills of Skye on the right hand, and, a little more astern, the strange isle of Rum.

THE RESCUE OF A CASTAWAY

Jules Verne

O N OCTOBER 10th the vessel was launched. Pencroft was radiant with joy: the operation was perfectly successful; the boat completely rigged, having been pushed on rollers to the water's edge, was floated by the rising tide, amid the cheers of the colonists, particularly of Pencroft, who showed no modesty on this occasion. Besides, his importance was to last beyond the finishing of the vessel, since, after having built her, he was to command her. The grade of captain was bestowed upon him with the approbation of all. To satisfy Captain Pencroft, it was now necessary to give a name to the vessel, and, after many propositions had been discussed, the votes were all in favor of the Bonadventure. As soon as the Bonadventure had been lifted by the rising tide, it was seen that she lay evenly in the water, and would be easily navigated. However, the trial trip was to be made that very day by an excursion off the coast. The weather was fine, the breeze fresh, and the sea smooth, especially toward the south coast, for the wind was blowing from the northwest.

"All hands on board," shouted Pencroft; but breakfast was first necessary, and it was thought best to take provisions on board, in the event of their excursion being prolonged until the evening.

Cyrus Harding was equally anxious to try the vessel, the model of which had originated with him, although on the sailor's advice he had altered some parts of it, but he did not share Pencroft's confidence in her, and as the latter had not again spoken of the voyage to Tabor Island, Harding hoped he had given it up. He would have indeed great reluctance in letting two or three of

from "The Mysterious Island" by Jules Verne

his companions venture so far in so small a boat, which was not of more than fifteen tons' burden.

At half-past ten everybody was on board, even Top and Jup, and Herbert weighed the anchor, which was fast in the sand near the mouth of the Mercy. The sail was hoisted, the Lincolnian flag floated from the masthead, and the Bonadventure, steered by Pencroft, stood out to sea.

The wind blowing out to Union Bay she ran before it, and thus showed her owners, much to their satisfaction, that she possessed a remarkably fast pair of heels, according to Pencroft's mode of speaking. After having doubled Flotsam Point and Claw Cape, the captain kept her close hauled, so as to sail along the southern coast of the island, when it was found she sailed admirably within five points of the wind. All hands were enchanted; they had a good vessel, which, in case of need, would be of great service to them, and with fine weather and a fresh breeze the voyage promised to be charming.

Pencroft now stood off the shore, three or four miles across from Port Balloon. The island then appeared in all its extent and under a new aspect, with the varied panorama of its shore from Claw Cape to Reptile End, the forests, in which dark firs contrasted with the young foliage of other trees, overlooked the whole, and Mount Franklin, whose lofty head was still whitened with snow.

"How beautiful it is!" cried Herbert.

"Yes, our island is beautiful and good," replied Pencroft. "I love it as I loved my poor mother. It received us poor and destitute, and now what is wanting to us five fellows who fell on it from the sky?"

"Nothing," replied Neb; "nothing, captain."

And the two brave men gave three tremendous cheers in honor of their island!

During all this time Gideon Spilett, leaning against the mast, sketched the panorama which was developed before his eyes.

Cyrus Harding gazed on it in silence.

"Well, Captain Harding," asked Pencroft, "what do you think of our vessel?"

"She appears to behave well," replied the engineer.

"Good! And do you think now that she could undertake a voyage of some extent?"

"What voyage, Pencroft?"

"One to Tabor Island, for instance."

"My friend," replied Harding, "I think that in any pressing emergency we need not hesitate to trust ourselves to the Bonadventure even for a longer voyage; but you know I should see you set off to Tabor Island with great uneasiness, since nothing obliges you to go there."

"One likes to know one's neighbors," returned the sailor, who was obstinate in his idea. "Tabor Island is a neighbor and the only one! Politeness requires us to go at least to pay a visit."

"By Jove," said Spilett; "our friend Pencroft has become very particular about the proprieties all at once!"

"I am not particular about anything at all," retorted the sailor, who was rather vexed by the engineer's opposition, but who did not wish to cause him anxiety.

"Consider, Pencroft," resumed Harding, "you cannot go alone to Tabor Island."

"One companion will be enough for me."

"Even so," replied the engineer, "you will risk depriving the colony of Lincoln Island of two settlers out of five."

"Out of six," answered Pencroft; "you forget Jup."

"Out of seven," added Neb; "Top is quite worth another."

"There is no risk at all in it, captain," replied Pencroft.

"That is possible, Pencroft; but I repeat it is to expose ourselves uselessly."

The obstinate sailor did not reply, and let the conversation drop, quite determined to resume it again. But he did not suspect that an incident would come to his aid and change into an act of humanity that which was at first only a doubtful whim.

After standing off the shore the Bonadventure again approached it in the direction of Port Balloon. It was important to ascertain the channels between the sand banks and reefs, that buoys might be laid down, since this little creek was to be the harbor.

They were not more than half a mile from the coast, and it was necessary to tack to beat against the wind. The Bonadventure was then going at a very moderate rate, as the breeze, partly intercepted by the high land, scarcely swelled her sails, and the sea, smooth as glass, was only rippled now and then by passing gusts. Herbert had stationed himself in the bows that he might indicate the course to be followed among the channels, when all at once he shouted:

"Luff, Pencroft, luff!"

"What is the matter?" replied the sailor; "a rock?"

"No—wait," said Herbert; "I don't quite see. Luff again—right—now."

So saying, Herbert, leaning over the side, plunged his arm into the water and pulled it out, exclaiming:

"A bottle!"

He held in his hand a corked bottle which he had just seized a few cables' length from the shore.

Cyrus Harding took the bottle. Without uttering a single word he drew the cork, and took from it a damp paper, on which were written these words: "Castaway. . . . Tabor Island: 153° W. long., 37° 11′ S. lat."

"A castaway!" exclaimed Pencroft; "left on this Tabor Island not two hundred miles from us! Ah, Captain Harding, you won't now oppose my going."

"No, Pencroft," replied Cyrus Harding; "and you shall set out as soon as possible."

"Tomorrow?"

"Tomorrow!"

The engineer still held in his hand the paper which he had taken from the bottle. He contemplated it for some instants, then resumed:

"From this document, my friends, from the way in which it is worded, we may conclude this: first, that the castaway on Tabor Island is a man possessing a considerable knowledge of navigation, since he gives the latitude and longitude of the island exactly as we ourselves found it, and to a second of approximation; secondly, that he is either English or American, as the document is written in the English language."

"That is perfectly logical," answered Spilett; "and the presence of this castaway explains the arrival of the case on the shores of our island. There must have been a wreck, since there is a castaway. As to the latter, whoever he may be, it is lucky for him that Pencroft thought of building this boat and of trying her this very day, for a day later and this bottle might have been broken on the rocks."

"Indeed," said Herbert, "it is a fortunate chance that the Bonadventure passed exactly where the bottle was still floating!"

"Does not this appear strange to you?" asked Harding of Pencroft.

"It appears fortunate, that's all," answered the sailor. "Do you see anything extraordinary in it, captain? The bottle must go somewhere, and why not here as well as anywhere else?"

"Perhaps you are right, Pencroft," replied the engineer, "and yet——"

"But," observed Herbert, "there's nothing to prove that this bottle has been floating long in the sea."

"Nothing," replied Gideon Spilett; "and the document appears even to have been recently written. What do you think about it, Cyrus?"

"It is difficult to say, and besides we shall soon know," replied Harding.

During this conversation Pencroft had not remained inactive. He had put the vessel about, and the Bonadventure, all sails set, was running rapidly toward Claw Cape.

Every one was thinking of the castaway on Tabor Island. Should they be in time to save him? This was a great event in the life of the colonists! They themselves were but castaways, but it was feared that another might not have been so fortunate, and their duty was to go to his succor.

Claw Cape was doubled, and about four o'clock the Bonadventure dropped her anchor at the mouth of the Mercy. That same evening the arrangements for the new expedition were made. It appeared best that Pencroft and Herbert, who knew how to work the vessel, should undertake the voyage alone. By setting out the next day, the 11th of October, they would arrive on the 13th, for with the present wind it would not take more than forty-eight hours to make this passage of a hundred and fifty miles. One day in the island, three or four to return, they might hope therefore that on the 17th they would again reach Lincoln Island. The weather was fine, the barometer was rising, the wind appeared settled, everything then was in favor of these brave men whom an act of humanity was taking far from their island.

Thus it had been agreed that Cyrus Harding, Neb, and Gideon Spilett, should remain at Granite House, but an objection was raised, and Spilett, who had not forgotten his business as reporter to the New York *Herald*, having declared that he would go by swimming rather than lose such an opportunity, he was admitted to take a part in the voyage. The evening was occupied in transporting on board the Bonadventure articles of bedding, utensils, arms, ammunition, a compass, provisions for a week, and this business being rapidly accomplished, the colonists ascended to Granite House.

The next day, at five o'clock in the morning, the farewells were said, not without some emotion on both sides, and Pencroft setting sail made toward Claw Cape, which had to be doubled in order to proceed to the southwest.

The Bonadventure was already a quarter of a mile from the coast, when the passengers perceived on the heights of Granite House two men waving their farewells; they were Cyrus Harding and Neb.

"Our friends," exclaimed Spilett, "this is our first separation for fifteen months."

Pencroft, the reporter, and Herbert waved in return, and Granite House soon disappeared behind the high rocks of the cape.

During the first part of the day the Bonadventure was still in sight of the southern coast of Lincoln Island, which soon appeared just like a green basket, with Mount Franklin rising from the center. The heights, diminished by distance, did not present an appearance likely to tempt vessels to touch there. Reptile End was passed in about an hour, though at a distance of about ten miles.

At this distance it was no longer possible to distinguish anything of the western coast, which stretched away to the ridges of Mount Franklin, and three hours after the last of Lincoln Island sank below the horizon.

The Bonadventure behaved capitally. Bounding over the waves she proceeded rapidly on her course. Pencroft had hoisted the foresail, and steering by the compass followed a rectilinear direction. From time to time Herbert relieved him at the helm, and the lad's hand was so firm that the sailor had not a point to find fault with.

Gideon Spilett chatted sometimes with one, sometimes with the other; if wanted he lent a hand with the ropes, and Captain Pencroft was perfectly satisfied with his crew.

In the evening the crescent moon, which would not be in its first quarter until the 16th, appeared in the twilight and soon set again. The night was dark but starry, and the next day again promised to be fine.

Pencroft prudently lowered the foresail, not wishing to be caught by a sudden gust while carrying too much canvas; it was perhaps an unnecessary precaution on such a calm night, but Pencroft was a prudent sailor and cannot be blamed for it.

The reporter slept part of the night. Pencroft and Herbert took turns for a spell of two hours each at the helm. The sailor trusted Herbert as he would himself, and his confidence was justified by the coolness and judgment of the lad. Pencroft gave him his directions as a commander to his steersman, and Herbert never allowed the Bonadventure to swerve even a point. The night passed quietly, as did the day of the 12th of October. A southeasterly direction was strictly maintained; unless the Bonadventure fell in with some unknown current she would come exactly within sight of Tabor Island.

As to the sea over which the vessel was then sailing, it was absolutely deserted. Now and then a great albatross or frigate bird passed within gunshot, and Gideon Spilett wondered if it was to one of them that he had confided his last letter addressed to the New York *Herald*. These birds were the only beings that appeared to frequent this part of the ocean between Tabor and Lincoln Islands.

"And yet," observed Herbert, "this is the time that whalers usually proceed toward the southern part of the Pacific. Indeed I do not think there could be a more deserted sea than this."

"It is not quite so deserted as all that," replied Pencroft.

"What do you mean?" asked the reporter.

"We are on it. Do you take our vessel for a wreck and us for porpoises?" And Pencroft laughed at his joke.

By the evening, according to calculation, it was thought that the Bonadventure had accomplished a distance of a hundred and twenty miles since her departure from Lincoln Island, that is to say, in thirty-six hours, which would give her a speed of between three and four knots an hour. The breeze was very slight and might soon drop altogether. However it was hoped that the next morning by break of day, if the calculation had been correct and the course true, they would sight Tabor Island.

Neither Gideon Spilett, Herbert, nor Pencroft slept that night. In the expectation of the next day they could not but feel some emotion. There was so much uncertainty in their enterprise. Were they near Tabor Island? Was the island still inhabited by the castaway to whose succor they had come? Who was this man? Would not his presence disturb the little colony till then so united? Besides, would he be content to exchange his prison for another? All these questions, which would no doubt be answered the next day, kept them in suspense, and at the dawn of day all fixed their gaze on the western horizon.

"Land!" shouted Pencroft at about six o'clock in the morning.

And it was impossible that Pencroft should be mistaken; it was evident that land was there. Imagine the joy of the little crew of the Bonadventure. In a few hours they would land on the beach of the island!

The low coast of Tabor Island, scarcely emerging from the sea, was not more than fifteen miles distant.

The head of the Bonadventure, which was a little to the south of the island, was set directly toward it, and as the sun mounted in the east his rays fell upon one or two headlands.

"This is a much less important isle than Lincoln Island," observed Herbert, "and is probably due like ours to some submarine convulsion."

At eleven o'clock the Bonadventure was not more than two miles off, and Pencroft, while looking for a suitable place at which to land, proceeded very cautiously through the unknown waters. The whole of the island could now be surveyed, and on it could be seen groups of gum and other large trees, of the same species as those growing on Lincoln Island. But the astonishing thing was that no smoke arose to show that the island was inhabited, not a signal appeared on any part of the shore whatever!

And yet the document was clear enough; there was a castaway, and this castaway should have been on the watch.

In the meanwhile the Bonadventure entered the winding channels among the reefs, and Pencroft observed every turn with extreme care. He had put Herbert at the helm, posting himself in the bows, inspecting the water, while he held the halyard in his hand, ready to lower the sail at a moment's notice. Gideon Spilett with his glass eagerly scanned the shore, though without perceiving anything.

However, at about twelve o'clock the keel of the Bonadventure grated on the bottom. The anchor was let go, the sails furled, and the crew of the little vessel landed.

And there was no reason to doubt that this was Tabor Island, since according to the most recent charts there was no island in this part of the Pacific between New Zealand and the American coast.

The vessel was securely moored, so that there should be no danger of her being carried away by the receding tide; then Pencroft and his companions, well armed, ascended the shore, so as to gain an elevation of about two hundred and fifty or three hundred feet which rose at a distance of half a mile.

"From the summit of that hill," said Spilett, "we can no doubt obtain a complete view of the island, which will greatly facilitate our search."

"So as to do here," replied Herbert, "that which Captain Harding did the very first thing on Lincoln Island, by climbing Mount Franklin."

"Exactly so," answered the reporter; "and it is the best plan of proceeding."

While thus talking the explorers had advanced along a clearing which terminated at the foot of the hill. Flocks of rock-pigeons and sea-swallows, similar to those of Lincoln Island, fluttered around them. Under the woods which skirted the glade on the left they could hear the bushes rustling and see the grass waving, which indicated the presence of timid animals, but still nothing to show that the island was inhabited.

Arrived at the foot of the hill, Pencroft, Spilett, and Herbert climbed it in a few minutes, and gazed anxiously round the horizon. They were on an islet which did not measure more than six miles in circumference, its shape not much bordered by capes or promontories, bays or creeks, being a lengthened oval. All around, the lonely sea extended to the limits of the horizon. No land nor even a sail was in sight. This woody islet did not offer the varied aspects of Lincoln Island, arid and wild in one part, but fertile and rich in the other. On the contrary this was a uniform mass of verdure, out of which rose two or three hills of no great height. Obliquely to the oval of the island ran a stream through a wide meadow falling into the sea on the west by a narrow mouth.

"The domain is limited," said Herbert.

"Yes," rejoined Pencroft. "It would have been too small for us."

"And moreover," said the reporter, "it appears to be uninhabited."

"Indeed," answered Herbert, "nothing here betrays the presence of man."

"Let us go down," said Pencroft, "and search."

The sailor and his two companions returned to the shore, to the place where they had left the Bonadventure.

They had decided to make the tour of the island on foot before exploring the interior, so that not a spot should escape their investigations. The beach was easy to follow, and only in some places was their way barred by large rocks, which, however, they easily passed round. The explorers proceeded toward the south, disturbing numerous flocks of sea-birds and herds of seals, which threw themselves into the sea as soon as they saw the strangers at a distance.

"Those beasts yonder," observed the reporter, "do not see men for the first time. They fear them, therefore they must know them."

An hour after their departure they arrived on the southern point of the islet, terminated by a sharp cape, and proceeded toward the north along the western coast, equally formed by sand and rocks, the background bordered by thick woods.

There was not a trace of a habitation in any part, not the print of a human foot on the shore of the island which after four hours' walking had been gone completely round.

It was to say the least every extraordinary, and they were compelled to believe that Tabor Island was no longer inhabited. Perhaps, after all, the document was already several months, or several years, old and it was possible in this case either that the castaway had been able to return to his country or that he had died of misery.

Pencroft, Spilett, and Herbert, forming more or less probable conjectures, dined rapidly on board the Bonadventure so as to be able to continue their excursion until nightfall. This was done at five o'clock in the evening, at which hour they entered the wood. Numerous animals fled at their approach, being principally, one might say, only goats and pigs, which it was easy to see belonged to European species. Doubtless some whaler had landed them on the island, where they had rapidly increased. Herbert resolved to catch one or two living, and take them back to Lincoln Island.

It was no longer doubtful that men at some period or other had visited this islet, and this became still more evident when paths appeared trodden through the forest, felled trees, and everywhere traces of the hand of man; but the trees were becoming rotten, and had been felled many years ago; the marks of the ax were velveted with moss, and the grass grew long and thick on the paths, so that it was difficult to find them.

"But," observed Gideon Spilett, "this not only proves that men have landed on this island, but also that they lived on it for some time. Now, who were these men? How many of them remain?"

"The document," said Herbert, "only spoke of one castaway."

"Well, if he is still on the island," replied Pencroft, "it is impossible but that we shall find him."

The exploration was continued. The sailor and his companions naturally followed the route which cut diagonally across the island, and they were thus obliged to follow the stream which flowed toward the sea.

If the animals of European origin, if works due to a human hand, showed incontestably that men had already visited the island, several specimens of the vegetable kingdom did not prove it less. In some places, in the midst of clearings, it was evident that the soil had been planted with culinary plants, at probably the same distant period.

What, then, was Herbert's joy, when he recognized potatoes, chicory, sorrel, carrots, cabbages, and turnips, of which it was sufficient to collect the seed to enrich the soil of Lincoln Island.

"Capital, jolly!" exclaimed Pencroft. "That will suit Neb as well as us. Even if we do not find the castaway, at least our voyage will not have been useless, and God will have rewarded us."

"Doubtless," replied Gideon Spilett; "but to see the state in which we find these plantations, it is to be feared that the island has not been inhabited for some time."

"Indeed," answered Herbert, "an inhabitant, whoever he was, could not have neglected such an important culture!"

"Yes," said Pencroft, "the castaway has gone."

"We must suppose so."

It must then be admitted that the document has already a distant date?"

"Evidently."

"And that the bottle only arrived at Lincoln Island after having floated in the sea a long time."

"Why not?" returned Pencroft. "But night is coming on," added he, "and I think that it will be best to give up the search for the present."

"Let us go on board, and tomorrow we will begin again," said the reporter.

This was the wisest course, and it was about to be followed when Herbert, pointing to a confused mass among the trees, exclaimed:

"A hut!"

All three immediately ran toward the dwelling. In the twilight it was just possible to see that it was built of planks and covered with a thick tarpaulin.

The half-closed door was pushed open by Pencroft, who entered with a rapid step.

The hut was empty!

Pencroft, Herbert, and Gideon Spilett remained silent in the midst of the darkness.

Pencroft shouted loudly.

No reply was made.

The sailor then struck a light and set fire to a twig. This lighted for a moment a small room, which appeared perfectly empty. At the back was a rude fireplace, with a few cold cinders, supporting an armful of dry wood. Pencroft threw the blazing twig on it, the wood cracked and gave forth a bright light.

The sailor and his two companions then perceived a disordered bed, of which the damp and yellow coverlets proved that it had not been used for a long time. In the corner of the fireplace were two kettles, covered with rust, and an overthrown pot. A cupboard, with a few moldy sailor's clothes; on the table a tin plate and a Bible, eaten away by damp; in a corner a few tools, a spade, pick-ax, two fowling-pieces, one of which was broken; on a plank, forming a shelf, stood a barrel of powder, still untouched, a barrel of shot, and several boxes of caps, all thickly covered with dust, accumulated, perhaps, by many long years.

"There is no one here," said the reporter.

"No one," replied Pencroft.

"It is a long time since this room has been inhabited," observed Herbert.

"Yes, a very long time!" answered the reporter.

"Mr. Spilett," then said Pencroft, "instead of returning on board, I think that it would be well to pass the night in this hut."

"You are right, Pencroft," answered Gideon Spilett, "and if its owner returns, well! perhaps he will not be sorry to find the place taken possession of."

"He will not return," said the sailor, shaking his head.

"You think that he has quitted the island?" asked the reporter.

"If he had quitted the island he would have taken away his weapons and his tools," replied Pencroft. "You know the value which castaways set on such articles as these, the last remains of a wreck? No! no!" repeated the sailor, in a tone of conviction, "no, he has not left the island! If he had escaped in a boat made by himself, he would still less have left these indispensable and necessary articles. No! he is on the island!"

"Living?" asked Herbert.

"Living or dead. But if he is dead, I suppose he has not buried himself, and so we shall at least find his remains!"

It was then agreed that the night should be passed in the deserted dwelling, and a store of wood found in a corner was sufficient to warm it. The door closed, Pencroft, Herbert, and Spilett remained there, seated on a bench, talking little but wondering much. They were in a frame of mind to imagine anything or expect anything. They listened eagerly for sounds outside. The door might have opened suddenly and a man presented himself to them without their being in the least surprised, notwithstanding all that the hut revealed of abandonment, and they had their hands ready to press the hands of this man, this castaway, this unknown friend, for whom friends were waiting.

But no voice was heard, the door did not open. The hours thus passed away.

How long the night appeared to the sailor and his companions! Herbert alone slept for two hours, for at his age sleep is a necessity. They were all three anxious to continue their exploration of the day before, and to search the most secret recesses of the islet! The inferences deduced by Pencroft were perfectly reasonable, and it was nearly certain that, as the hut was deserted, and the tools, utensils, and weapons were still there, the owner had succumbed. It was agreed, therefore, that they should search for his remains, and give them at least Christian burial.

Day dawned; Pencroft and his companions immediately proceeded to survey the dwelling. It had certainly been built in a favorable situation, at the back of a little hill, sheltered by five or six magnificent gum-trees. Before its front and through the trees the ax had prepared a wide clearing, which allowed the view to extend to the sea. Beyond a lawn, surrounded by a wooden fence falling to pieces, was the shore, on the left of which was the mouth of the stream.

The hut had been built of planks, and it was easy to see that these planks had been obtained from the hull or deck of a ship. It was probable that a disabled vessel had been cast on the coast of the island, that one at least of the crew had been saved, and that by means of the wreck this man, having tools at his disposal, had built the dwelling.

And this became still more evident when Gideon Spilett, after having walked round the hut, saw on a plank, probably one of those which had formed the armor of the wrecked vessel, these letters already half-effaced:

"Br-tan—a."

"Britannia," exclaimed Pencroft, whom the reporter had called; "it is a common name for ships, and I could not say if she was English or American!"

"It matters very little, Pencroft!"

"Very little, indeed," answered the sailor; "and we will save the survivor of the crew if he is still living, to whatever country he may belong. But before beginning our search again let us go on board the Bonadventure."

A sort of uneasiness had seized Pencroft upon the subject of the vessel. Should the island be inhabited after all, and should some one have taken possession of her? But he shrugged his shoulders at such an unreasonable supposition. At any rate the sailor was not sorry to go to breakfast on board. The road already trodden was not long, scarcely a mile. They set out on their walk, gazing into the wood and thickets through which goats and pigs fled in hundreds.

Twenty minutes after leaving the hut Pencroft and his companions reached the western coast of the island, and saw the Bonadventure held fast by her anchor, which was buried deep in the sand.

Pencroft could not restrain a sigh of satisfaction. After all this vessel was his child, and it is the right of fathers to be often uneasy when there is no occasion for it.

They returned on board, breakfasted, so that it should not be necessary to dine until very late; then the repast being ended, the exploration was continued and conducted with the most minute care. Indeed, it was very probable that the only inhabitant of the island had perished. It was therefore more for the traces of a dead than of a living man that Pencroft and his companions searched. But their searches were vain, and during the half of that day they sought to no purpose among the thickets of trees which covered the islet. There was then scarcely any doubt that, if the castaway was dead, no trace of his body now remained, but that some wild beast had probably devoured it to the last bone.

"We will set off tomorrow at daybreak," said Pencroft to his two companions, as about two o'clock they were resting for a few minutes under the shade of a clump of firs.

"I should think that we might without scruple take the utensils which belonged to the castaway," added Herbert.

"I think so too," returned Gideon Spilett; "and these arms and tools will make up the stores of Granite House. The supply of powder and shot is also most important."

"Yes," replied Pencroft; "but we must not forget to capture a couple or two of those pigs, of which Lincoln Island is destitute——"

"Nor to gather those seeds," added Herbert, "which will give us all the vegetables of the old and the new worlds."

"Then perhaps it would be best," said the reporter, "to remain a day longer on Tabor Island, so as to collect all that may be useful to us."

"No, Mr. Spilett," answered Pencroft, "I will ask you to set off tomorrow at daybreak. The wind seems to me to be likely to shift to the west, and after having had a fair wind for coming we shall have a fair wind for going back."

"Then do not let us lose time," said Herbert, rising.

"We won't waste time," returned Pencroft. "You, Herbert, go and gather the seeds, which you know better than we do. While you do that, Mr. Spilett and I will go and have a pig hunt, and even without Top I hope we shall manage to catch a few!"

Herbert accordingly took the path which led toward the cultivated part of the islet, while the sailor and the reporter entered the forest.

Many specimens of the porcine race fled before them, and these animals, which were singularly active, did not appear to be in a humor to allow themselves to be approached.

However, after an hour's chase, the hunters had just managed to get hold of a couple lying in the thicket, when cries were heard resounding from the northern part of the island. With the cries were mingled terrible yells, in which there was nothing human.

Pencroft and Gideon Spilett were at once on their feet, and the pigs by this movement began to run away, at the moment when the sailor was getting ready the rope to bind them.

"That's Herbert's voice!" said the reporter.

"Run!" exclaimed Pencroft.

And the sailor and Spilett immediately ran at full speed toward the spot from whence the cries proceeded.

They did well to hasten, for at a turn of the path near a clearing they saw the lad thrown on the ground and in the grasp of a savage being, apparently a gigantic ape, who was about to do him some great harm.

To rush on this monster, throw him on the ground in his turn, snatch Herbert from him, then bind him securely, was the work of a minute for Pencroft and Gideon Spilett. The sailor was of herculean strength, the reporter also very powerful, and in spite of the monster's resistance he was firmly tied so that he could not even move.

"You are not hurt, Herbert?" asked Spilett.

"No, no!"

"Oh, if this ape had wounded him!" exclaimed Pencroft.

"But he is not an ape," answered Herbert.

At these words Pencroft and Gideon Spilett looked at the singular being who lay on the ground. Indeed it was not an ape, it was a human being, a man! But what a man! A savage in all the horrible acceptation of the word, and so much the more frightful that he seemed fallen to the lowest degree of brutishness!

Shaggy hair, untrimmed beard descending to the chest, the body almost naked except a rag round the waist, wild eyes, enormous hands with immensely long nails, skin the color of mahogany, feet as hard as if made of horn—such was the miserable creature who yet had a claim to be called a man. But it might justly be asked if there were yet a soul in this body, or if the brute instinct alone survived in it!

"Are you quite sure that this is a man, or that he has ever been one?" said Pencroft to the reporter.

"Alas! there is no doubt about it," replied Spilett.

"Then this must be the castaway?" asked Herbert.

"Yes," replied Gideon Spilett, "but the unfortunate man has no longer anything human about him!"

The reporter spoke the truth. It was evident that if the castaway had ever been a civilized being, solitude had made him a savage, or worse, perhaps a regular man of the woods. Hoarse sounds issued from his throat between his teeth, which were sharp as the teeth of a wild beast made to tear raw flesh. Memory must have deserted him long before, and for a long time also he had forgotten how to use his gun and tools, and he no longer knew how to make a fire! It could be seen that he was active and powerful, but the physical qualities had been developed in him to the injury of the moral qualities. Gideon Spilett spoke to him. He did not appear to understand or even to hear. And yet on looking into his eyes the reporter thought he could see that all reason was not extinguished in him. However, the prisoner did not struggle, nor even attempt to break his bonds. Was he overwhelmed by the presence of men whose fellow he had once been? Had he found in some corner of his brain a fleeting remembrance which recalled him to humanity? If free, would he attempt to fly, or would he remain? They could not tell, but they did not make the experiment; and after gazing attentively at the miserable creature:

"Whoever he may be," remarked Gideon Spilett; "whoever he may have been, and whatever he may become, it is our duty to take him with us to Lincoln Island."

"Yes, yes!" replied Herbert; "and perhaps with care we may arouse in him some gleam of intelligence."

"The soul does not die," said the reporter; "and it would be a great satisfaction to rescue one of God's creatures from brutishness."

Pencroft shook his head doubtfully.

"We must try at any rate," returned the reporter; "humanity commands us."

It was indeed their duty as Christians and civilized beings. All three felt this, and they well knew that Cyrus Harding would approve of their acting thus.

"Shall we leave him bound?" asked the sailor.

"Perhaps he would walk if his feet were unfastened," said Herbert.

"Let us try," replied Pencroft.

The cords which shackled the prisoner's feet were cut off, but his arms remained securely fastened. He got up by himself and did not manifest any desire to run away. His hard eyes darted a piercing glance at the three men, who walked near him, but nothing denoted that he recollected being their fellow, or at least having been so. A continual hissing sound issued from his lips, his aspect was wild, but he did not attempt to resist.

By the reporter's advice the unfortunate man was taken to the hut. Perhaps the sight of the things that belonged to him would make some impression on him! Perhaps a spark would be sufficient to revive his obscured intellect, to rekindle his dull soul. The dwelling was not far off. In a few minutes they arrived there, but the prisoner remembered nothing, and it appeared that he had lost consciousness of everything.

What could they think of the degree of brutishness into which this miserable being had fallen, unless that his imprisonment on the islet dated from a very distant period, and after having arrived there a rational being solitude had reduced him to this condition?

The reporter then thought that perhaps the sight of fire would have some effect on him, and in a moment one of those beautiful flames, that attract even animals, blazed up on the hearth. The sight of the flame seemed at first to fix the attention of the unhappy object, but soon he turned away and the look of intelligence faded. Evidently there was nothing to be done, for the time at least, but to take him on board the Bonadventure. This was done, and he remained there in Pencroft's charge.

Herbert and Spilett returned to finish their work; and some hours after they came back to the shore, carrying the utensils and guns, a store of vegetables, of seeds, some game, and two couples of pigs.

All was embarked, and the Bonadventure was ready to weigh anchor and sail with the morning tide.

The prisoner had been placed in the fore-cabin, where he remained quiet, silent, apparently deaf and dumb.

Pencroft offered him something to eat, but he pushed away the cooked meat that was presented to him and which doubtless did not suit him. But on the sailor showing him one of the ducks which Herbert had killed he pounced on it like a wild beast, and devoured it greedily.

"You think that he will recover his senses?" asked Pencroft. "It is not impossible that our care will have an effect upon him, for it is solitude that has made him what he is, and from this time forward he will be no longer alone."

"The poor man must no doubt have been in this state for a long time," said Herbert.

"Perhaps," answered Gideon Spilett.

"About what age is he?" asked the lad.

"It is difficult to say," replied the reporter; "for it is impossible to see his features under the thick beard which covers his face; but he is no longer young, and I suppose he might be about fifty."

"Have you noticed, Mr. Spilett, how deeply sunk his eyes are?" asked Herbert.

"Yes, Herbert; but I must add that they are more human than one could expect from his appearance."

"However, we shall see," replied Pencroft; "and I am anxious to know what opinion Captain Harding will have of our savage. We went to look for a human creature, and we are bringing back a monster! After all, we did what we could."

The night passed, and whether the prisoner slept or not could not be known; but at any rate, although he had been unbound, he did not move. He was like a wild animal which appears stunned at first by its capture and becomes wild again afterward.

At daybreak the next morning, the 15th of October, the change of weather predicted by Pencroft occurred. The wind having shifted to the northwest favored the return of the Bonadventure, but at the same time it freshened, which would render navigation more difficult.

At five o'clock in the morning the anchor was weighed. Pencroft took a reef in the mainsail, and steered toward the northeast, so as to sail straight for Lincoln Island.

The first day of the voyage was not marked by any incident. The prisoner remained quiet in the fore-cabin, and as he had been a sailor it appeared that the motion of the vessel might produce on him a salutary reaction. Did some recollection of his former calling return to him? However that might be, he remained tranquil, astonished rather than depressed.

The next day the wind increased, blowing more from the north, consequently in a less favorable direction for the Bonadventure. Pencroft was soon obliged to sail close-hauled, and without saying anything about it he began to be uneasy at the state of the sea, which frequently broke over the bows. Certainly, if the wind did not moderate, it would take a longer time to reach Lincoln Island than it had taken to make Tabor Island.

Indeed, on the morning of the 17th, the Bonadventure had been forty-eight hours at sea, and nothing showed that she was near the island. It was impossible, besides, to estimate the distance traversed, or to trust to the reckoning for the direction, as the speed had been very irregular. Twenty-four hours after there was yet no land in sight. The wind was right ahead and the sea very heavy. The sails were close-reefed, and they tacked frequently. On

About two o'clock in the morning he started forward. "A light! a light!" he shouted.

the 18th a wave swept completely over the Bonadventure; and if the crew
had not taken the precaution of lashing themselves to the deck, they would
have been carried away.

On this occasion Pencroft and his companions, who were occupied with
loosing themselves, received unexpected aid from the prisoner, who emerged
from the hatchway as if his sailor's instinct had suddenly returned, and broke
a piece out of the bulwarks with a spar, so as to let the water which filled the
deck escape. Then the vessel being clear, he descended to his cabin without
having uttered a word. Pencroft, Gideon Spilett, and Herbert, greatly astonished, let him proceed.

Their situation was truly serious, and the sailor had reason to fear that he
was lost on the wide sea without any possibility of recovering his course.

The night was dark and cold. However, about eleven o'clock, the wind
fell, the sea went down, and the speed of the vessel, as she labored less, greatly
increased.

Neither Pencroft, Spilett, nor Herbert thought of taking an hour's sleep.
They kept a sharp lookout, for either Lincoln Island could not be far distant
and would be sighted at daybreak, or the Bonadventure, carried away by currents, had drifted so much that it would be impossible to rectify her course.
Pencroft, uneasy to the last degree, yet did not despair, for he had a gallant
heart, and grasping the tiller he anxiously endeavored to pierce the darkness
which surrounded them.

About two o'clock in the morning he started forward.

"A light! a light!" he shouted.

Indeed, a bright light appeared twenty miles to the northeast. Lincoln
Island was there, and this fire, evidently lighted by Cyrus Harding, showed
them the course to be followed. Pencroft, who was bearing too much to the
north, altered his course and steered toward the fire, which burned brightly
above the horizon like a star of the first magnitude.

AN UNKNOWN SPECIES OF WHALE

Jules Verne

THE YEAR 1866 was signalized by a remarkable incident, a mysterious and inexplicable phenomenon, which doubtless no one has yet forgotten. Not to mention rumors which agitated the maritime population, and excited the public mind, even in the interior of continents, seafaring men were particularly excited. Merchants, common sailors, captains of vessels, skippers, both of Europe and America, naval officers of all countries, and the governments of several states on the two continents, were deeply interested in the matter.

For some time past, vessels had been met by "an enormous thing," a long object spindle-shaped, occasionally phosphorescent, and infinitely larger and more rapid in its movements than a whale.

The facts relating to this apparition (entered in various log-books) agreed in most respects as to the shape of the object or creature in question, the untiring rapidity of its movements, its surprising power of locomotion, and the peculiar life with which it seemed endowed. If it was a cetacean, it surpassed in size all those hitherto classified in science. Taking into consideration the mean of observations made at divers times—rejecting the timid estimate of those who assigned to this object a length of two hundred feet, equally with the exaggerated opinions which set it down as a mile in width and three in length—we might fairly conclude that this mysterious being surpassed greatly all dimensions admitted by the ichthyologists of the day, if it existed at all. And that it did exist was an undeniable fact; and, with that tendency which

from "Twenty Thousand Leagues Under the Sea" by Jules Verne disposes the human mind in favor of the marvelous, we can understand the excitement produced in the entire world by this supernatural apparition. As to classing it in the list of fables, the idea was out of the question.

Captain Farragut was a good seaman, worthy of the frigate he commanded. His vessel and he were one. He was the soul of it. On the question of the cetacean there was no doubt in his mind, and he would not allow the existence of the animal to be disputed on board. He believed in it as certain good women believe in the leviathan—by faith, not by reason. The monster did exist, and he had sworn to rid the seas of it. He was a kind of Knight of Rhodes, a second Dieudonné de Gozon, going to meet the serpent which desolated the island. Either Captain Farragut would kill the narwhal, or the narwhal would kill the captain. There was no third course.

The officers on board shared the opinion of their chief. They were ever chatting, discussing, and calculating the various chances of a meeting, watching narrowly the vast surface of the ocean. More than one took up his quarters voluntarily in the cross-trees, who would have cursed such a berth under any other circumstances. As long as the sun described its daily course, the rigging was crowded with sailors, whose feet were burned to such an extent by the heat of the deck as to render it unbearable; still the Abraham Lincoln had not yet breasted the suspected waters of the Pacific. As to the ship's company, they desired nothing better than to meet the unicorn, to harpoon it, hoist it on board, and dispatch it. They watched the sea with eager attention.

Besides, Captain Farragut had spoken of a certain sum of two thousand dollars, set apart for whoever should first sight the monster, were he cabin-boy, common seaman, or officer.

I leave you to judge how eyes were used on board the Abraham Lincoln.

The 20th of July, the tropic of Capricorn was cut by 105° of longitude, and the 27th of the same month we crossed the equator on the 110th meridian. This passed, the frigate took a more decided westerly direction, and scoured the central waters of the Pacific. Commander Farragut thought, and with reason, that it was better to remain in deep water, and keep clear of continents or islands, which the beast itself seemed to shun (perhaps because there was not enough water for him! suggested the greater part of the crew). The frigate passed at some distance from the Marquesas and the Sandwich Islands, crossed the tropic of Cancer, and made for the China Seas. We were on the theater of the last diversions of the monster; and to say truth, we no longer *lived* on board. Hearts palpitated, fearfully preparing themselves for future incurable aneurism. The entire ship's crew were undergoing a nervous excitement, of which I can give no idea; they could not eat, they could not sleep: twenty times a day, a misconception or an optical illusion of some sailor seated on the taffrail would cause dreadful perspirations, and these emotions, twenty times repeated, kept us in a state of excitement so violent that a reaction was unavoidable.

And truly, reaction soon showed itself. For three months, during which a day seemed an age, the Abraham Lincoln furrowed all the waters of the Northern Pacific, running at whales, making sharp deviations from her course, veering suddenly from one tack to another, stopping suddenly, putting on steam, and backing ever and anon at the risk of deranging her machinery; and not one point of the Japanese or American coast was left unexplored.

The warmest partisans of the enterprise now became its most ardent detractors. Reaction mounted from the crew to the captain himself, and certainly, had it not been for resolute determination on the part of Captain Farragut, the frigate would have headed due southward. This useless search could not last much longer. The Abraham Lincoln had nothing to reproach herself with, she had done her best to succeed. Never had an American ship's crew shown more zeal or patience; its failure could not be placed to their charge—there remained nothing but to return.

This was represented to the commander. The sailors could not hide their discontent, and the service suffered. I will not say there was a mutiny on board, but after a reasonable period of obstinacy, Captain Farragut (as Columbus did) asked for three days' patience. If in three days the monster did not appear, the man at the helm should give three turns of the wheel, and the Abraham Lincoln would make for the European seas.

This promise was made on the 2nd of November. It had the effect of rallying the ship's crew. The ocean was watched with renewed attention. Each one wished for a last glance in which to sum up his remembrance. Glasses were used with feverish activity. It was a grand defiance given to the giant narwhal, and he could scarcely fail to answer the summons and "appear."

Two days passed, the steam was at half-pressure; a thousand schemes were tried to attract the attention and stimulate the apathy of the animal in case it should be met in those parts. Large quantities of bacon were trailed in the wake of the ship, to the great satisfaction (I must say) of the sharks. Small craft radiated in all directions round the Abraham Lincoln as she lay to, and did not leave a spot of the sea unexplored. But the night of the 4th of November arrived without the unveiling of this submarine mystery.

The next day, the 5th of November, at twelve, the delay would (morally speaking) expire; after that time, Commander Farragut, faithful to his promise, was to turn the course to the southeast and abandon forever the northern regions of the Pacific.

The frigate was then in 31° 15′ north latitude and 136° 42′ east longitude. The coast of Japan still remained less than two hundred miles to leeward. Night was approaching. They had just struck eight bells; large clouds veiled the face of the moon, then in its first quarter. The sea undulated peaceably under the stern of the vessel.

At that moment I was leaning forward on the starboard netting. Conseil, standing near me, was looking straight before him. The crew, perched in the ratlines, examined the horizon, which contracted and darkened by degrees. Officers with their night-glasses scoured the growing darkness; sometimes the ocean sparkled under the rays of the moon, which darted between two clouds, then all trace of light was lost in the darkness.

In looking at Conseil, I could see he was undergoing a little of the general influence. At least I thought so. Perhaps for the first time his nerves vibrated to a sentiment of curiosity.

"Come, Conseil," said I, "this is the last chance of pocketing the two thousand dollars."

"May I be permitted to say, sir," replied Conseil, "that I never reckoned on getting the prize; and, had the government of the Union offered a hundred thousand dollars, it would have been none the poorer."

"You are right, Conseil. It is a foolish affair after all, and one upon which we entered too lightly. What time lost, what useless emotions! We should have been back in France six months ago."

"In your little room, sir," replied Conseil, "and in your museum, sir; and I should have already classed all your fossils, sir. And the Babiroussa would have been installed in its cage in the Jardin des Plantes, and have drawn all the curious people of the capital!"

"As you say, Conseil. I fancy we shall run a fair chance of being laughed at for our pains."

"That's tolerably certain," replied Conseil quietly; "I think they will make fun of you, sir. And—must I say it?——"

"Go on, my good friend."

"Well, sir, you will only get your deserts."

"Indeed!"

"When one has the honor of being a savant as you are, sir, one should not expose one's self to——"

Conseil had not time to finish his compliment. In the midst of general silence a voice had just been heard. It was the voice of Ned Land shouting.

"Look out there! the very thing we are looking for—on our weather beam!"

At this cry the whole ship's crew hurried toward the harpooner—commander, officers, masters, sailors, cabin-boys; even the engineers left their engines, and the stokers their furnaces.

The order to stop her had been given, and the frigate now simply went on by her own momentum. The darkness was then profound; and however good the Canadian's eyes were, I asked myself how he had managed to see, and what he had been able to see. My heart beat as if it would break. But Ned Land was not mistaken, and we all perceived the object he pointed to. At two cables' lengths from the Abraham Lincoln, on the starboard quarter, the sea seemed to be illuminated all over. It was not a mere phosphoric phenomenon. The monster emerged some fathoms from the water, and then threw out that very intense but inexplicable light mentioned in the report of several captains. This magnificent irradiation must have been produced by an agent of great *shining* power. The luminous part traced on the sea an immense oval, much elongated, the center of which condensed a burning heat, whose overpowering brilliancy died out by successive gradations.

"It is only an agglomeration of phosphoric particles," cried one of the officers.

"No, sir, certainly not," I replied. "Never did pholades or salpæ produce such a powerful light. That brightness is of an essentially electrical nature. Besides, see, see! it moves; it is moving forward, backward, it is darting toward us!"

A general cry arose from the frigate.

"Silence!" said the captain; "up with the helm, reverse the engines."

The steam was shut off, and the Abraham Lincoln, beating to port, described a semicircle.

"Right the helm, go ahead," cried the captain.

These orders were executed, and the frigate moved rapidly from the burning light.

I was mistaken. She tried to sheer off, but the supernatural animal approached with a velocity double her own.

We gasped for breath. Stupefaction more than fear made us dumb and motionless. The animal gained on us, sporting with the waves. It made the round of the frigate, which was then making fourteen knots, and enveloped it with its electric rings like luminous dust. Then it moved away two or three miles, leaving a phosphorescent track, like those volumes of steam that the express trains leave behind. All at once from the dark line of the horizon whither it retired to gain its momentum, the monster rushed suddenly toward the Abraham Lincoln with alarming rapidity, stopped suddenly about twenty feet from the hull, and died out—not diving under the water, for its brilliancy did not abate—but suddenly, and as if the source of this brilliant emanation was exhausted. Then it reappeared on the other side of the vessel, as if it had turned and slid under the hull. Any moment a collision might have occurred which would have been fatal to us. However, I was astonished at the maneuvers of the frigate. She fled and did not attack.

On the captain's face, generally so impassive, was an expression of unaccountable astonishment.

"Mr. Aronnax," he said, "I do not know with what formidable being I have to deal, and I will not imprudently risk my frigate in the midst of this darkness. Besides, how attack this unknown thing, how defend one's self from it? Wait for daylight, and the scene will change."

"You have no further doubt, captain, of the nature of the animal?"

"No, sir; it is evidently a gigantic narwhal, and an electric one."

"Perhaps," added I, "one can only approach it with a gymnotus or a torpedo."

"Undoubtedly," replied the captain, "if it possesses such dreadful power, it is the most terrible animal that ever was created. That is why, sir, I must be on my guard."

The crew were on their feet all night. No one thought of sleep. The

Abraham Lincoln, not being able to struggle with such velocity, had moderated its pace, and sailed at half speed.   For its part, the narwhal, imitating the frigate, let the waves rock it at will, and seemed decided not to leave the scene of the struggle.   Toward midnight, however, it disappeared, or, to use a more appropriate term, it "died out" like a large glow-worm.   Had it fled?   One could only fear, not hope it.   But at seven minutes to one o'clock in the morning a deafening whistling was heard, like that produced by a body of water rushing with great violence.

The captain, Ned Land, and I were then on the poop, eagerly peering through the profound darkness.

"Ned Land," asked the commander, "you have often heard the roaring of whales?"

"Often, sir; but never such whales the sight of which brought me in two thousand dollars.   If I can only approach within four harpoon lengths of it!"

"But to approach it," said the commander, "I ought to put a whaler at your disposal?"

"Certainly, sir."

"That will be trifling with the lives of my men."

"And mine too," simply said the harpooner.

Toward two o'clock in the morning, the burning light reappeared, not less intense, about five miles to windward of the Abraham Lincoln.   Notwithstanding the distance, and the noise of the wind and sea, one heard distinctly the loud strokes of the animal's tail, and even its panting breath.   It seemed that, at the moment that the enormous narwhal had come to take breath at the surface of the water, the air was ingulfed in its lungs, like the steam in the vast cylinders of a machine of two thousand horsepower.

"Hum!" thought I, "a whale with the strength of a cavalry regiment would be a pretty whale!"

We were on the *qui vive* till daylight, and prepared for the combat.   The fishing implements were laid along the hammock nettings.   The second lieutenant loaded the blunderbusses, which could throw harpoons to the distance of a mile, and long duck-guns, with explosive bullets, which inflicted mortal wounds even to the most terrible animals.   Ned Land contented himself with sharpening his harpoon—a terrible weapon in his hands.

At six o'clock, day began to break; and with the first glimmer of light, the electric light of the narwhal disappeared.   At seven o'clock the day was sufficiently advanced, but a very thick sea-fog obscured our view, and the best spy-glasses could not pierce it. That caused disappointment and anger.

I climbed the mizzen-mast. Some officers were already perched on the mast-heads. At eight o'clock the fog lay heavily on the waves, and its thick scrolls rose little by little. The horizon grew wider and clearer at the same time. Suddenly, just as on the day before, Ned Land's voice was heard.

"The thing itself on the port quarter!" cried the harpooner.

Every eye was turned toward the point indicated. There, a mile and a half from the frigate, a long blackish body emerged a yard above the waves. Its tail, violently agitated, produced a considerable eddy. Never did a caudal appendage beat the sea with such violence. An immense track, of a dazzling whiteness, marked the passage of the animal, and described a long curve.

The frigate approached the cetacean. I examined it thoroughly.

The reports of the Shannon and of the Helvetia had rather exaggerated its size, and I estimated its length at only two hundred and fifty feet. As to its dimensions, I could only conjecture them to be admirably proportioned. While I watched this phenomenon, two jets of steam and water were ejected from its vents, and rose to the height of 120 feet; thus I ascertained its way of breathing. I concluded definitely that it belonged to the vertebrate branch, class mammalia.

The crew waited impatiently for their chief's orders. The latter, after having observed the animal attentively, called the engineer. The engineer ran to him.

"Sir," said the commander, "you have steam up?"

"Yes, sir," answered the engineer.

"Well, make up your fires and put on all steam."

Three hurrahs greeted this order. The time for the struggle had arrived. Some moments after, the two funnels of the frigate vomited torrents of black smoke, and the bridge quaked under the trembling of the boilers.

The Abraham Lincoln, propelled by her powerful screw, went straight at the animal. The latter allowed it to come within half a cable's length; then, as if disdaining to dive, it took a little turn, and stopped a short distance off.

This pursuit lasted nearly three-quarters of an hour, without the frigate gaining two yards on the cetacean. It was quite evident that at that rate we should never come up with it.

"Well, Mr. Land," asked the captain, "do you advise me to put the boats out to sea?"

"No, sir," replied Ned Land; "because we shall not take that beast easily."

"What shall we do then?"

"Put on more steam if you can, sir. With your leave, I mean to post myself under the bowsprit, and if we get within harpooning distance, I shall throw my harpoon."

"Go, Ned," said the captain. "Engineer, put on more pressure."

Ned Land went to his post. The fires were increased, the screw revolved forty-three times a minute, and the steam poured out of the valves. We heaved the log, and calculated that the Abraham Lincoln was going at the rate of 18½ miles an hour.

But the accursed animal swam too at the rate of 18½ miles.

For a whole hour, the frigate kept up this pace, without gaining six feet. It was humiliating for one of the swiftest sailers in the American navy. A stubborn anger seized the crew; the sailors abused the monster, who, as before, disdained to answer them; the captain no longer contented himself with twisting his beard—he gnawed it.

The engineer was again called.

"You have turned full steam on?"

"Yes, sir," replied the engineer.

The speed of the Abraham Lincoln increased. Its masts trembled down to their stepping-holes, and the clouds of smoke could hardly find way out of the narrow funnels.

They heaved the log a second time.

"Well?" asked the captain of the man at the wheel.

"Nineteen miles and three-tenths, sir."

"Clap on more steam."

The engineer obeyed. The manometer showed ten degrees. But the cetacean grew warm itself, no doubt; for, without straining itself, it made 19³⁄₁₀ miles.

What a pursuit! No, I cannot describe the emotion that vibrated through me. Ned Land kept his post, harpoon in hand. Several times the animal let us gain upon it. "We shall catch it! we shall catch it!" cried the Canadian. But just as he was going to strike the cetacean stole away with a rapidity that could not be estimated at less than thirty miles an hour, and even during our maximum of speed it bullied the frigate, going round and round it. A cry of fury broke from every one.

At noon we were no further advanced than at eight o'clock in the morning.

The captain then decided to take more direct means.

"Ah!" said he, "that animal goes quicker than the Abraham Lincoln. Very well! we will see whether it will escape these conical bullets. Send your men to the forecastle, sir."

The forecastle gun was immediately loaded and slewed round. But the shot passed some feet above the cetacean, which was half a mile off.

"Another more to the right," cried the commander, "and five dollars to whoever will hit that infernal beast."

An old gunner with a gray beard—that I can see now—with steady eye and grave face, went up to the gun and took a long aim. A loud report was heard, with which were mingled the cheers of the crew.

The bullet did its work; it hit the animal, but not fatally, and, sliding off the rounded surface, was lost in two miles' depth of sea.

The chase began again, and the captain, leaning toward me, said:

"I will pursue that beast till my frigate bursts up."

"Yes," answered I; "and you will be quite right to do it."

I wished the beast would exhaust itself, and not be insensible to fatigue, like a steam-engine! But it was of no use. Hours passed, without its showing any signs of exhaustion.

However, it must be said in praise of the Abraham Lincoln, that she struggled on indefatigably. I cannot reckon the distance she made under three hundred miles during this unlucky day, November the 6th. But night came on, and overshadowed the rough ocean.

Now I thought our expedition was at an end, and that we should never again see the extraordinary animal. I was mistaken. At ten minutes to eleven in the evening, the electric light reappeared three miles to windward of the frigate, as pure, as intense as during the preceding night.

The narwhal seemed motionless; perhaps, tired with its day's work, it slept, letting itself float with the undulation of the waves. Now was a chance of which the captain resolved to take advantage.

He gave his orders. The Abraham Lincoln kept up half-steam, and advanced cautiously so as not to awake its adversary. It is no rare thing to meet

We were not a hundred feet from the burning focus, the light of which increased and dazzled our eyes.

in the middle of the ocean whales so sound asleep that they can be success-
fully attacked, and Ned Land had harpooned more than one during its sleep.
The Canadian went to take his place again under the bowsprit.

The frigate approached noiselessly, stopped at two cables' length from
the animal, and following its track. No one breathed; a deep silence reigned
on the bridge. We were not a hundred feet from the burning focus, the
light of which increased and dazzled our eyes.

At this moment, leaning on the forecastle bulwark, I saw below me Ned
Land grappling the martingale in one hand, brandishing his terrible harpoon
in the other, scarcely twenty feet from the motionless animal. Suddenly his
arm straightened, and the harpoon was thrown; I heard the sonorous stroke
of the weapon, which seemed to have struck a hard body. The electric light
went out suddenly, and two enormous waterspouts broke over the bridge of
the frigate, rushing like a torrent from stem to stern, overthrowing men, and
breaking the lashing of the spars. A fearful shock followed, and, thrown over
the rail without having time to stop myself, I fell into the sea.

This unexpected fall so stunned me that I have no clear recollection of my
sensations at the time. I was at first drawn down to a depth of about twenty
feet. I am a good swimmer (though without pretending to rival Byron or
Edgar Poe, who were masters at the art), and in that plunge I did not lose my
presence of mind. Two vigorous strokes brought me to the surface of the
water. My first care was to look for the frigate. Had the crew seen me
disappear? Had the Abraham Lincoln veered round? Would the captain
put out a boat? Might I hope to be saved?

The darkness was intense. I caught a glimpse of a black mass disappearing
in the east, its beacon-lights dying out in the distance. It was the frigate! I
was lost.

"Help! help!" I shouted, swimming toward the Abraham Lincoln in des-
peration.

My clothes encumbered me; they seemed glued to my body, and paralyzed
my movements.

I was sinking! I was suffocating!

"Help!"

This was my last cry. My mouth filled with water; I struggled against being drawn down the abyss. Suddenly my clothes were seized by a strong hand, and I felt myself quickly drawn up to the surface of the sea; and I heard, yes, I heard these words pronounced in my ear:

"If master would be so good as to lean on my shoulder, master would swim with much greater ease."

I seized with one hand my faithful Conseil's arm.

"Is it you?" said I, "you?"

"Myself," answered Conseil; "and waiting master's orders."

"That shock threw you as well as me into the sea?"

"No; but being in my master's service, I followed him."

The worthy fellow thought that was but natural.

"And the frigate?" I asked.

"The frigate?" replied Conseil, turning on his back; "I think that master had better not count too much on her."

"You think so?"

"I say that, at the time I threw myself into the sea, I heard the men at the wheel say, 'The screw and the rudder are broken.'"

"Broken?"

"Yes, broken by the monster's teeth. It is the only injury the Abraham Lincoln has sustained. But it is a bad lookout for us—she no longer answers her helm."

"Then we are lost!"

"Perhaps so," calmly answered Conseil. "However, we have still several hours before us, and one can do a good deal in some hours."

Conseil's imperturbable coolness set me up again. I swam more vigorously; but, cramped by my clothes, which stuck to me like a leaden weight, I felt great difficulty in bearing up. Conseil saw this.

"Will master let me make a slit?" said he; and slipping an open knife under my clothes, he ripped them up from top to bottom very rapidly. Then he cleverly slipped them off me, while I swam for both of us.

Then I did the same for Conseil, and we continued to swim near to each other.

Nevertheless, our situation was no less terrible. Perhaps our disappearance had not been noticed; and if it had been, the frigate could not tack, being without its helm. Conseil argued on this supposition, and laid his plans accordingly. This phlegmatic boy was perfectly self-possessed. We then decided that, as our only chance of safety was being picked up by the Abraham Lincoln's boats, we ought to manage so as to wait for them as long as possible. I resolved then to husband our strength, so that both should not be exhausted at the same time; and this is how we managed: while one of us lay on our back, quite still, with arms crossed, and legs stretched out, the other would swim and push the other on in front. This towing business did not last more than ten minutes each; and relieving each other thus, we could swim on for some hours, perhaps till daybreak. Poor chance! but hope is so firmly rooted in the heart of man! Moreover, there were two of us. Indeed, I declare (though it may seem improbable) if I sought to destroy all hope, if I wished to despair, I could not.

The collision of the frigate with the cetacean had occurred about eleven o'clock the evening before. I reckoned then we should have eight hours to swim before sunrise—an operation quite practicable if we relieved each other. The sea, very calm, was in our favor. Sometimes I tried to pierce the intense darkness that was only dispelled by the phosphorescence caused by our movements. I watched the luminous waves that broke over my hand, whose mirror-like surface was spotted with silvery rings. One might have said that we were in a bath of quicksilver.

Near one o'clock in the morning, I was seized with dreadful fatigue. My limbs stiffened under the strain of violent cramp. Conseil was obliged to keep me up, and our preservation devolved on him alone. I heard the poor boy pant; his breathing became short and hurried. I found that he could not keep up much longer.

"Leave me! leave me!" I said to him.

"Leave my master? never!" replied he. "I would drown first."

Just then the moon appeared through the fringes of a thick cloud that the wind was driving to the east. The surface of the sea glittered with its rays. This kindly light reanimated us. My head got better again. I looked at all the points of the horizon. I saw the frigate! She was five miles from us, and looked like a dark mass, hardly discernible. But no boats!

I would have cried out. But what good would it have been at such a distance? My swollen lips could utter no sounds. Conseil could articulate some words, and I heard him repeat at intervals, "Help! help!"

Our movements were suspended for an instant; we listened. It might be only a singing in the ear, but it seemed to me as if a cry answered the cry from Conseil.

"Did you hear?" I murmured.

"Yes! yes!"

And Conseil gave one more despairing call.

This time there was no mistake! A human voice responded to ours! Was it the voice of another unfortunate creature, abandoned in the middle of the ocean, some other victim of the shock sustained by the vessel? Or rather was it a boat from the frigate, that was hailing us in the darkness?

Conseil made a last effort, and leaning on my shoulder, while I struck out in a despairing effort, he raised himself half out of the water, then fell back exhausted.

"What did you see?"

"I saw," murmured he—"I saw—but do not talk—reserve all your strength!"

What had he seen? Then, I know not why, the thought of the monster came into my head for the first time! But that voice? The time is past for Jonahs to take refuge in whales' bellies! However, Conseil was towing me again. He raised his head sometimes, looked before us, and uttered a cry of recognition, which was responded to by a voice that came nearer and nearer. I scarcely heard it. My strength was exhausted; my fingers stiffened; my hand afforded me support no longer; my mouth, convulsively opening, filled with salt water. Cold crept over me. I raised my head for the last time, then I sank.

At this moment a hard body struck me. I clung to it then I felt that I was being drawn up, that I was brought to the surface of the water, that my chest collapsed: I fainted.

It is certain that I soon came to, thanks to the vigorous rubbings that I received. I half opened my eyes.

"Conseil!" I murmured.

"Does master call me?" asked Conseil.

Just then, by the waning light of the moon, which was sinking down to the horizon, I saw a face which was not Conseil's, and which I immediately recognized.

"Ned!" I cried.

"The same, sir, who is seeking his prize!" replied the Canadian.

"Were you thrown into the sea by the shock of the frigate?"

"Yes, professor; but, more fortunate than you, I was able to find a footing almost directly upon a floating island."

"An island?"

"Or, more correctly speaking, on our gigantic narwhal."

"Explain yourself, Ned!"

"Only I soon found out why my harpoon had not entered its skin and was blunted."

"Why, Ned, why?"

"Because, professor, that beast is made of sheet-iron."

The Canadian's last words produced a sudden revolution in my brain. I wriggled myself quickly to the top of the being, or object, half out of the water, which served us for a refuge. I kicked it. It was evidently a hard, impenetrable body, and not the soft substance that forms the bodies of the great marine mammalia. But this hard body might be a bony carapace, like that of the antediluvian animals; and I should be free to class this monster among amphibious reptiles, such as tortoises or alligators.

Well, no! the blackish back that supported me was smooth, polished, without scales. The blow produced a metallic sound; and incredible though it may be, it seemed, I might say, as if it was made of riveted plates.

There was no doubt about it! this monster, this natural phenomenon that had puzzled the learned world, and overthrown and misled the imagination of seamen of both hemispheres, was, it must be owned, a still more astonishing phenomenon, inasmuch as it was a simply human construction.

We had no time to lose, however. We were lying upon the back of a sort of submarine boat, which appeared (as far as I could judge) like a huge fish of steel. Ned Land's mind was made up on this point. Conseil and I could only agree with him.

Just then a bubbling began at the back of this strange thing (which was evidently propelled by a screw), and it began to move. We had only just time to seize hold of the upper part, which rose about seven feet out of the water, and happily its speed was not great.

"As long as it sails horizontally," muttered Ned Land, "I do not mind; but if it takes a fancy to dive, I would not give two straws for my life."

The Canadian might have said still less. It became really necessary to communicate with the beings, whatever they were, shut up inside the machine. I searched all over the outside for an aperture, a panel, or a man-hole, to use a technical expression; but the lines of the iron rivets, solidly driven into the joints of the iron plates, were clear and uniform. Besides, the moon disappeared then, and left us in total darkness.

At last this long night passed. My indistinct remembrance prevents my describing all the impressions it made. I can only recall one circumstance. During some lulls of the wind and sea, I fancied I heard several times vague sounds, a sort of fugitive harmony produced by distant words of command. What was then the mystery of this submarine craft of which the whole world vainly sought an explanation? What kind of beings existed in this strange boat? What mechanical agent caused its prodigious speed?

Daybreak appeared. The morning mists surrounded us, but they soon cleared off. I was about to examine the hull, which formed on deck a kind of horizontal platform, when I felt it gradually sinking.

"Oh, confound it!" cried Ned Land, kicking the resounding plate; "open, you inhospitable rascals!"

Happily the sinking movement ceased. Suddenly a noise, like iron works violently pushed aside, came from the interior of the boat. One iron plate was moved, a man appeared, uttered an odd cry, and disappeared immediately.

Some moments after, eight strong men with masked faces appeared noiselessly, and drew us down into their formidable machine.

THE BALLAD OF THE "CLAMPHERDOWN"

Rudyard Kipling

It was our war-ship "Clampherdown"
 Would sweep the Channel clean,
Wherefore she kept her hatches close
When the merry Channel chops arose,
 To save the bleached marine.

She had one bow-gun of a hundred ton,
 And a great stern-gun beside;
They dipped their noses deep in the sea,
They racked their stays and staunchions free
 In the wash of the wind-whipped tide.

It was our war-ship "Clampherdown,"
 Fell in with a cruiser light
That carried the dainty Hotchkiss gun
And a pair o' heels wherewith to run,
 From the grip of a close-fought fight.

She opened fire at seven miles—
 As ye shoot at a bobbing cork—
And once she fired and twice she fired,
Till the bow-gun drooped like a lily tired
 That lolls upon the stalk.

from "Barrack Room Ballads" by Rudyard Kipling

"Captain, the bow-gun melts apace,
  "The deck-beams break below,
" 'Twere well to rest for an hour or twain,
"And botch the shattered plates again."
    And he answered, "Make it so."

She opened fire within the mile—
    As ye shoot at the flying duck—
And the great stern-gun shot fair and true,
With the heave of the ship, to the stainless blue,
    And the great stern-turret stuck.

"Captain, the turret fills with steam,
    "The feed-pipes burst below—
"You can hear the hiss of helpless ram,
"You can hear the twisted runners jam."
    And he answered, "Turn and go!"

It was our war-ship "Clampherdown,"
    And grimly did she roll;
Swung round to take the cruiser's fire
As the White Whale faces the Thresher's ire,
    When they war by the frozen Pole.

"Captain, the shells are falling fast,
    "And faster still fall we;
"And it is not meet for English stock,
"To bide in the heart of an eight-day clock,
    "The death they cannot see."

"Lie down, lie down my bold A. B.,
    "We drift upon her beam;
"We dare not ram for she can run;
"And dare ye fire another gun,
    "And die in the peeling steam?"

It was our war-ship "Clampherdown"
   That carried an armor-belt;
But fifty feet at stern and bow,
Lay bare as the paunch of the purser's sow,
   To the hail of the Nordenfeldt.

"Captain, they lack us through and through;
   "The chilled steel bolts are swift!
"We have emptied the bunkers in open sea,
"Their shrapnel bursts where our coal should be."
   And he answered, "Let her drift."

It was our war-ship "Clampherdown,"
   Swung round upon the tide,
Her two dumb guns glared south and north,
And the blood and the bubbling steam ran forth,
   And she ground the cruiser's side.

"Captain," they cry, "the fight is done,
   They bid you send your sword."
And he answered, "Grapple her stern and bow.
"They have asked for the steel. They shall have it now;
   "Out cutlasses and board!"

It was our war-ship "Clampherdown,"
   Spewed up four hundred men;
And the scalded stokers yelped delight,
As they rolled in the waist and heard the fight,
   Stamp o'er their steel walled pen.

They cleared the cruiser end to end,
   From conning-tower to hold.
They fought as they fought in Nelson's fleet;
They were stripped to the waist, they were bare to the feet,
   As it was in the days of old.

It was the sinking "Clampherdown"
    Heaved up her battered side—
And carried a million pounds in steel,
To the cod and the corpse-fed conger-eel
    And the scour of the Channel tide.

It was the crew of the "Clampherdown"
    Stood out to sweep the sea,
On a cruiser won from an ancient foe,
As it was in the days of long-ago,
    And as it still shall be.